METROPOLITAN COLLEGE OF NY
LIBRARY, 12TH FLOOR
431 CANAL STREET
NEW YORK, NY 10013

A Clamor for EQUALITY

METROPOLITAN COLLEGE OF NY
LIBRARY, 12TH FLOOR
431 CANAL STREET
NEW YORK, NY 10013

The author is solely responsible for all translations from Spanish.

F
870
.M5
G73
2012

A Clamor for EQUALITY
Emergence and Exile of Californio Activist Francisco P. Ramírez

PAUL BRYAN GRAY

Foreword by Gordon Morris Bakken

Texas Tech University Press

METROPOLITAN COLLEGE OF NY
LIBRARY, 12TH FLOOR
431 CANAL STREET
NEW YORK, NY 10013

Copyright © 2012 by Paul Bryan Gray
All rights reserved. No portion of this book may be reproduced in any form or by any means, including electronic storage and retrieval systems, except by explicit prior written permission of the publisher. Brief passages excerpted for review and critical purposes are excepted.
This book is typeset in Minion Pro. The paper used in this book meets the minimum requirements of ANSI/NISO Z39.48-1992 (R1997). ∞

Designed by Kasey McBeath
Cover photographs reprinted by permission of the Huntington Library, San Marino, California, and the University of Southern California Special Collections.

Library of Congress Cataloging-in-Publication Data
Gray, Paul Bryan.
  A clamor for equality : emergence and exile of Californio activist Francisco P. Ramírez / Paul Bryan Gray ; foreword by Gordon Morris Bakken.
       p. cm. — (American liberty & justice)
  Summary: "A biography of Francisco P. Ramírez, Mexican American rights activist and publisher of *El Clamor Público*, a Spanish-language newspaper that circulated in Los Angeles, California, from 1855 to 1859"—Provided by publisher.
  Includes bibliographical references and index.
  ISBN 978-0-89672-763-2 (hardcover : alk. paper) 1. Ramírez, Francisco P., 1837-1908. 2. Mexican Americans—California—Biography. 3. Political activists—California—Biography. 4. Mexican American journalists--California--Biography. 5. Clamor público. 6. Lawyers—California—Los Angeles—Biography. 7. Mexican Americans—Civil rights—California—History. 8. California—Ethnic relations—History. 9. California—Politics and government—1850-1950. 10. Exiles—Mexico—Ensenada (Baja California)—Biography. I. Title.
         F870.M5G73 2012
         979.4'04092—dc23
      [B]   2012020658

Printed in the United States of America
12 13 14 15 16 17 18 19 20 / 9 8 7 6 5 4 3 2 1

Texas Tech University Press
Box 41037 | Lubbock, Texas 79409-1037 USA
800.832.4042 | ttup@ttu.edu | www.ttupress.org

To my wife, Feli;
and my grandchildren,
Erik, Paul, Rosealee, Haley,
Kaya, and Henry

CLAMOR PUBLICO

Periódico Independiente y Literario.

LOS ANGELES, CALIFORNIA, MARTES, JUNIO 19 DE 1855.

COMISION DE LOS ESTADOS UNIDOS
PARA LA APROBACION DE LOS TITULOS DE TERRENOS.

[Sesion de 22 de mayo de 1855.]

Opinion del Comisionado Farwell.

APROBADOS.

N.° 250.—El título del Sr. M. G. Vallejo por 16 leguas cuadradas y 5 mas en el condado de Petaluma.

N.° 291.—Otro del mismo, por un terreno en el condado de Solano.

N.° 291.—El título de John Rose, seis leguas cuadradas en el condado de Yuba.

N.° 462.—El título de los herederos de Juan B. Alvarado, por el Rincon del Diablo en el condado de San Diego.

N.° 550.—El título de Jno P. Davison, cuatro leguas cuadradas en Santa Paula y Santicoy, condado de Sta. Barbara.

N.° 461.—El título de Juan Foster ocho leguas cuadradas en el valle de S. Felipe, condado de San Diego.

N.° 664.—El título de los herederos de David Litlejohn, una legua cuadrada en Los Carneros, condado de Monterey.

N.° 509.—El título de Samuel G. Reid, tres leguas cuadradas en el rancho del Puerto, condado de San Joaquin.

N.° 248.—El título de Chas Convilland, parte de 1 leguas concedidas primero á J. A. Sutter. Concesion por recompensa y con condiciones en 1841. El terreno esta situado en Feather River.

DESAPROBADO.

N.° 683.—El título de Temple y Alexander, pc 100 varas cuadradas en el condado de Los Angeles. Concedidas provisionalmente en 1854.

Mexico.

El General Alvarez ha espedido el siguiente decreto para favorecer á las personas que deseen emigrar á Mexico para esplotar los ricos placeres de oro que se han descubierto en Ajutechlan, cerca de Acapulco:

El Capitan Juan Alvarez, General de Division de la República Mexicana y en Gefe del ejército restaurador de la Libertad á los habitantes de la República, sabed:

Que usando de las amplias facultades que me concede el "Plan de Ayutla," para promover por cuantos medios me sean posibles la prosperidad y engrandecimiento de la nacion, he tenido á bien decretar:

Art. 1. El laboreo de los placeres de San Francisco del Oro, situados en el distrito de Ajutechlan del departamento de Guerrero, se declara libre para mexicanos y extranjeros desde la publicacion de este decreto.

Art 2. Todo individuo, ya sea nacional ó extranjero, que se dirija al distrito mencionado con objeto de trabajar los placeres, se presentará á las autoridades políticas para obtener de ellas "gratis," sus correspondientes resguardos.

Art. 3. Es libre de todo derecho la introduccion que se haga por el puerto de Acapulco, de maquinaria, instrumentos y provisiones para el trabajo de las minas.

Art. 4. Los metales preciosos del distrito mineral, que se extraigan fuera de la república, solo pagarán al erario el 1 por 100, cayendo en pena de comiso los que contravengan á esta disposicion.

Art. 5. Todo trabajador de placeres referidos, ya sea nacional ó extranjero, que desee adquirir terrenos para fabricar ó dedicarse á la agricultura, ocurrirá á la autoridad política, que facilitará de los terrenos valdíos que le pidiere, á precios convencionales ó equitativos.

Art. 6. Las diferencias que ocurran entre los mineros, se resolverán por quien corresponda con sujecion á la ordenanza de esta disposicion.

Por tanto, etc. Dado en cuartel general del Ejército Restaurador en Texca, á 20 de Abril de 1855. JUAN ALVAREZ.

Sud America.

CHILE.—Segun las últimas noticias continúa su marcha pacífica y progresiva. Las elecciones para miembros del Congreso han pasado sin ocurrencia alguna notable. Entre los Senadores electos vemos con suma satisfaccion el nombre del ilustre colombiano D. Andrés Bello.

PERU.—El general Flores habia llegado á Lima, y protestado contra el tratado que celebró Echenique con el gobierno del Ecuador, por el cual se le niega á aquel el asilo en el Perú. Parece que el gobierno provicional tiene por ominoso el tratado, y lo concidera humillante para el honor nacional. Pero el ministro del Ecuador protestó, y le han seguido los demas Ministros de la América septentrional residentes en Lima. Piden que Flores salga del Perú inmediatamente. "Si Flores (dice un diario del Sur) ha sido siempre una amenaza para los Estados Colombianos, hoy es mayor esa amenaza, mediante la expedicion que se quedaba formando en los Estados Unidos por él, con el fin de tomar las islas de los Galápagos."

Es un hecho imposible que salga de aquí expedicion contra el Ecuador, por mas que hagan Flores y su edecan Clemens.

BOLIVIA.—No son menores las inquietudes en Bolivia con motivo del anunciado regreso del general Santa Cruz. El Presidente Belzu ha dictado un decreto, ordenando el secuestro de los bienes de todo el que tome parte en alguna sedicion, invacion etc. etc. Uno de los artículos de ese decreto manda considerar sin efecto las transacciones que se hubieren celebrado sobre dichos bienes, desde seis años antes de cometido el delito, en cuando fueren aquellos necesarios para la indemnizacion al gobierno y á los particulares de los perjuicios causados por los perturbadores. Se ha dado á luz una carta que se dice dirijida por el general Santa Cruz al coronel Penh, fechada en Bruselas á 15 de setiembre del año próximo pasado, y en la cual manifiesta el Protector su determinacion de "regresar á America ú oponerse á la reeleccion en que está empeñado Belzu, adoptando al efecto el sistema de Rosas."

BRASIL Y PARAGUAY.—Por los extractos que ofrecen los diarios del Istmo de Panamá sabemos que la guerra del imperio del Brasil contra el Uruguay se está haciendo, y segun parece, sin una declaratoria que la precediera, "siendo lo mas extraño (dice el Panameño) ver que la marina de guerra de los Estados Unidos ayude á S. M. I; en su agresion contra los paraguayos. Estos, empero, oponen fuerzas considerables á sus adversarios, y hasta ahora alcanzan el triunfo en los combates habidos." He aquí lo que dice el Constitucional de Mendoza, en el asunto: " Se hacia serio nos informa uno de los pasajeros llegados en la mensajeria, el conflicto del Paraguay, atacado por una fuerte escuadra brasilera y un vapor norteamericano; dos potencias poderosas han llevado la guerra contra esta naciente y pequeña república; el Almirante del Paraguay, hijo del Presidente Lopez, de dos vapores que habian comprado en Europa, no habia conseguido introducir sino uno antes que la escuadra brasilera ocupase los rios. Habia tenido lugar un combate entre el vapor norteamericano que hemos mencionado y una batería paraguaya, la que causó con sus fuegos algunas averias en el vapor matándole dos hombres además. Este desmontó algunas piezas de aquella. En la frontera con el Brasil, en las guardias ó fuertes se trataban encuentros parciales entre paraguayos y brasileros, en los que aquellos habian salido vencedores."

Los periódicos de Buenos Ayres dan la noticia de que una fuerza paraguaya de 8,000 hombres habia obtenido á inmediaciones de Villareal un triunfo sobre las fuerzas brasileras invasoras. Sobre el Paraná ténian los paraguayos 20,000 hombres estacionados, habian tapado de las tres bocas del rio Paraguay, echando á pique piraguas armadas de piedras, y estan los

Francia.

Un decreto del Emperador aumenta al ejército en 90,000 hombres.—Cada regimiento de línea tendrá un refuerzo de 900.

Esperando la visita de la Reina Victoria á Paris, el Emperador ha mandado poner el Liceo Imperial en un pie de espléndida magnificencia.

Por decreto de 31 de marzo, Mr. de Thouvenel Ministro Plenipotenciario de primera clase y director de los asuntos políticos, se encargará durante la auciencia del Ministro Secretario de Estado de Negocios Extranjeros, Mr. Drouyn de Lhuys, de la direccion de los trabajos de ese departamento y de la correspondencia diplomática.

El gobierno francés se ha quejado oficialmente al belga, á instancias del Príncipe Napoleon, por un opúsculo publicado contra el Emperador sobre la guerra y que se atribuyó al Príncipe.

EL PROXIMO CONGRESO.—Hasta hoy los miembros electos para el próximo Congreso son como sigue: Administracion 31; Oposicion 129. Todavía resta que elejir 37 miembros en los Estados donde las elecciones congresionales aun no han tenido lugar.

INTERESANTE.—Un astrónomo Aleman dice que en veinte millones de años la tierra será destruida por una cometa!

LA MEDALLA RUSA.—En los cuerpos de algunos soldados rusos que cayéron en Eupatoria se encontró la medalla de plata de la decoracion de San Jorge. En un lado está grabada el águila con dos cabezas teniéndose los piés al globo terrestre y el cetro de las tempestades; y el águila está coronada por una paloma iluminada. Sobre ella suspende las alas el condor de grecia — Lengua rusa —
"Arrodillense, idolatras, porque Dios es con vosotros."
En el otro lado tiene la siguiente divisa tambien en ruso:
"Para la sumision de Hungria y Transilvania."

Dícese que casi todo el vino de la Moselle ha sido comprado por el gobierno Francés para mandarlo al ejército de Crimea.

La Union de Sacramento hablando del San Francisco Chronicle dice: "No se encuentra dentro de los límites de este Estado otro periódico mas cortéz, independiente y elegante."

Los soldados heridos y enfermos que han muerto en Liverpool, (Inglaterra) serán enterrados en un mismo lugar, sobre el cual se erijirá un monumento por suscricion pública.

PISCATORIO.—Mr. Joseph S. McIntyre, de la armada de los E. U. estacionada en Benicia, publica una carta en el Herald de San Francisco, anunciando que sacó un pescado, y abriéndolo encontro un látigo de veinte pulgadas y media de largo y montado en plata. No ha dudado mucho la veracidad de esta historieta.

POZO ARTESIANO.—Se ha cavado un nuevo pozo artesiano en San José, y segun el Tribune es una curiosidad.

CONVENCION DEMOCRATICA.—El día 27 de Junio tendrá lugar una convencion democratica en Sacramento con el objeto de nombrar oficiales para la eleccion general en Setiembre próximo.

EL CENSO.—La Constitucion del Estado previene que se tome el censo este año, pero como la legislatura no dispuso nada sobre esto, se tomara el año de 1860.

PELEGRINOS PARA PALESTINA.—Una caravana de pelegrinos se embarcó recientemente en Marsella para la Tierra Santa.—Antes de su salida fuéron invitados al palacio por el Obispo y cada uno recibió una crucesita de plata, con la fecha de su partida. Se esta organizando otra

La ley del Domingo.

SECCION I. Toda diversion bulliciosa será en lo sucesivo prohibida en los dias domingos.

SEC. 2. Todo individuo que ayudase á abrir en este dia un establecimiento público, tal como teatro, juego, cuarto ó salon, juego de lugares propios para carreras ó combate de osos, de toros, de gallos, diversiones bárbaras y bulla, siendo prendido por un delito especificado por la ley, y despues de convicto, será sujeto á una multa cuyo mínimum será de cuenta pesos y el máximum de 500.

SEC. 3. Todo individuo que venda un billete de entrada á uno de las diversiones enumeradas en la segunda seccion de esta acta, será castigado con una multa de 10 pesos al mínimum, y de cincuenta al máximum.

SEC. 4. Los jueces de paz en todos casos de infraccion á las prescripciones de esta ley.

SEC. 5. Esta ley estará en poder desde Junio de 1855.

PAPEL DE TULE.—El Exmo. Gobernador BIGLER en su último mensaje, habla de los terrenos inundados y anega presa como sigue:

"Y ya que estoy tocando este acaso no sea fuera de lugar el que llegan á tener buen éxito los experimentos que se están haciendo en el Atlántico, no tan solo serán sino que aumentará necesariamente el valor. Nadie ignora que una gran parte de los terrenos adquiridos por el virtud de la ley de Setiembre está cubierta de lozano Tule, este suelo, y que por término de 6 toneladas por acre.

"Durante el último otoño esto sido cuidadosamente ecsaminado fabricantes esperimentados, quienes presado que, en su opinion, se puede en el papel de calidad muy superior.

"Puesto que el tallo del Tule está maduro y antes que se derrita la lluvia, es casi blanco, se cree que el blanqueo seria comparativamente pequeño. Estando cubierto y compacta fibra, é interiormente un tejido celular con numerosas fibras longitudinales, se cree tiene todas las calidades requeridas.

"Se han remitido varias partes de Tule á algunos fabricantes de papel de los Estados del Atlántico, con el objeto que hagan ensayos con él, y pronto se sabrá el resultado de estos importantes esperimentos.

"A fin de poder apreciar debidamente la importancia de este esperimento, en caso que tenga feliz ésito, se hace necesaria la explicacion de algunos hechos referentes.

"El precio medio, en los Estados Atlánticos, del material con que las fábricas de papel hacen el papel, es de unos seis centavos la libra. A dos centavos la libra, tercera parte del precio actual de los trapos, cada acre produciria unos ochenta pesos ($80) ó sea doce cientos pesos ($12,800) cada cien acres, y esto, sin mas gastos que los que se orijinen al tiempo de la siega y despues que haya completamente durado.

"Sin embargo, cualquiera que sultado de los esperimentos que se haciendo acerca de la primera cualidad del papel de cartas ó de imprenta duda han los hombres que han entendido han ocupado de esta materia de que del Tule se puede fabricar papel de buena calidad."

CONTENTS

Illustrations   *xi*
Foreword   *xiii*
Acknowledgments   *xv*
Introduction   *xvii*

1
A Precocious Journalist   3

2
A Militant Mexican Newspaper   33

3
The Demise of *El Clamor Público*   51

4
An Interlude in Sonora   69

5
Homecoming   83

6
A Contest for the State Senate   97

7
San Francisco and *El Nuevo Mundo*   109

8
A Lawyer in Los Angeles   141

9
Stanford and Ramírez   177

10
The Independent Movement and Prosperity 203

11
Panic, Death, and Dissolution 221

12
Politics and Crime 253

13
El Partido Norte 283

14
Exile in Ensenada 317

Notes *347*
Bibliography *365*
Index *373*

ILLUSTRATIONS

Los Angeles Plaza, 1849	3
Map of Los Angeles, 1849	4
Map of Avila vineyard	5
Los Angeles Plaza, 1873	7
Ramírez homestead, 1857	8
Ramírez homestead, 1890	8
Vignes winery, 1857	9
Vignes vineyard, 1865	11
Portion of Los Angeles, 1872	12
Joseph Lancaster Brent	19
Francisco P. Ramírez	21
El Clamor Público, June 19, 1855	24
Henry Hamilton and William McKee	40
Mexican children in Sonoratown, c. 1890	61
La Estrella de Occidente, May 24, 1861	74
Mexican district of San Francisco, 1865	111
Vallejo Street, 1868	111
Geary Avenue, 1865	122
El Nuevo Mundo, December 22, 1864	123
Dashaway Hall, 1869	128
Artesian well, Riverside Country, c. 1900	145
Judge Ignacio Sepúlveda	157
Chinese tenements, c. 1885	167
Scene of the 1871 Chinese massacre	169
An American neighborhood south of the plaza, c. 1880	170
A hardware store south of the plaza	170

Illustrations

Sonoratown, c. 1885	172
Adobe in Sonoratown, c. 1875	172
Mexicans on Aliso Street, c. 1880	173
Indian shelters at Mission San Gabriel	174
Owner of the Shumacher Ranch	175
Volney E. Howard	178
The lower plaza, c. 1870	190
The Pico House Hotel and the Temple Block, 1880	190
The Clocktower Courthouse, 1872	191
Eulogio de Celis	194
A train and covered wagons at Promontory Point, Utah, 1869	240
Mexican riders in a Los Angeles parade, 1897	242
A Los Angeles fiesta, 1890	242
Reginaldo del Valle	261
Lastania Abarta	273
Aliso Street, 1885	280
Downtown Los Angeles, c. 1880	280
Spring Street, 1880	281
Manuel Clemente Rojo	289
San Rafael Valley, c. 1886	293
Residents of Real del Castillo, c. 1886	298
The main street of Real del Castillo, c. 1890	298
Tourists in Real del Castillo, 1903	299
El Fronterizo, January 14, 1882	302
Train passengers arriving in Los Angeles, 1885	313
Judge Ignacio Sepúlveda	316
Ensenada, c. 1887	322
Ensenada near the Hotel Iturbide, c. 1888	322
Headquarters of the American company, c. 1886	323
La Voz de la Frontera de la Baja California, March 24, 1888	325
George Ryerson and Guadalupe Serrano	329
Ensenada, 1891	333
María Saint Raymond	339
Francisco P. Ramírez in 1901	341
Ramírez homestead as an Italian restaurant, c. 1920	344
Lorenzo Ramírez	345
Hotel Ramírez, 1983	345

FOREWORD

Paul Bryan Gray's biography of Francisco P. Ramírez is a unique masterpiece of research, writing, and interpretation of American liberty and justice. Ramírez was a brilliant critic of racism in antebellum California. Southerners influenced much of Southern California society, yet Ramírez put into print scathing editorials against slavery and racism. Equally strident, his insistence for equality for Mexicans, free elections, and female education resonates more with the twentieth century than with antebellum Los Angeles. He was one of the first Mexican American lawyers in Los Angeles and a civil rights newspaper editor far ahead of his times.

Ramírez continued his advocacy in San Francisco as a newspaper editor. He was involved in every major political and social movement of his times. He practiced law in Los Angeles and Mexico, a truly transborder attorney and civil rights activist in the nineteenth century.

Visually, this book is magnificent, with images known to only a few. For example, the Abarta image is a family treasure, and although I wrote two book chapters involving Abarta, I never saw her image until Paul Bryan Gray had one sent to me in August 2011. Other images of Los Angeles and Mexico are unique and from collections private and scholarly. This collection of images is a monument to a scholar on both sides of the border.

Ramírez's San Francisco was a diverse community due to the gold rush. The flood of humanity that docked there, left there, or stayed there produced a city of cultural and ethnic diversity. The Irish and the Chinese were the labor that built the transcontinental railroad and populated the city. The Irish moved into politics and the Chinese into Chinatown. Jews, Irish, and Italians moved into the embedded mercantile elite. African Americans formed a small but vibrant community. Chinese and blacks sought legal counsel when threatened within their communities and on the streets. Charlotte Brown's lawsuits desegregated the San Francisco transit system in the 1860s. Another lawsuit desegregated the school system over a decade later. Lawyers challenged the anti-Chinese zoning ordinances in court, and the United States Supreme Court overturned them. Accommodations were not without rough spots, but diversity and accommodation became the mark of the city by the turn of the century. Not so in Los Angeles or many other cities of the West.

On our southern borders America has a clear Mexican American West that is both very urban and very sparsely settled. El Paso and San Diego are examples of our binational borderland of intensive interaction with a large cultural region of Hispanic settlement and enterprise. Ramírez was an early part of this border society.

Nineteenth-century and twentieth-century lawyers made their reputations as attorneys performing before a judge, jury, and audience made up of members of the bar, the press, and the public. Ramírez was part of this courtroom dance, but he was much more because of his public voice. His advocacy for civil rights was pathbreaking.

Enjoy the elegant prose, the profound interpretations, and the incredible images.

GORDON MORRIS BAKKEN
California State University, Fullerton

ACKNOWLEDGMENTS

This book could not have been written without the support of my wife, Feli. For more than ten years, while I spent hundreds of hours researching in libraries and archives, she was a steadfast source of support and encouragement. She bolstered my law practice and the domestic front by doing nearly everything I neglected. When I visited the archives in Baja California and Sonora, Mexico, she accompanied me and helped locate and analyze relevant material. To a very large extent, this book has been a shared effort. Her ideas and criticism over the years have been invaluable. Preparation of the final manuscript was mostly her work. I am deeply indebted to her, not only for this book, but for everything good in life.

I had the benefit of occasional advice from Dr. Doyce B. Nunis, Jr., distinguished professor emeritus of the University of Southern California. Until recently the editor of the *Southern California Quarterly*, he was for decades the ultimate arbiter of content and style in publishing California history. In addition to his own considerable body of work, his genius guided several generations of historians. He influenced my writing more than anyone else. His recent death took away an irreplaceable friend and scholar.

Several years ago I was surprised to discover that Donald Chaput knew more about Francisco P. Ramírez's career in Baja California than I did. Until we began a casual conversation at the Huntington Library, I thought I was the only person in the world who knew about Ramírez's disappearance from Los Angeles and his subsequent whereabouts. Don not only knew about Ramírez, he had a collection of newspaper clippings about him, together with other material. He gave me a computer printout of his collection, for which I am enormously grateful. His generous nature is shown by the donation of much of his material on Baja California to the archive of the Instituto de Investigaciones Históricas on the Tijuana campus of the Universidad Autónoma de Baja California, where he is honored as the contributor of an important group of documents known as the Colección Donald Chaput.

Preparation of this work was materially assisted by a grant from the California Supreme Court Historical Society. I hope the book justifies at least part of their extraordinary generosity.

Abraham Hoffman gave up much of his time to read the initial draft of the manuscript. His comments were an important factor in encouraging me to complete the book. I am greatly obliged to him as a friend and a noted historian.

I cannot mention all those who have lent me support. Some are academics; others are lawyers and judges. They know who they are and that I have respect and affection for all of them. A few have passed out of this life, leaving a void that can never be filled. I remember with nostalgia afternoons spent at the Huntington Library with Martin Ridge, Siegfried Demke, Frank Q. Newton, and Carl Chaffin.

Part of my research led me to Baja California and the Instituto de Investigaciones Históricas in Tijuana. There, I was tremendously impressed with the quality of the historical writing of Antonio Padilla, David Piñera, and Hilarie Heath, who in my opinion are world-class historians. I was especially helped at the start of my research in Baja California by my friend Jesús Cueva Pelayo of the Instituto Tecnológico de Tijuana. My induction into the membership of Ensenada's Seminario de Historia de Baja California while writing this book was a proud moment. The organization has long actively promoted the writing and study of history in the region. Its members include Dr. Miguel Tellez and Dr. Fernando Araujo, both of whom have shown me great kindness and become close friends over the years.

INTRODUCTION

The first edition of the Spanish-language newspaper *El Clamor Público* was distributed in Los Angeles on June 19, 1855, to a curious group of initial subscribers. The weekly publication was produced almost single-handedly by a brilliant and astonishingly precocious eighteen-year-old named Francisco P. Ramírez, who presented his journal as a champion of the Mexican people.

Ramírez's hopes for his newspaper were frustrated by its unpopular content. He often expressed radically liberal views on politics and race relations that both conservative Mexicans and Americans found offensive. Many readers recoiled at the unrestrained emotion presented in some of his editorials, a consequence of his extreme youth. Subscriptions and advertising gradually diminished until Ramírez, bankrupt and embittered, printed his last edition on December 31, 1859.

The brief existence of *El Clamor Público* was seldom mentioned by historians until the publication of Leonard Pitt's seminal book, *The Decline of the Californios*, in 1966. Pitt devoted an entire chapter to Ramírez and his work on *El Clamor Público*. Since then, social historians have realized the enormous significance of Ramírez's work in *El Clamor Público*. The editorials and essays he wrote for his newspaper are now seen as an invaluable presentation of the clash between American and Mexican cultures following the conquest of California. His protests against American discrimination toward the Spanish-speaking and his attempts to reconcile the differences between the two cultures remain relevant today as Mexicans have once again become the most numerous element in many parts of California, including Los Angeles County.

The last few decades have seen a rising interest in Ramírez's discourse in the pages of *El Clamor Público*. His work has become the subject of seminars, academic study, and mandatory reading in university classes. However, little has been written about Ramírez's life after his newspaper closed at the end of 1859. A few historians have traced his sojourn in Sonora, Mexico, from 1860 to 1862, only to lose track of him after his return to California, where he was appointed to a series of minor public offices. Even Pitt goes no further than to mention that Ramírez edited the Spanish-language weekly *La Crónica* for a time in 1872, "but thereafter one hears nothing of him in Los Angeles."

Nevertheless, from 1869 to 1881, Ramírez was highly visible in Los Angeles as a lawyer and prominent politician. Among the distinguished scholars commenting on the lack of biographical material concerning California Mexicans like Ramírez is Abraham Hoffman, who has identified figures from the past worthy of more attention in a valuable essay published by the Historical Society of Southern California, entitled "Needs and Opportunities in Los Angeles Biography," which can be read on the society's website. He notes: "Another person more mentioned than profiled, was Francisco P. Ramírez, a figure who truly cries for more biographical information."

This book attempts to present a complete picture of Ramírez's life. It will explore his sudden emergence as a public figure in Los Angeles during the 1850s, as well as the reasons for his later obscurity. As a kind of microhistory, it hopefully adds something to our understanding of the great social and political events in which Ramírez was both an observer and participant. It will also put to rest the curiosity of those of us who have wondered about the final destiny of this initially sympathetic young man, so far ahead of his time and once regarded as a youth of brilliant promise.

A Clamor for EQUALITY

CLAMOR PUBLICO.

Periódico Independiente y Literario.

LOS ANGELES, CALIFORNIA, MARTES, JUNIO 19 DE 1855.

COMISION DE LOS ESTADOS UNIDOS
PARA LA APROBACION DE LOS TITULOS DE TERRENOS.
[Sesion de 22 de mayo de 1855.]
Opinion del Comisionado Farwell.

APROBADOS.

N.º 250—El título del Sr. M. G. Vallejo por 10 leguas cuadradas y 5 mas en el condado de Petaluma.

N.º 291—Otro del mismo, por un terreno en el condado de Solano.

N.º 291—El título de John Rose, seis leguas cuadradas en el condado de Yuba.

N.º 462—El título de los herederos de Juan B. Alvarado, por el Rincon del Diablo en el condado de San Diego.

N.º 550—El título de Jno P. Davison, cuatro leguas cuadradas en Santa Paula y Santicoy, condado de Sta. Barbara.

N.º 461—El título de Juan Foster ocho leguas cuadradas en el valle de S. Felipe, condado de San Diego.

N.º 664—El título de los herederos de David Litteyohn, una legua cuadrada en Los Carneros, condado de Monterey.

N.º 509—El título de Samuel G. Reid, tres leguas cuadradas en el rancho del Puerto, condado de San Joaquin.

N.º 248—El título de Chas Convilland, parte de 1 leguas concedidas primero á J. A. Sutter Concesion por recompensa y con condiciones en 1841. El terreno esta situado en Feather River.

DESAPROBADO.

N.º 688—El título de Temple y Alexander, por 100 varas cuadradas en el condado de Los Angeles. Concedidas provisionalmente en 1854.

Mexico.

El General Alvarez ha espedido el siguiente decreto para favorecer á las personas que deseen emigrar á Mexico para esplotar los ricos placeres de oro que se han descubierto en Ajutechlan, cerca de Acapulco:

El Capitan Juan Alvarez, General de Division de la República Mexicana y en Gefe del ejército restaurador de la Libertad—á los habitantes de la República, sabed:

Que usando de las amplias facultades que me concede el "Plan de Ayutla," para promover por cuantos medios me sean posibles la prosperidad y engrandecimiento de la nacion, he tenido á bien decretar:

ART. 1.º El laboreo de los placeres de San Frácisco del Oro, situados en el distrito de Ajutichlan del departamento de Guerrero, se declara libre para mexicanos y extrajeros desde la publicacion de este decreto.

ART. 2.º Todo individuo, ya sea nacional ó extranjero, que se dirija al distrito mencionado con objeto de trabajar los placeres, se presentará á las autoridades políticas para obtener de ellas "gratis," sus correspondientes resguardos.

ART. 3.º Es libre de todo derecho la introduccion que se haga por el puerto de Acapulco, de maquinaria, instrumentos y provisiones para el trabajo de las minas.

ART. 4.º Los metales preciosos del distrito mineral, que se extraigan fuera de la república, solo pagarán al erario el 1 por 100, ayendo en pena de comiso los que contrevengan á esta disposicion.

ART. 5.º Todo trabajador de placeres referidos, ya sea nacional ó extranjero, que desee adquirir terrenos para fabricar ó dedicarse á la agricultura, ocurrirá á la autoridad política, que facilitará de los terrenos valdíos el que se le pidiere, á precios convencionales ó equitativos.

ART. 6.º Las diferencias que ocurran entre los mineros, se resolverán por quien corresponda con sujecion á la ordenanza del ramo.

Por tanto, etc. Dado en cuartel general del Ejército Restaurador en Texca, á 20 de Abril de 1855. JUAN ALVAREZ.

Sud America.

CHILE.—Segun las últimas noticias continúa su marcha pacífica y progresiva. Las elecciones para miembros del Congreso han pasado sin ocurrencia alguna notable. Entre los Senadores electos vemos con suma satisfaccion el nombre del ilustre colombiano D. Andrés Bello.

PERU.—El general Flores habia llegado á Lima, y protestado contra el tratado que celebró Echenique con el gobierno del Ecuador, por el cual se le niega á aquel el asilo en el Perú. Parece que el gobierno provicional tiene por ominoso el tratado, y lo considera humillante para el honor nacional. Pero el ministro del Ecuador protestó, y le han seguido los demás Ministros de la América septentrional residentes en Lima. Piden que Flores salga del Perú inmediatamente. "Si Flores (dice un diario del Sur) ha sido siempre una amenaza para los Estados Colombianos, hoy es mayor esa amenaza, mediante la expedicion que se quedaba formando en los Estados Unidos por él, con el fin de tomar las islas de los Galápagos."

Es un hecho imposible que salga de aquí expedicion contra el Ecuador, por mas que hagan Flores y su edecan Clemens.

BOLIVIA.—No son menores las inquietudes en Bolivia con motivo del anunciado regreso del general Santa Cruz. El Presidente Belzu ha dictado un decreto, ordenando el secuestro de los bienes de todo el que tome parte en alguna sedicion, invacion. etc. etc. Uno de los artículos de ese decreto manda considerar sin efecto las transacciones que se hubieren celebrado sobre dichos bienes, desde seis meses antes de cometido el delito, en cuando fueren aquellos necesarios para indemnizar al Gobierno y á los particulares de los perjuicios causados por los perturbadores. Se ha dado á luz una carta que se dice dirijida por el general Santa Cruz al coronel Puch, fechada en Bruselas á 15 de noviembre del año próximo pasado, y en la cual manifiesta el Protector su determinacion de "regresar á America y oponerse á la reeleccion en que está empeñado Belzu, adoptando al efecto el sistema de Rosas."

BRASIL Y PARAGUAY.—Por los extractos que ofrecen los diarios del Istmo de Panamá sabemos que la guerra del imperio del Brasil contra el Uruguay se está haciendo, y segun parece, sin una declaratoria que la precediera. "Siendo lo mas extraño (dice el *Panameño*) ver que la marina de guerra de los Estados Unidos ayude á S. M. I.; en su agresion contra los paraguayos. Estos, empero, oponen fuerzas considerables á sus adversarios, y hasta ahora alcanzan el triunfo en los combates habidos."—He aquí lo que dice el *Constitucional* de Mendoza, en el asunto: "Se hacia serio nos informa uno de los pasajeros llegados en la mensajería, el conflicto del Paraguay, atacado por una fuerte escuadra brasilera y un vapor norteamericano; dos potencias poderosas han llevado la guerra contra esta naciente y pequeña república; el Almirante del Paraguay, hijo del Presidente Lopez, de dos vapores que habian comprado en Europa, no habia conseguido introducir sino uno antes que la escuadra brasilera ocupase los rios. Habia tenido lugar un combate entre el vapor norteamericano que hemos mencionado y una batería paraguaya, la que causó con sus fuegos algunas averías en el vapor matándole dos hombres ademas. Este desmontó algunas piezas de aquella. En la frontera con el Brasil, en las guardias ó fuertes se trababan encuentros parciales entre paraguayos y brasileros, en los que aquellos habian salido vencedores."

Los periódicos de Buenos Ayres dan la noticia de que una fuerza paraguaya de 8,000 hombres habia obtenido é inmediaciones de Villareal un triunfo sobre las fuerzas brasileras invasoras. Sobre el Paraná tenian los paraguayos 20,000 hombres estacionados, habian tapado dos de las tres bocas del rio Paraguay, echando á pique

FRANCIA.—Un decreto del Emperador aumenta al ejército en 90,000 hombres.—Cada regimiento de línea tendrá un refuerzo de 900.

Esperando la visita de la Reina Victoria á Paris, el Emperador ha mandado poner el Liceo Imperial en un pie de espléndida magnificencia.

Por decreto de 31 de marzo, Mr. de Thouanevel Ministro Plenipotenciario de primera clase y director de los asuntos políticos, se encargará durante la audiencia del Ministro Secretario de Estado de Negocios Extranjeros, Mr. Drouyn de Lhuys, de la direccion de los trabajos de ese departamento y de la correspondencia diplomática.

El gobierno francés se ha quejado oficialmente al belga, á instancias del Príncipe Napoleon, por un opúsculo publicado contra el Emperador sobre la guerra y que se atribuyó al Príncipe.

EL PROXIMO CONGRESO.—Hasta hoy los miembros electos para el próximo Congreso son como sigue: Administracion 31; Oposicion 129. Todavía resta que elejir 37 miembros en los Estados donde las elecciones congresionales aun no han tenido lugar.

INTERESANTE.—Un astrónomo Aleman dice que en veinte millones de años la tierra será destruida por una cometa!

LA MEDALLA RUSA.—En los cuerpos de algunos soldados rusos que cayéron en Eupatoria se encontró la medalla de plata de la decoracion de San Jorge. En un lado está grabada el águila rusa, con dos cabezas, teniendo en los pies el globo terrestre y el cetro del soberano; sobre el águila esta la corona imperial y una paloma iluminada. Sobre estas figuras tiene las siguientes palabras en lengua rusa:

"Arrodillense, idolatras, porque Dios es con nosotros."

Y en el otro lado tiene la siguiente divisa tambien en ruso:

"Para la sumision de Hungria y Transilvania."

☞ Dícese que casi todo el vino de la Moselle ha sido comprado por el gobierno Francés para mandarlo al ejército de Crimea.

☞ La *Union* de Sacramento hablando del San Francisco *Chronicle* dice: "No se encuentra dentro de los límites de este Estado otro periódico mas cortés, independiente y elegante."

☞ Los soldados heridos y enfermos que han muerto en Liverpool, (Inglaterra) serán enterrados en un mismo lugar, sobre el cual se erijirá un monumento por suscricion pública.

PISCATORIO.—Mr. Joseph S. McIntyre, de la armada de los E. U. estacionada en Benicia, publica una carta en el *Herald* de San Francisco, anunciando que sacó un pescado y abriéndolo encontro un látigo de veinte pulgadas y media de largo y montado en plata. Se ha dudado mucho la veracidad de esta historieta.

POZO ARTESIANO.—Se ha cavado un nuevo pozo artesiano en San José, y segun el *Tribune* es una curiosidad.

CONVENCION DEMOCRATICA.—El dia 27 de Junio tendrá lugar una convencion democratica en Sacramento con el objeto de nombrar oficiales para la eleccion general en Setiembre próximo.

EL CENSO.—La Constitucion del Estado previene que se tome el censo este año, pero como la legislatura no dispuso nada sobre esto, se tomara el año de 1860.

PELEGRINOS PARA PALESTINA.—Una caravana de pelegrinos se embarcó recientemente en Marsella para la Tierra Santa.—Antes de su salida fuéron invitados al palacio por el Obispo y cada uno recibió una crucesita de plata, con la fecha de su par-

La ley del Domingo

SECCION 1. Toda diversion bolíciosa será en lo sucesivo prohibida en los dias domingos.

SEC. 2. Todo individuo que ayudase á abrir un casa de divertimiento público, tal como teatro, juego, cuarto ó saton, juego de bolos, lugares propios para carreras ó combate de osos, de toros, de gallos ó diversiones barbaras y bulliciosas, siendo prendido por un delito específico contra esta ley, y despues de convicto, será sujeto á una multa cuyo minimum sera cincuenta pesos y el maximum doscientos cuenta.

SEC. 3. Todo individuo que tenga un billete de entrada á uno de las diversiones enumeradas en la segunda seccion de esta acta, será igualmente castigado con una multa del mismo al minimum, y de cincuenta al máximum.

SEC. 4. Los jueces de paz en todos casos de infraccion á las disposiciones de esta ley.

SEC. 5. Esta ley estará en vigor desde Junio 15 de 1855.

PAPEL DE TULE.—El Exmo. Sr. BIGLER en su último mensage, sobre los terrenos inundados y anegadizos dice como sigue:

"Y ya estoy tocando un punto que acaso no sea fuera de lugar el que no lleguen á tener buen éxito los esfuerzos que ahora se están haciendo en el lado del Atlántico, no tan solo serán, sino que aumentarán necesariamente nuestros valores. Nadie ignora que una gran parte de los terrenos adquiridos por el Estado en virtud de la ley de Setiembre de 1850 está cubierta de lozano *Tule*, que produce este suelo, y que por término medio cuatro toneladas por acre.

"Durante el último otoño se han hecho cuidadosamente examinaciones por fabricantes esperimentados, y han espresado, que en su opinion, se puede fabricar con él un papel de calidad bien superior.

"Puesto que el tallo del *Tule* está maduro y antes que comience la lluvia, es casi blanco, se cree que el blanqueo seria comparativamente pequeño. Estando cubierto con una compacta fibra, é interiormente con un tejido celular con numerosas fibras longitudinales, se cree que todas las cualidades requeridas.

"Se han remitido varias piezas de *Tule* á algunos fabricantes en los Estados del Atlántico, con el objeto que hagan ensayos con él, y pronto se verá el resultado de estos importantes esperimentos.

"A fin de poder apreciar con mas importancia de este esperimento, puesto que tenga feliz éxito, se hace necesaria la explicacion de algunos hechos referentes.

"El precio medio, en los Estados Atlánticos, del material con que se fabrica el papel es de unos seis pesos la libra. A dos centavos la libra, tercera parte del precio actual de los trapos, cada acre produciria ochenta pesos ($12,800) ó sea doce cientos pesos ($12,800) cada cien acres, y esto, sin mas gastos que se orijinen al tiempo de la siega no despues que haya completado su durado.

"Sin embargo, cualquiera que sea el sultado de los esperimentos que se están haciendo acerca de la primera papel de cartas ó de imprentar no duda han los hombres que han entendido de esta materia á que el *Tule* se puede fabricar papel de buena calidad.

CHAPTER ONE
A Precocious Journalist

Francisco P. Ramírez was the child of Juan Ramírez and Petra Avila. His paternal grandfather, also named Francisco, was a carpenter who arrived in Alta California in 1794 with a party of settlers from Sonora, Mexico. A native of Tepic, the elder Francisco Ramírez and his wife, Rosa Quijada, settled at the Mission Santa Barbara, where Juan Ramírez was born in 1801.[1] By 1828 the latter had moved to Los Angeles, where in 1830 he married Petra Avila, a member of a prominent family. She was the granddaughter of Cornelio Avila, a Sonoran who had led a caravan of settlers from northern Mexico to Alta California in 1786. Petra's father, Francisco Avila, once the mayor of Los Angeles, built the Avila adobe in 1818. This structure still stands on Olvera Street, renowned as the oldest house in the city.

Juan Ramírez did not accumulate much wealth in his lifetime. He had no family connections or political influence great enough to obtain one of the

Drawing of the Los Angeles Plaza by William Hutton as it appeared in 1849, when Francisco P. Ramírez was twelve years old. Reprinted by permission of the University of Southern California Special Collections.

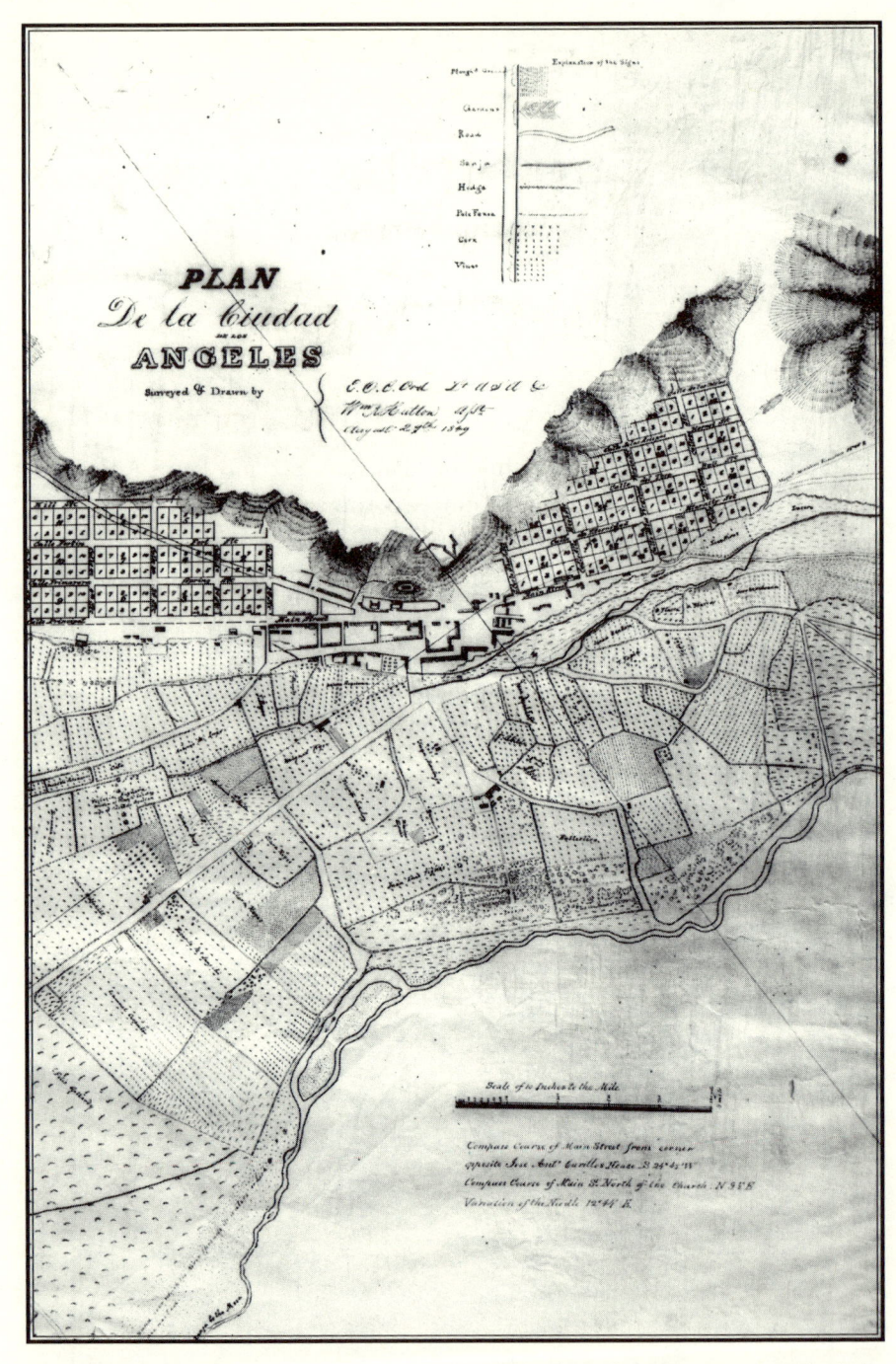

Map of Los Angeles surveyed by Edward O. C. Ord and drawn by William Hutton in 1849. The thick lines around the plaza represent rows of adobe houses, not walls. The uniform rectangular lots above the pueblo were not yet developed. Reprinted by permission of the University of Southern California Special Collections.

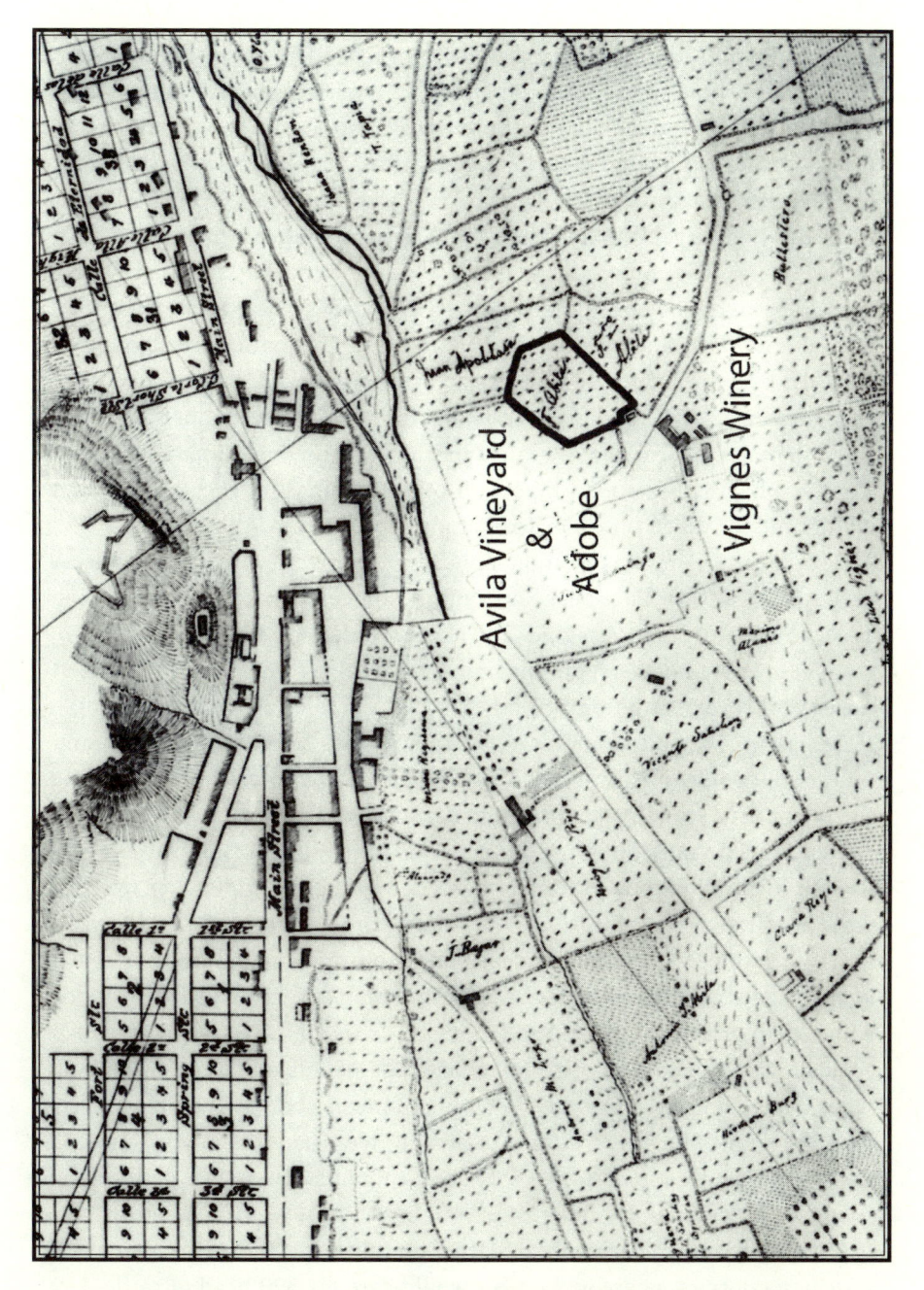

An enlargement of a portion of Ord's map. The various plots of land are vineyards worked by Indian labor. The vineyard shown in bold outline belonged to Francisco Avila, Ramírez's grandfather. It was inherited by his mother, who allowed it to become the Ramírez homestead. The vineyard and home of Jean Louis Vignes are adjacent. Reprinted by permission of the University of Southern California Special Collections.

large land grants issued by Mexican governors. Ramírez obtained possession of a modest vineyard for commercial winemaking from his wife's family. With the help of Indian labor, he built a large two-story adobe home on the property, a fairly pretentious structure at the time. His property was adjacent to the north side of Aliso Road and east of Alameda Street, about 700 yards from the Los Angeles plaza. The road was named after a giant, 400-year-old *aliso*—an alder or sycamore tree—standing over sixty feet high where the winery and vineyards of Jean Louis Vignes were located across the road from the Ramírez family property. Vignes was a prosperous French vintner who had become a naturalized Mexican citizen.[2] Over the years Vignes persuaded a few relatives and friends to join him in Los Angeles, but his wife refused to make the trip. Juan Ramírez had a nearly lifelong camaraderie with Vignes, which led to friendships with other members of the small French community centered on Aliso Road among the vineyards.

Jean Louis Vignes was an anomalous figure in the tiny Mexican pueblo. A native of Beguey, a village near Bordeaux, he appeared in Los Angeles during 1831, already fifty-one years old. The reasons for his middle-aged departure from France are not clear, but they must have been compelling since he left a wife and several children behind. After efforts to establish himself in the Hawaiian Islands and Monterey, California, Vignes bought 104 acres of land on the south side of Aliso Road, just west of the Los Angeles River. During the next thirty years he had phenomenal success producing wine from imported French vines. His wine, far superior to the old Mission variety, easily sold in Santa Barbara, Monterey, and San Francisco. Following 1851 his wine production was at least 32,000 gallons per year, which he sold for two dollars a gallon. Vignes also made lesser quantities of a famous brandy that sold for twice as much. Besides his wine and brandy, Vignes usually shipped some 5,000 oranges a year to San Francisco, as well as other kinds of fruit.[3]

Juan Ramírez could not compete with the genius of Vignes in making wine. Moreover, his vineyard of about seventeen acres was much smaller than the Vignes property. Ramírez seems to have had less interest in wine than livestock. He joined with Vignes on September 7, 1840, to petition the *subprefecto*, Santiago Arguello, for permission to raise Merino sheep on Santa Catalina Island.[4] Nearly a decade later, on July 8, 1849, the two men made a written contract whereby Ramírez would care for 390 head of cattle, 139 horses, and 359 sheep belonging to Vignes. At the end of one year, Ramírez would receive three fourths of the natural increase of the animals.[5] The livestock was located on land rented outside Los Angeles. This transaction sug-

The Los Angeles Plaza in 1873. The Ramírez homestead and vineyard are on the upper right side marked with the number 15. A cluster of other buildings stands a little behind and to the left. Reprinted by permission of the University of Southern California Special Collections.

gests that Ramírez was subordinate to Vignes economically, willing to abandon his vineyard to perform the contract. Ramírez must have known a great deal about cattle raising despite not owning a ranch. In addition to holding several minor public offices in Los Angeles, he was a *juez de campo*—judge of the plains—a prestigious position of great respect whose duties were to resolve disputes during roundups and other ranch activities.[6]

In a transaction with Isaac Hartman acting as agent, Juan Ramírez and his wife, Petra Avila de Ramírez, sold a little more than ten acres on the west end of their homestead to Matthew Keller on November 17, 1855.[7] They re-

(above) A drawing of the Ramírez homestead that appeared on the margin of a Los Angeles map drawn in 1857. Reprinted by permission of the University of Southern California Special Collections. (left) The Ramírez homestead in 1890, with the balcony gone and the walls sheathed in wood siding. The palm tree was a landmark on Aliso Road. Reprinted by permission of the University of Southern California Special Collections.

An 1857 drawing of the Vignes Winery across Aliso Road from the Ramírez homestead. Reprinted by permission of the University of Southern California Special Collections.

ceived $2,500 in exchange, giving up more than half of what they had originally owned. The boundaries of the parcel sold were Alameda Street to the west, the Ramírez homestead to the east, the vineyard of Juan Apablasa to the north, and Aliso Road to the south. The sale reduced the Ramírez holding to a plot of slightly less than seven acres, which the family retained for several decades thereafter.

All the land owned by Ramírez was inherited by his wife from her father, Francisco Avila, in 1833, but according to custom, she passively allowed it to fall into the dominion of her husband, who arranged the sale of a large part of it. Since their son, Francisco P. Ramírez, would master three languages and use them as a journalist, it is curious to note that both Juan Ramírez and his wife were illiterate. The deed to Keller was signed on their behalf by a witness who swore that, although they could not read or write, he saw them make their marks on the document.[8]

Juan Ramírez was not endowed with an enterprising nature. The sale of the western part of his property to Matthew Keller is evidence of this. Keller undertook an exhaustive study of viniculture. Within a short time he announced the formation of a business called the Rising Sun and Los Angeles Wineries. Keller managed to produce an excellent vintage that was sold in markets as far away as New York. Fully exploiting his opportunities, he promoted his product throughout the United States, eventually acquiring a fair amount of wealth.[9] Meantime, Juan Ramírez did little to improve his own vineyard.

Francisco P. Ramírez was born in Los Angeles on February 9, 1837, the fourth of thirteen children. His godfather was Jean Louis Vignes.[10] He was raised at his father's homestead on Aliso Road across from Vignes's estate. As a nine-year-old Ramírez may have witnessed the entry of American troops into the little town on January 10, 1847. In good marching order, the force passed by on Alameda Street, not far from the Ramírez adobe, a stirring event enhanced by a brass band, the first ever heard in the city. His maternal grandfather's widow, Encarnación Sepúlveda de Avila, fled to the home of Jean Louis Vignes, leaving her residence at the plaza unattended. An American officer who noticed the fine appearance and furnishings of the abandoned Avila adobe ordered it taken for use as a military headquarters.[11] The seizure of his grandfather's house by invading American forces was the first of many acts by which Ramírez learned, even as a child, that he belonged to a conquered people.

Ramírez grew up during an unstable period, when Los Angeles was evolving from a remote adobe village on the Mexican frontier to an American city. He was a remarkably intelligent boy, who quickly acquired an excellent knowledge of English from American settlers. Early in Ramírez's life Vignes taught him French, the result of the child's being a kind of surrogate son to his godfather. Ramírez's mastery of French and English, together with his native Spanish, made him conversant in three languages before he was fourteen years old.

In later years Ramírez provided the historian Hubert Howe Bancroft with a biographical "dictation," in which he said that his education was mainly acquired by "self-application to books."[12] He was undoubtedly tutored to some extent by Vignes, who encouraged him to read in the three languages he understood. There were no regular schools in early Los Angeles, and Ramírez's illiterate parents could do little to educate him in a traditional way. Ramírez had to learn what he could by himself. Except for what he picked up from Vignes, his education was mainly autodidactic. The results were impressive. His later writing appears to be the work of an unusually learned person. Without knowing his background, some historians have erroneously concluded that Ramírez must have been the product of a university education in Mexico.[13] In fact, he was a self-taught prodigy who never went to school outside California. His early intellectual pursuits left him with little interest in the mundane affairs of the family winemaking business.

During 1851 Ramírez was hired by the *Los Angeles Star* as a compositor.[14] The newspaper first appeared on May 17, 1851, to serve American residents,

A northern view of the Vignes vineyard in 1865. The large building in the far distance is a mill. The Ramírez homestead lies unseen to the right of it across Aliso Road. Vignes's winery and home are to the right among the trees. Reprinted by permission of the Los Angeles Public Library.

who were a distinct minority in a Mexican population. As a gesture toward its surroundings, the back page of the journal was printed in Spanish under the title *La Estrella de Los Angeles*. Ramírez's fourteenth birthday occurred just two months before the first edition of the *Star*. Despite his youth, he was a natural candidate for employment by the newspaper. Ramírez was one of the few people in Los Angeles who was at home with the printed word in both English and Spanish. He became an expert typesetter, absorbing the details of operating a newspaper.

Ramírez's experience at the *Star* greatly increased his general knowledge since the paper reprinted many articles culled from a variety of domestic and foreign publications. For the first time he had access to a vast source of information about the world at large. He was also brought into daily contact with men like Manuel Clemente Rojo, editor of the Spanish section, a sometime lawyer, politician, and poet of considerable learning.[15] Ramírez developed a friendship with the older man, whose worldliness must have been instructive. In this environment the boy's unusual attainments were appreciated. The August 23, 1851, issue of *La Estrella de Los Angeles* reprinted an article from a French newspaper, giving Ramírez credit for translating it into Spanish.

An enlarged part of an 1872 Los Angeles map. The Ramírez family homestead appears just below their name. The big building is the same mill appearing in the prior photograph. The Ramírez adobe, standing apart, is the second structure slightly above the mill to the right. The map maker even included the huge palm tree in front of the Ramírez adobe, showing that the entrance faced east. Reprinted by permission of the University of Southern California Special Collections.

While working for the *Los Angeles Star*, Ramírez discovered that the Catholic Church had opened Santa Clara College near San Jose. About a dozen students began instruction there in May 1851 under a Jesuit faculty, thus beginning one of California's first schools after statehood.[16] Ramírez quit his newspaper job in 1852 to investigate the new college. He went north, accompanied by his ten-year-old sister, Isabel. By previous arrangement she enrolled at Notre Dame College, a girl's school in San Jose, founded by Belgian nuns in 1851. Jean Louis Vignes paid her tuition according to school records. He also persuaded his nephew, Pierre Sainsevain, to act as a local guardian for Isabel and Francisco.[17] Vignes, the godfather of both children, took an unusual interest in their welfare. Sainsevain was a pioneer resident of San Jose, ideally situated to watch over his uncle's godchildren. Since Vignes paid Isabel's tuition, it is likely that he assumed Ramírez's expenses as well.

There is no firm evidence that Ramírez actually attended Santa Clara College, but student records from 1851 to 1854 are "incomplete and drawn from sometimes conflicting contemporary sources."[18] If he did register at the college, the experience may have been disappointing. The founder of the school, an Italian Jesuit named Giovanni Nobili, wrote in 1852, "We do not now claim for it even the name of a college but have looked upon it merely as a select boarding and a day school."[19] Some of the students were as young as eight years old. The first bachelor's degree was not awarded until 1857, several years after Ramírez had departed.

Perhaps Ramírez was not placed in Santa Clara College at all. Instead, he could have taken instruction at a small adobe structure adjacent to St. Joseph's Church in San Jose. The Jesuits established a school at this location in 1850 called St. Joseph's College. In the early 1850s Father Giovanni Nobili operated both the church with its tiny school and Santa Clara College.[20] During their formative period both colleges, housed in rude adobes, were short of money and understaffed. Neither was an institution of higher learning in the modern sense and provided gifted students with few intellectual challenges. Ramírez may have received some advanced tutoring, but he could hope for little else. He was already trilingual, widely read, and a veteran of newspaper work alongside adults. Perhaps disillusioned by his classes and resistant to Jesuit discipline, he stayed for less than a year.

Ramírez next moved to San Francisco, where he took employment on the *Catholic Standard*, a newspaper first published on May 6, 1853.[21] It was directed toward Catholic laymen and affiliated with the church in some manner. Ramírez's passage from a Jesuit college to a Catholic newspaper seems more than coincidental. A sympathetic teacher may have helped him extend an apprenticeship begun on the *Los Angeles Star*.

In 1853 San Francisco had sixteen of the thirty-eight newspapers in California.[22] Some were highly profitable, a fact that stimulated a series of short-lived publications seeking a share of the city's readership. Most could not compete with established newspapers and soon disappeared. The *Catholic Standard* was one of them, collapsing within a few months of its maiden edition. Not a single copy of it has survived.

Ramírez's residence in San Francisco corresponded to the brief existence of the *Catholic Standard*. His exposure to big-city journalism gave him the opportunity to see how newspapers formed public opinion and wielded political power. Journalism was one of the few occupations in which Ramírez's intellectual prowess was valued. It was potentially a source of influence and wealth, as demonstrated by the San Francisco press. Ramírez began to think about starting his own newspaper, a goal that would await his return to Los Angeles.

When the *Catholic Standard* went bankrupt in early 1854, Ramírez did not leave for home immediately. Instead, he went to Marysville, where he was employed by the *Weekly California Express*, a newspaper begun in 1852. The town of about 4,500 people stood at the juncture of the Feather and Yuba rivers, with direct communication by steamboat to Sacramento. It was a supply point for the gold fields, which brought Ramírez into contact with American miners. The region had a history of intense hatred toward Mexicans, whom the miners frequently expelled or killed. Ramírez was affected to some extent by this hostility. In later years protests against American violence toward the Spanish-speaking would be a frequent theme in the journalism he practiced.

Ramírez could have been brought to work on Marysville's newspaper through the efforts of Charles Covillaud, a respected French settler and cofounder of the town named after his wife, Mary Murphy, a survivor of the Donner party. Covillaud was acquainted with Ramírez's godfather, Jean Louis Vignes, and his guardian, Pierre Sainsevain. The Frenchmen very likely placed Ramírez under the protection of Covillaud during his brief stay near the mining country.

Toward the end of 1854, Ramírez left Marysville, returning to Los Angeles. His experiences in northern California had an enormous impact on him. He was only seventeen years old but highly skilled in newspaper work and far more sophisticated than his age would suggest. These qualities induced James S. Waite, owner of the *Los Angeles Star*, to offer Ramírez the editorship of his paper's Spanish page, *La Estrella de Los Angeles*.[23] Since the departure of Manuel Clemente Rojo in 1854, *La Estrella* had been largely neglected. It contained little more than legal notices, statutes, and abstracts from American periodicals, translated into Spanish.

Ramírez transformed *La Estrella* into a lively source of local news and items of interest to Spanish-speaking readers. The young editor's work attracted the notice of other newspapers. The February 2, 1855, issue of San Francisco's *Alta California* remarked: "The editor of the Spanish page of the *Los Angeles Star* is a native Californian named Francisco Ramírez, only fifteen years of age. Those versed in the Castilian language say that *La Estrella* is a model for purity of style." Actually, Ramírez was only a week short of his eighteenth birthday when this item was published, but it shows that he was acquiring a reputation among journalists as something of a phenomenon. As one writer observed, "Ramirez achieved a modicum of fame as the editor of the Spanish page of the *Star*."[24]

Ramírez was not long content as the editor of *La Estrella*. He aspired to begin his own Spanish-language newspaper in Los Angeles. This ambition was encouraged by Waite. Despite the enhanced quality of *La Estrella* through Ramírez's efforts, Waite regarded the *Star*'s Spanish appendage as a liability. He thought that profits could be increased by abandoning the Spanish page altogether in order to use the extra space for English advertising. Waite did not believe that a Spanish-language competitor would have any effect on the *Star*'s circulation. Based on these considerations, Waite allowed Ramírez to publicize his proposed newspaper in the pages of the *Star*. Ramírez chose to call his newspaper *El Clamor Público*, a name already in use by one of Madrid's great journals.

Throughout May 1855 the *Star* announced the forthcoming appearance of *El Clamor Público*, a newspaper to be "devoted exclusively to the service and interests of native Californians." The *Star* also printed notices that all Spanish-language advertising would be transferred to the new publication. At the same time, Ramírez solicited subscribers for *El Clamor Público* at the rate of five dollars a year. Several editions of *La Estrella* contained a prospectus in which Ramírez advised potential readers that his enterprise depended on receiving money in advance: "About one hundred subscribers are needed to begin, and all persons desiring to remit payment are requested to do so at this office."

Only Ramírez knew if one hundred citizens found their way to the *Star*'s office on Main Street to pay five dollars each. He may have begun his newspaper with fewer than the desired number of subscribers, subsidized instead by his godfather and supporter, Jean Louis Vignes. Beginning on June 16, 1855, Waite stopped publishing *La Estrella*, leaving Ramírez free to work on his own Spanish-language newspaper. According to plan, Ramírez moved to Temple's adobe near the corner of Main and Commercial streets, where he produced the first edition of *El Clamor Público* on June 19, 1855. A week later, on June 27, the *Daily Alta California* in San Francisco passed favorable judgment:

> We received yesterday, the first number of *El Clamor Público*, a newspaper printed wholly in the Spanish language. It is edited and published

[16]   A Clamor for Equality

> by Francisco P. Ramírez, a native Californian, a mere youth in years (only sixteen), but uncommonly talented and well educated. *El Clamor Público* is a handsomely printed sheet and published at the low rate of $5 per annum. We trust the Spanish people of the South will give this newspaper a liberal support.

Ramírez's age, always confused in the San Francisco press, was actually eighteen years and four months when *El Clamor Público* first appeared. Modern writers have thought he was seventeen years old at the time, an error based on misstatements in the English version of the *Los Angeles Star*.

The experiment with *El Clamor Público* arose from Ramírez's apprenticeship on American newspapers and his status as a California Mexican. In San Francisco he had observed that newspapers could be effective in the defense of special interests. Every ethnic group with a newspaper was identified as a participant in the struggle for political and social ascendancy. Newspapers such as the California *Staats-Zeitung*, the *Hebrew Observer*, *Le Phare*, *La Crónica*, and *L'Echo du Pacifique* circulated in San Francisco in the early 1850s. They were a crucial element in advancing the status of the minorities they represented. These publications attracted the attention of men like David C. Broderick, a leader of the San Francisco Free Soil Democrats, who made accommodations to naturalized foreign immigrants in exchange for their votes. Candidates for political office actively sought support from ethnic newspapers. Editors of the foreign-language press prospered by providing their readers with increased political and social standing.

Ramírez probably intended *El Clamor Público* to be an ethnic newspaper based on models he had observed in San Francisco. It is highly doubtful that he was influenced by the example of the Mexican press, where there was no tradition of responsible journalism. After its independence in 1821, every government in that country was installed through a violent revolution. Except for official gazettes and literary journals, most Mexican periodicals were ephemeral organs of insurrection and agitation. In contrast, *El Clamor Público* called for orderly social change, with editorials that attempted to influence readers in the same manner as an American newspaper. Its format was nearly identical to any of the state's three dozen or so other newspapers. Ramírez's understanding of journalism was clearly the result of his experience working in the American press.

While his newspaper experiences taught Ramírez much about American society, he could not accept the position of Spanish-speaking people within it. He was aware that white Americans had the most alarming attitudes toward racial differences. English-speaking immigrants of European descent genuinely believed that Mexicans were some kind of inferior race. Their treatment of Spanish-speaking people frequently involved negative behavior and ranged from an air of bemused superiority to unprovoked physical violence.

A pioneer resident from Maryland, describing Los Angeles in 1851, noted that there was "the strongest race prejudice" among the Americans against Mexicans.[25] Anglo-Saxon racism was the central problem in Ramírez's life. During his boyhood in Los Angeles and his residency in northern California, he must have been on good terms with a few Americans, but he was separated from many of them by their disdain for Mexicans. He understood that the inevitable result of American bias would be the subordination of Spanish-speaking people. His response was to publish *El Clamor Público* as an organ of Mexican resistance and political action.

The success of Ramírez's newspaper was jeopardized, however, because he was out of touch with the profoundly conservative Mexican community in Los Angeles. At some point Ramírez had embraced the principles of nineteenth-century liberalism, especially the variety encountered in Mexico. He probably read the work of Mexicans like José María Luis Mora and other ideologues of the liberal movement headed by Benito Juárez. One writer suspects that Ramírez "traveled in Mexican revolutionary circles."[26] Another believes that while in Mexico, he was "exposed to revolutionary ideology."[27] Such opinions are conjectural since there is no evidence of early visits to Mexico by Ramírez. However, they illustrate the radical nature of the political and social content of his newspaper.

Several recurrent themes in the pages of *El Clamor Público* were drawn directly from Mexican liberalism. Among them was a fervent belief in racial equality and the abolition of slavery. Others included the impartial administration of justice and full political rights for every citizen. Such ideals were incorporated in the United States Constitution, a document greatly admired by Ramírez but which he believed was largely nullified by American racism and slavery.

The traditional Mexican society of Los Angeles was not amenable to the views espoused by Ramírez. Most of its members did not share his radical liberalism. They were joined by Americans who increasingly formed a significant part of the community. The majority of those arriving from the United States were Southerners, who supported slavery and regarded the abolitionists as part of a lunatic fringe. The most damaging opposition to

El Clamor Público came from wealthy Spanish-speaking landowners, who made up only about three percent of California Mexicans.[28] This influential group resided in adobe townhouses adjacent to the plaza in Los Angeles when not visiting their outlying ranches. Sometimes known as the "ranchero elite," they controlled the economic, political, and social life of Mexican Los Angeles.

The first American political leaders cultivated an alliance with the ranchero elite. One early politician, a young lawyer named Joseph Lancaster Brent, learned to speak fluent Spanish and set about recruiting prominent rancheros into the Democratic Party. Brent, a Catholic from Maryland, captivated many wealthy Mexican families through his personal charm, shared religious beliefs, and ability to speak the native language. He represented a branch of the Democratic Party originating in the Deep South, known as the Chivalry, which zealously supported slavery and its extension into the territories acquired after the Mexican-American War.[29] Many of the ranchero elite found the Chivalry appealing. There was a certain analogy between their position as owners of vast estates supported by Indian labor and the aristocratic plantations of the South worked by black slaves. By 1853 Brent had developed "a wonderful influence" over the wealthy Mexican element.[30]

Several white Southerners married into elite Mexican families. They found it more palatable to refer to their wives as "Spanish ladies" than to acknowledge "a heritage that was reserved only for lowly or despicable Indians or Mexicans."[31] The rancheros encouraged this fiction although most were racially identical to their workers. Long before the American conquest they were "obsessed with outward manifestations of status." This included claims that they could be distinguished from their Indian and mestizo workers by a mythical "Spanish" past that entitled them to wealth and high social standing. Their assertion of superiority was symbolized by the use of costly clothing and jewelry displayed on public occasions such as weddings and fiestas.[32] They exhibited a paternal but condescending attitude toward the lower classes who, they felt, were not their moral or intellectual equals. Both the ranchero elite and the Americans had little regard for Mexican laborers at the bottom of the social order. The rancheros thought of them as cholos, and Americans openly referred to the Spanish-speaking poor as "greasers."

The great majority of Mexicans in Los Angeles during the 1850s were members of the working class. In 1860 skilled and unskilled laborers made up about seventy-seven percent of the town's Mexican population.[33] Many were dependent on the ranchero elite for a living, stoically accepting their

Undated portrait of Joseph Lancaster Brent, a young proslavery lawyer in Los Angeles during the 1850s. A master of aristocratic Southern politics, he was the undisputed leader of the Chivalry until he left in 1862 to become a Confederate brigadier general. Reprinted by permission of the Los Angeles Public Library.

humble position as a normal part of the Mexican social order. Nevertheless, the relationships of most Hispanic landowners and their workers had an ancient element of reciprocity, which was rooted in Spanish feudalism. Mexican *patrones* often sponsored weddings, baptisms, and funerals for their employees. They were likely to be chosen as godfathers by their workers, a highly important undertaking in Mexican society that bound them to assume responsibility for the children should their parents die or become disabled. In times of crisis, rancheros might go to great lengths to intervene on behalf of those in their service. In such manner certain personal loyalties developed between master and servant that were unknown in American society. This helped the ranchero elite to gather the votes of those they employed. With the support of their relatives, friends, workers, and those dependent on them, rancheros elected candidates of the Chivalry Democrats to public office. As one writer notes, "In a system reminiscent of New Mexico's, the Democratic caciques of southern California operated through the *ricos* to reach underlings long accustomed to following their 'betters' in public matters."[34]

For the most part, working-class Mexicans had little interest in politics. *La Estrella de Los Angeles* noticed this fact on October 30, 1852, in a Spanish column written by the editor, Manuel Clemente Rojo: "We have seen with pain the great apathy that has existed on the occasion of elections. We have heard with surprise the statements of many people that election results are not important." Much as Francisco P. Ramírez would later do in the pages of *El Clamor Público*, the editor exhorted ordinary Mexican people in Los Angeles to participate in public affairs and vote for "honest and just men who will attend to your complaints." Over the years *La Estrella* made other similar appeals without apparent effect.

A large number of Mexican laborers outside the reach of ranchero influence were willing to sell their votes. The usual price was one dollar. This was a handsome bribe since the customary wage for *vaqueros*—cowboys—on surrounding ranches was only fifteen dollars a month.[35] Some traded their votes for liquor. They permitted themselves to be rounded up in places where the candidates could harangue them while keeping up a constant flow of alcohol. The most abased were "in a state of magnificent intoxication" during the night before the election. At sunrise the wretches were taken to the polling place and "as each staggered to the ballot-box, a ticket was held up and he was made to deposit it."[36]

Ramírez was not a member of the ranchero elite or the working class. His family belonged to a small number of agriculturists, merchants, and entrepreneurs who stood outside the traditional relationship between rancheros and their workers. As a liberal he tended to align himself with the laboring classes, hoping to raise their political awareness and induce them to vote for candidates who would somehow reduce discrimination and improve the condition of Spanish-speaking people. Yet, few of the Mexican poor subscribed to his newspaper or reflected on the merits of his work. A tremendous apathy existed on the part of most Mexicans toward political affairs,

Portrait of Francisco P. Ramírez about the time he was editor of *El Clamor Público*. Reprinted by permission of the Huntington Library, San Marino, California.

a fact that helped defeat the aspirations of Ramírez and caused him much personal anguish.

Beyond their nearly complete disinterest in public matters, Los Angeles Mexicans failed to support Ramírez for other reasons. Most would not subscribe to *El Clamor Público*, or any other newspaper, simply because they could not read. In 1850 far less than half of Spanish-speaking adults in Los Angeles were literate.[37] This situation had not changed much by the time that *El Clamor Público* appeared in 1855. Even if there had been a high level of interest in Ramírez's newspaper, he would not easily find the one hundred Mexican subscribers initially desired. Moreover, the Mexican community in Los Angeles was not stable enough to provide a cadre of loyal readers. There was a tendency for Mexicans to move in and out of the city in accordance with demands for their labor. Only a small number of Spanish-speaking families resided continuously in Los Angeles from 1850 to 1880.[38] This transient behavior was a severe handicap in soliciting support for a local newspaper.

Not surprisingly, Ramírez encountered difficulties in recruiting Mexican subscribers. In the first edition of *El Clamor Público*, on June 19, 1855, he wrote a column in which he regretted that "foreigners"—meaning the Americans and the French—had shown more interest in subscribing than had Mexicans. He made the first of many appeals for support from the Spanish-speaking community. His newspaper was "entirely dedicated" to that group's interests, and it would be "the best defense" of the Mexican people. Ramírez condemned those who took no part in matters of public interest. He challenged his countrymen to work together to see what "happy results" they could produce by their efforts.

In this first issue *El Clamor Público* was represented as an "independent newspaper, following the banner of no political party or religious sect." Ramírez wrote that it was "built on the foundation of liberal ideas" and its columns would always be open for "impartial discussion of all public affairs." The little sheet was generally published once a week, on Saturdays. It contained only four pages, but the annual subscription rate for 52 copies was five dollars, an amount equivalent to seventy-eight dollars in 1991. This must have discouraged Mexican laborers from subscribing since many earned about a dollar a day and sometimes even less.

Like other newspapers of the time, the first page usually displayed national and foreign news reprinted from periodicals around the world. Long-outdated reports on events in places like Constantinople, London, Moscow, Madrid, and Paris appeared with stories of wars and natural disasters in locales that tested the reader's knowledge of geography. Items from Washington D.C., New York, and Richmond could take weeks to arrive. Ramírez made a special effort to keep abreast of developments in Mexico and Latin America, frequently giving those events first-page priority. He supplemented his scrutiny of the Mexican press by correspondence with informants below the border and interviews with travelers passing through Los Angeles. The office of *El Clamor Público* eventually became a clearinghouse for intelligence on Mexico.

The second page, written almost entirely by Ramírez, was the heart of the newspaper. The left-hand column invariably contained editorials in which he expounded his political and social views. The rest of the page was devoted to news of state and local events. Developments in San Francisco, Sacramento, and the rest of northern California were closely examined. Ramírez wrote articles on Los Angeles, describing a sometimes turbulent daily life. He covered homicides, robberies, public drunkenness, political meetings, social events, religious celebrations, bullfights, and everything else in the little town that came to his attention. The third and fourth pages were reserved for legal notices and advertisements that Ramírez was paid to print.

The general format of *El Clamor Público* was not rigidly maintained. Sometimes poetry, fiction, and humorous anecdotes appeared at random throughout the newspaper. Ramírez was fond of reprinting bizarre items that he found in other journals, freakish events from around the world calculated to astound the reader. They might show up anywhere to occupy a little space. When news was scarce and his editorial muse failed him, he published material like weather tables, information from almanacs, and extracts from scientific journals to round out his four pages.

Despite the purported independent position of *El Clamor Público* on political matters, Ramírez immediately used his newspaper to attack the American Party, a growing force in California politics during 1855. The party began in Massachusetts as a protest against a huge wave of Irish immigration to the United States. Protestant Americans believed that poor and uneducated Irish Catholics would undermine American society because of their lack of democratic traditions and alleged overriding loyalty to the pope's foreign-church hierarchy. The American Party advocated restrictions on further immigration and the exclusion of Roman Catholics from public life. It tried to be a secret society whose members were instructed to keep silent on its activities and objectives. Because of this, those belonging to the party were soon called Know-Nothings.

In the July 3, 1855, issue of *El Clamor Público*, Ramírez sarcastically wrote that the Know-Nothings were "miserable and fanatic beings" who were intent on destroying the rights of every person "of whatever class or condition who has the *misfortune* to profess the Catholic religion." He urged his readers not to fall victim to their usual apathy: "Many of you believe that the right to vote is of little importance and completely fail to do so. But the right you view with so much indifference and lethargy is the only guarantee of our liberty."

The passive nature of the Mexican electorate greatly concerned Ramírez.

The first edition of *El Clamor Público*, June 19, 1855. Reprinted by permission of the Huntington Library, San Marino, California.

In the first edition he told his Mexican subscribers, "Until now you have been asleep, and taken very little part in matters of public interest." In subsequent issues he tried to arouse their interest in politics. Mexicans represented the majority of the population, and by voting together they had the potential to take control of their lives. Ramírez's July 3 editorial told them, "If we can unite our votes there will be no danger because we will concentrate our strength, but if we fail to unite we will be governed by Know-Nothings."

On July 10, 1855, Ramírez reprinted an article from *La Crónica*, a San Francisco Spanish-language newspaper. It was written by Javier Jofre, a Mexican liberal whom Ramírez had probably befriended while working on the *Catholic Standard*. Ramírez agreed with Jofre's observations that, "Californians of the Spanish race are the most threatened in their rights and property, yet blandly repose in the arms of the most profound indolence. Their apathy for all public affairs is one of the greatest causes of their misfortune and the reason for their having almost no influence on the current scene." Challenged by such comments, Ramírez continued to publish editorials on the Know-Nothings and argued for a large Mexican vote against them.

Americans in Los Angeles had little cause to complain about editorials in *El Clamor Público* criticizing the Know-Nothings. After all, most were Democrats as much opposed to the secretive new political party as Ramírez. But during the first few months of publication, the young editor began to present items that would provoke outrage among immigrants from other parts of the United States, especially those from the South.

As early as the fourth edition of *El Clamor Público*, on July 17, 1855, Ramírez reprinted an article from *La Prensa de la Habana* entitled "Impressions of Travel in the United States." Written by a Cuban journalist, it described a trip by steamboat from New Orleans to Louisville, Kentucky. Although cast in a humorous and satirical form, the piece depicted Southerners as stupid brutes with filthy personal habits. The author clearly regarded them as a lower form of humanity. To illustrate their backwardness, he claimed that they let giant hogs roam everywhere, even into hotel rooms and restaurants. The article ended, "May God save you from this swinish region and the people I have seen here." Most Americans living in Los Angeles were Southerners who regarded the remarks of the Cuban reporter as a malicious distortion of themselves and the region from which they came. However, Ramírez had few reservations about the insulting article. He soon published other items critical of Southerners.

In a July 24 editorial, Ramírez unburdened himself on slavery, an issue that deeply disturbed him. It was the first public expression of his unusually radical views:

> The idea of liberty in the United States is truly curious.... Certain people have no liberty at all. It is denied by the courts to every person of color.... But there is the great liberty of any white man to buy a human being in order to arbitrarily hang him or burn him alive. This happens in states where slavery is tolerated and the vilest despotism runs wild— this, in the center of the nation that calls itself a "model republic."

The next edition contained another editorial on slavery, in which Ramírez displayed an impressive knowledge of the subject. The Compromise of 1850 and the part that Henry Clay had played in it were discussed in depth. Ramírez mentioned protests against slavery published by ex-president John Quincy Adams and outlined the development of the abolitionist movement in New England. He deplored the suffering of slaves caused by separation from their families, the fact that they were sold like animals, and the occasional horrific mistreatment imposed at the whim of white masters.

These attacks on slavery were not favorably received by most Americans in Los Angeles. A few local people from the northeast quarter of the United States opposed slavery, but their objections were seldom based on humane considerations. They thought that bringing slaves into the West would degrade the value of free white labor and reduce wages. As one writer explains, "The opposition to the introduction of slavery into California was not the sign of an enlightened social attitude toward black people. It reflected a common belief that the presence of blacks or any nonwhite group associated with unfree labor posed a real or symbolic threat to the status of free white labor in the state."[39]

Ramírez's hatred of slavery was not caused by economic concerns. He was genuinely affected by the plight of blacks and sympathized with them on a human level. This was entirely consistent with his adherence to Mexican liberalism. Racial equality was an ideal introduced to Mexico by liberals who had begun to abolish slavery as early as 1810. They also attempted to give full juridical and civil rights to Indians. Although constant warfare between liberals and conservatives impeded such reforms, a belief in racial equality remained fundamental to Mexican liberal ideology. It was one of Ramírez's most deeply held convictions. He was a defender of every racial group in California.

Ramírez published a January 19, 1856, editorial opposing a bill in the legislature to exclude Chinese from the state, saying, "America is a free country and a haven for the oppressed of other nations, and it would not be reasonable or just to close its doors to an industrious people merely because their customs are different from ours and they have another color." At this time there was virtually no popular support for the Chinese, who were willing to work for greatly reduced wages. But beyond being a champion of this maligned group, Ramírez was an almost solitary voice of protest against the mistreatment of Indians. Such advanced views on race directly challenged the pretensions of the ranchero elite and repudiated the American belief in white supremacy.

The radical tone of *El Clamor Público* provoked criticism from the community. Without identifying those responsible or stating the nature of their grievances, on November 6, 1855, Ramírez wrote: "We have been attacked by every means possible . . . but to those who have done so, both in our presence and outside it, we offer only our contempt." He defiantly continued, "As journalists, private citizens, and honest men, we have a right to go about with our heads held high and not bow to anyone for any reason." A few months later, on February 2, 1856, Ramírez complained that "some people consider themselves censors of everything written or spoken by the editor and threaten him with death and all manner of tortures worthy of the inquisition."

American indignation toward *El Clamor Público* may have been mollified during the first year of its existence by occasional articles expressing admiration for the United States. Ramírez felt a close connection with American democracy. He understood that both Mexican liberalism and the United States political system arose from a common European origin. In some respects they were nearly identical, but America had achieved a level of stability and respect for the electoral process that was unknown in Mexico. One of Ramírez's earliest editorials, on July 3, 1855, praised the United States Declaration of Independence, presenting a remarkably detailed account of the men and events that had inspired it. The same edition reprinted the entire text of the document translated into Spanish. Ramírez wrote another laudatory column on August 28, saying that the government of the United States was "formed by men of such greatness and profound wisdom that they have no parallel in history." Three weeks later, *El Clamor Público* published a short biography of every American president.

There was a strange juxtaposition of articles in the newspaper on May 24, 1856. One article, written by Ramírez, described the phenomenal development of commerce, the railroads, and the telegraph systems on the east coast of the United States. This progress was attributed to America's democratic form of government. Immediately next to this article was an item reprinted from San Francisco's *El Eco del Pacífico*, reporting the slaughter of seventeen Chileans and three Mexicans by an American mob near Coulterville in the gold country. It was the latest in a long series of unpunished atrocities committed by Americans in northern California against Latins. The two articles stood side by side in utter contrast, one portraying Americans as founders of a great democracy and the other describing them as murderous enemies of Spanish-speaking people. Whether by coincidence or not, this issue marked the end of articles expressing an exalted opinion of the United States.

At this time Ramírez took on José Elias González as a partner. For a while after August 25, 1855, both men appeared on the newspaper's masthead as editors. González seems to have had little influence on Ramírez or his newspaper, and their brief association lasted only six months.

Ramírez was now struggling to identify with some element of the American political system. He had earlier felt obliged to support the Democratic Party against the anti-Catholic Know-Nothings. In the September 5, 1855, election the Know-Nothings were defeated in Los Angeles, but they won elsewhere in the state, placing their candidate, J. Neely Johnson, as governor. Of the 1,813 votes cast in Los Angeles County, only a minuscule number could have been influenced by *El Clamor Público*. Its circulation probably did not exceed one hundred subscribers, little more than five percent of the county electorate. At first Ramírez tried to align himself with the Free Soil wing of the Democratic Party, headed by David C. Broderick, which opposed slavery. However, dominance of the party passed to the Chivalry Democrats, led by Senator William M. Gwin, whose members supported slavery with an almost fanatical enthusiasm. Ramírez was appalled when the Chivalry began to prevail over the Free Soilers.

Beyond the Chivalry's advocacy of slavery, Ramírez rejected it because Senator Gwin was the architect of the Land Act of 1851, a measure passed by Congress that required California landowners claiming under Mexican grants to prove that their titles were originally valid under Mexican law in order to be recognized by the United States. A petition had to be presented before a three-man commission in San Francisco, which decided on a case-by-case basis whether a particular land grant had been properly issued under the old regime. Successful petitioners received a United States land patent confirming the validity of their Mexican title. Those who lost before the commission forfeited their lands to the United States government. The owners had the burden of proof, were subject to ruinously expensive legal fees, and had to endure uncertain, time-consuming appeals. The cost of such proceedings bankrupted many Mexicans regardless of the merit of their claims.[40]

Ramírez considered the Land Act of 1851 as an instance of American injustice, often citing it when venting his anger against the new government. For the most part only wealthy Mexicans in California were greatly affected. The protests of Ramírez on their behalf did not result in any significant increase in support for his newspaper by landowners. They failed to respond to articles like the one appearing on June 19, 1856, in which Ramírez wrote: "Gwin is a Democrat and justly deserves the hatred of the people for having originated the Land Commission which has ruined and retarded the progress of California." The majority of the ranchero elite continued to accept the Chivalry leader and his representative in Los Angeles, the popular lawyer Joseph Lancaster Brent.

The rise of the Chivalry throughout the state greatly distressed Ramírez. It seemed to confirm the hopelessly racist nature of the American public. His unhappiness led him to embrace a proposal that Spanish speakers leave California to establish a colony in Mexico. On February 7, 1855, several leading California Mexicans conducted a formal meeting at the St. Francis Hotel in San Francisco to discuss the misfortunes they were experiencing under American rule. A former Mexican governor, Juan Alvarado, presided. Many of those attending were northern California landowners in peril of losing their property. They had been suddenly overwhelmed by thousands of aggressive newcomers during the Gold Rush. The swiftly ensuing chaos had never permitted them to form social or political connections with Americans like the southern California ranchero elite. After reviewing the enormous expense required to prove legal title to their ranches under the Land Act of 1851, the high taxes, and the uncontrollable invasion of their holdings by squatters, they concluded that it would be in their interest to escape American influences by moving to northern Mexico. In addition to the erosion of their property rights, those attending could see no end to the discrimination and violence directed toward Mexicans in California. They formed an organization to encourage a Mexican departure from California called the "Society for the Promotion of the Emigration of Native Californians to Sonora."[41]

Jesús Islas, a native of Mazatlan, was chosen to locate a suitable place in the northwest border state of Sonora for the establishment of a colony in Mexico. The movement to Sonora began under the auspices of landowners but quickly evolved into a working-class enterprise. Ramírez's October 23, 1855, edition contained a prospectus sent by Islas, outlining a plan for a Mexican withdrawal from California. It declared that one of the basic reasons for abandoning the state was the bad treatment received "from certain classes of the American people."

Islas turned out to be a persistent and highly effective leader. In early 1856 he appeared in San Jose with a small convoy of immigrants ready to depart for Sonora. On February 16 *El Clamor Público* gave notice that Islas would pass through Los Angeles on his way south. It also published official documents from the state government of Sonora, welcoming the arrival of the proposed colony. Islas intended to recruit additional colonists as he moved toward Sonora. He had already acquired land rights for his colony on Rancho Búsanic, near the abandoned village of Sáric, about twenty miles southwest of Nogales, Arizona.

As Islas approached Los Angeles, Ramírez became increasingly fired with enthusiasm for the exodus to Sonora. The May 10, 1856, edition of *El Clamor Público* reported the arrival of Islas and predicted that 200 to 300 persons would eventually leave with him. Ramírez tried to persuade Los Angeles Mexican residents to join the caravan southward, rhapsodizing about Sonora's advantages and the fertile fields destined to support "a free people of Spanish descent." He wrote that for the Mexican people in California, "there is no justice, no equality, no liberty. . . . We ask in the name of reason and common sense if it would not be better for us all to immigrate to the only asylum that guarantees our liberty."

A handful of Los Angeles families decided to accompany Islas, but most residents rejected the migration south and Ramírez's efforts to promote it. Various letters were sent to *El Clamor Público*, expressing concern for the turbulent politics and poor living conditions in Sonora. Some worried that immigrants from Los Angeles would be conscripted and forced to fight in one of the region's endless political insurrections. Others feared the constant unseen presence of Apache marauders. In any event, few cared to risk their futures with Islas in Sonora.

After the party of California Mexicans reached Sonora, they settled in the village of Sáric, an adobe wreck with the remnants of a church built by Father Eusebio Kino in 1702. It had been abandoned years before the arrival of the colony because of incursions by Apaches, who were still in the area. Islas wrote several letters to Ramírez expressing the hope that more Californians would come to his colony. Those who went to Sáric from California rebuilt the village and stayed for several decades. Some twenty-seven years after the arrival of the Mexican American colonists, a Sonora state official who visited Sáric in 1883 reported that its inhabitants were engaged in agriculture and still "retained the characteristics of colonists."[42] The Tucson Spanish-language newspaper *El Fronterizo* published an article on October 19, 1889, concerning the California origin of Sáric. It related that "the colony prospered and shows today a settlement of 800 inhabitants, laborious, strong in peace and war, and as patriotic as the best, chiefly engaged in agriculture, mining, trade, and raising of cattle." The item noted that two daughters of Jesús Islas had married Americans and were living in Tucson, an ironic turn of events for a man who struggled so hard to distance himself from the United States.

Today, residents of Sáric have no memory of the California colonists, nor do they claim descent from them. Local research on the colony is difficult. According to the mayor and city council, the municipal archives were destroyed by vandals in 1956. Church records from the nineteenth century are mysteriously absent. The area suffered a prolonged drought in the 1940s, which caused the virtual abandonment of the village for several years. The descendants of the colonists were forced to disperse to other parts of the border area, especially Nogales. Modern residents of Sáric, even municipal officials, are immigrants from other points in Mexico who repopulated the village within the last few decades.

If Ramírez was disappointed by the small number of families that left California with Islas, he made no mention of it in his newspaper. His June 14, 1856, edition marked the first anniversary of *El Clamor Público*. With surprising candor he wrote, "We have to ask the indulgence of our readers for the errors we have incurred during our editorship, which can be attributed to our age and limited experience." Referring to the lack of interest in his newspaper by the Spanish-speaking population, he observed, "During our short experience we have noted that our race is little concerned with the support of such enterprises." But he gratefully saluted "the brave sons of France" for their liberal backing of his newspaper through subscriptions and advertising. Ramírez proclaimed that "with hand on heart, we again launch into the sea of public opinion."

CLAMOR PUBLICO

Periódico Independiente y Literario.

LOS ANGELES, CALIFORNIA, MARTES, JUNIO 19 DE 1855.

COMISION DE LOS ESTADOS UNIDOS
PARA LA APROBACION DE LOS TITULOS DE TERRENOS.

[Sesion de 22 de mayo de 1855.]

Opinion del Comisionado Farwell.

APROBADOS.

N.° 250.—El título del Sr. M G. Vallejo por 10 leguas cuadradas y 5 mas en el condado de Petaluma.

N.° 291.—Otro del mismo, por un terreno en el condado de Solano.

N.° 291.—El título de John Rose, seis leguas cuadadas en el condado de Yuba.

N.° 462.—El título de los herederos de Juan B. Alvarado, por el Rincon del Diablo en el condado de San Diego.

N.° 550.—El título de Jno P. Davison, cuatro leguas cuadradas en Santa Paula y Santicoy, cudado de Sta. Barbara.

N.° 461.—El título de Juan Foster ocho leguas cuadradas en el valle de S. Felipe, condado de San Diego.

N.° 664.—El título de los herederos de David Litsejohn, una legua cuadrada en Los Carneos, condado de Monterey.

N.° 509.—El título de Samuel G. Reid, tres leguas cuadradas en el rancho del Puerto, condado de San Joaquin.

N.° 248.—El título de Chas Convilland, parte de 1 leguas concedidas primero a J. A. Sutter Concesion por recompensa y con condiciones en 1841. El terreno esta situado en Feather River.

DESAPROBADO.

N.° 685.—El título de Temple y Alexander, po 100 varas cuadradas en el condado de Los Angeles. Concedidas provisionalmente en 1854.

Mexico.

El Genral Alvarez ha espedido el siguiente dereto para favorecer a las personas que deseen emigrar a Mexico para esplotar los ricos placeres de oro que se han descubierto en Ajutechlan, cerca de Acapulco:

El Capitan Juan Alvarez, General de Division de la República Mexicana y en Gefe del ejército restaurador de la Libertad á los habitantes de la República, sabed:

Que hacido de las amplias facultades que me concede el "Plan de Ayutla," para promover por cuantos medios me sean posibles la prosperidad y engrandecimiento de la nacion, he tenido á bien decretar:

ART. 1. El laboreo de los placeres de San Fracisco del Oro, situados en el distrito de Ajutchlan del departamento de Guerrero, se declara libre para mexicanos y extranjeros desde la publicacion de este decreto

ART. 2. Todo individuo, ya sea nacional ó estranjero, que se dirija al distrito mencionado con objeto de trabajar los placeres se presentará a las autoridades políticas para obtener de ellas "gratis," sus correspondientes resguardos.

ART. 3. Es libre de todo derecho la introduccion que se haga por el puerto de Acapulco, de maquinaria, instrumentos y provisiones para el trabajo de las minas.

ART. 4. Los metales preciosos del distrito mineral, que se extraigan fuera de la república, solo pagarán al erario el 1 por 100, ayendo en pena de comiso los que contravengan a esta disposicion.

ART. 5. Todo trabajador de placeres referidos, ya sea nacional ó extranjero, que desere adquirir terrenos para fabricar ó dedicarse a la agricultura, ocurrirá a la autoridad política, que facilitara de los terrenos valdíos el que se le pidiere, a precios convencionales y equitativos.

ART. 6. Las diferencias que ocurran entre los mineros, se resolverán por quien corresponda con sujecion a la ordenanza del ramo.

Pr tanto, etc. Dado en cuartel general del Ejército Restaurador en Texca, a 20 de Abril de 1855. JUAN ALVAREZ.

Sud America.

CHILE.—Segun las últimas noticias continúa su marcha pacifica y progresiva. Las elecciones para miembros del Congreso han pasado sin ocurrencia alguna notable. Entre los Senadores electos vemos con suma satisfaccion el nombre del ilustre colombiano D. Andrés Bello.

PERU.—El general Flores habia llegado á Lima, y protestado contra el tratado que celebró Echenique con el gobierno del Ecuador, por el cual se le niega a aquel el asilo en el Perú. Parece que el gobierno provisional tiene por ominoso el tratado, y lo considera humillante para el honor nacional. Pero el ministro del Ecuador protestó, y le han seguido los demas Ministros de la América septentrional residentes en Lima. Piden que Flores salga del Perú inmediatamente. "Si Flores (dice un diario del Sur) ha sido siempre una amenaza para los Estados Colombianos, hoy es mayor esa amenaza, mediante la expedicion que se quedaba formando en los Estados Unidos por él, con el fin de tomar las islas de los Galápagos."

Es un hecho imposible que salga de aquí expedicion contra el Ecuador, por mas que hagan Flores y su edecan Clemens.

BOLIVIA.—No son menores las inquietudes en Bolivia con motivo del anunciado regreso del general Santa Cruz. El Presidente Belzu ha dictado un decreto, ordenando el secuestro de los bienes de todo el que tome parte en alguna sedicion, invacion etc. Uno de los artículos de ese decreto manda conciderar sin efecto las transacciones que se hubieren celebrado sobre dichos bienes, desde seis meses antes de cometido el delito, en cuando fueren aquellos necesarios para indemnizar al Gobierno y a los particulares de los perjuicios causados por los perturbadores. Se ha dado a luz una carta que se dice dirijida por el general Santa Cruz al coronel Puch, fechada en Bruselas a 15 de nobiembre del año próximo pasado, y en la cual manifiesta el Protector su determinacion de "regresar a America á oponerse á la reeleccion en que está empeñado Belzu, adoptando al efecto el sistema de Flores."

BRASIL Y PARAGUAY.—Por los extractos que ofrecen los diarios del Istmo de Panama sabemos que la guerra del imperio del Brasil contra el Uruguay se está ya haciendo, y segun parece, sin una declaracion que la precediera, "siendo lo mas extraño (dice el *Panameno*) ver que la marina de guerra de los Estados Unidos ayude a S. M. I; en su agrecion contra los paraguayos. Estos, empero, oponen fuerzas considerables á sus adversarios, y hasta ahora alcan el triunfo en los combates habidos." He aquí lo que dice el *Constitucional* de Mendoza, en el asunto: "Se hacia serio nos informa uno de los pasajeros llegados en la mensajería, el conflicto del Paraguay, atacado por una fuerte escuadra brasilera y un vapor norteamericano; dos potencias poderosas han llevado la guerra contra esta naciente y pequeña república; el Almirante del Paraguay, hijo del Presidente Lopez, de dos vapores que habian comprado en Europa, no habia conseguido introducir sino uno antes que la escuadra brasilera ocupase los rios. Habia tenido lugar un combate entre el vapor norteamericano que hemos mensionado y una batería paraguaya, la que causó con sus fuegos algunas averias en el vapor matándole dos hombres ademas. Este desmontó algunas piezas de aquella. En la frontera con el Brasil, en las guardias ó fuertes se trataban encuentros parciales entre paraguayos y brasileros, en los que aquellos habian salido vencedores."

Los periódicos de Buenos Ayres dan la noticia de que una fuerza paraguaya de 8,000 hombres habia obtenido á inmediaciones de Villareal un triunfo sobre las fuerzas brasilerias invasoras. Sobre el Paraná tenian los paraguayos 20,000. hombres estacionados, habian tapado dos de las tres bocas del rio Paraguay, echando á pique piraguas cargadas de piedras, y están le

Francia.

FRANCIA.—Un decreto del Emperador aumenta al ejército en 90,000 hombres.—Cada regimiento de línea tendrá un refuerzo de 900.

Esperando la visita de la Reina Victoria á Paris, el Emperador ha mandado poner el Liceo Imperial en un pie de espléndida magnificencia.

Por decreto de 31 de marzo, Mr. de Thouenevel Ministro Plenipotenciario de primera clase y director de los asuntos políticos, se encargará durante la audiencia del Ministro Secretario de Estado de Negocios Extranjeros, Mr. Drouyn de Lhuys, de la direccion de los trabajos de su departamento y de la correspondencia diplomática.

El gobierno francés se ha quejado oficialmente al belga, á instancias del Príncipe Napoleon, por un opúsculo publicado contra el Emperador sobre la guerra y que se atribuyó al Príncipe.

EL PROXIMO CONGRESO.—Hasta hoy los miembros electos para el próximo Congreso son como sigue: Administracion 31; Oposicion 129. Todavia resta que elejir 37 miembros en los Estados donde las elecciones congresionales aun no han tenido lugar.

INTERESANTE.—Un astrónomo Aleman dice que en veinte millones de años la tierra será destruida por una cometa!

LA MEDALLA RUSA.—En los cuerpos de algunos soldados rusos que cayeron en Eupatoria se encontró la medalla de plata de la decoracion de San Jorge. En un lado está grabada el águila rusa, con dos cabezas, teniendo en los pies el globo terrestre y el cetro del soberano; sobre el águila esta la corona imperial y una paloma iluminada. Sobre estas figuras tiene las siguientes palabras en lengua rusa:

"Arrodillense, idolatras, porque Dios es con nosotros."

En el otro lado tiene la siguiente divisa tambien en ruso:

"Para la sumision de Hungria y Transilvania."

☞ Dícese que casi todo el vino de la Moselle ha sido comprado por el gobierno Francés para mandarlo al ejército de Crimea.

☞ La *Union* de Sacramento hablando del San Francisco *Chronicle* dice: "No se encuentra dentro de los límites de este Estado otro periódico mas cortéz, independiente y elegante."

☞ Los soldados heridos y enfermos que han muerto en Liverpool, (Inglaterra) serán enterrados en un mismo lugar, sobre el cual se erijirá un monumento por suscricion pública.

PISCATORIO.—Mr. Joseph S. McIntyre, de la armada de los E. U. estacionada en Benicia, publica una carta en el *Herald* de San Francisco, anunciando que sacó un pescado y abriéndolo encontro un látigo de veinte pulgadas y media de largo y montado en plata. Se ha dudado mucho la veracidad de esta historieta.

POZO ARTESIANO.—Se ha cavado un nuevo pozo artesiano en San José, y segun el *Tribune* es una curiosidad.

CONVENCION DEMOCRATICA.—El dia 27 de Junio tendrá lugar una convencion democratica en Sacramento con el objeto de nombrar oficiales para la eleccion general en Setiembre próximo.

EL CENSO.—La Constitucion del Estado previene que se tome el censo este año, pero como la legislatura no dispuso nada sobre esto, se tomara el año de 1860.

PELEGRINOS PARA PALESTINA.—Una caravana de pelegrinos se embarcó recientemente en Marsella para la Tierra Santa.—Antes de su salida fuéron invitados al palacio por el Obispo y cada uno recibió una crucesita de plata, con la fecha de su partida. Se esta organizando otra caravana

La ley del Doming

SECCION 1. Toda diversion bulliciosa será en lo sucesivo dias domingos.

SEC. 2. Todo individuo que ayudase a abrir un establecimiento público, tal como teatro, juego, cuarto ó salon, juego de lugares propios para carreras combate de osos, de toros, de diversiones barbaras y bul prendido por un delito especial, y despues de convicto, a una multa cuyo minimun cuenta pesos y el maximum cuenta.

SEC. 3. Todo individuo que un billete de entrada á uno de las diversiones enumera gunda seccion de esta acta, se castigado con una multa al minimum, y de cincuenta

SEC. 4. Los jueces de en todos casos de infraccion ciones de esta ley.

SEC. 5. Esta ley estará en desde Junio de 1855.

PAPEL DE TULE.—El Exmo BIGLER en su último mensaje los terrenos inundados y an presa como sigue:

"Y ya que estoy tocando acaso no sea fuera de lugar el llegan a tener buen éxito los que ahora se están haciendo del Atlántico, no tan solo sino que aumentará necesaria lor. Nadie ignora que una los terrenos adquiridos por virtud de la ley de Setiem está cubierta de lozano Tule este suelo, y que por término toneladas por acre.

"Durante el último otoño sido cuidadosamente ecsamin bricantes esperimentados, qu presado que, en su opinion, s con él un papel de calidad b perior.

"Puesto que el tallo del está maduro y antes que se la lluvia, es casi blanco, se d del blanqueo seria compe pequeño. Estando cubierto d y compacta fibra, ó interiorm un tejido celular con numero fibras longitudinales, se cre todas las cualidades requerid

"Se han remitido varias Tule á algunos fabricantes de Estados del Atlántico, y es p hagan ensayos con él, y pron el resultado de estos importa mentos.

"A fin de poder apreciar c la importancia de este esperim que tenga feliz éxito, se hace explicacion de algunos hecho rentes.

"El precio medio, en los Atlántico, del material con q fabrica el papel es de unos x la libra. A dos centavos en la tercera parte del precio actual los trapos, ada acre producir ochenta pesos ($80) ó sea do cientos pesos ($12,800) cada c acres, y esto, sin mas gastos se orijinen al tiempo de la si no despues de que haya complet durado.

"Sin embargo, cualquiera q sultado de los esperimentos q haciendo acerca de la primera papel de cartas ó de imprent duda han los hombres entend han ocupado de esta materia el *Tule* se puede fabricar pape na calidad.

CHAPTER TWO
A Militant Mexican Newspaper

A little more than two months after urging a withdrawal to Sonora, Ramírez manifested a startling change in attitude toward relations with Americans. In an editorial of July 19, 1856, he wrote about complaints from American law enforcement officials that Mexicans protected members of their race from arrest. Ramírez noted that the law against harboring fugitives had never been published in Spanish. He translated the relevant statute in his newspaper and asked readers to join with Americans in following the law:

> Californians! Americans! Citizens of every origin and class! Let us all unite to see that the laws are obeyed and that our officials are aided in carrying them out when necessary. By doing this we will soon see the regeneration of our country and peacefully enjoy our rights to life and property.

This was a peculiar pronouncement for someone who had recently advocated the total separation from Americans by moving to Mexico.

Strangely, Ramírez's appeal on July 19 for harmony between the races was published on the very day an event occurred that shattered the peace in Los Angeles. On that Saturday morning, at about 10:00 a.m., Deputy Marshal William W. Jenkins went to the adobe home of Antonio Ruiz with a writ of execution to collect a judgment of fifty dollars. He seized Ruiz's guitar toward payment of the debt. As he was about to leave, Ruiz's common-law wife, María Candelaria Pollorena, remembered she had a letter from her mother in the guitar and asked Jenkins to return it. When Jenkins refused, she tried to snatch the guitar from his hands. At that moment Jenkins drew a pistol and aimed it at her. Ruiz grabbed Jenkins's arms from behind in a frantic effort to protect his wife. The deputy marshal pointed the gun backwards, firing a round into Ruiz's chest.

Although the wound was fatal, death did not come until 5:00 p.m. the next day. Ruiz remained conscious long enough to bid farewell to a procession of tearful friends. He was thirty-three years old, a poor but respected man who had given the oration at the previous Mexican Independence Day celebration. His patriotic speech had been well received and was published on October 2, 1855, in *El Clamor Público*. The killing of Ruiz by an American officer provoked spontaneous demonstrations of outrage by the Mexican people for several days. Jenkins was placed in jail, largely for his own protection. The July 26, 1856, edition of *El Clamor Público* was almost completely taken up with reporting the events of a week that Ramírez described as one "not seen in California since the war between Mexico and the United States."

There was a grand funeral for Ruiz on July 21, the largest ever seen in the city and one that included a band playing "sad and solemn airs." After the ceremony a group of Mexicans went to the jailhouse to place a watch over Jenkins. They feared that Ruiz's death would not be avenged because Jenkins would be allowed to escape. Most believed that the Americans would never punish one of their own for killing a Mexican. After a tense encounter at the jail, an American deputy sheriff persuaded the Mexicans to leave. During Tuesday, July 22, the town was electrified by rumors of an impending Mexican attack on the jail to lynch Jenkins. Ramírez observed, "From an early hour everyone went about with weapons in hand." This dangerous situation caused most businesses to close and "commerce was completely paralyzed." That night a force of angry Mexicans met on Fort Hill to discuss an assault on the jail to hang Jenkins. They were led by Ferdinand Carriega, one of several Frenchmen who sided with the Mexicans. About midnight some one hundred of them made a quick foray into the plaza, discharging their weapons, only to scatter when confronted by a small group of American defenders. No one was hurt except Marshal William C. Getman, who miraculously survived a grazing bullet wound of his right temple.

The Americans rapidly moved to take back control of Los Angeles. Fourteen Mexicans who had nothing to do with the attack on the plaza were arrested the next morning and spent the day in jail. Jenkins was released on a bail bond posted by his friends. The Americans convened a public meeting in the plaza where four military companies were organized to round up and disarm Mexican dissidents. A vigilante-style committee of twenty men was appointed to coordinate the suppression of disturbances and decide the fate of those captured by the military companies. Although the great majority of people in Los Angeles were Spanish speaking, only four Mexicans were appointed to the committee. Each was a conservative member of the wealthy ranchero elite and a trusted Chivalry Democrat. Mexicans of lesser standing had little part in the proceedings.

The death of Ruiz and the disorders that followed were fully described in the July 26, 1856, edition of *El Clamor Público* along with a commentary on the events of the week. Ramírez understood the anger of ordinary Spanish-speaking people, saying, "It is becoming common to assassinate and outrage Mexicans with impunity." The Ruiz affair was called "murder, nothing more or less." Yet Ramírez continued the conciliatory tone of the previous edition: "We regret that this incident has increased the differences between Americans and Mexicans. The disturbance of last Tuesday has only served to widen the distance that has existed for so long between the races." He expressed the hope that Mexicans roaming the streets would return to their homes.[1]

Ramírez's calm reaction to the uprising changed the next week. He printed an August 2 editorial in which he reflected on the unhappy condition of Mexicans in California, concluding with an emotional outburst:

> We are convinced that *California is lost to all hispanic-americans*; and here in Los Angeles, because of the recent *revolution* (?), if they had to ask for favors before, now they will beg on their knees for *justice* and *liberty* to carry on their lives. Almost all the newspapers from the north are continually filled with reports of lynchings in the mines. And, oh fatality! only Mexicans are the victims of the people's insane fury! Mexicans alone have been sacrificed on gallows raised to launch their poor souls into eternity. Is this the *liberty* and *equality* of the country we have adopted?

Despite the passionate nature of this editorial, Ramírez's general reaction to the uprising was more measured. He began to urge greater cooperation between Mexicans and Americans as a means of reducing racial conflict. In the August 16 issue, he wrote, "It is necessary that there be *union* in this city in order to have security. Let us all work together in the same spirit to carry out the laws."

When Jenkins was brought to trial on charges of manslaughter, Ramírez devoted almost his entire August 23 issue to a meticulous presentation of the proceedings. Every detail of the testimony was given, together with an explanation of the American jury trial for the benefit of his Mexican readers. However, those in the Spanish-speaking community who cynically believed that Jenkins would never be punished were vindicated. Twelve Americans were placed on the jury without a single Mexican among them. Predictably, they returned a verdict of not guilty in less than fifteen minutes. Ramírez's reaction to the trial's outcome was uncharacteristically complacent: "No one will deny that it had bad effects on the community; but time will erase them, and we will return to living in harmony, each class working to establish and perpetuate the fraternal sentiments that ought to govern a well-regulated society."

Ramírez's approach to race relations was undergoing a dramatic change during the summer of 1856. His editorials were becoming less critical of Americans, even urging accommodation with them. This new outlook was caused by the spectacular rise of the Republican Party. Its sudden appearance on the national scene revealed a side of the American people that Ramírez had never seen. Based on violent Northern opposition to the Kansas-Nebraska Bill of 1854, which allowed slavery in those territories, the party rapidly spread across the United States. The cardinal principle of Republicans was a prohibition of slavery in all the western territories, especially those acquired after the Mexican-American War. Seven prominent individuals met in Sacramento on March 8, 1856, to plan the formation of the party in California. Republican clubs were organized throughout the state with an April 30 convention held in Sacramento.[2] Ramírez printed the convention's platform on May 31, 1856. Its antislavery stance was expanded to include a plank defending the rights of immigrants and a call for a transcontinental railroad.

Ramírez realized that Republican hostility to slavery was largely the result of a desire to protect free white labor. There was often little concern for blacks as human beings. Even so, Republican sentiment against slavery was a revelation to Ramírez. It was the first time he found himself in complete agreement with the aims of a popular American political movement.

When the Republicans nominated John Charles Frémont as their presidential candidate in Philadelphia on June 19, 1856, Ramírez's enthusiasm soared. Frémont's career was closely associated with California, where he was regarded as a sympathetic friend of its Spanish-speaking people. At the outbreak of the Mexican-American War, Frémont was present in California as a U.S. Army officer in charge of a party charting the Pacific slope. He was already famous for two previous topographical expeditions into the North American wilderness. It was Frémont who received Mexican emissaries to discuss surrender at Cahuenga, near Los Angeles, on January 13, 1847. The supreme military authorities in California were unaware of Frémont's negotiations with the Mexicans until he sent them Articles of Capitulation that were already signed. Frémont acceded to nearly all of the demands made by the Mexicans. It was a magnanimous peace that left the native Californios with their property and honor intact. His sensitive handling of the surrender made him extremely popular among the Mexican people.

In early 1847 Frémont briefly served as the American military governor of California. Headquartered in Los Angeles, he treated Mexicans as equals and seemed to enjoy their company. One writer notes that during this period Frémont was "winning many friends among the natives by joining in their festivities and adopting to some extent their ways of dress and life."[3] Unfortunately, a conflict with General Stephen Watts Kearny caused Frémont's removal from office and a court-martial for insubordination in Washington, D.C. Frémont chose to resign from the army. He returned to live in Rancho Las Mariposas, a property in the northern California gold country that he had acquired earlier. His adoption of Mexican dress was more than an affectation to gain native support while governor. Even after Frémont became a private citizen, a newspaper reporter found him in San Francisco "wearing a sombrero and California jacket."[4]

At the end of 1849, the state constitutional convention elected Frémont as one of the first United States senators from California. Since his term was extremely short, he was back from the capital to seek reelection during January 1851. At that time United States senators were elected by state legislatures, not by popular vote. While Frémont was away in Washington, D.C., the political scene in California radically changed. The legislature was soon dominated by Chivalry Democrats who refused to reelect him because he had done little while a senator other than introduce bills opposing slavery. The abolitionist tendencies of Frémont were anathema to the majority in the legislature. He had no chance of returning to the United States Senate. Nevertheless, as proof of the high regard of California Mexicans for Frémont, the few Spanish-speaking members of the legislature never wavered in their support of him. San Francisco's *Alta California* marveled on January 7, 1851: "The native Californian members of the Senate and Assembly voted for Frémont and stuck to him from the first to the last ballot."

After finally withdrawing as a candidate for the Senate, Frémont devoted himself to gold mining operations on Rancho Las Mariposas. This land, originally a Mexican grant, was the subject of a bitter legal contest with the federal government that only concluded when the U.S. Supreme Court ruled in Frémont's favor. His efforts to preserve Rancho Las Mariposas united him with Mexican landowners in their struggle against the Land Act of 1851.

Frémont later took up residence in New York, leaving his California property in the care of others. During 1855 he traveled through Europe, where he was feted for his trail-blazing exploits in charting the North American continent and for his skills as a naturalist. He was favorably compared with the explorer Sir Richard Burton and other celebrated figures engaged in opening Africa for the British Empire. Frémont's world fame as the "Pathfinder" elevated him to the status of an American hero. His political failure in California had little effect on his national image.

From Ramírez's point of view, Frémont's presidential candidacy was a fantastic stroke of luck for the Mexican people. Not only did Frémont relate well to California Mexicans, he had a kind of Latin element in his own personality. His father, Louis René Frémont, a native French speaker, was from either France or Quebec, according to equally plausible sources. Although born of an Anglo-American mother in Savannah, Georgia, and raised in Charleston, South Carolina, Frémont was heavily influenced by his father's background. He sometimes used the French language and always placed an accent on his last name, a trait that emphasized his Latin roots.

Frémont insisted on having a cosmopolitan company of men for his explorations of North America. His command included Indians, blacks, and mixed-blood frontiersmen, who were fiercely loyal to him. He was accustomed to sharing life on the trail with men of widely differing backgrounds and races. It is not surprising that Frémont endeared himself to the California Mexicans by his easy acceptance of their lifestyle. His opposition to slavery and his sympathy for Mexicans was well known. During the presidential campaign of 1856, mocking placards appeared in San Francisco, reading, "Frémont: Free Niggers and Frijoles."[5] But Frémont's enlightened attitudes and vaguely Latin air aroused the greatest admiration on the part of Ramírez. He believed that Frémont's election would bring a friend of the Mexican people to the White House.

Beginning with his August 30, 1856, edition, Ramírez hammered Spanish-speaking readers with arguments in favor of voting for the Republicans in the election scheduled for November 4, 1856. Besides their promise to limit slavery, the Republicans would eliminate the difficulty of confirming title to Mexican land grants and stop filibustering expeditions to Latin America. The last issue was important to many Spanish-speaking people. Privately organized groups of armed Americans, known as filibusterers, had already invaded parts of Mexico and Nicaragua without official sanction. These adventurers had hopes of getting rich and ultimately claiming new areas for the United States. It was widely believed that the Mexican state of Sonora would soon be overrun by them. News of such aggressive movements offended California Mexicans who still resented the loss of their territory to the United States. At this time William Walker's filibusterers occupied Nicaragua, where they operated an extralegal government. Many local Mexicans felt a need to defend the sovereignty of people below the border.

Ramírez's advocacy of Frémont and the Republicans brought him the enmity of several leading citizens. None was a more relentless antagonist than Henry Hamilton, the new editor of the *Los Angeles Star*. Hamilton, who purchased the newspaper in June 1856, was an Irishman born in Londonderry who arrived in America during 1848, at the age of twenty-two. After following the newspaper trade in northern California, he took up residence in Los Angeles, a town congenial to his temperament.[6] He was as much devoted to antebellum ideals as the most ardent Southerner and had a virulent hatred of blacks. Hamilton's antipathy toward them was unusually pronounced, even for a partisan of the Chivalry. As the *Star*'s editor he became the Democratic Chivalry's leading spokesman, a highly influential figure in local politics.

The endorsement of Frémont and the Republicans by *El Clamor Público* started a protracted feud between Hamilton and Ramírez. When Hamilton learned that *El Clamor Público* had obtained a printing contract from Los Angeles authorities, he called the city council "nigger-worshippers" for supporting a newspaper with abolitionist views. Over the objections of Ramírez, the city contract was soon rescinded. The *Star* then launched a series of personal attacks on Frémont, accusing him of keeping a "harem" of Mexican women and stealing money while acting as military governor in Los Angeles.[7] Ramírez responded energetically to Hamilton's charges. The two men exchanged insults throughout the period leading up to the presidential election.

Hamilton feigned ignorance of the true underpinnings of the Republican movement. Instead of recognizing that the new party opposed the expansion of slavery as a threat to free white labor, he pretended that their position was based on an unusual affection for Africans by whites. He almost always referred to members of the opposition as "Black Republicans," an emotionally charged term used by many Chivalry politicians.

Despite pressures to quash the Republican Party, some Los Angeles residents supported it. "A large and enthusiastic meeting of the friends of Frémont" was noticed on September 13 in *El Clamor Público*. Several prominent citizens from the northern part of the United States—such as Alexander Bell, Lewis Granger, and Obed Macy—formed a Republican club.

Henry Hamilton, editor of the *Los Angeles Star*, on the right. William McKee, a school teacher who refused to take a loyalty oath to the Union, on the left, date unknown. Reprinted by permission of the University of Southern California Special Collections.

Beginning with the September 27 edition, *El Clamor Público* ran a series of pages in English to help the Republican campaign. Numerous articles in favor of Frémont were contributed by John O. Wheeler, a former newspaper editor known for his acerbic wit. Ramírez's conversion to the Republican Party necessarily involved collaboration with Americans. Now he placed his newspaper at their disposal.

During the last few weeks before the election, *El Clamor Público* became a bilingual propaganda sheet for the Republican Party. An article written by Wheeler in English, which appeared on November 1, 1856, demonstrates the reasons that the Republican Party appealed to Ramírez and a number of other Mexicans in Los Angeles:

> This election is to determine the great question whether Filibusterism, Slavery, and robbery and "greaser laws" shall, as heretofore disgrace our nation and blight our own individual interest; or whether by the election of John C. Frémont we shall inaugurate a new era in the history of our country characterized by equal rights, equal justice, equality between Californians and Americans, freedom of speech, a free press, and a Pacific Railroad.

The purported Republican goal of "equality between Californians and Americans" set forth by Wheeler had no counterpart in Chivalry rhetoric. Their openly racist attitudes brought several despairing Mexicans over to the Republican side. One of these, José Rubio, published a letter in *El Clamor Público* on October 4, saying in part: "When we remember the bad treatment we have received from Democratic officials during the past seven years, it is incredible that any native Californian could continue with this damned party unless he has lost all self-respect and submits to being led around by the nose."

Rubio's letter appeared in the same edition as word of an unexpected source of support for the Republicans. Pío Pico, California's last Mexican governor, announced in the paper that he favored Frémont for president. The names of thirty-two Mexicans who joined Pico's endorsement accompanied the item. Pico's support was based on his friendship with Frémont, as well as on ideological considerations. However, despite Pico's stellar position within the ranchero elite, most of his class remained firmly committed to the Chivalry.

The Republican campaign in Los Angeles was more than an effort to gather votes for Frémont. It was also a movement to control local politics. The Chivalry kept many Mexicans in line by exploiting their traditional submission to the ranchero elite. Those dependent on wealthy landowners loyal to the Chivalry usually voted as requested. Ramírez tried to persuade ordinary Mexicans that such behavior was self-defeating. By casting their ballots for the Chivalry, they supported an oppressive minority of white Southerners who cared little for the welfare of Mexicans outside the ranchero elite. In the October 4 edition of *El Clamor Público*, he offered an alternative: "From now on we should operate independently. . . . We have enough votes among ourselves to control the elections in this county and we have the power to elect candidates who will work for our interests."

Ramírez believed that a coalition of Mexicans and Republicans would improve the situation of Spanish-speaking people in Los Angeles. Based on dialogues with local and state Republican leaders, he was convinced that a new era of equality was at hand. As early as July 26, he counseled his readers to contain their rage over the killing of Ruiz since "a more favorable order of things is coming to this city." He was not surprised, therefore, when Los Angeles Republicans nominated Pío Pico, Manuel Requeña, and Vicente Lugo as candidates for the five-man county board of supervisors in the week of October 18, 1856. In this way, the Republicans offered the majority of seats on the board to the Mexican community. In contrast, the Chivalry proposed to place the wealthy rancheros Tomás Sánchez and Manuel Dominguez on the board, while reserving the three decisive seats for themselves. Unlike the Chivalry, Republicans were willing to actually share power with Mexicans in exchange for their votes. Ramírez fully appreciated this fact and did his utmost to seize the opportunities for Mexican advancement presented by the new party.

There is little doubt that Ramírez's advocacy of the Republicans led to their providing him with financial support during the election campaign. This would by no means diminish the sincerity of his commitment to their cause. He failed to publish the edition of *El Clamor Público* scheduled for September 20 because he left Los Angeles to confer with Republican leaders in northern California on tactics and finances. During this same week the *San Francisco Herald*, a Chivalry newspaper, published a September 22 item that saw increased activity and spending by the opposition party:

> The Black Republicans are moving heaven and earth to carry California—money is being lavished with an open hand everywhere. The Blacks are also working stealthily, and have their paid agents and hireling spies all over the state.

The Chivalry press suspected that Ramírez was paid for his services to the Republicans. Shortly after the election the San Francisco *Herald* ran an article on the Republican campaign that referred to the role of *El Clamor Público*: "This same party purchased a paper at Los Angeles, printed both in English and Spanish. It was the most violent of all the Free-Nigger organs in the state." The *Los Angeles Star* reprinted the item on December 6. However, with uncharacteristic aloofness, Ramírez did not refute his adversaries.

Toward the end of the campaign, *El Clamor Público* began making desperate, almost hysterical attacks on the Democratic presidential nominee, James Buchanan. He was portrayed as a filibusterer, an enemy of the Spanish-speaking, who favored the annexation of much of Latin America. Ramírez vilified Buchanan as a racist who believed that the Mexican people were indistinguishable from African slaves. The newspaper repeatedly published a statement attributed to Buchanan that blacks who escaped to Mexico would find a haven there since, "the Mexican nation is composed of Spanish, Indians, and Negroes mixed with one another to such an extent that our slaves will be received by them on terms of perfect social equality." Los Angeles Mexicans were urged to avenge these "insults" by voting against Buchanan.

In California the presidential election of November 4, 1856, was a disaster for the Republicans. On a statewide level less than twenty percent of the voters favored Frémont. In Los Angeles Frémont did better, losing by 722 to 522 votes. The Chivalry swept the local elections, defeating every Republican candidate. The challenge of Ramírez and his colleagues was crushed with embarrassing ease.

On November 9, a stunned Ramírez confided, "We were certain that this county would give a tremendous majority to Frémont." He blamed the Republican loss on election fraud, refusing to accept the popular rejection of his party. A week later Ramírez made a more detached analysis. The November 15 edition of *El Clamor Público* recognized that traditional Mexican behavior was an important factor in the Republican rout. Ramírez complained about the tendency of Spanish-speaking voters to blindly accept leadership from the conservative ranchero elite. However, as might be expected, Ramírez gave notice that he was not through with politics: "They have won on this occasion, but we promise that we will prevail when the public is better informed."

Publication of the November 15 issue of *El Clamor Público* was delayed several hours so Ramírez could respond to an item appearing in the *Los Angeles Star* on the same day. The *Star* presented a column in Spanish addressed to the Mexican people, a rare occurrence for the paper. Although printed anonymously, the article was obviously written by a member of the Mexican elite who supported the Chivalry. He accused *El Clamor Público* of stirring up Mexican hatred against "our American Democratic brothers." According to the article, Ramírez was "only a boy" and not to blame for the content of *El Clamor Público*. Instead, some unknown "evil genius" was behind the "diabolical writing" in the newspaper.

Ramírez was exasperated by the unusual article in the *Star*. Its refusal to recognize his legitimate role as editor of *El Clamor Público* offended his vanity. He affirmed that he was solely responsible for the newspaper despite his youth. The rest of the item was dismissed with sarcasm: "We were amused to see that we are charged with creating a division between Californios and our 'American Democratic brothers.' We wonder how long our brothers will continue to call us 'greasers,' a name the Democrats have always used for us."

Ramírez did not permit himself any public signs of discouragement after the Republican defeat. Rather than despair, he looked forward to the state elections set for September 3, 1857, when Republicans would run a candidate for the governorship of California. Although handicapped by his extreme youth, his efforts in the recent campaign had earned him favor within the party's leadership. He sensed a coming shift of political power toward the Republicans that would benefit the Mexican people and brighten his own future. Accordingly, at the opening of 1857, Ramírez was biding his time until the next election and closely watching the Chivalry opposition.

By remaining faithful to the Republican political machine, Ramírez was tied to Americans who were fellow party members. His editorials continued to call for unity among the races. He was working to effect a fusion of Republican, Mexican, and French voters into a majority that would expel the Chivalry from power in Los Angeles. Unfortunately, a sudden outbreak of racial violence in early 1857 interfered with his agenda.

During the morning of January 23, 1857, Sheriff James R. Barton, along with three members of his five-man posse, was ambushed and killed just north of San Juan Capistrano. Barton was an enormously popular officer, known for his bravery. News of this event caused an American panic in Los Angeles. Residents had long suspected that the Mexican uprising after the death of Antonio Ruiz had created a permanent band of rebels responsible for the murder of several Americans. They believed that there was now a larger, more determined Mexican force approaching from the south to pillage and kill with Sheriff Barton's posse as its first victims. When word of Barton's fate reached Los Angeles, "the frenzy was indescribable."[8]

Several armed companies were dispatched toward San Juan Capistrano to investigate the ambush. A company of Mexican lancers under Andrés Pico was the first to arrive. Local residents told them that the settlement had been looted by several young men and a teenage boy who fatally shot a storekeeper named George Pflugardt and killed Sheriff Barton's men. Pico liberated his brother-in-law, John Forster, and several families from the Mission San Juan Capistrano, where they had barricaded themselves during the excitement.

The next day a group of Americans from El Monte arrived to join Pico's company in searching for the bandits. They were located in a mountainous area toward the northeast, where most were taken prisoner. Their leaders were Juan Flores, an escaped twenty-one-year-old convict, and a horse thief named Pancho Daniel. The Americans took Flores and Daniel to their camp for the night, leaving three other prisoners in the custody of the Mexican company. The next morning the Americans were chagrined to find that Flores and Daniel had escaped. This infuriated Pico, who immediately hanged his prisoners from a nearby sycamore. Although Flores was recaptured, Pancho Daniel managed to remain at large.

The captured outlaws, including Flores, were brought to Los Angeles, where they were summarily hanged by a committee of leading citizens who bypassed the local court and its delays. One fugitive, an eighteen-year-old named José Jesús Espinosa, was arrested in San Buenaventura. A party from Los Angeles went north to take him from local authorities for execution. Moments before he was hanged, Espinosa allowed a priest to record his confession. He confirmed that only ten youths were involved in the crime spree at San Juan Capistrano. Apart from the murders committed, they stole about $120 and ten horses.[9] The little criminal band, however vicious, never posed a threat to Los Angeles.

Ramírez supported the capture and execution of the Flores gang. He wrote an editorial on January 31, 1857, appealing to his readers for a united front against the outlaws: "Our society is formed in such a way that we are indissolubly linked with American citizens. Let us all unite on this occasion to see that our laws are respected and to protect our lives, property, and families."

However, the same edition reported an incident just thirteen miles from Los Angeles that suggested angry Americans were engaging in acts of violence not clearly connected with the murder of Barton. On January 29, 1857, three Mexicans were lynched in the little settlement of San Gabriel. At the same time, a fourth was fatally shot, dying in the arms of his anguished wife. The victims were longtime residents with families. The Americans claimed they were involved in Barton's ambush since personal articles belonging to dead members of the posse were found in their possession. Ramírez was skeptical about the evidence behind the lynchings, demanding to see proof of the victims' guilt. In the next edition, February 7, 1857, Ramírez wrote that there was "general indignation" among Mexicans over the San Gabriel incident because "recent discoveries show that the victims were not guilty of the crimes imputed to them."

The situation was made worse a few days later when a group of Americans suspected a Mexican named Miguel Soto of carrying a shotgun belonging to Sheriff Barton. Soto was chased into a swamp where he buried himself among mud and brush until the Americans set a fire that exposed his position. He was then shot through the heart. Soto's body was brought to San Gabriel where a maddened American justice of the peace purportedly cut the head off the corpse and stabbed it several times in the chest. His savage behavior was described in the February 7, 1857, edition of *El Clamor Público*. Ramírez wondered why Mexican suspects were not arrested and dealt with by the proper authorities, instead of being killed on the spot. He was incensed by the fact that the Americans could have arrested Soto but instead "pursued one of their fellow men as if they were hunting an animal."

Although several Mexicans and Americans accused of crimes were illegally hanged in Los Angeles over the years, such executions were generally sanctioned by the community at large. Rather than rely on slow, unpredictable local courts, public meetings were convened where a committee of leading citizens, including a few Mexicans, determined the guilt or innocence of those accused and decided whether they should be hanged. The violence at San Gabriel marked the first time that a group of American vigilantes, acting alone, had seized Mexicans from their homes and killed them without the pretense of a public meeting. While such lynchings were common in northern California, most notably in the gold country, they were a shocking development in southern California.

Spanish-speaking residents in the Los Angeles area no longer felt secure, especially since few had firearms for self-defense. Their lack of weapons is revealed by the fact that during the uprising after the death of Antonio Ruiz, Mexican malcontents could only arm themselves by digging up old weapons that had been hidden in the Plaza Church since the Mexican-American War.[10] Even the Mexican company organized by Andrés Pico to find the killers of Sheriff Barton was described by the *Los Angeles Star* as being "barely armed."[11] Incredibly, most of its members had no weapons beyond some homemade lances. In contrast, nearly all Americans possessed a private arsenal of rifles, pistols, and shotguns. Their firepower was far greater than anything the Mexicans could muster. It is for this reason that a handful of

Americans could terrorize the village of San Gabriel and kill its residents with impunity.

A meeting in Los Angeles of "all persons of the Spanish race in this county" was announced in the February 21 edition of *El Clamor Público*. Its purpose was to protest "the horrifying murders of three innocent Mexicans in the vicinity of San Gabriel." The same edition reported the discovery of two Mexicans' bodies hanging from a tree in Los Nietos. Ramírez believed they were also victims of American vigilantes, and he called on those responsible to justify their actions. He wrote, "In the name of truth, justice, and humanity, we demand an explanation for this black mark on the American character." An ominous tension prevailed in Los Angeles that threatened to explode into armed conflict. Both sides speculated about a coming "war of the races."

Ramírez's reaction to the sudden wave of American violence was more analytical than might be expected. Editorials in *El Clamor Público* addressing vigilantism advocated a two-pronged approach to the problem. Ramírez simultaneously urged a rigid adherence to the law and the abrogation of all distinctions between Americans and Mexicans. Obviously, the lynchings carried out by Americans were illegal. The best defense against them would be the intervention of law enforcement officers prepared to defend Mexican people by breaking up mob action and punishing those responsible. Ramírez felt that such officers could be elected if only ordinary Mexicans would shake off their apathy and vote in accordance with their own interests.

In a February 14, 1857, editorial, he told his readers that it was their duty to sustain public order: "If we fail to respect the law, we renounce our honor and dignity. It would be to destroy the law, abolish the courts, demolish the jail, and raise the banner of anarchy and chaos." He spoke of the evils of lynching in the February 21 issue, reminding his subscribers that after Cipriano Sandoval was hanged without legal authority in 1852, it was discovered that "he was entirely innocent of the crime imputed to him." Three weeks later, Ramírez produced a list of several other hanging victims who had committed no crimes. By March 14 the furor over Barton's death had subsided. That day Ramírez's editorial was a reflection on lynchings: "How can we let life itself, the greatest gift of God to man, drift like a feather in the wind, a plaything of chance, dependent on changing moods of vengeance, fear, or resentment?"

Ramírez published a May 9 article entitled "War of the Races," an expression he heard being used to describe the state of local ethnic relations. He did not mention the Mexican insurrection after the killing of Antonio Ruiz some ten months before or the brutal lynchings of innocent people in the aftermath of Sheriff Barton's ambush. Instead, he denied that there was a race war, calling the notion "ridiculous to rational men who calmly look about Los Angeles and see how our society is composed." Clearly, Ramírez wished to build political and social bridges between disparate elements in Los Angeles. He believed that the evils of racism could be controlled by electing public officials committed to the fair treatment of Mexicans. He wrote, "Equality of the Spanish-speaking depends on the will of the people manifested in the electoral urn."

As the crisis of vigilantism in Los Angeles faded, Ramírez turned to other issues affecting Mexicans. The April 4, 1857, edition of *El Clamor Público* indignantly reported that Manuel Dominguez, one of southern California's wealthiest landowners and a delegate to the 1849 California constitutional convention, was not allowed to testify as a witness in a San Francisco court because of his "Indian" appearance. His disqualification was based on a law enacted in 1851, one of the first passed by American legislators.[12] It prevented all persons having one-fourth part or more of Indian blood, and any person with one-half or more Negro blood from testifying in civil cases against white men. At the time Dominguez's testimony was refused, he was a respected citizen serving on the Los Angeles County board of supervisors.

Joseph Lancaster Brent had recruited Dominguez into the Chivalry several years before. As a member of the legislature, Brent sent a letter to the state senate, protesting the treatment of Dominguez. He referred to coverage of the incident in *El Clamor Público*, saying, "I would not call this matter to your attention were it not for the fact that it has been the subject of comment by one of my county's local newspapers with the object of disseminating sentiments of treason and hatred among the native population of California." The letter was reprinted in full by Ramírez on May 2. He replied, "If it is treason to speak out from the abyss of our misfortune, demanding justice which is denied us, then we admit to treason." Meantime, Dominguez remained barred from giving testimony. His status as one of the ranchero elite protected by the Chivalry in Los Angeles did not exempt him from indignity and humiliation elsewhere in the state.

Repressive laws received more attention in the April 11, 1857, edition of *El Clamor Público*. Ramírez discussed the effect of a statute passed by the legislature to control vagrancy. The measure was clearly intended to operate solely against Mexicans.[13] The legislature even allowed it to be officially published as the "Greaser Law," the name by which it was popularly known. The statute permitted local law officials to arrest persons "without a legal occupation" and force them to work on public projects. In this way wandering Mexicans whose behavior did not conform to American expectations could be taken into custody. Ramírez reported that several Mexicans arrested under the new law in Los Angeles had been performing forced labor for over two months. He asked if there were no vagrants other than Mexicans to arrest. According to Ramírez, professional gamblers among the Americans had no "legal occupation" and could therefore be "forced to help clean the town water ditch." But this would never happen: "Oh no! they are gentlemen, well-dressed, and guaranteed the rights of Americans." He observed that only poor and friendless Mexicans were victims of the law.

Beyond concern for his own people, Ramírez was troubled by other manifestations of American racism. The May 2 edition contained a report on the Dred Scott case decided by the U.S. Supreme Court, which remarked that a black man had "no rights that a white man is bound to respect." Not even slaves who obtained their freedom were permitted to exercise rights of citizenship. On May 23, Ramírez described a proposal in the California legislature to prohibit the immigration of free blacks to the state. The bill barely passed the assembly by a vote of thirty-three to thirty-one, with most Republicans opposing it. Ramírez praised those who had voted against the law since "they were guided only by principles of justice and humanity." He noted that Los Angeles assemblyman and Chivalry leader Joseph Lancaster Brent had voted in favor of excluding free blacks from California.

While Ramírez found few encouraging developments at this time, he was pleased to hear that American filibusterers were being defeated in Latin America. On May 2, *El Clamor Público* gave an account of a battle between an invading American expedition and Mexicans at Caborca, Sonora. Led by Henry Crabb, a former California state senator, the large American party was killed by aroused natives of the area. Crabb's head was cut off and preserved in pickle brine, an act which provoked revulsion among Americans who heard of it. Soon afterward, the famous filibusterer William Walker was defeated and his company of American adventurers driven from Nicaragua. News of these events elated Ramírez. An editorial of June 27, 1857, rejoiced: "Honor and gratitude to all those who have so brilliantly carried out their duty as loyal patriots."

The same issue marked the second anniversary of *El Clamor Público*.

Ramírez used the occasion to write a guarded opinion about the future of his newspaper: "As we enter our third year, we feel that our prospects are as favorable as could be expected." This mild comment replaced the exuberant optimism he had expressed when his newspaper first started. After two years of publication, Ramírez undoubtedly realized that most members of the Mexican community had not accepted his ideas. Nevertheless, he was determined to persevere. Ramírez was then twenty years and five months old, just seven months away from attaining his majority.

CHAPTER THREE
The Demise of *El Clamor Público*

Ramírez added a French-language page to the July 4, 1857, edition of *El Clamor Público*. It was an enterprising move calculated to increase the paper's circulation. The French community, numbering about 400 persons, had provided him with some of his first subscribers. French businessmen proved more inclined than Mexicans or Americans to advertise in his newspaper. Much of this support was probably generated by Ramírez's godfather, Jean Louis Vignes, an influential figure among the French in Los Angeles.

Immigrants from France were far more likely to accept Ramírez's liberal ideals than were traditional Mexicans. His July 25 edition contained a long article in the French language on the triumph of liberal democracy in France during the Revolution of 1789. A week later a sophisticated essay appeared in French on the role of poetry in revolutionary movements. The French page was separately written and designed to appeal to a special class of readers. It was not a mere translation of the paper's Spanish content. Preparing articles in two languages must have taxed Ramírez's energy. However, despite the extra work, he did not notice an increase in French subscribers and advertising. Perhaps this source of revenue had already been fully exploited. The August 8 issue announced the suspension of the French page, "due to the indisposition of the person helping us to edit it." The person alluded to was Jean Louis Vignes, now about seventy-six years old, enfeebled, and showing signs of senile dementia.[1] The unrewarding experiment had lasted less than a month.

The Republican state convention took place in Sacramento on July 8, 1857, beginning the party's campaign for the governorship. The platform adopted at the convention was published in Ramírez's July 25 edition. The party continued to press for the limitation of slavery, a national railroad, the settlement of controversies over Mexican land grants, and a policy of open admission for new immigrants to the United States. Ramírez was no doubt gratified to see that it also urged a reversal of the Dred Scott decision as a flagrant injustice against black people.

An editorial in the same edition of July 25 tried to prepare local Mexicans for the coming elections. Ramírez expressed his constant concern over their apathy and submission to the ranchero elite:

> The majority of our countrymen, through a lamentable abandonment of their rights, have almost always regarded elections with indifference. They have allowed corrupt politicians and the owners of large estates to manipulate their votes. Had they not done this, capable men of good will would have been elected, and all of us spared much crime and hardship.

On August 1 Ramírez dutifully placed the name of the Republican gubernatorial candidate, Edward Stanly, on the political masthead of *El Clamor Público*. He was obviously unfamiliar with the man since several issues misspelled his name as "Stanley." A column described Stanly's service as a congressman representing North Carolina, where he associated with Daniel Webster, Henry Clay, John Quincy Adams, and other icons of the American past. However, Ramírez evinced little enthusiasm for Stanly. His endorsement was a halfhearted effort, containing none of the passion of the editorials written on behalf of Frémont. Ramírez padded much of his August 1 edition with laudatory quotes about Stanly from Republican newspapers in northern California. A smaller space was given to David W. Cheesman, the candidate for lieutenant governor, whose name Ramírez consistently misspelled as "Cheeseman."

For the next three weeks scarcely any mention of the Republicans or their candidates appeared in *El Clamor Público*. This unusual silence was explained in the August 22 edition. Ramírez printed a letter from Stanly to an organization of small farmers, which made it clear that he favored squatters over the owners of large Mexican land grants. According to Stanly's letter, he backed a proposal to prevent the sale of land by grant owners unless squatters were first reimbursed for the cost of improvements and taxes incurred. At this time rancheros were struggling to retain their holdings in the face of the Land Act of 1851, which forced them to prove that their titles were originally valid under Mexican law. Squatters frequently took possession of Mexican ranch land in anticipation of its reverting to the public domain. Others had no such expectation but held it anyway, demanding exorbitant amounts of money to withdraw their claims.

Stanly's position on payment to squatters created a situation where those who successfully confirmed title to Mexican land grants would face yet another challenge. After the anxiety and enormous cost of proving valid ownership before the federal courts, the rancheros would still have to deal with American squatters seeking exaggerated amounts of compensation. In some cases, the money needed to pay them could exceed the value of the land. Failure to settle might result in state lawsuits lasting for several years while squatters continued to occupy the property.

When Ramírez learned of Stanly's views on squatters' rights, he immediately withdrew his support for the Republican candidate. Stanly's name was stricken from the endorsements of *El Clamor Público* on August 22, 1857. At the same time Ramírez explained his rejection of Stanly to his readers. He pointed out that Mexican land grants were increasingly damaged by the encroachment of squatters, but Stanly "had declared himself in favor of these usurpations and it can be seen that he will provide no relief to landowners." Ramírez bitterly wrote, "No one of our race in possession of his reason will vote in favor of Stanley [*sic*]."

After removing Stanly's name from the top of his newspaper's political masthead, Ramírez left an oddly decapitated list of Republican candidates for state office. His lack of enthusiasm for the party's election was shared by others in Los Angeles. No county convention was held to nominate Republican candidates for local office. The election of September 2, 1857, was purely a contest between rival Democrats in Los Angeles. Listless Republicans observed that their party's candidate for governor was rebuffed in the county by a vote of 1,294 to 82.[2]

The election had at least one result that Ramírez welcomed. Without any effort by the Republicans, the Chivalry's monopoly on local political power suddenly showed signs of breaking down. An emerging group of antislavery Democrats mounted a rebellion within the party, demanding restrictions on bringing slaves to the West. Although this was a Republican position, many working-class members of the Democratic Party were beginning to express concern about the possible competition of slavery with white labor.

Antislavery Democrats in Los Angeles tended to be hard-working farmers and merchants disgusted with the pretensions of the Rosewater, a name used for certain leaders of the Chivalry claiming to be Southern gentlemen. The Rosewater believed themselves possessed of learning and refinement that placed them above ordinary laboring white men. This attitude was engendered by the aristocratic culture of the antebellum South from which they came. One enemy of the Rosewater called it "a little nucleus of tooth powder, hair oil, pin-backed jewelry and Shanghai coats."[3] Most of its members were lawyers and public officials whose participation in the Chivalry gave them access to public monies in the form of salaries and fees.

During the 1857 election the Los Angeles Democratic Party revealed its lack of unity when the antislavery element proposed its own slate of candidates in opposition to the Chivalry. Henry Hamilton, editor of the *Star*, ridiculed the insurgents as "a band of guerrillas."[4] Nevertheless, the Rosewater candidates, John W. Shore and John Reed, lost their bid for election as city clerk and sheriff. Antislavery Democrats celebrated with a procession down Main Street, carrying banners with unflattering caricatures of Hamilton and the defeated candidates.[5]

Ramírez's disenchantment with the Republicans caused a noticeable change in the content of *El Clamor Público*. Earlier pronouncements favoring racial unity and brotherhood vanished from his newspaper. During his campaign for Frémont in 1856, he had strongly advocated harmony between Americans and the Spanish speaking. He tried to encourage a coalition between Republican and Mexican voters in order to control local politics. Ramírez was committed to this strategy. He continued it until the elections of September 1857. His efforts to promote goodwill between the two groups even survived the Mexican uprising after the death of Antonio Ruiz and the outburst of American lynchings to avenge the murder of Sheriff Barton.

Near the beginning of 1858, Ramírez dropped his attempts to unify Mexican and Republican voters. He was profoundly disappointed by the failure of the Republicans to support Mexican landowners against squatters. His editorial policy of racial accommodation had lasted for over a year, largely based on political considerations. Now, despite all his work on their behalf, the Republicans no longer seemed an ally of the Spanish speaking. Disillusioned, Ramírez began to reassess the situation in Los Angeles.

Meantime, the January 23, 1858, edition of *El Clamor Público* described some unfinished business related to the death of Sheriff Barton. Pancho Daniel, the last fugitive of the outlaws who had ambushed the sheriff's posse, was discovered near Santa Clara and brought to Los Angeles. No effort was made to lynch Daniel. Instead, he was lodged in the city jail, then brought before Judge Benjamin I. Hayes, who scheduled a date for his trial. From Ramírez's point of view, the administration of criminal justice in Los Angeles was improving. Two other defendants charged with murder had already received jury trials without the intervention of a lynch mob. These men, Thomas King and Luciano Tapia, were lawfully convicted and hanged by the sheriff. In a February 20, 1858, article Ramírez approved of these proceedings since their trial and punishment had been conducted legally. However, he was now totally opposed to any executions not sanctioned by law. Mexicans were the usual victims of lynching, a fact he found truly disturbing. Ramírez began to monitor the case of Pancho Daniel to see that he would not suffer death without a proper trial.

Ramírez's March 27, 1858, edition welcomed the appearance of the *Southern Vineyard*, an English-language newspaper begun by J. J. Warner, a pioneer who arrived in California during 1831. A native of Connecticut, he was born Jonathan Trumbull Warner.[6] In early California he became a naturalized Mexican citizen after being baptized into the Catholic faith under the name Juan José. With the advent of American rule, he soon reclaimed United States citizenship but retained the initials of his adopted Spanish name. Warner was a leader of the antislavery Democrats in opposing the Chivalry Rosewater. His newspaper was intended to be a voice of this disaffected element. It would engage in vicious competition with the proslavery *Star*.

Ramírez was attracted to Warner's first edition by a pronouncement that the newspaper would try to allay hostilities between Americans and Mexicans. Warner complimented *El Clamor Público* for its past advocacy of better race relations. Ramírez responded with wishes of success to the new editor for "the arduous task of journalism on which he has embarked."[7] However, these pleasantries were of short duration. The *Southern Vineyard* soon accused *El Clamor Público* of being "a seditious and anti-American organ." This evoked a gentle June 26, 1858, response from Ramírez, who praised Warner as a man of "elevated sentiments" who had been misled by others respecting the nature of *El Clamor Público*. Ramírez wrote, "If we are called seditious, it is because we defend our race against injustice; this has always been the purpose of our humble publication, one which we consider as our duty."

In fact, Ramírez was becoming more critical of Americans. He probably had less concern about offending them since giving up efforts to merge the Mexican and Republican vote. An article published on June 6, 1858, in *El Clamor Público* described the lynching in San Luis Obispo of some Mexicans accused of murder and robbery. Ramírez reported the incident with remarks similar to those he had made before joining the Republican Party: "This is how justice is done in this country, where it is claimed that there are laws, rights, and liberty! They lie! . . . Here, when a mob punishes a crime, another crime is committed worse than the first!"

[56]   A Clamor for Equality

The July 3, 1858, issue remarked on the third anniversary of *El Clamor Público*. Ramírez optimistically wrote, "We see no obstacle in the future to prevent our continuing in the same manner as we began." In the next issue he described a happy occasion in which he seemed to be lighthearted and thoroughly enjoying himself. He reported that he had spent the Fourth of July holiday with "a large number of French citizens" at a picnic under some trees near Aliso Road. After lunch several toasts were made in honor of France's role in the American Revolution, then the crowd, bearing a French flag, marched off to the bar at the Hotel Montgomery near the plaza, singing patriotic French songs. There they met Myron Norton, a lawyer and former judge noted for heavy drinking and a gift of oratory. By providing him with a few shots of bourbon, the Frenchmen induced Norton to give an impromptu speech in English suitable for the occasion, which Ramírez simultaneously translated to French. It was a performance that "greatly gratified the French patriots."

Ramírez was not an introvert given only to working on his paper. He often displayed a gregarious nature, seeming to enjoy social events during this phase of his life. After his twenty-first birthday on February 9, 1858, he began to consider running for public office. He hoped that his social activities and his work on *El Clamor Público* had made him a political contender. Although alienated from the Republican Party, Ramírez believed he might win election in Los Angeles as an independent candidate. His August 7, 1858, edition contained an announcement in English entitled "Declaration to the People," in which he stated, "At the urging of many of my friends, I have resolved to present myself in the general elections next September as a candidate for the state Assembly." He explained that he would be an independent candidate since "I have learned by experience that little faith should be placed in political parties."

Beginning with the edition of August 21, the masthead of *El Clamor Público* displayed the names of the candidates endorsed by the newspaper. Those contending for the assembly were Andrés Pico, Henry Hancock, and Ramírez. Pico and Hancock were incumbent Chivalry Democrats running for another term. Only two candidates could be elected to represent Los Angeles County in the assembly at Sacramento. Ramírez indicated his choice for the assemblymen by placing the name of Andrés Pico on the paper's masthead alongside his own. The two men made an odd combination. Pico was the forty-eight-year-old brother of Pío Pico. He was a wealthy, conservative rancher who had early embraced the Chivalry. Andrés Pico was greatly esteemed by Americans because of his leadership in suppressing Mexican outlaws. As already seen, it was Pico who led a force of Mexican lancers to San Juan Capistrano in search of those responsible for the death of Sheriff Barton. Soon afterward, the Americans expressed their gratitude by electing him to the assembly, and Governor J. Neely Johnson appointed Pico to the rank of brigadier general in the state militia.[8] Like other members of his class, Pico had little sympathy for Ramírez's radical liberalism. He was probably not grateful for the endorsement that appeared in *El Clamor Público*.

Ramírez's strategy in the election was to present the Mexican vote with two Spanish-speaking candidates, himself and Andrés Pico. He hoped that most Mexicans would prefer to vote for their own rather than the third candidate, the American incumbent, Henry Hancock. Ramírez was forced to rely on Mexican support. The majority of Americans in Los Angeles were members of the Chivalry, who thoroughly disliked Ramírez's liberal views and would not vote for him. Antislavery Democrats who opposed the Chivalry's Rosewater leaders would also find him unattractive. They were far more likely to back candidates approved by J. J. Warner in his recently established newspaper, the *Southern Vineyard*. It has already been seen that Warner accused *El Clamor Público* of being a "seditious and anti-American organ." His friends among the antislavery Democrats had similar feelings. Perhaps the only Americans willing to support Ramírez would be members of the Republican Party. While he could count on a few of them, such as John O. Wheeler, they had little influence. Besides, some Republicans must have resented his abandonment of their party during the last election.

Ramírez's best hope for election to public office was the vote of the Mexican people combined with members of the French community. If the Spanish speaking united in his favor, there was a chance he could win. The Mexican element was still the largest group in Los Angeles County, but their voting habits were problematic. The failure of common Mexicans to take an active part in public life was the subject of much criticism by Ramírez. He must have realized that the conservative ranchero elite, loyal to the Chivalry, would use all its influence to turn the passive Spanish-speaking vote against him.

As a candidate Ramírez implored Mexicans not to sell their votes. He wrote an August 28, 1858, editorial saying, "There are no words strong enough to condemn a man who sells his vote and vilely prostitutes his conscience and his personal rights." He denounced those who cast their votes in exchange for money and drinks or as favors to wealthy employers. Since political parties and candidates were allowed to print their own ballots in different sizes and colors, it was possible to see which way a particular individual was voting by the kind of ballot he carried to the electoral urn, which was exposed to public view. Although Ramírez railed against such practices, he never stated the precise nature of his objective in running for political office as an independent candidate or how his election would benefit the people of Los Angeles. He merely asked his readers to vote for individuals they considered "best suited to direct public affairs."

As might be expected, Ramírez was not elected. According to results published on September 4, 1858, he received only 499 votes while Pico received 1,234 and Hancock 1,013. The *Los Angeles Star* sneered: "We congratulate our friend of *El Clamor Público*, Mr. F. P. Ramírez, for the compliment his friends have paid him for his consistent defense of pernicious principles."[9] Already hurt by rejection, Ramírez protested the sarcastic comment on his loss. In the September 4 edition of his newspaper, he called it a "grotesque felicitation" and challenged the *Star*'s editor, Henry Hamilton, to explain why the Democratic Party always elevated men to power who worked against the interests of ordinary Mexicans. Ramírez angrily pledged to continue opposing the Democrats and "all undertakings which lead to ruin, misery, and destruction of native Californians."[10]

During the last part of 1858, Ramírez's interest in a migration to Sonora by California Mexicans revived. His October 2, 1858, edition contained a letter from a colonist in Sáric. It was the first mention of this subject in two years. The colonist reported that 300 persons, including women and children, were living there, "breathing the pure agreeable air of this beautiful climate." This letter preceded an October 16 article in *El Clamor Público* announcing the formation in Los Angeles of a new organization to promote a migration to Sonora. Ramírez approved of the movement, saying: "The tranquility of Sonora is the salvation of Hispano-Americans suffering in California." Subsequent editions described the development of a "Junta for the Promotion of Hispano-American Migration to Sonora." Its president was Manuel Retes, a Mexican citizen residing in Los Angeles, who had contributed several articles to *El Clamor Público*. Ramírez printed a copy of an elaborate resolution establishing the junta. His October 23 issue called the project "a praise-worthy enterprise." However, the effort to shift California Mexicans to Sonora eventually failed when proposed colonists were assigned land in the Yaqui River Valley by the Mexican government. The area was a theatre of war against all Mexicans by the Yaqui Indians. Few local residents desired to risk annihilation in that hostile place.

The year 1858 closed with a most unfortunate incident for Ramírez and the future of his newspaper. On December 4 *El Clamor Público* reported that Pancho Daniel, still awaiting trial for the murder of Sheriff Barton, had been taken from his cell during the early morning hours of November 30 and furtively strung up over the gate of the jail yard. This lynching was committed by a group of Americans frustrated with the delay of the local court in processing Daniel's case. The event apparently affected Ramírez's stability. In an editorial published December 18, 1858, his emotions went completely out of control. Ramírez blamed California Mexicans for Daniel's death. Their apathy and failure to elect officials willing to protect Mexicans from American violence triggered a hysterical attack on his own people:

> And you, imbecile Californians! You are responsible for the lamentable acts we are witnessing. We are tired of saying: "Open your eyes, now is the time to assert your rights and interests." It is shameful, but necessary to admit that you are the sarcasm of humanity. When the time comes to vote, the first of your rights, you go about the streets in the carriages of candidates, and you will not cast your votes unless you are paid for them. . . . You are cowardly and stupid, inspiring nothing but disdain.

Readers of *El Clamor Público* must have thought Ramírez was becoming unhinged. These insults drastically reduced his credibility among the Spanish speaking. It was a suicidal commentary that would help accelerate the demise of *El Clamor Público*.

Ramírez's newspaper began to unravel in early 1859 as subscriptions to *El Clamor Público* dwindled to their lowest point. Never popular with most Americans, the paper now had fewer Mexican subscribers because of Ramírez's attacks on the Spanish-speaking community. As his fortunes declined, Ramírez became increasingly hostile toward those who opposed him. An editorial on February 12, 1859, referred to the *Star*'s editor, Henry Hamilton, as "Mickey Dimikrat." This attempt to ridicule Hamilton's Irish background was the only instance of Ramírez resorting to an ethnic slur against his enemies. In the same edition he harshly criticized an article in the *Southern Vineyard* written by J. J. Warner, calling him "Mr. Delirium Tremens." On February 19 Ramírez described the efforts of a San Francisco newspaper to draw a parallel between Andrew Jackson and President James Buchanan, "like trying to compare Alexander the Great with a Hottentot chief." This affront to an incumbent president of the United States by an upstart Mexican youth was certain to offend a large part of the American community.

Ramírez directed most of his animosity toward Chivalry Democrats. His February 26 editorial again attacked the Land Act of 1851. He blamed its creator, "the imbecile Senator Gwin," leader of the state Chivalry, for "irreparable damage committed against the natives of California." Gwin was charged with maintaining a corps of Southern "gentlemen" in public office who idled in luxury, "while ordinary people live by the sweat of their brow." According to Ramírez, public money was being misappropriated by Gwin to finance the acquisition of a Chivalry empire in Cuba, Mexico, and Central America.

Ramírez asserted that the Chivalry's projected expansion was based on slavery. He believed that even California was not exempt from Gwin's machinations. A February 26 item reported on a resolution presented in the assembly by Andrés Pico, which proposed that all of southern California below a line near San Luis Obispo be separated from the rest of the state. The southern portion would be removed from statehood and converted to the "Territory of Colorado." This scheme was the handiwork of Gwin and his Chivalry associates. Ramírez feared that the Chivalry would introduce slavery into southern California soon after it was reduced to territorial status. His concerns were not irrational. Indeed, many Americans suspected that division of the state was a Chivalry maneuver to bring slavery to California's southern counties.[11]

Ramírez set politics aside on March 5, 1859, to discuss public education. His views were considered excessively liberal at the time, but except for his romanticism, they somewhat resemble modern thought on the subject. He argued that public education should "penetrate to the very bottom of the masses who seem destined to misery, ignorance, and complete abjection." He asked: "What is to be done with mud-covered children without parents who only seem to be awaiting prison or the gallows steps? There is much to do, but nothing is done!" His faith in romantic nineteenth-century liberalism led him to write, "When these children are lifted from ignorance, some of them might exhibit great genius like brilliant meteors that appear in certain ages to illuminate the world."

In the same article, Ramírez chided Los Angeles authorities for not making public education their first priority. "Is it not essential for government to create good citizens of children immersed in ignorance?" The cost of schooling was of little concern. "Our public officials are willing to spend immense sums to erect public buildings *we do not need* while ignorance and misery reign among our children, principally those of the Mexican race." He re-

Mexican children in Sonoratown, circa 1890. Ramírez thought that universal education for both boys and girls might make some of them "like meteors that appear in certain ages to illuminate the world." Reprinted by permission of the University of Southern California Special Collections.

minded his readers that "ignorance is the sister of all vices and the great breeding ground of revolutions." In earlier articles, such as those appearing on January 26 and February 9, 1856, Ramírez forcefully argued for the education of girls as well as boys. His advanced ideas on public instruction were not unique, but nevertheless they were unusual for the time and place.

Ramírez had opinions on other local affairs that would not set well with public officials, especially members of the Chivalry Rosewater accustomed to receiving large emoluments of office. He was disgusted with municipal government, based on what he saw in the streets of Los Angeles. In the April 23, 1859, edition of his newspaper, he complained:

> Few cities have the resources that we do for public education, clean streets, road repair, law enforcement, and distribution of water for

household and agricultural uses. But what do we see around us? A crowd of depraved and demoralized children, streets filled with filth and abominations, flooded roads, fights, drunkenness, and misery.

Ramírez blamed city officials for these conditions. He charged that local government had plenty of money since "exorbitant license fees and taxes now oppress business and industry, enough to attend to all the needs of municipal government." Yet, he observed, those in charge of the city threatened bankruptcy and took ever-increasing loans.

The solution proposed by Ramírez must have struck city officials as a form of anarchy. He favored abolition of the city charter and a general refusal to pay further taxes. Instead, he asked private citizens to cooperate in providing funds for public necessities without paying taxes that financed the high salaries of "insatiably rapacious" officials. Ramírez used the occasion to prod for a change of city officers, and he admonished Mexican voters: "Think of your own interest and welfare—reflect on the well-being of your family." Referring to the influence of the ranchero elite and the purchase of votes, he advised, "Let no outside influence affect your actions, select a fair-minded person for mayor and men of honor and good-will for the city council."

Toward the middle of 1859, Ramírez was forced to confront the growing problems of his newspaper. As subscriptions and advertising sagged, it was becoming impossible to pay overhead costs. Such expenses mainly involved the purchase of paper and ink shipped from San Francisco, together with the acquisition of numerous publications from all over the world that he needed for material to reprint in *El Clamor Público*. Labor costs were largely avoided since Ramírez produced the paper single-handedly, often an exhausting ordeal. He tried, with limited success, to generate additional income by commercial printing and offering his services as an interpreter. The only assets of *El Clamor Público* were a printing press and related equipment housed in a brick building owned by Jean Louis Vignes at the northeast corner of Aliso and Alameda streets. In any event, the cost of producing *El Clamor Público* was not great, a fact that partially accounts for the paper's relative longevity. As a young bachelor Ramírez cut his costs by living at his family's adobe. Still, however slight his personal expenses, the time had come when he could no longer ignore the demands of creditors.

Ramírez now made a series of desperate moves that he hoped would save his newspaper. The June 18, 1859, edition of *El Clamor Público* was virtually a manifesto of how he intended to rescue himself. The issue contained many surprises. As an opening gambit he warmly endorsed the candidates for state office nominated by the Republican convention at Sacramento on June 3, 1859. He placed the whole ticket on his paper's masthead in a special place of honor. It was an announcement that he would again campaign for the Republicans in southern California. Ramírez probably expected that this would cause him to receive financial support from the party's state leadership. It would not be the first time. Ramírez had almost certainly been compensated to some degree for his efforts on behalf of Frémont and the Republican ticket in 1856. In fact, he had never given up on Frémont. From the beginning of 1859, every edition contained a statement on the masthead urging "Frémont for President, Subject to the Republican Convention." The general content of *El Clamor Público* created the appearance of a Republican journal before Ramírez formally returned to the party.

This same edition revealed that Ramírez had been industriously gathering support for his newspaper from Republican sources for months. Copies of *El Clamor Público* had been sent to editors of Republican newspapers across the country, asking for aid and subscriptions. Many of them responded to the appeal from what seemed to be an isolated Republican outpost in Los Angeles. Communications arrived from northern California, New York, Illinois, Ohio, and Iowa. The editors effusively praised Ramírez and his newspaper. The June 18 edition of *El Clamor Público* contained excerpts of their highly complimentary remarks. At least a few of these Republican newspapers may have contributed some financial support to sustain Ramírez's work.

Beginning on June 18, 1859, Ramírez published a large part of *El Clamor Público* in English. He hoped that English-language columns in his newspaper would attract a small but affluent number of Americans in Los Angeles who sympathized with the Republicans. Since the local party organization was moribund, Ramírez tried to rekindle Republican enthusiasm. He pressed the name of Frémont on his readers, suggesting that he would again be the party's candidate for president. Frémont had been a popular figure in Los Angeles during the election of 1856, despite his defeat. Nearly three years later Ramírez was trying to recreate some of the excitement of that campaign. The purpose of emphasizing English-language articles in *El Clamor Público* was made clear in the June 18 edition. Ramírez connected the needs of his newspaper with the upcoming election by asking American residents for money in their own language: "We earnestly invoke our friends to lend us their aid—'material aid'—to carry out our designs in the present highly important conjuncture of affairs."

Finally, Ramírez gave notice in the June 18 issue that he would make another run for the office of state assemblyman. Neither Andrés Pico nor Henry Hancock chose to stand for reelection, a fact that may have encouraged Ramírez's entry into a new field of candidates. With *El Clamor Público* on the point of collapse, he had little to lose by another attempt at public office. Ramírez now geared up for an aggressive campaign that would last until the elections of September 7, 1859.

On June 25, Ramírez printed more copies of *El Clamor Público* than were needed in Los Angeles. He mailed the extra copies to Republicans all over California. The edition contained a prominent article in English entitled "To Our Republican Friends." It was a frank solicitation for money combined with an unlikely scheme for increasing subscriptions. After pointing out that *El Clamor Público* was "the only Republican press in Southern California," Ramírez wrote:

> Our expenses are heavy, and we ask only a fair remuneration for our services. Will not our Republican friends everywhere through-out the state aid us in the present emergency? Let every one of them to whom this extra is sent cut out this appeal, paste it on a white slip of paper, and obtain for us three or five or ten subscribers and forward the list and money to us at their earliest convenience.

Like efforts to raise money from Republican newspapers across the United States, this appeal was directed to sources outside southern California. Ramírez now acknowledged that he had lost nearly all support from the local Spanish-speaking community. He printed a June 25 column in Spanish that resentfully told his Mexican readers, "In the midst of innumerable obstacles we have persevered in our career without a moment's rest. Those who ought to have helped us with advice, influence, and pecuniary aid have abandoned us without the assistance we have vainly solicited."

On July 9, 1859, *El Clamor Público* reported that Ramírez had gone to San Francisco "to attend to business and purchase printing materials." The more likely purpose of this unusual trip was to meet with Republican state leaders to request money at the party's fountainhead. He must have been at least partly successful in getting funded. Soon afterward, his paper increased agitation on behalf of the Republican cause.

For the next several weeks, *El Clamor Público* contained little not related to the approaching elections. The newspaper appeared much as it did during the campaign of 1856. Considerable space was given to English-language columns written by John O. Wheeler. On July 16, 1859, Wheeler announced that he would be a Republican candidate for the office of county clerk. Both Wheeler and Ramírez, each in his own native language, wrote inflammatory articles denouncing the Democrats. The Spanish columns contained familiar exhortations to Mexican voters:

> Wake up from your lethargy and make greater efforts in favor of your own interest.... Carefully consider those for whom you will vote. You are free and independent men! Do not let it be said that you vilely sell your votes for a little money or some trinket. Your families and personal honor require that you do not turn your right to vote into a shameful commerce.... Republicans! It is necessary to strike a blow against the Democratic Party that has oppressed us with odious laws, taxes, and all the evils from which we now suffer. Long live liberty! Down with monopoly, deceit, fraud and hypocrisy!

Ramírez occasionally extended such bombast to the French language. Just before the election, a curious array of political columns in Spanish, English, and French were spread throughout the pages of *El Clamor Público*.

While pumping for the Republican Party, Ramírez did his best to promote his own candidacy for the state assembly. In a political advertisement of June 25, 1859, he proclaimed in English: "I will serve as a Legislator for California—my Native State, and with which every fiber of my heart is inseparably intertwined—with all the zeal and ability a faithful representative of the public welfare can inspire." The August 13 edition ran an article in Spanish by Ramon Carrillo, one of the few prominent Mexicans in Los Angeles as fervently devoted to liberalism as Ramírez. He declared, "The Republican Party adheres to the same principles that inspired Washington, Bolivar, Hidalgo, and other great leaders of North and South America to liberate the soil of their birth from the yoke of oppressors, and to fight for humanity, civilization, and the sacred rights of Man." Carrillo exalted Ramírez as a candidate: "He has earned the esteem of his friends and the respect of his opponents. His cause should be our cause."

Ramírez's competition for a seat in the assembly came from a dominant, but badly divided Democratic Party. The Chivalry nominated one slate of candidates and the Northern antislavery faction selected another. Each claimed to represent the Democratic Party, and they held separate county conventions in Los Angeles. The choice of the Chivalry for the two vacancies in the assembly were Andrew J. King and Murray Morrison. The Northerners promoted J. J. Warner and James F. Burns for the same offices. The rivalry between the two groups led to ferocious attacks. Among other things the Chivalry accused Warner of being a traitor during the Mexican-American War. E. J. C. Kewen, a Chivalry candidate for county district attorney, made a memorable speech at a barbecue in El Monte, in which he eloquently assailed the leading Northern candidate: "This trifling fellow, Warner, is so notoriously corrupt and villainous, as to wholly exclude him from every consideration except that which would prompt a man to kick a snarling cur that intercepts his path."[12] These insulting remarks were published several times by Henry Hamilton in the *Los Angeles Star*. They epitomized the invective used by both factions in their contest to control the Democratic Party. Each side was too deeply involved in their own conflict to pay much attention to Ramírez and his little band of Republicans.

The elections of September 7, 1859, confirmed that Los Angeles remained a Chivalry stronghold. The party captured nearly every local office. Except for electing J. J. Warner as one of the two assemblymen, the Northern Democrats failed to defeat any of the Chivalry Southerners. Warner was successful only because one of the Chivalry candidates for the assembly, Murray Morrison, withdrew at the last moment.

The Republicans had little impact on the elections. Their candidate for governor, Leland Stanford, was trounced by a local vote of 1,916 to 220. No Republicans were elected to office in Los Angeles. Ramírez placed fourth in a field of six candidates for the assembly. Andrew J. King, a Chivalry Democrat, led the contest with 968, followed by J. J. Warner with 805. These two men were elected just ahead of the Northern Democrat, James F. Burns, who had 718 votes. Ramírez received 692 votes, the best showing of any Republican in Los Angeles County. He was trailed by two Americans running independently, Alphonso Tilden and David Lewis, who picked up 535 and 256 votes.[13]

John O. Wheeler lost his contest for the office of county clerk with results typical of the Republicans. He was overwhelmed by the Chivalry candidate, John W. Shore. Wheeler analyzed the election in a September 17, 1859, article written in English for *El Clamor Público*. He partly blamed the Republican rout on a "large foreign admixture of our population, who vote the Democratic ticket from prejudice or inclination." But Wheeler concluded that the basic reason for the Chivalry landslide was "the large immigration from the South who feel a strong attachment to the 'peculiar institution' under which they were raised and for which they bear a paternal regard."

Ramírez's prospects in Los Angeles were severely diminished after his defeat. At least a place in the assembly would have provided a measure of income while the legislature was in session. By now *El Clamor Público* had become an impossible financial burden. He began to spend less time on his insolvent newspaper. Ramírez supplied *El Clamor Público* with fewer original articles, filling it instead with an unusually large number of items copied from other newspapers. The derivative content of *El Clamor Público* reflected his distraction over the collapse of his career in Los Angeles.

On December 17, 1859, Ramírez's newspaper advertised the sale of his printing press and equipment. A complete inventory was set forth that listed nearly everything he owned. The announcement gave notice that publication of *El Clamor Público* was about to end. Within a few days Charles R. Conway and Alonzo Waite purchased Ramírez's assets. The two men formed a partnership to operate another newspaper, the *Semi-Weekly Southern News*. The first edition appeared on January 18, 1860, printed with the press that Ramírez had sold them shortly before.

Ramírez agreed to deliver his equipment to Conway and Waite after publishing the final edition of *El Clamor Público* on December 31, 1859. In the meantime he printed an item on December 24 advising his friends and readers that he had accepted an offer from the governor of Sonora, Ignacio Pesqueira, to serve as editor of the Mexican border state's official newspaper, *La Estrella de Occidente*. Ramírez's talents probably came to the attention of Governor Pesqueira through Manuel Retes, the organizer of a movement to emigrate Mexicans from California to Sonora. Retes was a native of Mexico connected with officials in the Sonora state government. Ramírez encouraged Retes, just as he had endorsed the successful efforts of Jesús Islas to establish a colony of Mexican Americans in Sáric during 1856. The movement headed by Retes was centered in Los Angeles, where an organizing committee prepared numerous formal resolutions dealing with the proposed migration that were published in *El Clamor Público*. Copies of the newspaper found their way to Sonora, where public officials became aware of Ramírez and his work. Retes understood Ramírez's delicate position and the impending failure of his newspaper. While inspecting Sonora to locate a place for his colony, he touted Ramírez to highly placed friends as an ideal person to edit the official state newspaper.

In the same edition of December 24, 1859, Ramírez published a final word on his frustration with the complacent nature of Spanish-speaking residents. He mused on an article in the *San Francisco Herald*, a Chivalry newspaper, that called Mexicans "a degraded race" and speculated that, if slavery was brought to California, they would soon "amalgamate with Blacks," becoming slaves themselves. Ramírez cited the editorial as an example of the true opinion held by the Chivalry about his people. He reproached Mexicans who backed the Southern faction despite their undisguised racism: "It is unbelievable that after so many insults and affronts, one still sees the sad spectacle in California of Hispanic Americans supporting the slavery party with their votes and influence." In this manner Ramírez acknowledged that his four-and-a-half-year crusade had ended without much effect on the Mexican people.

The final issue of *El Clamor Público* appeared December 31, 1859. Ramírez placed a column on the front page—a sullen message of farewell. He pointed out that he had written the text and done all the hard printing work by himself, otherwise "the paper would not have lasted three months." His efforts extended to articles in French and English, but all he received in return was "drudgery and misery." Ramírez directed a sarcastic last word to his readers: "I take leave of my good and dear friends who have viewed with complacency my efforts to give them a moment's distraction through reading. If they had an idea of the work and expense this publication has caused me, they would be less severe in their criticism of the errors I have made and which are impossible to avoid."

CHAPTER FOUR
An Interlude in Sonora

Ramírez did not leave for Sonora immediately after the last edition of *El Clamor Público*. He lingered in Los Angeles for two months, helping Conway and Waite set up the first few editions of the *Semi-Weekly Southern News*. More than two decades later Ramírez told an investigator for the historian Hubert Howe Bancroft that he briefly served as an editor of the newspaper during this period, but his name does not appear on any of its editions.[1]

The March 14, 1860, *Semi-Weekly Southern News* printed a notice from Ramírez and his brother, Juan de la Resurrección, advising that, "During our absence from this State, Mr. A. Ignacio Sepúlveda is our authorized attorney to transact all business in our name." This announcement marked the approximate date of Ramírez's departure, accompanied by his brother, who was two years younger. They could have traveled to Sonora by one of the coastal steamers to the port of Guaymas, then proceeded northeast to the state capital in Ures, where Ramírez would commence his work as editor of the official state newspaper, *La Estrella de Occidente*. This would have been far less arduous than crossing the great Sonoran desert by horseback. Nevertheless, Ramírez chose the more adventurous overland route. This is shown by a letter he sent to Conway and Waite that was mentioned in the *Semi-Weekly Southern News* on May 9, 1860. The letter, dated April 5, reported that Ramírez was then passing through Altar, Sonora. His presence at a place north of Ures and so distant from the sea proves that he was traveling by land.

The overland journey from Los Angeles on plodding horses and mules necessarily involved considerable hardship and danger. Even the best-organized expeditions sometimes suffered from thirst and exhaustion while traversing the enormity of Sonora. A constant watch for Apaches, Seris, Yaquis, and other hostile Indians could be extremely stressful, especially at night. Contact with any of these groups might be fatal. Random killings by Indians were a major problem in Sonora until the beginning of the twentieth century. Travelers who set out alone or in small groups often disappeared forever in Sonora's immense wastelands. Of necessity, Ramírez and his brother must have left Los Angeles with a caravan of homeward-bound Sonorans who knew the desert, its perils, and the places where water could be found.

Striking toward Yuma, they would cross the Colorado River, then move eastward 240 miles to Sonoita on a desert trail called El Camino del Diablo because of the bleached bones of animals and men scattered along the way. Sonoita, a tiny Spanish outpost long abandoned to the Apaches, was the only dependable source of water and pasture within hundreds of miles. The trail then turned southeast through 180 miles of cactus and mesquite to Caborca, the town where Henry Crabb and his American filibusterers were killed in 1857.

Once at Sonoita, Ramírez may not have taken the rest of El Camino del Diablo to Caborca. By continuing to press nearly straight east 120 miles, he would come to Sáric, the Mexican American colony organized by Jesús Islas. It was situated in a hilly area above the usually dry Altar River, about twenty miles below the Arizona border. Ramírez had enthusiastically promoted emigration to Sáric in *El Clamor Público*. It was represented as an idyllic refuge from American racism and oppression. Ramírez's decision to travel overland was probably based in part on a desire to see Sáric, but he may have become disillusioned after observing the isolated colony's struggle to coax a living from the region's scant resources and its exposure to Apaches. About the time he made his visit, a village official was killed in an Apache raid and several head of cattle were stolen.[2]

From Sáric Ramírez had to follow a sixty-mile trail leading south to the town of Altar. It followed the empty Altar River, passing through the tiny adobe settlements of Tubutama, Atíl, and Oquitoa, begun by the Jesuit missionary Eusebio Kino during the late seventeenth century. While these villages still exist, the arid nature of their surroundings has prevented them from prospering. All these places, including Sáric, still appear much the same as Ramírez would have seen them, barely subsisting on cattle and uncertain crops along the river bottom.

After writing his letter of April 5, 1860, to Conway and Waite from Altar, Ramírez would take an established road east to Magdalena. This little town was on an important trade route between Tucson and Hermosillo. It was a hard trip of 140 miles across desert and low mountain ranges from Magdalena southward to the city of Hermosillo on the Sonora River. Hermosillo was

Sonora's largest urban center, monopolizing the state's commercial activities. The capital, Ures, was a provincial town in the uplands of the Sonora River, about forty miles northeast of Hermosillo. Set above the desert near a water source, it was an agricultural center where even sugar cane thrived. While Hermosillo is now a dynamic industrialized city, Ures remains a small agricultural town. Many ancient houses still have patios that open to quaintly narrow streets through a *zaguán*, or foyer, with colonial wrought iron grilles and carved doors. Ramírez arrived there during May 1860. It would not take long to discover that, despite the rustic attractions of Ures, he was in a far more difficult and hostile place than he could have imagined.

Sonora suffered from a pervasive climate of fear and violence. There were few times when warfare was not taking place somewhere in the state.[3] The region was plagued by armed conflicts that constantly disrupted commerce and government. In large part conditions in Sonora reflected a power struggle occurring in central Mexico. Since 1857 a bloody contest between liberals and conservatives called the War of Reform had convulsed the country. While Sonora's isolation prevented direct participation in the conflict, the state's wealthy elite divided into the same liberal and conservative factions as the rest of the nation. These groups engaged in a prolonged battle for control of Sonora. The liberals gained the upper hand when Ignacio Pesqueira overthrew the conservative governor Manuel Gándara in 1857. Pesqueira's state government was the only semblance of authority in the region since national institutions were paralyzed by civil war. During Pesqueira's regime, which lasted for twenty years, he was challenged by several conservative uprisings that killed numerous combatants on both sides.

Although political disorders contributed to an atmosphere of insecurity, the first of many threats to Mexican people in Sonora was the presence of a large population of dangerously hostile Indians. The Yaquis, an indigenous nation centered in a river valley south of Guaymas, had a long history of resistance to encroachment on their land. They developed an unremitting enmity toward outsiders. Sometimes angry Yaquis carried out attacks well beyond their territory, even menacing towns like Guaymas, Alamos, and Hermosillo. The Yaqui population numbered in the thousands, withstanding all attempts to subdue them until the late nineteenth century. In the north members of Indian groups like the Seris, Ópatas, and Tohono O'odham (formerly Pápagos) occasionally posed a danger to Mexicans. Except for the Seris, who completely rejected Mexican society, most tribal Indians were at least partially reconciled to the presence of settlers. Some, like the Yaquis, had a complicated and delicate relationship with non-Indians. While capable of explosive violence to defend their territory, the Yaquis frequently worked as laborers outside their homeland. Unless provoked to take up arms, they constituted the most important element of Sonora's work force.[4]

The Mexican population lived in a state of constant anxiety since no part of Sonora was safe from sudden Indian attack. This situation was occasionally made terrifying by Apache raiders from the north. Their incursions into Sonora caused enormous dread. Based on 1850 contemporary estimates, an authority on Sonora wrote that each year one thousand residents lost their lives fighting Apaches.[5] The lightly populated region could not afford such losses. Towns were established as "self-sufficient, defensible enclaves."[6] In such places the homes of wealthy families stood next to impoverished hovels since "the need to defend against Indian attacks compelled elites and common folk to share the same urban space."[7] Apache raiding parties often penetrated deep into the interior of Sonora without detection, making ambush a terrible possibility everywhere. Northern Sonora was nearly depopulated by their persistent attacks.

Apart from Indian depredations and political warfare, Sonora was overrun with uncontrollable crime. As one historian notes, "Confronting extremely harsh conditions of life and taking advantage of the weak state authority, many Sonorans turned to banditry to improve their lot."[8] Predatory Mexican *bandoleros* made normal life impossible. The movement of essential trade goods from the port of Guaymas to the rest of the state had to be protected by armed guards. Only large caravans could pass through Sonora without fear of some hostile encounter. Wandering outlaws further complicated chaotic conditions during the nineteenth century and helped deter the region from developing a stable social order.

Despite Sonora's turbulence the official state newspaper, *La Estrella de Occidente*, adhered to a regular publication schedule. It appeared on Friday of each week for distribution throughout the state wherever possible. Like most papers of the time, it consisted of only four pages. As an organ of the state, the first page invariably displayed official notices, statutes, and budgets. Sonora was divided into nine administrative districts, each headed by a prefect appointed by the governor. Reports from the district prefects were also placed on the front page. They presented detailed descriptions of daily life touching on matters such as commerce, mining, agriculture, taxes, public amusements and military affairs. A striking feature of every report was a category entitled "*Bárbaros*," a sobering narrative by the prefects, describing the deaths of those most recently killed by Indians. The other pages of the journal were taken up with news about the rest of the world copied from periodicals arriving from Arizona and the port of Guaymas.

The state printing office was in a fortress-like building called the *Casa de Correcciones*, which, as the name implies, was mainly used as a jail. However, the massive stone structure also housed government offices and a small detachment of a military force called the National Guard. Several printing office employees relieved Ramírez of the arduous labor he had endured while working alone in Los Angeles. The position of state printer and editor of the official newspaper was considered well up in the government hierarchy. Ramírez's predecessor, an unrelated Sonoran named Cirilo Ramírez, was an influential politician who acted as the private secretary of Governor Pesqueira as well as the editor of the newspaper. This same individual later became interim governor. After the departure of Ramírez, the editorship was assumed by Francisco D. Tena, a highly placed official who was the prefect for the district of Ures. Therefore, at the age of twenty-four, Ramírez occupied a prestigious position in the local scheme of things. He was assigned a room as his living quarters adjacent to the printing office in the Casa de Correcciones. Despite his relatively high standing, Ramírez's accommodations were fairly Spartan, a situation not ameliorated by regular payments of his salary. The state government was notorious for its failure to properly compensate public employees.

The first issue of *La Estrella de Occidente* edited by Ramírez appeared on May 25, 1860. No changes were made in the newspaper's format. His presence as the new editor was not noticeable until June 22, 1860, when he wrote a column introducing himself to his readers. It was a long piece portraying Sonora as a place of fabulous mineral wealth "destined to seize the cornucopia, the golden horn of plenty, which is now ready to pour its rich storehouse of wealth and industry into our laps." He foresaw commerce along what would later be called the Pacific Rim: "The close proximity of Mexico with China and Japan is a marked feature in our road to greatness. We occupy a highly favorable position on the Pacific side to open an immense trade with these two ancient and populous countries." Ramírez called on Sonora to foster railroads, steam ships, religious liberty, tolerance of political opinions, universal education, a better postal service, and a free press. He concluded: "For the attainment of these objects we shall labor zealously

The official newspaper of Sonora, Mexico, as it appeared under Ramírez's editorship, May 24, 1861. Courtesy of the Archivo Histórico del Gobierno del Estado de Sonora, Hermosillo.

and faithfully; we shall devote our whole energies in developing these views, these aims, these purposes, and we appeal with confidence to the loyal and noble-hearted people of Sonora to rally to our aid; to come to the rescue, and help us one and all to carry out this great design."

Ramírez's message had a distinctively American ring about it. Almost any progressive newspaper editor imported from the United States would have produced a similar litany of ideals. In fact, it was not intended for a Sonoran audience since it was published in English! The motive for Ramírez's extraordinary departure from the Spanish language was revealed several months later in the edition of December 28, 1860. That issue reprinted comments from newspapers in the United States congratulating Ramírez on his undertaking in Sonora. It included editorial good wishes from points as far away as Boston. Obviously, copies of *La Estrella de Occidente* with its maiden editorial in English had been sent north by Ramírez to keep American colleagues posted on his career. He even sent a copy to his old antagonist in Los Angeles, Henry Hamilton. The July 7, 1860, *Star* mentioned receipt of the Mexican journal containing "an address to the people of Sonora by Mr. Ramírez on the occasion of entering on his duties as an editor."

In one of his first issues, that of June 15, 1860, Ramírez announced that the state government of Sonora had authorized the purchase of a new printing press. The *Semi-Weekly Southern News* in Los Angeles published a rumor on July 27 that Ramírez was then in San Francisco buying a new "printing establishment which is to be conducted on the American plan." If he made such a trip, it was not mentioned in *La Estrella de Occidente*. Instead, it appears that Ramírez was in Sonora at the time, perhaps feeling homesick. He copied many items from the Los Angeles press, far more than were appropriate. For example, on August 3 he mentioned that Henry Mellus had been elected as a city councilman there, something of no interest to his Sonora readers. Other editions, such as the one published on August 17, had whole columns devoted to events taking place in Los Angeles. A week later Ramírez spoke directly to acquaintances in his hometown on the subject of Abraham Lincoln's presidential campaign. His remarks suggested a certain degree of nostalgia: "We ardently hope that our friends in Los Angeles, including Pio Pico, Ramon Carrillo, Juan Avila, Juan María Sepúlveda, José Antonio Carrillo, etc., will use their influence to elect the Republican candidate despite all opposition. Brothers, we greet you from here!"

Articles concerning Los Angeles began to disappear from the newspaper, possibly in response to criticism from Ramírez's superiors. In any event he gradually started to pay more attention to Sonora. The September 7, 1860, edition of *La Estrella de Occidente* published a dramatic story that illustrated the harsh realities of life in the region. Under the headline "Yaqui War!," Ramírez reported the latest uprising of the formidable and independent native people. Earlier in the week, they had suddenly attacked government forces near Alamos. Governor Pesqueira himself led a relief column to join elements of the National Guard there commanded by his brother-in-law, Colonel Jesús García Morales. Before arriving, Pesqueira was surprised by a large number of Yaquis, who scattered his men and shot his horse out from under him. Only a daring lieutenant kept Pesqueira from being killed. News of the event created alarm in Ures until it was learned that the governor was safe. According to Ramírez, word of Pesqueira's rescue provoked a spontaneous celebration: "A relieved and overjoyed public manifested their happiness by playing music and shooting off fireworks in the streets."[9] Pesqueira returned to Ures and prepared to defend against a Yaqui offensive, but the crisis subsided when the Indians withdrew to their own territory.

About three weeks after Pesqueira's Yaqui scare, a group of conservatives met in the town of Magdalena to plot the overthrow of the liberal government. Several of the conspirators were relatives of Manuel Gándara, a wealthy conservative who was the governor until removed from office by Pesqueira. The conspirators drafted a document called the *Plan de Magdalena*, which accused Pesqueira of being a tyrant who ignored the property rights of landowners and imposed unjust special taxes. The rebels proposed one of their leaders, Dionisio Rivera, as the new governor. To bolster their forces, Rivera took 200 men toward the Yaqui River Valley to recruit Indian support for the movement. Both conservatives and liberals frequently induced the Yaquis to join their battles. The Yaquis, oblivious to Mexican political differences, would fight for whichever side they thought best suited their interests at the time. While Rivera headed for Yaqui country, another force commanded by Manuel Sosa proceeded toward Ures to attack the capital. On September 30, at about 9:00 a.m., the Casa de Correcciones on the plaza at Ures was the scene of a two-hour firefight between government defenders and the insurgents.[10]

Ramírez wrote a description of the incident in a letter to Conway and Waite, editors of the *Semi-Weekly Southern News* in Los Angeles. He thought the attackers were Yaquis, but they were actually a mixed group of mestizos, Yaquis, and some Ópata Indians, led by their famous captain, Refugio Tánori. An article based on Ramírez's communication appeared in the Los

Angeles paper on November 30, 1860. It reported: "A revolutionary band of Yaquis, numbering 150, attacked Ures, the capital of the State, but could not take the House of Corrections, which served as a fort, and where the Government printing office is located." The newspaper stated that during the fight "the editor Don Francisco Ramirez was not in his room."

Seven rebels were killed, but there were no casualties on the government side. Ramírez published an account of the battle on October 12, 1860. Judging by his article, he was greatly disturbed: "We dare not describe in detail the fear and anguish of the town's population or the horrible consequences that faced them if the perverted beings who made up the attackers had triumphed." It was his introduction to the shock of combat. Whether or not personally under fire, Ramírez was severely affected, if not traumatized, by corpses in the street and bullet holes throughout the building where he lived.

In the next issue, on October 19, Ramírez presented an emotional editorial on the conservative rebellion. He accused its adherents of being men with "corrupt minds and blood-stained hands," who were intent on "destroying Sonora's towns and cities through murderous pillage and vandalism." But he had faith in the people of the state "who are enlightened, and therefore liberal." He believed they would "inexorably crush the traitors." The rebels would find that the "blue sky had turned to brass and the flames of hell were erupting beneath their feet." As Ramírez predicted, the main conservative force was defeated at El Buey, near Hermosillo, on October 22. Their leaders fled toward Arizona, pursued by a Pesqueira loyalist, Colonel Federico A. Ronstadt. On November 23 Ramírez reported, "This part of the state now enjoys the tranquility so much desired by good citizens."

Soon after the conservative rebellion, Ramírez announced that he was going home. He had been in Sonora for only seven months. A column in the December 28 edition notified his readers that "personal business claiming all my attention requires that I leave Sonora." His intent to depart was impeccably stated. He made no criticism or complaint. Ramírez wrote, "Wherever fortune takes me, I will always have pleasant memories of Sonora's kind and generous people." The edition presented numerous quotations from American newspapers praising his work on *La Estrella de Occidente*. It was a souvenir issue designed to commemorate his brief turn as editor of the official newspaper.

There was good cause to withdraw from Sonora. Not only was Ramírez seldom paid, the attack on the Casa de Correcciones had proved that the state government could not guarantee his safety. However, his sudden decision to leave was also influenced by the election of Abraham Lincoln. The elating news of Lincoln's triumph arrived just before Ramírez's message of farewell. On his return to California, he could claim a reward from the new Republican administration for past services. But whatever the reason for the announcement, Ramírez then changed his mind and decided to stay at his post. He continued to produce the official newspaper as if he had never published his resignation.

At the beginning of 1861, Ramírez made an error in judgment that embroiled him in considerable difficulty. He wrote an article charging wealthy merchants in the town of Alamos with "unpatriotic behavior" because they objected to a special tax that Pesqueira intended to levy for a new campaign against the Yaquis.[11] Ramírez learned of their opposition through private letters indiscreetly circulated in Hermosillo. Some of the correspondence from Alamos accused Ramírez of being a paid propagandist for the Pesqueira regime because he had written editorials favoring the tax. Ramírez was deeply offended by the views set forth in the letters. He refuted the merchants on January 18, 1861, by proclaiming, "We are the owners of our opinions and we express them as we see fit, without fear or a desire to ingratiate ourselves with anyone."

Miguel Urrea was one of the merchants in Alamos who rejected the proposed tax. A wealthy and influential liberal, Urrea had been Pesqueira's lieutenant governor in 1857. He feared that Pesqueira might use the tax for purposes other than to make war on the Yaquis. Urrea privately printed a circular defending the Alamos tax protest. His publication mentioned Ramírez's efforts to promote the tax in the official newspaper but dismissed the young editor as a lackey who had failed in California and was driven by hunger to sell his services to Pesqueira. Ramírez's feelings were injured by these contemptuous remarks. In the February 22 edition his wounded pride led him to make an injudicious attack on Urrea's circular: "It provoked supreme disdain for the author of this imbecile confusion of lies and stupidity." He claimed it was an "ugly little paper that turned the stomach of those who read it."

Ramírez reported on April 12, 1861, that Urrea had filed a lawsuit against him for libel in the Court of the First Instance in Ures. The attorney for Urrea was José de Aguilar, a distinguished lawyer trained in Mexico City, who had once been a liberal governor of Sonora. Although Ramírez ridiculed the court proceedings against him, he was well out of his depth. Much of his bombast against Urrea had been a demonstration of loyalty to Pesqueira.

However, later in the year the governor visited Urrea in Alamos where he reconciled with his old colleague. Ramírez was left with nothing from the incident but Urrea's personal enmity.

During April 1861, the state congress granted 45,000 pesos to Pesqueira from a special tax imposed over the objections of Urrea and his colleagues in Alamos. Pesqueira used the money for a military campaign he hoped would finally break Yaqui defiance of Mexican authority. He spent the next three months in the field, but his troops and artillery could not defeat the elusive and tenacious Indians. Meantime, the state constitution called for elections in the month of July. Ramírez printed a slate of candidates for state office on May 17. There was no pretense of conducting a democratic election. The only candidates were men chosen by Pesqueira for their loyalty to him and the liberal cause. Every liberal candidate was unopposed and guaranteed to be elected. The conservatives were regarded as traitors who could not be allowed to participate, especially after their recent armed revolt. Their most militant leaders had already been killed or driven to exile in Arizona and California.

Despite the absence of a conservative opposition, *La Estrella de Occidente* took on the appearance of a highly partisan newspaper engaged in a close political contest. For editorial purposes Ramírez indulged in the fiction that the liberals needed to fight to win the election. In terms identical to those he had used in Los Angeles, he exhorted Sonorans to vote. Ramírez had brought some copies of *El Clamor Público* to Ures, from which he reprinted whole columns of campaign rhetoric. For example, on June 28, 1861, he told his readers, "You are free and independent men! Your families and your honor require that you do not make a shameful commerce of your vote!" These words, taken from a passage published in *El Clamor Público* two years before, on July 16, 1859, were not relevant in Sonora. There was no need to buy votes when the outcome of the election was already certain. State officials may have found Ramírez's pronouncements inappropriate for Sonora, but they were nevertheless gratified by the show he put on for the voters and his unstinting praise of liberal candidates.

Pesqueira was the only contender for office who encountered any resistance. He had a ruthless side to his personality, a quality suited to Sonora's unsettled conditions, but one that adversely affected his popularity. Ramírez was an unabashed admirer of the governor and entirely overlooked his defects. A column he wrote on June 28, 1861, just before the elections, exemplifies the extreme adulation of the governor that appeared in the official newspaper:

[80] A Clamor for Equality

> The name of PESQUEIRA is pronounced with affection and admiration in all parts of the world where the cause of humanity and liberty has friends and martyrs. His great heart beats in harmony with the most noble impulses of Mankind. He disdains oppression and tyranny. His principles are just and his political opinions are those of a liberal statesman. His courage and energy have been the salvation of Sonora and always will be!

Pesqueira's opponents questioned the basis for such unrestrained glorification. Many of them were members of the Club de la Reforma, a small liberal organization in Hermosillo that persuaded Fernando Cubillas to challenge the incumbent governor for election. Although the politics of Pesqueira and Cubillas were nearly identical, the latter had a less abrasive personality. The club published a statement criticizing Pesqueira for hiring Ramírez. It cited the official newspaper's slavish devotion to the governor as evidence that Ramírez was being paid from public funds to aggrandize Pesqueira.

The negative statements of the Club de la Reforma marked the second time within six months that Sonorans had raised doubts about Ramírez's integrity. In response, much of the July 5 edition of *La Estrella de Occidente* consisted of communications by Pesqueira's followers in defense of Ramírez. The governor's personal secretary wrote that the editor was not "a miserable adventurer" who had come to Mexico "with no more credentials than a desire to satisfy his hunger." Instead, he was "respectfully and repeatedly" invited to become editor of the official newspaper after the governor had noticed Ramírez's work on *El Clamor Público* as well as his "courageous and intelligent defense of the Mexican people in California." Based on his journalistic talents Ramírez could easily sustain himself in the United States, "a fact which proves that he is not here as a beggar looking for money, but rather as an editor expressing his own original and independent ideas."

Pesqueira had no trouble turning back the challenge mounted by Cubillas and his supporters in the Club de la Reforma. On July 26, 1861, Ramírez published election results showing that the governor had won by a nearly two-thirds majority. However, the elections had hardly concluded before Sonora was stunned by the news that a conservative army from the state of Sinaloa under Colonel Antonio Esteves had entered the southern part of the state and captured the town of Alamos.[12] Nearly the whole edition of the official newspaper on August 30 was devoted to reporting the invasion. Ramírez observed, "In this month of August, we begin yet another time of tribulation for our state that will result in the sacrifice of more loyal and brave young men." Despite his concern over the killing that would ensue, Ramírez did not hesitate to urge the troops forward. On September 6 he wrote, "In the name of your families, may the curse of heaven fall upon the soldier who returns home before achieving a victory in this war!"

Led by Governor Pesqueira, the National Guard set up defenses around the plaza of Hermosillo, the state's most important city. On October 15, 1861, a conservative force of 500 men attacked the plaza, which was defended by 300 state troops. After five hours of fighting, the Sonorans defeated the invaders, capturing 100 prisoners and ten cannon.[13] The next day Ramírez hurriedly distributed a special bulletin announcing: "Complete defeat of the assassins! Long live the brave sons of Sonora! Long live the state government!"

When the conservatives from Sinaloa had previously occupied Alamos, they found several young Sonorans in the city prepared to join them. One such person, Toribio Almada, was a twenty-one-year-old from a prominent family, who was given the rank of captain in the invading army. After the victory at Hermosillo, Pesqueira refused to pardon Almada's disloyalty, although he had released similar prisoners on parole. Ignoring the appeals of Almada's wife with a newborn baby in her arms, Pesqueira had Almada shot in Alamos on November 29, 1861. As the hour for the execution approached, the governor, who was present in the city, ordered drums and bugles to drown out cries for mercy by the condemned man's relatives.[14] Ramírez must have been told this now-legendary story in Ures. It was a disturbing episode that revealed Pesqueira's implacable nature.

Most Sonorans considered Almada a misguided young man who ought to have been spared. The governor's insistence on revenge disgusted a large number of Sonorans. As one writer observes, "Pesqueira's lack of mercy would have far-reaching repercussions. Many who had once been committed to the liberal cause and loyal to the governor would now become vehemently anti-Pesqueira, going to any ends to unseat him."[15] As a general rule, Ramírez himself had no pity for those who provoked rebellions. On September 20, 1861, he commented, "Revolutions will increase unless those who instigate them are refused clemency and punished as prescribed by law—death by firing squad." Nevertheless, he disapproved of Pesqueira's actions in the Almada case. After the execution laudatory remarks about the governor began to disappear from the official newspaper.

At this time Ramírez was again thinking of a return to California. His personal situation in Sonora continued to be prejudiced by the state's failure to pay his salary. Earlier, on May 17, 1861, he had written an article condemning delay in payment to public officials as "immoral and fraudulent." The item was published on behalf of all those working for the state, but it was also a kind of protest by Ramírez himself. Apparently he lived under difficult circumstances because of the state's nearly bankrupt condition. Still, even in the absence of compensation, he was a loyal and articulate spokesman for the liberal government. Now, as 1861 came to a close, conditions in California were especially favorable for a homecoming. The Republican candidate for governor, Leland Stanford, was poised to win election, bringing his party to power. Ramírez was personally acquainted with Republican leaders who could provide him with a political appointment after their victory.

Throughout his editorship in Sonora, Ramírez was able to follow developments in the United States. Newspapers and correspondence arriving through Arizona and the port of Guaymas brought valuable news, even if several weeks late. For example, on February 8, 1861, Ramírez reported the secession of South Carolina, an event that had occurred six weeks before. A similar period passed before he could describe the Confederate attack on Fort Sumter in the May 31 issue. Since news from California took less time to receive, Ramírez probably learned of Leland Stanford's election as governor during October 1861.

On February 14, 1862, Ramírez printed an announcement of his departure "with gratitude to the people of Sonora and the state government." He was probably delayed in leaving by efforts to collect some of his back salary to pay for the passage home and arranging for an escort to travel safely outside the capital. In any event, it took him a month to finally make his way to Guaymas, where he boarded a coastal steamer bound for Los Angeles.

CHAPTER FIVE
Homecoming

The March 28, 1862, *Semi-Weekly Southern News* noticed that Ramírez had arrived in the city by the last steamer. The editors announced, "We are pleased to welcome our friend Frank to his home and friends after a long absence." Henry Hamilton of the *Los Angeles Star* was less gracious. Aware that Ramírez had been paid little of his salary in Sonora, Hamilton remarked in his March 29 edition that his former rival returned "not much improved in worldly goods."

As Ramírez wandered through Los Angeles, reconnecting with friends and relatives, he would have noticed dozens of American buildings constructed in his absence. They were evidence of a growing number of immigrants. These industrious newcomers had become a definite majority of the population, which now stood at a little less than 5,000 people.[1] A few years earlier the Mexican community had ignored Ramírez's proposals in *El Clamor Público* to vote as a bloc to counteract American discrimination. This strategy might have succeeded when the electorate was mainly Spanish speaking, but now the American vote was too large to overcome.

The conversion of Mexicans to a minority was accompanied by a chronic uneasiness between the races. Ordinary Mexicans were aware that most Americans did not regard them as equals, a fact that engendered anger and resentment. Many Spanish-speaking families expressed their discomfort by moving north of the plaza to the adobe Mexican quarter called Sonoratown. Meantime, the Americans occupied an expanding area southwest of the plaza, characterized by brick-and-wood frame construction. The two groups established a pattern of residential segregation that has persisted, in one form or another, down to modern times.

Several prominent members of the old Mexican ranchero elite remained in their town houses on the plaza, but it was becoming apparent that this indigenous aristocracy could not long survive the new economy brought by the Americans. During the 1850s the gold rush created a desperate need for beef cattle in the San Francisco market, a need that brought Mexican rancheros in southern California huge amounts of cash. They used this windfall for lavish displays of wealth to validate their high social standing. Whenever the flow of money abated, they took loans from Americans at ruinous rates of interest and continued spending. Now, however, the demand for the cattle they drove northward was beginning to disappear in the face of competition from ranches in northern California, Nevada, Texas, and even the Missouri frontier. As prices in a glutted market dropped to alarming levels, the ranchero elite found it impossible to repay the loans they had improvidently taken.[2]

While Ramírez was still in Mexico, an unprecedented month-long rainstorm during December 1861 had caused floods that severely damaged landowners. The San Bernardino County communities of Agua Mansa and Placita were entirely washed away. "Scores of adobe buildings became saturated and collapsed; dry washes grew into raging torrents; nearly every stream cut a new channel to the sea; turbid rivers carried away hundreds of acres of vineyards and gardens."[3] The disaster exacerbated the financial problems of elite Mexican families, and their misfortunes were reflected in the changing appearance of the plaza. Based on economic reverses, Ignacio del Valle retreated with his family to Rancho Camulos in Ventura County during 1861. His town house at the southeast corner of the plaza stood vacant by the time of Ramírez's return. Not long after del Valle's departure, Vicente Lugo transferred his magnificent two-story home on the plaza, together with its mortgage and tax liabilities, to the Catholic church. This transaction nearly coincided with the loss of Lugo's other property to the lending firm of Bachman & Co. in 1862.[4] The Lugo place, just north of del Valle's, was converted to a Catholic boys' school.

Across the plaza, on the south side of the church, stood the town house of Andrés Pico. His financial difficulties were dramatically revealed in early 1862 when American creditors seized all his cattle on the Rancho San Fernando by judicial order. Soon afterward, he conveyed his San Fernando property and one-half the giant Rancho Santa Margarita to his brother, Pío Pico, to avoid foreclosing creditors.[5] It must have been evident to Ramírez that the wealth and prestige of the Mexican elite was beginning to deteriorate.

Although Ramírez had kept posted on local events while in Sonora by reading the Los Angeles press, he was probably not prepared for the degree of tension between Americans caused by the Civil War. The outbreak of hostilities provoked emotional demonstrations of support for the Confederacy in the streets of Los Angeles. Most Americans were people from the South who openly identified with the secessionists. The Bella Union Hotel was a gathering place for Southerners, who placed a huge portrait of the Confederate hero from Louisiana, General Pierre Gustave Beauregard, over the bar in the saloon. Those passing the hotel on Main Street could hear the drunken singing of rebel lyrics to the tunes of popular airs. One such number was called "We'll Hang Abe Lincoln to a Tree."[6]

Outnumbered Unionists worried that the fervor of the secessionists might lead to a violent uprising. The sole U.S. Army officer in Los Angeles, Captain Winfield Scott Hancock, was warned of a possible raid on his quartermaster stores. He reacted by recruiting a small group of civilians with Union loyalties to help guard government property. An urgent letter dated May 4, 1861, from Hancock to his superiors requested cannon for the use of his volunteers. He was concerned about rumors of a secessionist militia being organized in El Monte to capture Los Angeles. Hancock was therefore relieved when Major James Henry Carlton, with fifty troopers of Company K, 1st Dragoons from Fort Tejon, arrived on May 14. In less than three weeks, a further force of two companies from the 6th Infantry Regiment came from Fort Mojave and San Diego to impose federal authority on the area. According to a leading writer on the period, "Los Angeles became a garrison town, with soldiers in blue patrolling the streets during the daytime to the stares of a largely hostile populace."[7] Eventually a large army post called Drum Barracks was built in Wilmington, which served as a military headquarters for southern California and Arizona. It was an impressive federal installation designed to safeguard Los Angeles.

Despite the fears of local Unionists, no secessionist insurrection took place in Los Angeles. Even the most militant Southerners were aware that political and geographical realities prevented a successful rebellion in California. The northern part of the state, which contained the vast majority of the population, was overwhelmingly in favor of the Union. Since it was obvious that Los Angeles rebels could never defeat the number of troops at the disposal of federal officials in San Francisco, resistance to Union authority occurred in other ways. Scores of Southerners expressed their rejection of the Union government by joining the Confederate Army, an act that local Unionists did their utmost to prevent. Perhaps as many as 250 residents of Los Angeles County eluded capture, quietly slipping away to fight for the South.[8] The route they had to take was a miserably hard one across the deserts of southeast California, then onward through the barren wastes of

Arizona and New Mexico toward the refuge of Confederate Texas. Those who remained at home formed secret societies such as the Knights of the Columbian Star and Knights of the Golden Circle. Both groups had handshakes and passwords known only to their members. If favorable conditions appeared, they were sworn to strike a blow for the Confederacy.[9]

While the presence of federal troops in Los Angeles precluded open rebellion, it had little effect on local politics. Union authorities in San Francisco did not regard Confederate sympathizers in the southern California "cow counties" as a threat great enough to justify martial law. Chivalry Democrats continued to dominate regular elections for municipal and county offices. Most Los Angeles residents took comfort in knowing that the city remained under the control of a political faction devoted to familiar antebellum Southern values.

At the time of Ramírez's return in 1862, the Los Angeles delegation to the state legislature consisted of James R. Vineyard, state senator, together with Murray Morrison and Jack Watson, assemblymen. These Chivalry members, especially Watson, were coldly received in Sacramento, where they were suspected of disloyalty to the Union. Newspapers in northern California routinely referred to Watson as a "secessionist" and a "copperhead."[10] The officials elected in Los Angeles strongly contrasted with men like Leland Stanford, the Republican choice for governor. A Unionist and opponent of Chivalry ideals, Stanford won election based on the northern California vote. In Los Angeles voters attuned to the Chivalry had rejected Stanford in favor of the "Regular Democrat," John McConnell, by a vote of 1,087 to 455.[11]

The few federal officeholders in Los Angeles during 1862 were appointed by President Abraham Lincoln. They were a beleaguered cadre of loyalists dedicated to carrying out their duties in the face of popular opposition. Such men included Henry D. Barrows, United States marshall; Kimball H. Dimmick, federal attorney; Oscar Macy, customs collector; and Antonio María Pico, register of the land office. Despite a Chivalry lock on local politics, these authorities were not entirely without support. During May 1861 a Union Club was organized by a small number of residents, who declared, "We, the citizens of Los Angeles, declare our devotion to the Union and to the Government, sustain and support the Constitution; and will to the extent of our lives and means resist treasonable spirit."[12]

At about this time both Republicans and pro-Union Democrats recognized a need to jointly support the federal government. Following the example of the national Union Party, which had developed in the northeastern states, the California Republican Central Committee issued a statement changing its organization's name to the Union Party and inviting "the whole people of California, without distinction of party, or reference to partisan issues, to stand with us by our country and our flag." The Union Party soon swelled with Republicans and loyal Democrats. This coalition, under Republican leadership, would last until the conclusion of the Civil War. A People's Union Convention was held in Los Angeles on August 5, 1861, and was supported by both Republican stalwarts such as John O. Wheeler and pro-Union Democrats like J. J. Warner.[13]

The editors of the Los Angeles *Semi-Weekly Southern News*, Charles R. Conway and Alonzo Waite, tried to maintain a certain neutrality during the first stages of the Civil War, but they wholeheartedly embraced the Union Party after the September 5, 1861, local elections. They believed the Chivalry victory in that election was tantamount to treason. Their September 6 editorial denounced the Chivalry triumph: "Secession and disunion have carried the day, and years of repentance cannot wash out the stain. Abroad we shall be set down as a county not to be relied upon; and as a county containing naught but traitors and conspirators against the government." In this way the *Semi-Weekly Southern News* set itself in opposition to the *Los Angeles Star* under Henry Hamilton, a paper that espoused the cause of the Confederacy without restraint.

Comments in the *Star* on Lincoln's war tax were typical of its position. In the August 31, 1861, edition, the paper claimed that the tax was "to enable the administration to carry on a wholesale butchery of the people of the Southern States, who have the temerity to ask to be let alone, and allowed to govern themselves." Hamilton's criticism of Lincoln and the Union government never abated, not even after postal authorities excluded the *Star* from the U.S. mail during February 1862 on the grounds that it was "used for the purpose of overthrowing the Government of the United States."[14]

In the midst of the turmoil in Los Angeles, one of Ramírez's concerns was finding a way to make a living. Henry Hamilton was correct when he remarked that Ramírez had returned "not much improved in worldly goods." Ramírez's parents could offer him little since they were experiencing the same economic distress as the rest of the Mexican community. Their vineyard and adobe homestead were heavily mortgaged to Americans. A small lot on Aliso Street had already been sold out of necessity a few years before. No assistance was available from Ramírez's former protector, Jean Louis Vignes. The old man was now about to die; he was suffering from hopeless senile dementia and under the care of Manuel Requeña, a court-appointed guardian.

Although he had little money, Ramírez was not without prospects. Among other things he was in a position to claim a reward from Governor Stanford's administration for past services to the Republican Party. Except for a lapse—when he refused to support Edward Stanly as a candidate for governor—Ramírez had done good work. He had undoubtedly been promised a suitable political appointment by the Republican leadership when they came to power. Unfortunately, when the Republicans won control of California, Ramírez was in Sonora unable to campaign for them. This fact placed him outside the circle of those whose work for the party in the elections of 1861 earned them the most desirable offices. Nevertheless, Ramírez knew that the party would extend some favor to him upon his return to Los Angeles.

When he arrived home, one of Ramírez's first acts was to apply for a commission as a notary public. At that time the office was not the inconsequential matter it is today. The number of notaries was limited, giving those with commissions a monopoly on notarial fees. A special law authorized each county a certain number of notaries based on population. The County of San Francisco was assigned twenty, while Los Angeles County was permitted eight. A statute fixed the fee for an acknowledgment of a deed or other instrument at one dollar for each signature. Drawing legal documents brought forty cents per folio of one hundred words. The charge for protesting a note, bill, or check was two dollars.[15] These were generous fees at a time when common laborers were often paid less than a dollar a day.

The February 17, 1864, edition of the *Alta California* reported a debate on a bill in the state senate to reduce notary fees. One member complained that a notary in San Francisco "made ten thousand dollars per annum" and sometimes "as high as $20,000." However, another believed that outside the Bay Area "the great majority of Notaries only gained a comfortable livelihood." The senate voted to reduce notary fees in San Francisco by one-half but not to change them in the rest of the state. Some senators thought that the monopoly enjoyed by notaries led to abuses and unseemly profits, but the system giving a privileged position to notaries was sustained by an unspoken recognition that it was a convenient way of rewarding political service.

The selection of notaries was taken seriously. Petitions for the office were submitted to the governor and supported by recommendations from leading citizens attesting to the applicant's merits and political contributions. Since the term of a notary commission was only two years, each new administration was besieged by another round of office seekers. A typical applicant was William G. Still, who was granted a notary commission for Los Angeles County by Governor Leland Stanford in 1862. Earlier, during 1860, Still ran for justice of the peace, although his Republican sentiments isolated him from the mainstream of Chivalry voters. Without property or a profession, Still advertised in the *Semi-Weekly Southern News* that he sought the office "because I am poor, and am desiring of making an honest living thereby." His situation vastly improved under the new Republican administration when he became a notary public. He rented a room next to the post office, where he offered his services and operated a news depot selling various publications and maps of "mineral districts." The August 15, 1862, *Semi-Weekly Southern News* announced that he also offered "blank forms of deeds, mortgages, leases, powers of attorney, and gutta percha pen holders."

William G. Still was exceedingly active in the Union Party, the coalition directed by Republicans. He frequently served as chairman of its county central committee. During 1863, based on his political connections, he obtained a federal appointment as postmaster of Los Angeles, a post that provided a small salary. Men like Still belonged to a class of minor officials commonly found in the nineteenth century, men whose livelihood and status in the community depended on local politics. They were generally respected. Ramírez had no compunction about joining them.

Ramírez's application to become one of the eight notaries in Los Angeles County was approved within a few weeks of his arrival, the appointment accelerated as a political favor. He took up headquarters on Main Street in Temple's Row, sharing an office with Joseph R. Gitchell, a pioneer lawyer who had once been the U.S. district attorney. A contemporary of Gitchell wrote of him that "he was a jolly old bachelor and was popular although he did not attain eminence."[16] The older man could have been useful to Ramírez by helping him attract business in the legal community. Lawyers always needed notaries to take oaths, record depositions, and prepare affidavits. Ramírez made his presence in Gitchell's office known to the public through an advertisement in the Los Angeles *Semi-Weekly Southern News*, which first appeared June 18, 1862:

> F. P. Ramirez
> Notary Public
> Commissioned by Gov. Stanford. Translator and Interpreter of the French, Spanish and English. All legal documents neatly drawn up. Collections made, &c.
>
> Office with J. R. Gitchell, Esq., Temple's Row.

Gitchell was a "Douglas Democrat," another name for the Northern faction of the party opposed to the Chivalry. The August 15 *Semi-Weekly Southern News* reported the election of Gitchell to the Douglas County Committee but also announced that no convention would be held during 1862. There was no need for a convention since members of the group were shifting their entire support to the Union Party.

Ramírez must have been gratified by the rise of the Union Party. It resembled the kind of coalition he had earlier advocated to defeat the Chivalry. In addition to political discussions with friends, he attended meetings of the Union Central Committee along with the editors of the *Semi-Weekly Southern News*, Conway and Waite. The Central Committee was composed of prominent Republicans and Northern Democrats, including Ramírez's fellow notaries William G. Still and Ozias Morgan, who alternated as chairmen. The usual question discussed was how to defeat the Chivalry in the coming elections. The political situation had changed little while Ramírez was gone. This fact was shown by editorials published in the *Semi-Weekly Southern News*. The August 20, 1862, issue complained, "Under the administration of this secession clique, the county has been plunged deeper and deeper in debt every year; all the money raised by taxation must go to swell the coffers of county officials and their tools and hangers on." This accusation of Chivalry graft was similar to one made by Ramírez in *El Clamor Público* three years earlier, on April 23, 1859.

Two days later an article appeared concerning Mexican voting habits, a theme that the newspaper had not touched on previously. Although Mexicans were no longer the majority of the population, their support of the Union Party could act as a swing vote to help overturn the Chivalry. The *Semi-Weekly Southern News* of August 22, 1862, addressed Mexican voters in terms almost identical to Ramírez's earlier editorials:

> To the native Californians who have so long been misled and deceived by unprincipled and designing men, who, obtaining their votes, treated their wishes with contempt, we would address a few words, advising them to throw off the yoke and influence of their leaders, be men and exercise their right of suffrage free from the control and dictation of the clique who have ruled this county so long by their votes. If the native Californians will but shake off the unprincipled leeches that they have so long supported for office in opposition to worthy and responsible men, a change for the better will take place in our county affairs.

This item, written in English, would not be read by many Mexicans. Few could read English and most had little interest in political arguments made by liberal Americans. Conway and Waite must have experienced the same frustration that Ramírez had felt a few years before when he could not persuade a Mexican majority to withdraw its support from the Chivalry.

The Union Party held a county convention reported in the August 22, 1862, *Semi-Weekly Southern News*. Two weeks later elections were held, resulting in the usual Chivalry triumph. This time, however, the vote was much closer than in the past. The Chivalry candidates for the assembly, Jack Watson and Edward John Cage Kewen, won by only a few votes. Henry Hamilton's *Star* blamed the narrow victory on the absence of Chivalry Democrats, who had gone to a gold strike at the Colorado River mines and on illegal voting by nonresident U.S. soldiers at Drum Barracks. It charged that some voters were driven from the polls at bayonet point by U.S. Army troops. The Chivalry was given special congratulations for winning since "notwithstanding all the bullying and illegal voting, their votes outnumbered the combinations formed against them."[17]

Meantime, the *Semi-Weekly Southern News* grimly encouraged continued opposition to the Chivalry. Reflecting on their party's loss, the newspaper's editors wrote on September 5, 1862, "Weak as we are, this same Union organization will put 'secesh' to some trouble to obtain what they now hold and control—every office in Los Angeles County—at the next fall election." In the October 10 issue the paper dropped the word "Southern" from its title, renaming the paper the *Los Angeles Semi-Weekly News*. The editors wrote, "The reason for the change has been obvious and necessary."

Despite unpopularity with Los Angeles voters, Unionists had means at their disposal to combat the secessionists. They occupied every position of federal authority in southern California, an advantage they turned against their opponents. The October 8, 1862, the *Semi-Weekly News* announced,

"Col. E. J. C. Kewen, member elect to the Assembly from this County was arrested yesterday by Capt. Grant and a guard and taken to Camp Drum." An affidavit signed by three witnesses accused Kewen of cheering for Jefferson Davis and using "treasonable language." He was taken to Alcatraz Island for two weeks but released after swearing allegiance to the United States and posting a $5,000 bond.

While Kewen was still in custody, the October 22 *Semi-Weekly News* published a report that the *Star's* editor, Henry Hamilton, had also been arrested. The newspaper stated that Hamilton "is now located on Alcatraz Island, where he will remain until the close of the war." The editors of the *Semi-Weekly News* heartily approved of their rival's incarceration: "The *Star* has been, since the commencement of the existing rebellion, one of the most, and perhaps the most, treasonable sheets in the loyal states, constantly vilifying and misrepresenting the Government and its course, and openly advocating the secession of California and the formation of a Pacific Republic." To the disappointment of the *Semi-Weekly News*, Hamilton was released after ten days. His return was celebrated by a barbecue in El Monte, a community of Texas immigrants noted for the exceptional purity of their Chivalry credo.[18] Hamilton's confinement had done little to deter him. Instead of being intimidated, he immediately resumed publishing attacks on the federal government.

While Americans on both sides were preoccupied with the Civil War during 1862, a network of organizations called *Juntas Patrióticas* suddenly erupted among Mexicans living in California. They were not a result of local conditions but rather a collective response to events occurring in Mexico. On April 27, 1862, nearly 6,000 troops of Napoleon III, emperor of the French, invaded Mexico from the port of Vera Cruz under the command of Brigadier General Ferdinand Latrille, Count of Lorencez. The liberal government of President Benito Juárez reacted to the crisis by sending 4,000 soldiers to stop the French at Puebla, a town on the road to the capital.

The Mexican defense was more effective than expected against one of the finest armies in the world. At a decisive battle on May 5, 1862, the French were forced to retreat. They would be unable to take Puebla until they returned a year later with a much greater number of troops. The initial victory at Puebla set off celebrations throughout Mexico. The liberal government honored General Ignacio Zaragoza, the thirty-three-year-old commander who defeated the French, by renaming the city Puebla de Zaragoza. Mexicans living in California were also jubilant over the success of their national army. Their joy extended to places like Colombia in Mariposa County, where they "cheered, fired salvos, and toasted the glory of Mexico."[19]

For most Mexicans the best source of news about their country appeared in a small Spanish-language newspaper published in San Francisco called *La Voz de Méjico*. It did not announce the French defeat at Puebla until May 27, 1862, three weeks after the event, since it took that long for news to arrive from central Mexico. The newspaper had been started only two months before by a French-speaking native of South Carolina named Henry Payot, a bookseller and publisher of almanacs in English, Spanish, French, and Italian. He began publishing *La Voz de Méjico* to promote the branch of his business specializing in the sale of Spanish publications, but Payot was little interested in Mexican politics. His editors, Antonio Mancillas and Manuel E. Rodriguez, both natives of Mexico, were passionately opposed to the French invasion. They bought out Payot during October 1862, then transformed *La Voz de Méjico* into an organ of Mexican nationalism and resistance to the French.

An item appearing on August 26, 1862 in *La Voz de Méjico* had an impact on California that no one could have predicted. The article was a reprint from the newspaper *El Monitor* in Mexico City entitled "An Invitation to Mexicans." It urged the formation of patriotic societies in Mexico to raise money for the war against the French. The idea of providing financial assistance to fight the invaders was enthusiastically adopted by Mexicans in California. From their position outside the theater of war, it was the only way they could do something to assuage their patriotic feelings. Within a week *La Voz de Méjico* received a letter from a group of Mexicans in the mining town of Placerville, stating that the article reprinted from *El Monitor* had inspired them to form an organization to collect funds for the war in Mexico. They called themselves La Junta Patriótica de Placerville. The letter listed the names of those who had joined the junta and the amount of money each had contributed. When the newspaper printed the letter from Placerville on September 2, 1862, it caused a sensation. Within a few weeks Mexican communities all over California had sent correspondence to *La Voz de Méjico*, announcing that they too had formed a junta patriótica.

The September 9 edition described the organization of a master Junta Central Directiva in San Francisco. Its members, prominent Mexican leaders, would coordinate the movement and receive funds from outlying juntas for transmission to the government of Benito Juárez. Suddenly juntas began to appear in cities, towns, and mining camps everywhere. New juntas were constantly announced in the newspaper with lists of their membership and contributions of money. Their rapid spread began to overwhelm *La Voz de Méjico* as it became simultaneously a source of news about Mexico and a medium of communication between individual juntas throughout the state. The newspaper published nearly everything it received from the juntas, such as copies of speeches, minutes of meetings, and a large assortment of letters containing comments intended for statewide distribution to other juntas.

The Mexican community in Los Angeles quickly adhered to the junta movement. The October 9, 1862, edition of *La Voz de Méjico* reported the formation of the Junta Patriótica de Los Ángeles. Ramírez attended meetings of the junta from the first and was elected its secretary, with instructions to write a constitution for the organization. After accepting a position of leadership in the junta, he never wavered in his wholehearted support of it. It represented something like the kind of Mexican political and social participation he had advocated while editor of *El Clamor Público* just a few years before. Partly because of Ramírez, the Los Angeles junta became the largest such organization in California. His leadership is shown by the fact that he was always chosen to represent the junta on public occasions. Ramírez constantly made speeches on its behalf, being held out by the membership as their spokesman.[20] His high standing in the junta movement would be of great importance later.

Ramírez's search for employment during 1862 eventually led to a federal appointment as register of the Los Angeles land office. A document to this effect was signed in Washington, D.C., by Caleb B. Smith, secretary of the interior, on September 29, 1862.[21] Less than two weeks later the November 19th *Semi-Weekly News* noticed that Ramírez had also been named U.S. commissioner of the federal court. This latter position was procured for Ramírez by John O. Wheeler, who had become clerk of the federal court for the Southern District, a reward for his service to the Republican Party. The federal judge was Fletcher M. Haight, whose jurisdiction extended from Monterey to San Diego. He succeeded Judge Isaac Stockton Keith Ogier, a popular Los Angeles resident who had died in 1861. Haight was elevated to the federal bench on August 5, 1861.[22] A historian of the Southern District court wrote of Haight's selection: "It is highly probable that the possession of Union sentiment was an important factor in the qualifications of the United States district judge, especially in remote California in the summer of 1861."[23] Although the federal court occupied seven rented rooms at the southeast corner of the old Temple Block's second floor, Judge Haight seldom held sessions there. He lived at the northern edge of his district on a ranch in the Carmel Valley, near Monterey, leaving the administration of Los Angeles affairs to his clerk, John O. Wheeler. The ability of Wheeler to obtain an appointment as U.S. commissioner for Ramírez was something that must have pleased both old friends.

U.S. commissioners were empowered to set bail, take affidavits, and determine whether cases involving a suspected felony should be presented to the grand jury. This last power was demonstrated by Ramírez's successor to the office when a Los Angeles official was accused of fraud, "but he was able to justify himself before the United States commissioner and the grand jury was never organized."[24] Ramírez exercised very few functions of the office because the federal court did little business. Wheeler frequently had to stay at the court's northern branch. He appointed Ramírez as his substitute in his absence, thereby making Ramírez both U.S. commissioner and deputy clerk of the federal court. On December 1, 1862, a rare Los Angeles session of Haight's court was reported in the *Semi-Weekly News*. The personnel consisted of "the Hon. Fletcher M. Haight presiding" and "John O. Wheeler, clerk, per F. P. Ramirez, deputy."

Ramírez now held several appointments based on personal and political considerations. None of these positions demanded much time. In combination, however, they kept him fully occupied and generated enough money to make a living. The position of receiver for the federal land office involved extremely little work but paid $125 each quarter, an amount of $500 per year. In comparison, William G. Dryden, judge of the Los Angeles County Court, received an annual salary of $1,500 for a demanding full-time schedule.[25] Besides Ramírez's official duties as receiver, U.S. commissioner, and deputy federal court clerk, every issue of the *Semi-Weekly News* advertised his services as a notary, translator, and bill collector.

It is ironic that Ramírez accepted an appointment as receiver of the federal land office. An editorial in *El Clamor Público* written six years before—on June 19, 1856, when he was nineteen years old—angrily charged that the land commission had "ruined and retarded the progress of California." Now he was an agent of the same land commission. Perhaps any negative feelings he had entertained were mollified by the fact that the land commission had already run its course. Ramírez acknowledged taking possession of the Los Angeles district office in a letter written December 2, 1862, to J. M. Edmunds, commissioner of the general land office in Washington, D.C. This began an official correspondence with Edmunds, in which Ramírez demonstrated an absolutely correct and solicitous attitude toward his superior. His letters to Washington, D.C., were elegantly written. They even contained appropriately bureaucratic phrases, evidence of his mastery of the English language. In one of his few letters to third persons, Ramírez answered an inquiry about a land claim from a certain A. D. Palmer of San Francisco, signing himself on December 5, 1862, as "Frank P. Ramirez." It was the only time the young Mexican experimented with anglicizing his signature. Except for his Spanish name, Ramírez's correspondence was indistinguishable from that of any well-educated American.[26]

By now, Ramírez had been in Los Angeles for only nine months. During that time he made a remarkable transition from being a state official and newspaper editor in Mexico to holding public office in Los Angeles. The young Mexican possessed a rare ability to function at a high level within both cultures. He was not quite twenty-six years old.

CHAPTER SIX
A Contest for the State Senate

At the beginning of 1863, Americans in Los Angeles tensely awaited news of the war on the other side of the continent. Lincoln's Emancipation Proclamation took effect on the first day of the year, provoking outrage among the local Chivalry. The *Star*'s January 3 edition voiced the opinion of most residents on the Union's abolition of slavery: "By the stroke of his pen, Mr. Lincoln frees every slave in rebeldom, robs every master of his servant, every household of its property. Was ever such an outrage perpetuated in the name of law, or such foul perjury committed, as by this man, sworn to maintain the Constitution and govern by its laws?" But the discontent of local Southerners was muted by an overwhelming federal military force and distractions imposed by nature.

No rain had fallen for over a year. By 1863 southern California was in the midst of a drought. Ranchers especially suffered the effects of exceedingly dry weather. Cattle began to die of thirst and starvation throughout the region. A Los Angeles ranch owner received a message from his foreman that typified conditions: "We have had no rain yet, there is no grass and the cattle are very poor; your Rancho men report a great many dying. Should we have no rain your cattle buyers will get nothing but hides and bones."[1] Weakened cattle could not endure a drive to the San Francisco market, a problem that caused money to evaporate from circulation. Local merchants who depended on trade with ranchers and their workers experienced a severe downturn in business.

Nearly all Mexican ranchers had their land heavily mortgaged to Americans at fantastic interest rates. Since the drought deprived them of cattle sales, they had no means to pay creditors. An avalanche of foreclosures ensued that stripped them of their property. The most prominent members of the ranchero elite saw their names in newspaper lists of those being reduced to poverty by foreclosure.[2] Americans who had formerly cultivated cordial relations with Mexican landowners now spurned those losing their wealth. The drought would lead to the downfall of most aristocratic families.

Just as economic distress set in at the beginning of 1863, a fatal epidemic of smallpox struck Los Angeles. During February of that year, there were some 278 cases of the disease in the city, mostly among Mexicans in Sonoratown. Ramírez must have been acquainted with many of the Spanish-speaking victims. The most tragically affected were native Indians, who lacked immune defenses to the white man's disease. They succumbed in large numbers, a misfortune that helped bring about their eventual extinction.[3]

To a certain extent Ramírez's political appointments exempted him from the hard times afflicting Los Angeles. His quarterly salary of $125 as receiver of the land office gave him $41.66 per month, an amount great enough to provide a modest living. The position also entitled him to the use of an office in the old Temple Block paid for by the government. Little was demanded from Ramírez in return. This was evident in a communication sent to his superior in Washington, D.C., dated January 1, 1863, advising that "no business of any kind has been transacted at this office." The letter was the first of many such reports attesting to the dormant state of the land office. The receiver's job was only one of Ramírez's income-producing activities. His earnings from other sources very likely exceeded his salary as receiver.

While the depressed economy did not improve, smallpox cases declined by the end of March 1863 to an almost normal level. Meantime, the Chivalry and Unionists continued their rivalry in Los Angeles. As early as March 27, 1863, the *Semi-Weekly News* expressed concern about the next statewide election, which would not occur for another five months. The paper warned Union Party members to arouse themselves since the opposition's campaign "has been opened for months past." The defeat of the Chivalry elsewhere left southern California as its last bastion, a galling situation for the paper's editors. The April 15, 1863, *Semi-Weekly News* tried to stir up Unionists against the Chivalry by publishing an editorial that verged on hysteria:

> We have in our midst a foul brood of traitors who seek but a fitting time and opportunity to bring upon us the horrors of civil war and internecine strife; who in the dark hours of night are perhaps concocting a plan to ruin the prosperity and blight the happiness of the people of this favored State; to cause bloodshed and devastation; to usurp the place of peace and plenty and make widows and orphans where now exist happy and contented families.

The hateful rhetoric of the *News* was matched by attacks on Lincoln and the Union government in Henry Hamilton's *Star*. Only a ghastly tragedy, the worst yet seen in Los Angeles, could temporarily silence the contending factions. Late in the afternoon of April 27, a ferry steamer, the *Ada Hancock*, exploded off the port of San Pedro, killing twenty-six people, including several members of prominent local families. Most of the survivors were badly injured or disfigured. Both newspapers in Los Angeles gave solemn accounts of the disaster in columns divided by heavy black borders. The horror of the incident diverted public attention from the May 5 city elections for mayor and common council. Just one day before the election, the *Semi-Weekly News* reported the arrival of newly found bodies from the *Ada Hancock*, including "a portion" of a deckhand's corpse. Flags hung at half-mast throughout the city as the May 6 *Semi-Weekly News* briefly reported yet another clean sweep of local offices by the Chivalry.

Three weeks after the city elections, an unusual excitement stirred the Mexican community, which was aware that the French had returned to Puebla, the scene of their defeat a year before, on May 5, 1862. Now heavily reinforced, the French were determined to conquer Puebla and move on to Mexico City. They laid siege to the place for over two months while the Mexican defenders, starving and nearly without ammunition, hung on in a suspenseful drama about which side would prevail. California Mexicans awaited the outcome with the utmost anxiety. Finally, a stage arrived in Los Angeles on the morning of May 25, 1863, bringing copies of *La Voz de Méjico* to local subscribers. It contained a letter dated April 25, 1863, written by the commander in Puebla, General Jesús González Ortega to Ignacio Comonfort, a former president of Mexico. The letter described how the Mexicans had repulsed a major French attack, killing 400 of the enemy. The letter was interpreted as meaning that the French had been decisively beaten at Puebla for a second time. The Junta Patriótica in Los Angeles immediately called for a massive public celebration to be held the next day. There were twenty-one-gun salutes, displays of Mexican flags, and a procession through the streets. Ramírez had an important part in this event. He was called upon by the junta to give a speech commemorating the Mexican victory before an audience of several hundred people. An item in the Wednesday, May 27 *Semi-Weekly News* described the proceedings:

> The Native Californians, Sonorians, and natives of other Mexican States, resident here, became quite jubilant, on the receipt of the news—by overnight mail on Monday—of the defeat of the French troops at Puebla, by

the Mexican forces. They assembled and had a good time generally, by a stirring revival of patriotism; commencing their ceremonies on Monday afternoon, they continued them until last evening. They were addressed by Mr. F. P. Ramirez, and concluded by marching in procession, through the principal streets, led by a band of music and carrying the American Flag under which was that of Mexico.

Unfortunately, the letter from General Gonzalez Ortega was misunderstood. It described only one engagement in a long battle. The truth of the matter was that the French had won at Puebla and were entering Mexico City even as the people in Los Angeles were celebrating. Nevertheless, a description of the proceedings and a full transcript of Ramírez's speech were published in *La Voz de Méjico* on June 6, 1863.

Since Ramírez's return from Sonora, his political activities had gone beyond working with Americans for the Union Party. He was now regarded as a leader and Mexican patriot among his own people. On August 23, 1863, he gave a solemn eulogy before a large Mexican audience in honor of General Ignacio Lallave after the junta patriótica learned of his death in operations against the French. Ramírez's address was published in *La Voz de Méjico* on September 15, 1863. With state elections just three months distant, Ramírez was in a position to take another run at political office. By devoting much of his time to local Mexican people as well as Americans, he was building a personal constituency on both sides of the plaza.

The elections of 1863 began to take shape when the Chivalry Democrats held a county convention on August 1 to select their candidates. Henry Hamilton was advanced as the party's choice for state senator because of his long service defending the Chivalry in the *Los Angeles Star*. E. J. C. Kewen and Ignacio Sepúlveda were chosen as assemblymen. Kewen, who had recently joined Hamilton in being arrested for sedition, was running for a second term. Sepúlveda was only twenty-one years old, with the distinction of being a native Californio educated on the east coast. His father, José Antonio Andrés Sepúlveda, was a great landowner and a wealthy member of the ranchero elite. A new lawyer, Sepúlveda had been admitted to the bar just prior to the election. Unlike Ramírez, he was unusually conservative, with little concern for social reform. However, his intellectual capacity and knowledge of the English language was similar to that of Ramírez.

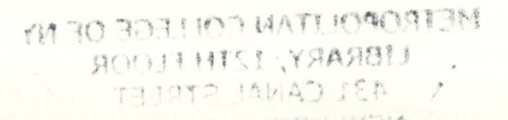

The Union Party delayed its convention until only eighteen days before the election, scheduled for September 2, 1863. William G. Still, the ubiquitous local politician and notary public, acted as chairman. According to the August 17 *Semi-Weekly News*, "Francisco P. Ramirez was nominated by acclamation for State Senator." Manuel Garfias and David Lewis were put forth as candidates for the state assembly. Some of those selected to run for office—such as William Wolfskill, nominee for public administrator, and Francis Pliny Fisk Temple, nominee for county supervisor—were important men in Los Angeles, whose presence added prestige to the ticket. A few positions like those of county clerk and county treasurer were contested, with the nominees emerging only after several ballots. The fact that Ramírez headed the party's ticket by acclamation shows that he had done some adroit maneuvering among the delegates.

Prior to his nomination Ramírez had divided his energies between the Union Party and the Mexican community. His increasing status among Los Angeles's Spanish-speaking people was reflected in his roles as a founding member of the junta patriótica and principal speaker at all their events. Instead of preaching from an editorial pulpit in *El Clamor Público*, he now personally engaged Mexican people in their homes and neighborhoods. The Union Party was persuaded that Ramírez had become their best hope of attracting Mexican voters. The August 26, 1862, *Semi-Weekly News* made an assessment of the Union Party's chances in the election: "We have not much hope of being able to elect our entire ticket, but the prospect is good for a portion of it, and a most determined effort will be made to effect that most desirable result."

Since the Union Party convention chose its nominees slightly more than two weeks before the election, its candidates had little time to campaign. Ramírez hurriedly made every effort to marshal support from both major groups in the city. On Sunday, August 30, he appeared at separate political functions, one Mexican and the other American. In the afternoon he attended a meeting of his own people described in the August 31 *Semi-Weekly News*:

> Union demonstration—Mr. F. P. Ramirez, the Union candidate for Senator, addressed a very large crowd of Native Californians yesterday afternoon, at the garden of Juan Apablasa. His address, and appeals to his brethren to rally round and support the government they have adopted, was most withering to traitors. The greatest enthusiasm and good humor pervaded the whole affair.

During the evening of the same day, a "grand rally of Union citizens" in front of the Lafayette Hotel on Main Street was reported in the August 31 *Semi-*

Weekly News as the "largest and most enthusiastic assemblage ever congregated in the city." The speakers were Ramírez, J. R. Gitchell, and J. J. Warner. Of course, both Gitchell and Warner were well known to Ramírez. Ramírez had started as a notary public in Gitchell's law office, while Warner was the leader of the pro-Union Democrats whom Ramírez had once insulted in *El Clamor Público* as "Mr. Delirium Tremens." Now all three joined in support of the Union Party and "the remarks of each of the speakers were in good taste, to the point, and were overflowing with patriotism." A brass band from the Fourth Infantry was present, whose "soul-stirring strains in the form of those old and familiar National airs brought forth a sentiment never before expressed in this community." The event did not conclude until after eleven o'clock, ending a long day for Ramírez.

Despite the efforts of the Union Party candidates, their challenge to the Chivalry failed in the elections of September 2, 1863. Like every other Union candidate, Ramírez lost his bid for public office. He received 761 votes while Hamilton got 922. The September 7 *Semi-Weekly News* remained hopeful for the future since the Southern majority appeared to be diminishing with each election. Commenting on the senate race, the editors wrote: "We have been beaten by a small majority, compared with former years, being but a fraction over one hundred." They were consoled by a great Union Party triumph outside southern California, in which Frederick F. Low was elected as governor. The *Semi-Weekly News* had a special correspondent in San Francisco who sent jubilant telegrams reporting on the progress of Low's huge victory as the ballots were counted. However, at the election's conclusion, the political situation for local residents was unchanged. Although California held firmly to the Union, the little town of Los Angeles stubbornly remained an isolated pocket of Confederate sympathy.

Regardless of his disappointment over his defeat, Ramírez made an appearance at a celebration of Mexican Independence Day less than two weeks after the election. He gave a speech in Spanish before an audience of more than one thousand. Ramírez shared the podium with Filomeno Ibarra, president of La Junta Patriótica de Los Ángeles. According to the September 18 *Semi-Weekly News*, "Mr. Ramirez also made an address in English." The newspaper reported, "Everything was conducted with propriety; the greatest respect for the Government of their adoption was shown, and heart-felt sentiment in behalf of the Union flowed freely from every breast."

Based on overwhelming Union sentiment in Sacramento, Ramírez decided to challenge the validity of Hamilton's election. The fiery Irishman's secessionist views would not be well received in the senate. Many members were aware of Hamilton's devotion to Southern ideals and his untempered criticism of the Union government. There was a fair chance they would refuse to seat a "copperhead" with such pronounced Confederate tendencies. His oath of allegiance while in custody on Alcatraz Island meant little since it had been given under coercion.

State law required Ramírez to contest the election by filing a notice with the county clerk. Two justices of the peace were then appointed by the clerk to hear witnesses and receive documents. All recorded testimony, affidavits, and other papers would be sent to the Senate Committee on Elections in Sacramento for a decision. Ramírez filed his election contest notice on September 24, 1863.[4] Thomas D. Mott, the county clerk, who had recently been elected on the Chivalry ticket, appointed his fellow party members, John D. Woodworth and Benjamin S. Eaton, both justices of the peace, to take evidence in the case. Ramírez was assisted in the proceedings by Paul R. Hunt, an early Republican with the dubious celebrity of having received only three votes when he ran for mayor of Los Angeles in 1855. Hunt was not a lawyer, but he was referred to in several documents as Ramírez's "attorney." Although one writer has labeled Hunt as an eccentric, Ramírez must have trusted him.[5]

At the first hearing before the justices of the peace, Hunt made a motion that witnesses be required to take a loyalty oath to the United States before testifying. Many of those called as witnesses were known to be secessionists. According to an affidavit filed by Hunt with the senate, Justice of the Peace Woodworth replied: "You can stick your motion up your god damned arse, and if you make another motion of the kind, we will send you to the County Jail."[6]

In this hostile environment Ramírez attempted to build a record for transmission to the state senate. His contest was grounded on charges that Hamilton was not a citizen, was disloyal, and had engaged in corrupt practices at the polls. The allegation of disloyalty was supported by extracts from inflammatory editorials in the *Star* condemning President Lincoln and the Union government. The accusations of misconduct at the polls consisted of testimony from several witnesses that the Chivalry had brought Mexicans from surrounding ranches into various precincts to vote with the knowledge that they were not citizens. The issue of whether Hamilton's supporters had procured illegal votes was the subject of much testimony by purported experts on the Mexican population, such as Sheriff Tomás Sánchez and ex-senator Andrés Pico. After several days of examining witnesses, the records of the proceeding were shipped to the Senate Committee on Elections in Sacramento for a ruling on who should be Los Angeles County's state senator.[7]

Ramírez's claim that Hamilton was not a citizen of the United States led to Union Party demands that the Irish editor's naturalization papers be produced. Beginning with the November 18 issue, the *Semi-Weekly News* published a series of short items headed "How About Them Papers Anyhow?" The first one read: "As the time for the meeting of the Legislature draws near, the query as to whether the Senator elect, from Los Angeles, can 'show papers' becomes more and more frequent. —'How about them papers anyhow?' The seat will be contested—the papers must be shown." Hamilton refused to present any proof of his citizenship, a deliberate omission that infuriated the *Semi-Weekly News*. The December 4 edition struck out against Hamilton, saying, "He set out at the commencement of the war to stir up rebellion in our midst, by a series of incendiary articles, which in any other country would have consigned him to a dungeon, at least." The newspaper thought Hamilton's disloyalty was "aggravated by the fact that he is a man born on foreign soil, perhaps not a citizen of our country."

The *Los Angeles Star* reported on November 28 that "Hon. H. Hamilton, our Senator elect took his departure yesterday for Sacramento, on the overland stage." A few days later Ramírez left for the capital by the *Brother Jonathan*, a coastal steamer, perhaps so he would not have to travel with Hamilton. With hearings pending before the Senate Committee on Elections, Ramírez wanted to be present to argue his position. His arrival was noted in a passenger list published by the *Daily Alta California* on December 6, 1863. Among those also on board were E. J. C. Kewen and Ignacio Sepúlveda, the Chivalry assemblymen from Los Angeles. Over a month went by before the press took notice of Ramírez's election contest. The *Alta California* printed the following item on January 13, 1864:

> The only contested election case which will come before the Legislature is that of Ramirez vs. Hamilton. The latter is the sitting senator from Los Angeles county. He claims to be elected by one hundred and forty-eight majority. The contesting party alleges eleven counts in his papers, the principal of which are that Hamilton is not a citizen, and that he is disloyal to the General Government. A Commission has been sitting in Los Angeles since the 19th ult., and it is expected that the case will come up before the Senate for a hearing in the course of next week.

Meantime, Hamilton was given a seat in the senate. As it turned out, his secessionist leanings were generally ignored because he could not affect a legislature completely controlled by Unionists. Hamilton was one of five "copperheads" in the legislature whose presence was considered more of a nuisance than a threat. He was relegated to some minor committees on state printing, commerce, and navigation where he could do no harm.

Contrary to expectations, the senate failed to promptly decide the election contest. The *Los Angeles Star* stated on January 23, 1864, that Ramírez had asked the Senate Elections Committee to subpoena Paul R. Hunt to appear before it since "Hunt's presence would be necessary to secure justice to his side of the case." Hunt was still in Los Angeles, leaving Ramírez to represent himself before the committee. The senators refused to pay the expenses needed to bring Hunt to Sacramento, and the former "attorney" of Ramírez did not appear.

Ramírez did not pay for Hunt's travel expenses himself, probably because he could not afford to do so. His quarterly salary of $125 as receiver of the Los Angeles land office was not due until March 31, 1864. It would be further delayed by the mail until after the middle of April. Worse yet, Ramírez was cut off from his income-producing activities in Los Angeles. He was forced to find some kind of employment while waiting for a decision from the Senate Committee on Elections. As a temporary measure he took a job in the state printing office at Sacramento. The March 19, 1864, *Los Angeles Star* reprinted an article from the *San Francisco Call* describing his situation: "Ramirez is setting type on Spanish work in the State Printing Office. Ramirez acts as his own counsel before the Elections Committee, and Sepúlveda of the Assembly, is counsel for Hamilton."

By this time Ramírez had been in Sacramento nearly three months. The senate's slow disposition of his case was doubtlessly a source of enormous frustration. His work as a typesetter at the printing office was of a menial nature, something Ramírez may have felt was embarrassingly incompatible with his pretensions to the office of state senator. The *Star* noted his problems with a certain satisfaction. The March 24 edition contained a satirical piece ridiculing Ramírez: "Mr. Hamilton was called away to the State Capital, and Mr. Ramirez being anxious to relieve his friend, as far as possible from official duties, followed him, and in order that he might be as near as possible to the object of his special attention, took up his abode at the office of the State Printer, and has ever since devoted his leisure hours to this laudable work."

Back home, the Los Angeles Union Party leadership tried to bolster Ramírez's standing. The local party elected him as a delegate to the state convention in Sacramento scheduled for March 24, 1864. They then passed a resolution supporting Ramírez, which was published in the *Semi-Weekly News* on March 16: "*Resolved,* That it is the desire of this convention that the State Senate, now in session at Sacramento, use all diligence in giving Mr. F. P. Ramirez—our Senator elect—his seat as Senator from Los Angeles County." The irritation of local Unionists over the election contest generated several unpleasant and probably false accusations in the *Semi-Weekly News*, such as one appearing on March 25: "Senator Hamilton, as we learn, re-adopted his 'first love,' took to the intoxicating bowl—red-eye—and has ever since continued inebriated to such an extent that he has been wholly unfit to vote on questions of importance."

Ramírez must have been intensely disappointed when the Senate Committee on Elections reserved its ruling until the end of the legislative session. Just before the senate adjourned for the year, a decision was issued denying Ramírez a seat in the senate. The following day, April 3, 1864, the *Alta California* gave the results of the committee's investigation:

> Señor Ramirez, the Union contestant for the seat now occupied by Hamilton, Copperhead, will not get it. The main charge, that Hamilton failed to receive a constitutional majority of the votes cast, is not made out by the evidence. Hamilton has held the seat throughout the session.

The Committee on Elections did not deal with the question of Hamilton's alleged lack of citizenship. On that issue it reported to the senate, "The only evidence is an affidavit of the Contestant and your committee did not feel called upon to investigate a charge thus gratuitously made."[8] The committee calculated that, even conceding that some Mexicans had voted illegally, Ramírez had still lost by 32 votes. No consideration was given to excerpts from the *Star* illustrating Hamilton's disloyalty to the federal government.

Ramírez had misjudged the realities of state politics. The outcome might have been different if the senate had been closely divided and needed his vote to defeat the opposition. However, the Union Party in the legislature had nothing to fear from Hamilton and the four other Copperheads, whom they could easily neutralize. On the other hand Ramírez was from Los Angeles, part of the region known as the "cow counties," a barely populated place with so few votes that it could have little effect on state elections. Most of northern California regarded the southern hinterland as a strange but inconsequential amalgam of secessionists and lowly Mexicans. It is significant that the *Alta California* reported the decision of the State Committee on Elections by calling the contestant "Señor Ramirez," an allusion to his Mexican origin not intended to be complimentary. His contact with the legislature had been an abrasive experience.

CLAMOR PUBLICO

Periódico Independiente y Literario.

LOS ANGELES, CALIFORNIA, MARTES, JUNIO 19 DE 1855.

COMISION DE LOS ESTADOS UNIDOS
PARA LA APROBACION DE LOS TITULOS DE TERRENOS.

[Sesion de 22 de mayo de 1855.]

Opinion del Comisionado Farwell.

APROBADOS.

N.° 250.—El título del Sr. M. G. Vallejo por 10 leguas cuadradas y 5 mas en el condado de Petluma.

N.° 291.—Otro del mismo, por un terreno en el condado de Solano.

N.° 291.—El título de John Rose, seis leguas cuadradas en el condado de Yuba.

N.° 462.—El título de los herederos de Juan B. Alvarado, por el Rincon del Diablo en el condado de San Diego.

N.° 550.—El título de Jno P. Davison, cuatro leguas cuadradas en Santa Paula y Santicoy, cudado de Sta. Barbara.

N.° 461.—El título de Juan Foster ocho leguas cuaradas en el valle de S. Felipe, condado de San Diego.

N.° 664.—El título de los herederos de David Litejohn, una legua cuadrada en Los Carneos, condado de Monterey.

N.° 509.—El título de Samuel G. Reid, tres leguas cuadradas en el rancho del Puerto, condado de San Joaquin.

N.° 248.—El título de Chas Convilland, parte de 1 leguas concedidas primero a J. A. Sutter Concesion por recompensa y con condiciones en 1841. El terreno esta situado a Feather River.

DESAPROBADO.

N.° 68.—El título de Temple y Alexander, por 100 varas cuadradas en el condado de Los Angeles. Concedidas provisionalmente en 1854.

Mexico.

El Genral Alvarez ha espedido el siguiente decreto para favorecer á las personas que deseen emigrar á Mexico para esplotar los ricos placeres de oro que se han descubierto en Ajutechlan, cerca de Acapulco:

El Capitan Juan Alvarez, General de Division de la República Mexicana y en Gefe el ejército restaurador de la Libertad á los habitantes de la República, sabed:

Que usando de las amplias facultades que me concede el "Plan de Ayutla," para promover por cuantos medios me sean posibles la prosperidad y engrandecimiento de la nacion, he tenido á bien decretar:

ART. 1.° El laboreo de los placeres de San Francisco del Oro, situados en el distrito de Ajutchlan del departamento de Guerrero, se declara libre para mexicanos y extrajeros desde la publicacion de este decreto.

ART. 2. Todo individuo, ya sea nacional ó extranjero, que se dirija al distrito mencionado con objeto de trabajar los placeres, se presentará á las autoridades políticas para obtener de ellas "gratis," sus correspondientes resguardos.

ART. 3. Es libre de todo derecho la introducion que se haga por el puerto de Acapulco, de maquinaria, instrumentos y provisiones para el trabajo de las minas.

ART. 4. Los metales preciosos del distrito mineral, que se estraigan fuera de la república, solo pagarán al erario el 1 por 100, hayendo en pena de comiso los que contravengan á esta disposicion.

ART. 5. Todo trabajador de placeres referidos, ya sea nacional ó extranjero, que desee adquirir terrenos para fabricar ó dedicarse á la agricultura, ocurrirá á la autoridad política, que facilitará los terrenos valdios el que se le pidiere, á precios convencionales ó equitativos.

ART. 6. Las diferencias que ocurran entre los mineros, se resolverán por quien corresponda con sujecion á la ordenanza del ramo.

Por tanto, etc. Dado en mi cuartel general del Ejército Restaurador en Texca, a 20 de Abril de 1855. JUAN ALVAREZ.

Sud America.

CHILE.—Segun las últimas noticias continúa su marcha pacífica y progresiva. Las elecciones para miembros del Congreso han pasado sin ocurrencia alguna notable. Entre los Senadores electos vemos con suma satisfaccion el nombre del ilustre colombiano D. Andrés Bello.

PERU.—El general Flores había llegado á Lima, y protestado contra el tratado que celebró Echenique con el gobierno del Ecuador, por el cual se le niega á aquel el asilo en el Perú. Parece que el gobierno provisional tiene por ominoso el tratado, y lo concidera humillante para el honor nacional. Pero el ministro del Ecuador protestó, y le han seguido los demas Ministros de la América septentrional residentes en Lima. Piden que Flores salga del Perú inmediatamente. "Si Flores (dice un diario del Sur) ha sido siempre una amenaza para los Estados Colombianos, hoy es mayor esa amenaza, mediante la expedicion que se quedaba formando en los Estados Unidos por él, con el fin de tomar las islas de los Galápagos."

Es un hecho imposible que salga de aquí expedicion contra el Ecuador, por mas que hagan Flores y su edecan Clemens.

BOLIVIA.—No son menores las inquietudes en Bolivia con motivo del anunciado regreso del general Santa Cruz. El Presidente Belzu ha dictado un decreto, ordenando el secuestro de los bienes de todo el que tome parte en alguna sedicion, invacion etc. Uno de los artículos de ese decreto manda concideran sin efecto las transacciones que se hubieren celebrado sobre dichos bienes, desde seis meses antes de cometido el delito, en cuando fueren aquellos necesarios para indemnizar al Gobierno y a los particulares de los perjuicios causados por los perturbadores. Se ha dado á luz una carta que se dice dirijida por el general Santa Cruz al coronel Puch, fechada en Bruselas á 15 de noviembre del año próximo pasado, y en la cual manifiesta el Protector su determinacion de "regresar á América á oponerse á la reeleccion en que está empeñado Belzu, adoptando al efecto el sistema de Rosas."

BRASIL Y PARAGUAY.—Por los extractos que ofrecen los diarios del Istmo de Panamá sabemos que la guerra del imperio del Brasil contra el Uruguay se está haciendo, y segun parece, sin una declaratoria que la precediera, "siendo lo mas extraño (dice el Panameño) ver que la marina de guerra de los Estados Unidos ayude á S. M. J; en su agresion contra los paraguayos. Estos, empero, oponen fuerzas considerables á sus adversarios, y hasta ahora alcanzan el triunfo en los combates habidos."—He aquí lo que dice el Constitucional de Mendoza, en el asunto: "Se hacía serio nos informa uno de los pasajeros llegados en la mensajería, el conflicto del Paraguay, atacado por una fuerte escuadra brasilera y un vapor norteamericano; dos potencias poderosas han llevado la guerra contra esta naciente y pequeña república; el Alpiraje del Paraguay, hijo del Presidente Lopez, de dos vapores que habian corrido el Parana, no habia conseguido introducir sino uno antes que la madera brasilera empezara los ataques. Se habla de un combate entre el vapor norteamericano y los vapores paraguayos, combate tenaz en que causó con sus fuegos algunas averías en el vapor matándole dos hombres ademas. Este desmontó algunas piezas de aquella. En la frontera con el Brasil, en las guardias ó fuertes se trataban encuentros parciales entre paraguayos y brasileros, en los que aquellos habian salido vencedores."

Los periódicos de Buenos Ayres dan la noticia de que una fuerza paraguaya de 8,000 hombres había obtenido é inmediaciones de Villareal un triunfo sobre las fuerzas brasileras invasoras. Sobre el Paraná tenian los paraguayos 20,000 hombres estacionados, habian tapado dos de las tres bocas del rio Paraguay, echando á pique piraguas cargadas de piedras, y están le-

Francia.

FRANCIA.—Un decreto del Emperador aumenta el ejército en 90,000 hombres.—Cada regimiento de línea tendrá un refuerzo de 900.

Esperando la visita de la Reina Victoria á Paris, el Emperador ha mandado poner el Liceo Imperial en un pié de esplendida magnificencia.

Por decreto de 31 de marzo, Mr. de Thouvenel Ministro Plenipotenciario de primera clase y director de los asuntos políticos, se encargará durante la ausencia del Ministro Secretario de Estado de Negocios Extranjeros, Mr. Drouyn de Lhuys, de la direccion de los trabajos de ese departamento y de la correspondencia diplomática.

El gobierno frances se ha quejado oficialmente al belga, á instancias del Príncipe Napoleon, por un opúsculo publicado contra el Emperador sobre la guerra y que se atribuyó al Príncipe.

EL PROXIMO CONGRESO.—Hasta hoy los miembros electos para el próximo Congreso son como sigue : Administracion 31 ; Oposicion 129. Todavía resta que elegir 37 miembros en los Estados donde las elecciones congresionales aun no han tenido lugar.

INTERESANTE.—Un astrónomo Aleman dice que en veinte millones de años la tierra será destruida por una cometa !

LA MEDALLA RUSA.—En los cuerpos de algunos soldados rusos que cayéron en Eupatoria se encontró la medalla de plata de la decoracion de San Jorge. En un lado está grabada el águila rusa, con dos cabezas, teniendo en los piés el globo terrestre y el cetro del soberano ; sobre el águila está la corona imperial y una paloma iluminada. Sobre estas figuras tiene las siguientes palabras en lengua rusa :

"Arrodíllense, idólatras, porque Dios es con nosotros."

En el otro lado tiene la siguiente divisa tambien en ruso :

"Para la sumision de Hungria y Transilvania."

☞ Dícese que casi todo el vino de la Moselle ha sido comprado por el gobierno Francés para mandarlo al ejército de Crimea.

☞ La Union de Sacramento hablando del San Francisco Chronicle dice : "No se encuentra dentro de los límites de este Estado otro periódico mas cortés, independiente y elegante."

☞ Los soldados heridos y enfermos que han muerto en Liverpool, (Inglaterra) serán enterrados en un mismo lugar, sobre el cual se erijirá un monumento por suscricion pública.

PISCATORIO.—Mr. Joseph S. McIntyre, de la armada de los E. U. estacionada en Benicia, publica una carta en el Herald de San Francisco, anunciando que sacó un pescado y cojiéndolo encontro un látigo de venado armado y media de largo y montado en plata? Se ha dudado mucho de la veracidad de esta historieta.

POZO ARTESIANO.—Se ha cavado un nuevo pozo artesiano en San José, y segun el Tribune es una curiosidad.

CONVENCION DEMOCRATICA.—El dia 27 de Junio tendrá lugar una convencion democratica en Sacramento con el objeto de nombrar oficiales para la eleccion general en Setiembre próximo.

EL CENSO.—La Constitucion del Estado previene que se tome el censo este año, pero como la legislatura no dispuso nada sobre esto, se tomará el año de 1860.

PELEGRINOS PARA PALESTINA.—Una caravana de pelegrinos se embarcó recientemente en Marsella para la Tierra Santa.—Antes de su salida fuéron invitados al palacio por el Obispo y cada uno recibió una crucesita de plata, con la fecha de su partida. Se esta organizando otra caravana

La ley del Dom——

SECCION 1. Toda diversion bulliciosa será en lo sucesi——— dias domingos.

SEC. 2. Todo individu—— ayudase á abrir uno de este—— miento público, tal como —— juego, cuarto ó salon, juego lugares propios para carre—— combate de osos, de toros, diversiones bárbaras y b—— prendido por un delito esp—— ley, y despues de convicto, á una multa cuyo mínimo cuenta pesos y el maximum—— cuenta.

SEC. 3. Todo individu—— un billete de entrada á uno—— de las diversiones enumer—— gunda seccion de esta acta te castigado con una multa al minimum, y de cincuen——

SEC. 4. Los jueces de—— en todos casos de infraciones de esta ley.

SEC. 5. Esta ley estará—— desde Junio de 1855.

PAPEL DE TULE.—El Ex—— BIGLER en su último mensa—— los terrenos inundados y presa como sigue :

"Y ya que estoy tocan—— acaso no sea fuera de lugar llegan á tener buen éxito lo que ahora se están haciendo del Atlántico, no tan sólo se sino que aumentará necesar—— Nadie ignora que una—— los terrenos adquiridos po—— virtud de la ley de Septi—— está cubierta de lozano T—— este suelo, y que por térmir toneladas por acre.

"Durante el último otoñ sido cuidadosamente ecsami bricantes esperimentados, o presado que, en su opinion, con él un papel de calidad perior.

"Puesto que el tallo de está maduro y antes que l la lluvia, es casi blanco, se to del blanqueo sería com pequeño. Estando culture y compacta fibra, ó interior un tejido ceular con numer fibras longitudinales, se c todas las cualidades requeri

"Se han remitido varia Tule á algunos fabricantes Estados del Atlántico, y con hagan ensayos con él, y r el resultado de estos impo mentos.

"A fin de poder apreciar la importancia de este esperi que tenga feliz éxito, se ha explicacion de algunos hec rentes.

"El precio medio, en lo Atlántico, del material con fabrica el papel es de unos la libra. A dos centavos la tercera parte del precio act los trapos, bastaría para esc ochenta pesos ($80) ó sea cientos pesos ($12,800) cada acres, y esto, sin mas gaste se orijinen al tiempo de la c no despues que haya produc durado.

"Sin embargo, cualquier sultado de los esperimentos haciendo acerca de la prim papel de cartas ó de mu duda han los hombres ente han ocupado de esta materi el Tule se puede fabricar p. calidad."

CHAPTER SEVEN
San Francisco and *El Nuevo Mundo*

Ramírez visited San Francisco during his stay in northern California to contest the senate seat. He had first become familiar with the city during 1853, when he worked there as a sixteen-year-old on the *Catholic Standard*. At that time a small Mexican community was concentrated in the North Beach district, within a few blocks bounded by Dupont (now Grant), Kearney, Pacific, and Vallejo streets.[1] Immediately toward the northeast was a small section called Little Chile, further extending a kind of Spanish-speaking barrio.[2] Besides this Latin American enclave, North Beach was occupied by French, Italians, and Portuguese, whose presence caused the area to be known as the Latin Quarter.[3] The heart of North Beach was just above Broadway Street, which separated the Latins from Chinatown.[4] South of Broadway, incorporating part of Chinatown, was the infamous center of gambling, opium, and prostitution known as the Barbary Coast. A little further down was a huge commercial and financial center radiating from Market and Montgomery streets and dominated by white Americans. The majority of San Francisco's citizens were Anglo-Celtic people who looked askance at the Latins in North Beach.

A well-known book on San Francisco published in 1855 estimated that some 1,500 Mexicans then resided in the city. They were described in terms that most white Americans of the era would readily accept:

> They show no ambition to rise beyond the station where destiny, dirt, ignorance, and sloth have placed them. They seem to have no wish to become naturalized citizens of the Union, and are morally incapable of comprehending the spirit and tendencies of our institutions. The most inferior class of all, the proper "greaser," is on a par with the common Chinese and the African; while many negroes far excel the first-named in all moral, intellectual and physical respects.[5]

This frank expression of racism, common for the time, was manifested in hostility toward San Francisco's Mexicans. It was natural for them to take refuge in the Latin Quarter, a place where they found low rents, compatible neighbors, and fewer contacts with Americans.

Largely confined to their own neighborhoods in North Beach, Latin nationalities discovered close cultural and linguistic affinities that helped promote a pattern of mutual cooperation. Beginning in 1854, the Italian community was allowed to publish a page in the Mexican newspaper, *La Crónica*, in its own language. In the same manner, *L'Echo du Pacifique*, an organ of the French colony, contained a page in Spanish. The Portuguese Benevolent Society arranged to send its sick members to the Italian hospital. The French Savings and Loan Society was joined by so many Italians that records had to be kept in two languages. The Church of Nuestra Señora de Guadalupe at 904 Broadway Street, named after Mexico's greatest religious icon and built for Spanish-speaking parishioners, was shared with Italians until 1884.[6]

By the time Ramírez revisited the Latin Quarter, the Mexican community in North Beach had moved a few blocks to occupy an area around the intersection of Powell and Vallejo streets. Most Americans referred to this place at the foot of Russian Hill as Little Mexico. It remained a Spanish-speaking district for more than seventy-five years. Although its history has never been properly recorded, references to Little Mexico occasionally appear, such as the piece about a tour of "quaint" Mexican restaurants—"not far from the Church of Nuestra Señora de Guadalupe"—that was published in the *San Francisco Examiner* on December 2, 1923. As late as 1939, a guidebook gave this description of a westerly stroll on Vallejo Street beyond Powell: "A little further on, the brown pottery in the windows and such names as the Xochimilco Cantina indicate that we are in the Mexican and Spanish Quarter, and at the base of Russian Hill." This neighborhood remained the core of San Francisco's Mexican population until the 1940s, when nearly all Spanish-speaking people moved to the Mission District south of downtown. The beautiful North Beach church, Nuestra Señora de Guadalupe, is the last reminder of the former Mexican colony.

At some point during early 1864, Ramírez met Antonio Mancillas, who showed him around the editorial offices of *La Voz de Méjico* at 622 Clay Street. By this time Mancillas was the sole owner of the newspaper, a fact published on January 19, 1864. He hired José Rentería and a young expatriate Mexican lawyer, Antonio García Pérez, to help him as editors. The paper gave extensive coverage to dozens of juntas patrióticas, while constantly announcing the formation of new juntas in California and Nevada. Lists

View of the Mexican district eastward from Russian Hill in 1865. Vallejo Street is in the middle. St. Joseph's Church is on the left side of Vallejo Street. Reprinted by permission of the San Francisco Public Library.

Vallejo Street in 1868, looking west toward Russian Hill. St. Joseph's Church is now on the right. Most of the Mexican readership of *El Nuevo Mundo* lived in areas like this. Reprinted by permission of the San Francisco Public Library.

of those donating money were printed, together with occasional acknowledgments that Juárez's *Ministerio de Hacienda* had received funds collected from the juntas. In addition to his editorial duties, Mancillas served as secretary of the Junta Patriótica de San Francisco and frequently published notices of meetings at his office.

Of course, like most newspapermen, Mancillas was aware of Ramírez's work on *La Estrella de Los Angeles, El Clamor Público,* and *La Estrella de Occidente*. He also knew of Ramírez's leading role in the Junta Patriótica de Los Ángeles. His paper had printed several of Ramírez's speeches there. He must have been especially impressed by Ramírez's turning up in San Francisco because he was contesting a senate seat at the state capital. Ramírez's intellectual gifts would have been obvious even in casual conversations at the cafés and bistros of the Latin Quarter. Before Ramírez left San Francisco, Mancillas offered him the editorship of *La Voz de Méjico*. A decision on this proposal had to await the ruling of the Senate Elections Committee, but Ramírez's later conduct demonstrates that he was attracted to the idea.

During 1864 San Francisco would have been a dynamic and exciting place for a young Mexican intellectual. The French intervention had forced many famous artists, politicians, and writers into exile. Several of these celebrities found their way to San Francisco, where they held court among local expatriates. One of the first to arrive was Ignacio Ramírez, popularly known as El Nigromante. He was forty-six years old when he disembarked from a steamer in San Francisco in November 1863. El Nigromante was a radically liberal politician, lawyer, and university professor who was responsible for many of the reforms in the Constitution of 1857, the culmination of a liberal movement revered in Mexico as *La Reforma*. During his career he had been elected to the Mexican congress and many other important public offices. He had been appointed Minister of Justice in 1861 by his friend Benito Juárez, as well as given various positions of power at the highest levels of the national government. In addition to politics, his literary talents brought him recognition.[7] As an essayist and poet Ignacio Ramírez remains one of Mexico's greatest writers. Nearly all standard reference works acknowledge his enduring place in Mexican literature.

Antonio Mancillas took advantage of El Nigromante's presence in San Francisco by obtaining some of his work for publication in *La Voz de Méjico*. One item that Mancillas printed was a letter that El Nigromante wrote on January 1, 1864, relating his impressions of San Francisco. It was one of a series of letters to Guillermo Prieto, a writer in Mexico, whom El Nigromante addressed by the fictitious name "Fidel." The letter was printed on January 21, 1864, in Mancillas's newspaper. El Nigromante was probably paid something for it since he was nearly destitute in exile. This letter and several others written over the years were collected and published as a book in Mexico under the title *Cartas a Fidel*, one of El Nigromante's most beloved works.

It is likely that Ramírez met El Nigromante while he was in San Francisco. Such an encounter would have been a memorable experience for the young Los Angeles Mexican. The writing of the older man, as one of the chief exponents of Mexican liberalism, must have influenced the formation of Ramírez's early radical beliefs. Since neither left a record of a meeting, we can only speculate about the extraordinary conversation that might have occurred. Other Mexican intellectuals fleeing the French were constantly arriving in San Francisco, and Ramírez certainly became well acquainted with many of them. They would provide far more exciting company than he could find in Los Angeles.

After the disappointing decision by the State Elections Committee in April 1864, Ramírez was not anxious to return home. He stayed in Sacramento for at least another month, sustained by his employment at the state printing office. He continued his excursions to San Francisco, taking the measure of the city and considering the possibilities it presented. About this time Ramírez learned that General Plácido Vega had arrived in San Francisco from Mazatlan on March 20, 1864, aboard the steamship *Oregon*. Vega had a confidential commission to raise money, purchase arms, and recruit volunteers to aid in the struggle against the French intervention. To the extent possible he was also instructed to promote American public support for the Juárista cause. Vega's orders, signed by the Mexican ministers of war and foreign relations, authorized him to finance his mission by drawing as much as $260,000 from receipts at the Mazatlan and Guaymas customhouses.[8]

Ramírez was familiar with Plácido Vega's background. He knew that Vega had taken the side of the liberals in the War of Reform provoked by a violent conservative reaction to the Constitution of 1857. A native of Sinaloa, Vega had organized an insurrectionary movement to depose the state's conservative governor in 1858. He was supported by Ignacio Pesqueira, the powerful liberal governor of Sonora, who personally joined Vega in an attack on Mazatlan. After defeating the conservatives, Pesqueira helped install Vega as governor of Sinaloa in 1859. Vega was then only twenty-nine years old. He consolidated his position by suppressing armed challenges to his authority led by Domingo Cajén and Manuel Lozada, "El Tigre de Alica." Vega was able to inform the Juárez government in 1860 that he had secured the state of Sinaloa for the liberal cause.[9] The grateful Juáristas responded by sending the young governor a commission as a general in their army.

Throughout his administration Vega maintained a close relationship with Governor Pesqueira, sometimes dispatching troops to help him in emergencies. One foray from Sinaloa to assist Pesqueira occurred in August 1861, during the Esteves revolt. Ramírez was then editor of *La Estrella de Occidente*, and he published several articles touching on Vega's career. When Vega accepted his assignment in San Francisco, he had no intention of giving up his governorship. He asked General Jesús García Morales, Pesqueira's brother-in-law, to act in his place until he returned.

Vega's mission to San Francisco was frustrated almost as soon as he arrived. In early April 1864 customs officials seized 3,000 rifles he had intended to send home on the American steamship *John L. Stephens*. The officials acted under an order signed by President Lincoln, prohibiting the export of arms from the United States.[10] This incident began a course of evasive maneuvers by Vega to avoid official interference with his plans.

The efforts of Vega to recruit Americans for the war against the French drew a remarkable number of letters and visitors to his headquarters in Frank's Building on Portsmouth Square. Most Americans soliciting a place in Juárez's army desired commissions, high pay, and land grants.[11] Vega also attracted the moral and financial support of prominent Californios such as Mariano Vallejo and Romualdo Pacheco. As the state treasurer Pacheco was the highest Spanish-speaking official in California. He introduced Vega to Governor Frederick F. Low and other state leaders while arranging financial contributions to the beleaguered Juárez government.[12]

Vega assumed that his official fundraising mission entitled him to collect donations from the juntas patrióticas. He opened correspondence with organizations throughout the state. For the most part these groups recognized his authority to deal with them, responding well to a stream of *oficios*—official memoranda—dispatched by Vega. Many exiles in San Francisco saw him as a greater source of assistance than the Mexican consulate. Vega generously distributed funds to exiles in need, including Ignacio Ramírez, "El Nigromante."

In complying with instructions to generate public support for the Juáristas, Vega partly subsidized Antonio Mancillas's newspaper, *La Voz de Méjico*. However, only three months after his arrival, Vega paid the costs of opening another Spanish-language newspaper called *El Nuevo Mundo*, which first appeared on June 28, 1864. Its editor was José María Vigil, one of the most famous exiles in San Francisco. Vigil had founded a liberal newspaper, *La Revolución*, in Guadalajara and was a political commentator, poet, and writer of national stature.[13] Vega recognized Vigil's need for an income while in exile by placing him in charge of *El Nuevo Mundo* under the business name of José M. Vigil & Co.

Ramírez returned to Los Angeles sometime in May 1864. While still in Sacramento he obtained a new notary commission from Governor Low for Los Angeles County. His appointment for another two years was mentioned by the May 26 issue of the *Tri-Weekly News*. During his absence, the federal court in Los Angeles had been abolished. The Southern District court remained permanently in Monterey after February 19, 1864, thereby eliminating Ramírez's positions as a local U.S. commissioner and deputy clerk. However, he continued as receiver of the federal land office throughout 1864. During his long stay in northern California, Ramírez made his few items of official correspondence with Commissioner Edmunds in Washington, D.C., appear as if they had originated from Los Angeles. After July the only communications he sent were monthly statements that no new business had been presented to the land office. Since the job was a political reward, the slightest activity was enough to assure a salary.

Not long after coming home, Ramírez learned that the situation in Mexico had further deteriorated. During May 1864 Archduke Ferdinand Maximilian of Austria claimed that he had become the "Emperor of Mexico." Earlier in the year a delegation of ultraconservative Mexicans, abetted by the French imperial government, persuaded Maximilian to come to their country to preside over a European-style monarchy. The ambitions of the blond, blue-eyed member of the Hapsburg family were enforced by French troops garrisoned in Mexico. With the support of Napoleon III, emperor of the French, Maximilian seemed to be in a position to rule Mexico indefinitely. This development caused great concern among Mexicans in California. There was a dramatic outburst of support for the republican government of Benito Juárez, which was holding out against the French from a temporary capital in Chihuahua.

On the second anniversary of the Mexican victory over the French at Puebla on May 5, 1862, the Junta Patriótica de Los Ángeles organized a great celebration, putting to one side the bitter loss that had occurred at the same place a year before. Practically the whole Mexican community turned out on May 5, 1864, in a demonstration of faith that Mexico would ultimately prevail over the French. Ramírez was the main speaker of the day, and his remarks were published in *La Voz de Méjico* on June 15, 1864. Besides the usual homilies about the purity of patriotism, the beauty of Mexico, and duty to country, Ramírez lamented that the world was being enveloped by the forces of darkness. In Mexico democracy and liberty were at risk of being extinguished by a monarch with the support of a powerful European emperor. In the United States a Confederate victory would perpetuate slavery, perhaps forever. Both Abraham Lincoln and Benito Juárez were in a universal struggle against oppression and despotism, each facing different facets of the same evil that was spreading everywhere. Ramírez told his audience: "The present war is not only directed against Mexico. It is a threat against all the American republics, against the United States, against Colombia, Peru, Chile, Bolivia, Ecuador, etc. We have a sacred duty to preserve the purity and robustness of the ideals of Washington, Bolivar, and Hidalgo!" He saw the dilemma of Mexico as part of a global attempt to crush human liberty.

Ramírez's American colleagues in Los Angeles were not preoccupied with the plight of Mexico. Looking toward the presidential election of 1864, Unionists formed a new organization called the Lincoln and Johnson Club, which was first reported in the July 21 *Tri-Weekly News*. A club room was provided by Abel Stearns in the Arcadia Block, a long brick building on the east side of his Main Street home, named after his Mexican wife, Arcadia Bandini de Stearns. Although Ramírez accepted a seat on the club's executive committee and acted as one of its delegates to the Union County convention on August 17, he was losing interest in Los Angeles affairs. His mind was now on what he had seen in San Francisco. He decided to accept the offer of Antonio Mancillas to take over the editorship of *La Voz de Méjico* and began preparations to leave Los Angeles for the great city in the north.

Ironically, Henry Hamilton also chose this time to depart from southern California. The September 1 edition of the *Tri-Weekly News* claimed that Hamilton had sold the *Star* and that "A. C. Russell is to take charge of its columns." The identity of the buyer proved inaccurate since Russell denied having made the transaction. Instead, Phineas Banning soon purchased the *Star*'s printing press for $1,100 and moved it to Wilmington. Hamilton, the old nemesis of Ramírez, went to Tucson, where he was a candidate for county recorder.

Just prior to leaving for San Francisco, Ramírez acted as the principal speaker at a fiesta commemorating the independence of Mexico. His speech on September 16, 1864, was printed by *La Voz de Méjico* two weeks later, on October 1. Ramírez again linked the war in Mexico with the struggle between the Union and Confederacy: "Let us refuse those who want Mexico to be a nation of abject subjects of a corrupt empire and those attempting to establish a slave empire in the south of the United States." It would be his last public appearance in Los Angeles for several years.

Ramírez left for San Francisco during October 1864. Advertisements in the Los Angeles *Tri-Weekly News* offering his services as a notary abruptly ended with the October 25 edition. His presence in San Francisco was noted in the October 18 issue of *El Nuevo Mundo*, which announced that Ramírez was scheduled to speak at 7:30 p.m. the next day before the Club Hispano-Americano de la Union at Terpsichore Hall on Pacific and Jackson streets. Ramírez's previous visits had created a highly favorable impression on the Spanish-speaking community, and he was welcomed as a kind of luminary.

Almost as soon as Ramírez arrived, Antonio Mancillas asked him to write a political tract on behalf of the Union Party for distribution among the state's Spanish-speaking voters. The Democrats had previously circulated a pamphlet in Spanish urging the election of their presidential candidate, George B. McClellan. The Union Party wanted a similar work supporting Abraham Lincoln's reelection. It contracted to pay Mancillas for the production of a Spanish language rejoinder to the Democrats. Ramírez was given two hundred dollars to write the eight-page tract, far more than he was accustomed to earning. Mancillas printed the document on the press of his newspaper. A list of several well-known Mexicans who endorsed the reelection of Lincoln appeared at the end of the pamphlet. They included Romualdo Pacheco, the California state treasurer, and Ramon J. Hill, a half-Mexican assemblyman from Santa Barbara, who was an orator much in demand at Union Party functions. Ramírez's name appeared at the top of the list, a recognition not only of his authorship but also of his growing status among the state's Spanish-speaking population.[14]

Ramírez's association with Antonio Mancillas at *La Voz de Méjico* lasted less than a month. A growing dislike developed between the two men that turned into mutual hatred. Mancillas, as Ramírez learned, was not a popular figure. He had antagonized members of the San Francisco Junta Patriótica by various acts committed while secretary of the organization and as editor of *La Voz de Méjico*. A broadside written by the junta president, Gerardo López del Castillo, once circulated among members, accusing Mancillas of failing to publish notice of a meeting because he feared its purpose was to replace him as secretary.[15] Four other broadsides by different members followed, alleging that Mancillas was trying to manipulate the organization for personal gain.[16] Mancillas had an unpleasant personality that tended to generate controversy and bad feelings. His standing in the Mexican community frequently suffered because of offensive behavior.

When Ramírez decided to separate from Mancillas, his attention turned to the situation of San Francisco's other Spanish-language newspaper, *El Nuevo Mundo*. As we have seen, General Plácido Vega had financed the opening of the journal during June 1864 and installed the prestigious Mexican writer José María Vigil as its editor. From a second floor office at the southwest corner of Jackson and Sansome streets, Vigil tried to publish a daily newspaper. In exile he wrote extensive attacks on Maximilian and the Mexican "traitors" who joined his government. News of French activities in Mexico were bitterly reported, along with editorials exhorting greater resistance to their intrusion in Mexico. Much space was devoted to a spectacular number of juntas patrióticas springing up all over California and parts of Nevada. Even remote mining camps formed juntas that appeared in the pages of *El Nuevo Mundo*. Nearly every edition contained lists of widely scattered groups that had donated money to the Juárez government.

Vigil was unfamiliar with the business practices of American newspapers. Advertisers in *El Nuevo Mundo* were too limited to provide an adequate income. Typical of those buying space in the paper were a grocery store called Los Dos Amigos at 1336 Dupont near Green Street; a restaurant, La Fonda Mejicana, on Kearney between Pacific and Broadway; a drug store, Botica Mexicana, on Kearney and Sacramento; La Union Groceries at 540 Vallejo; and a theatre, El Teatro Español, on Montgomery between Washington and Jackson. All these advertisers were marginal enterprises located in a small area around the Mexican district. Vigil needed more lucrative sponsors, but operating a successful newspaper in San Francisco was not his first priority. He was already planning to return home.

Near the end of August 1864, less than sixty days after becoming editor of *El Nuevo Mundo*, Vigil withdrew from the newspaper. The September 6 edition announced that ownership of *El Nuevo Mundo* had passed to a committee called the Defenders of the Republic. This group consisted of the staff remaining after Vigil's departure. It appears that General Plácido Vega was now unwilling or unable to further subsidize the newspaper. In an attempt to survive, the Defenders of the Republic invited readers to purchase shares in a corporation that would take over the newspaper. As might be expected, neither subscribers to *El Nuevo Mundo* nor San Francisco investors responded well to the shaky proposition of the anonymous ad hoc committee.

The situation of *El Nuevo Mundo* was severely prejudiced by the reluctance of its new editors to identify themselves. They were fearful that creditors might force them to take personal responsibility for the debts of the newspaper. However, Ramírez had no such timidity. He saw the floundering enterprise as a chance to establish himself in San Francisco. During November 1864, he opened negotiations to acquire *El Nuevo Mundo* from the ineffectual successors of José María Vigil. Since he had little money, Ramírez agreed to publicly assume the paper's debts in exchange for the transfer of its assets to him. The December 22, 1864, edition had a notice on the front page, boldly stating that it had been purchased by "F. P. Ramirez and Co."

Beginning on December 28 *El Nuevo Mundo* took on a different appearance. Under Ramírez's direction its pages were made much larger, and the newspaper was suddenly filled with new advertisers. Along with Mexican businesses the paper now carried advertisements from national firms, such as Grover and Baker sewing machines, Van Buskirk tooth powder, and the Occidental Insurance Company. Ramírez also persuaded local American companies like Baldwin Jewelry, the International Hotel, and the College of the Union to buy publicity in his newspaper.

Ramírez's developing plans were made quite clear in the content of *El Nuevo Mundo*. He intended to make himself a leader of the growing network of juntas patrióticas in California and Nevada. His newspaper would be the focal point of this effort. The first step toward this goal was an attempt to become the general treasurer of all the juntas patrióticas. The office was part of a Junta Central Directiva organized in San Francisco to coordinate the state's juntas. The idea was that local organizations would recognize the leadership of the Junta Central, including a treasurer to receive donations and forward them to the Juárez government. The treasurer was the most significant member of the Junta Central. Its president had little authority over the voluntary and sometimes ephemeral associations he was supposed to direct. In contrast the treasurer had large amounts of cash to disburse, which gave him considerable power.[17]

Ramírez envisioned the junta patriótica movement as more than a means of sending money to Mexico. He understood that it had great political potential. President Lincoln's administration refused to recognize the legitimacy of Maximilian's government, a position that gratified California Mexicans and caused juntas patrióticas everywhere to support the Union Party. It was the first time that formally organized groups of Mexicans had actively taken a political stance in California. This phenomenon was demonstrated at a Union Party rally in Los Angeles reported in the October 18, 1864, *Tri-Weekly News*, where Filomeno Ibarra, president of the local junta patriótica, made a speech in Spanish that equated support for the Union Party with loyalty to Mexico. In northern California General Plácido Vega, a person of great influence among Mexicans, set an example by becoming vice president of the San Francisco Union Club and campaigning for Lincoln's reelection, even though he was a foreigner.[18]

In one of his first editions of *El Nuevo Mundo*, on January 6, 1865, Ramírez acknowledged the political side of the junta movement: "The juntas patrióticas can do a great deal of good for Mexicans in this country. Together they make a formidable body whose opinion can have great political influence on the government of the United States when we make our voice heard to demand the redress of injustices and abuse." Such statements indicate the direction that Ramírez wanted the juntas to take. A large number of Mexicans in California were citizens who could vote. Ramírez hoped that, in addition to supporting the Union Party because it refused to recognize Maximilian's government, the juntas would evolve into a permanent voting bloc, becoming a factor in California politics. If Ramírez was perceived as a leader who delivered the Mexican vote, he would become a kind of political broker with access to the power and influence he seemed to desire.

Just two weeks after taking over *El Nuevo Mundo*, Ramírez printed the first notice that he aspired to be treasurer of the Junta Central. The office was available since Manuel E. Rodriguez had resigned, a fact known to Ramírez even before he came to San Francisco. The January 6, 1865, edition contained a communication from the Los Angeles Junta Patriótica advancing Ramírez's name for the position. The document, which was sent to juntas all over California, nominated Ramírez in the following terms:

> This Junta proposes Francisco P. Ramirez as General Treasurer. He is one of those who first organized this Junta and who has been its secretary ever since. He founded *El Clamor Público*, a newspaper devoted to the interest of Mexicans, and has spent his life, at the cost of great sacrifices, defending the cause of Mexico. He is now the editor of *El Nuevo Mundo*, with the sole object of defending our beloved country. He deserves our complete confidence.

Various articles promoting Ramírez's candidacy as general treasurer appeared in *El Nuevo Mundo* for several months. His ambition for the office was so great that his newspaper stubbornly rejected all other candidates, even at the cost of creating dissension within San Francisco's Junta Central. He almost certainly arranged for the Los Angeles junta to nominate him.

Beyond his intention to use the junta movement as a political base, Ramírez probably thought it would subsidize his newspaper. He was aware that when Manuel E. Rodriguez was both an editor of *La Voz de Méjico* and treasurer of the Junta Central, he used $200 from donations for operating expenses of his newspaper. The February 13, 1864, edition of *La Voz de Méjico*, acknowledging what Rodriguez had done, printed correspondence from the Los Angeles and San Luis Obispo juntas defending Rodriguez. Both groups thought Rodriguez was justified in taking the money since the junta movement needed a newspaper and *La Voz de Méjico* was "about to collapse for lack of funds." They proposed that part of the donations received be used by the general treasurer to support a statewide newspaper as an organ of the juntas patrióticas. Ramírez undoubtedly wanted *El Nuevo Mundo* to assume such a role.

While Ramírez saw the juntas as a political platform and source of money, he also realized they were a means of increasing the circulation of his newspaper. All the patriotic clubs in California and Nevada were potential subscribers, as well as many of their individual members. To exploit this source of readers and subscriptions, Ramírez needed to supplant *La Voz de Méjico* as the leading newspaper among such organizations. The only other Spanish-language paper in San Francisco, *El Eco del Pacífico*, offered little competition. It was a single page, published as part of *L'Echo du Pacifique*, a French journal owned by Étienne Derbec. Few Mexicans read the little sheet since it openly endorsed Emperor Maximilian and the French intervention.

Although Ramírez was principally concerned with tying his newspaper to the junta movement, he astutely recognized the importance of attracting local subscribers beyond San Francisco's Mexican colony. One of the largest groups of Spanish-speaking residents was a Chilean community in North Beach adjacent to the Mexican district. Ramírez associated a Chilean activist, Felipe Fierro, as an assistant editor of *El Nuevo Mundo*.[19] Fierro's presence helped expand circulation among his countrymen. Nearly every edition contained news relating to Chile and its citizens residing in San Francisco. Articles on other Latin American countries often appeared in the newspaper. Immigrants from Central America, Argentina, Columbia, Venezuela, Ecuador, and Peru might find references printed about their homeland with enough frequency to justify a subscription. Ramírez moved the paper's office to 603 Front Street, rooms 3 and 4, at the northwest corner with Jackson. Instead of taking up residence in the North Beach Mexican district, Ramírez lived downtown at 33 Geary, between Dupont (now Grant) and Kearny. This was just a few doors west of Market Street near one of the city's busiest intersections.[20] The place was a boarding house where Ramírez stayed in San Francisco.

The January 25, 1865, edition of *El Nuevo Mundo* began Ramírez's push to become treasurer of the Junta Central. This effort was combined with a challenge to Antonio Mancillas and his newspaper, *La Voz de Méjico*, for supremacy among the state's juntas. On the same date *El Nuevo Mundo* reported that, despite promises to do so, Mancillas had refused to print a notice of Ramírez's nomination as general treasurer by the Los Angeles Junta Patriótica. Ramírez accused Mancillas of trying to thwart his candidacy. His supporters in Los Angeles were warned that "they now know what side their friends are on." The next edition of *El Nuevo Mundo*, on January 30, contained an even stronger resolution from the Los Angeles junta, nominating Ramírez and demanding that its proceedings be published in *La Voz de Méjico*.

The growing contention over the office of general treasurer was demonstrated in a letter from Jesús Camarena published on February 3, 1865, in *El Nuevo Mundo*. Camarena wrote that Plácido Vega, backed by numerous juntas, had appointed him general treasurer some four months before. He assumed that Vega's mission to collect funds on behalf of Mexico gave him

The street in the foreground is a part of Geary Avenue, just west of Market Street. This 1865 photograph shows the block where Ramírez lived in a boarding house at 33 Geary Avenue. The church in the background is the Jewish Temple El-Emmanuel. Reprinted by permission of the San Francisco Public Library.

The first edition of *El Nuevo Mundo* under Ramírez's editorship, December 22, 1864. Reprinted by permission of the Huntington Library, San Marino, California.

authority to designate a general treasurer for the juntas. Although he had declined the appointment, Camarena was confident that "other persons are well able to carry out the office of general treasurer such as Francisco P. Ramírez, already nominated by the junta of Los Angeles."

Although grateful for Camarena's endorsement, Ramírez used the occasion to question Vega's power to appoint a statewide treasurer. The Mexican general's assertion of control over the juntas threatened Ramírez's ambition to lead them. He wrote, "The juntas should not delegate their right to conduct elections to anyone. It is not just nor reasonable that Mr. Vega interfere in matters purely of concern to the juntas." Ramírez criticized Vega for "a stream of officious communications that keep the juntas in a state of alarm with no understanding of how to respond to his orders and demands."

A week later, on February 10, 1865, Ramírez published an open letter anonymously signed by "Various True Liberals," that badly denigrated Plácido Vega. It came shortly after Vega announced that he had appointed yet another general treasurer, Julio Valade, based on powers of attorney, proxies, and other written authority from junta members in California and Nevada. The letter suggested that Vega wanted a treasurer he could control in order to loot donations from the juntas. It charged that Vega's appointment was made to benefit "his own interests" and "private enterprises." Moreover, the unilateral appointment by Vega "would create anarchy among the juntas." The item claimed that some organizations like those in Sacramento, Jackson, Sonora, and La Porte would approve of Vega's selection of Valade, but others in Los Angeles, Wilmington, San Luis Obispo, West Point, and Pinole were committed to Ramírez. Without a statewide election for the office of general treasurer, "we see nothing in the future except complete separation or dissolution of the juntas." All this was part of an "infernal plan" concocted by Vega to destroy the independence of the junta movement.

While engaged in a fight to become general treasurer of the juntas, Ramírez did not foreclose the possibility of further political appointments from Republican leaders in the Union Party. His departure from Los Angeles was not noticed by federal authorities, who gave him an appointment as postmaster there on October 22, 1864. By then Ramírez was already in San Francisco and unable to exercise the office. The February 10, 1865, *Alta California* printed an item well after the appointment, saying: "Mr. Ramirez is a native born Californian, and a gentleman of fine education and a high order of talent, as appears from his reports to the Land Office. They are very much praised in that department and Mr. Ramirez deserves some higher appointment than that of Postmaster." Ramírez reprinted these comments in *El Nuevo Mundo* on the same day they appeared in the *Alta California*. He may have had a hand in getting these favorable remarks published in the American newspaper for the benefit of Republican leaders. It was an advertisement of his availability for employment. He had sent his resignation as receiver of the Los Angeles federal land office on December 1, 1864, more than a month after moving to San Francisco. He made it effective on March 31, 1865, a clever move that not only provided the government with notice but also gave Ramírez an extra four months' salary. Meantime, Ramírez remained on a list of those being considered by the Republicans for political appointment, a fact that was demonstrated later in the year.

The conflict over the office of general treasurer seemed at an end when Ramírez printed an article on February 22, 1865, conceding that Vega's appointment of Julio Valade was supported by a majority of juntas. The hopelessness of further struggle was confirmed when the Mexican consul, José A. Godoy, sent a circular to the juntas urging unanimous acceptance of Valade. *El Nuevo Mundo* had praised the integrity and good sense of Godoy so often that it could hardly now oppose him. However, Ramírez openly expressed contempt for Antonio Mancillas. It was apparent that General Plácido Vega was largely subsidizing Mancillas's newspaper. Ramírez wrote that the editorial opinions of *La Voz de Méjico* were suspect and "the juntas should punish Mancillas" for his lack of independence and servility to Vega.

Ramírez's anger at Mancillas was indicative of his capacity for hatred. He had already demonstrated this unhappy characteristic in his treatment of Henry Hamilton in Los Angeles and Miguel Urrea in Sonora. Now, with his political and personal ambitions frustrated, he turned his considerable negative feelings toward Antonio Mancillas and Plácido Vega. Ramírez was further disturbed when Vega sent two lieutenants demanding to know who was responsible for the letter published on February 10 and signed "Various True Liberals." As we have seen, the item accused Vega of nothing less than wanting to control the general treasury of the juntas in order to steal money. Surprisingly, Ramírez asked to see Vega personally.

Their interview was described by Ramírez in his February 24, 1865, edition. He was led by two men to a room at the International Hotel since it was hard to locate Vega "because of the mysterious life he leads." According to Ramírez, little of substance was exchanged during a fairly civil meeting. He vaguely promised to provide more information about the offending letter after speaking to his Chilean editor, Felipe Fierro. However, the next day members of Vega's staff told Antonio Mancillas that Ramírez had used the occasion to ask Vega for help in becoming general treasurer of the juntas. In light of Ramírez's challenging, even arrogant posture toward Vega in public, rumors that he had humbled himself by asking Vega for a favor related to the juntas might have been humiliating.

Whatever the cause of the meeting between the men at the International Hotel, nothing positive came of it. When Vega consented to see Ramírez, it was probably to rebuke him for publishing the insulting letter in *El Nuevo Mundo*. Of course, Vega believed that if Ramírez really had the welfare of the Juárez government at heart, he would have worked with him as its official representative. Much more could be done for Mexico through cooperation than malicious bickering over who should hold office on the Junta Central. Vega viewed Ramírez as a nuisance whose ambitions obstructed his mission.

A May 19, 1865, article in *El Pájaro Verde*, a semiofficial gazette of the Mexican empire published daily in Mexico City, identified Ramírez and Vega as enemies because both were operating against Maximilian in San Francisco. It mistakenly claimed that Vega had given Ramírez $200 to defray the expenses of his newspaper, *El Nuevo Mundo*. Ramírez would have been pleased to know about the item in the imperial press. His reputation as a loyal Juárista had spread to Mexico City and beyond.

Within a few days Ramírez discovered that Antonio Mancillas had been actively working against his becoming general treasurer. Mancillas made the mistake of sending a letter to the Junta Patriótica de Wilmington, criticizing Ramírez as not being "the most suitable person for the office since he is unable to obtain a bond to guarantee the proper management of funds under his care." He also charged that Ramírez would divert donations from the juntas to support *El Nuevo Mundo*. In light of this, he had refused to publish Ramírez's nomination in *La Voz de Méjico* to prevent a "bad election." The president of the Wilmington group, Trinidad Nerio, sent a copy of the letter to Ramírez, who published it in the March 8 edition of *El Nuevo Mundo*. Ramírez accused both Mancillas and his patron, Plácido Vega, of forming a conspiracy to block his election. He regarded the letter as an attack on his character since it alleged that he would embezzle money entrusted to him. He wrote that the letter "has wounded the most delicate fibers of my heart with its miserable calumnies." For several weeks afterward Ramírez expressed his rage against Mancillas by printing the name of his newspaper upside down.

The highly impolitic treatment of Vega by Ramírez's newspaper, together with his efforts to undermine the general's position among the juntas, caused enormous resentment. The depth of Vega's hostility was made clear in an incident that occurred on March 26, 1865, at the Dashaway Hall on Post Street. Both Vega and Ramírez were present at a meeting of the Club Patriótico Mexicano. Julio Valade, Vega's choice for general treasurer of the juntas, made a motion that the club refuse admission to Mexicans who had adopted American citizenship after the French invaded Mexico. He alleged that changing nationalities during the crisis was an act of disloyalty to the homeland. Ramírez argued that many Mexicans had become citizens in order to support Abraham Lincoln and the Union Party, Mexico's greatest allies against Maximilian's government. It was widely believed that Lincoln would enforce the Monroe Doctrine by turning the U.S. Army toward the French once the Civil War was over. According to Ramírez, Mexicans who had become American citizens to vote for Lincoln had done nothing inimical to their native country.

A vote was taken that defeated Valade's proposition. For some reason Vega was upset over this outcome. At an earlier meeting not attended by Ramírez, the club had passed Valade's motion. Now Ramírez had convinced members to reverse their previous decision. Vega may have thought Ramírez argued against Valade's position solely to spite him personally. It was commonly understood that Valade was entirely controlled by Vega. The attempted change of membership rules was undoubtedly Vega's idea.

When the meeting was over, Ramírez stepped onto the sidewalk outside Dashaway Hall and headed toward his office. Vega came up behind him and knocked Ramírez to the ground. According to an article in *El Nuevo Mundo* the following day, Vega fell on Ramírez and tried to "gouge out his eyes." The article, entitled "Brutal Assault," shrilly complained that "Mr. Ramírez had no defense in such a critical situation other than to seize the beard of General Vega with both hands." Members of the Club Patriótico Mexicano were too stunned to quickly intervene "in such an unequal encounter." A pair of policemen immediately arrived and took the grappling men into custody. At the police station both were required to post bail pending investigation of the incident. The Mexican Consul, José A. Godoy, put up the money for Ramírez, while Vega paid his own bail under the pseudonym "Santos Rodriguez."

One day later Ramírez tried to assess his feelings about the matter. His March 27 editorial mused, "We do not envy the situation in which Mr. Vega finds himself. If his heart is capable of human emotion, he will regret yester-

Dashaway Hall in 1869. General Plácido Vega attacked Ramírez on the sidewalk here on March 26, 1865. Reprinted by permission of the San Francisco Public Library.

day's episode as long as he lives." He went on to speculate that, "Mr. Vega's public career will terminate based on the errors in carrying out his commission, his interference with the juntas, and now this shameful street attack in plain sight of his friends against a defenseless editor of *El Nuevo Mundo*." Despite Ramírez's wishful predictions, however, Vega appears to have suffered few, if any, consequences. For the next several weeks he continued to attend meetings of the Club Patriótico Mexicano at Dashaway Hall as if nothing had happened. Ramírez, however, was not present. He avoided meetings of the organization for several months afterward. Perhaps the club's membership had some degree of sympathy for Vega, believing that Ramírez's defamatory articles about him had provoked an unfortunate, but understandable response.

The stories Ramírez printed relating to his struggle with Vega and Mancillas were interpreted by juntas outside San Francisco as a breakdown of the state leadership. Several local organizations sent letters to *El Nuevo Mundo* expressing dissatisfaction with the discord at the highest level of the junta movement. A few outlying juntas supported Ramírez, asking for unity under his direction. Such letters were published in *El Nuevo Mundo* along with Ramírez's declarations of gratitude. A message from the president of the junta in Mariposa, appearing in the April 5 edition, endorsed Ramírez as a general treasurer but complained, "All the juntas have placed San Francisco at the head of our movement as the point most suitable to deposit our funds, but now we see a falling out between our most illustrious men and a failure to perform their duties." To a large extent such letters reflected difficulties that Ramírez himself had created in his drive to become general treasurer.

The question of who would control the money generated by junta donations was temporarily put to rest with Vega's appointment of Julio Valade as general treasurer. Nevertheless, Ramírez continued to publish letters from juntas that supported him for the office, and he did not moderate his criticism of Vega. His ambition to lead the junta movement was briefly sidetracked, but not forgotten. Ramírez never abandoned his efforts to become general treasurer even though he could not quite muster all the support he needed. During this period he did all he could to enhance his image among California Mexicans. The April 7 edition of his newspaper reprinted an item from *La Estrella de Occidente* praising *El Nuevo Mundo* and its editor. It read in part, "Francisco P. Ramirez is one of the most intelligent and enthusiastic defenders of our country's cause and the authority of his editorial pen is well-known to the people of Sonora." The comment was probably induced by Ramírez's sending copies of *El Nuevo Mundo* to acquaintances in Ures and Hermosillo.

Larger issues replaced the contest for power in the junta movement beginning with the April 10, 1865, edition of *El Nuevo Mundo*. On that date the newspaper reported that the Union Army had taken the city of Richmond, capital of the Confederacy. Ramírez expected that a Union victory over the South would result in the destruction of Maximilian's government. He thought that, once the Civil War was concluded, the United States would crush the French in Mexico. He called the occupation of Richmond "a positive step toward enforcement of the Monroe Doctrine." The end of the Confederacy would free the slaves from "the bastard Democrats of the south" and extinguish "the last vestige of feudalism in America."

Two days later Ramírez jubilantly published a translation of Robert E. Lee's letter of surrender to Ulysses S. Grant. Reports of the South's defeat dominated the April 12 edition, but even in the midst of dealing with such momentous news, Ramírez remained fixed on his personal feud with Plácido Vega. On the same date he printed an item purporting to be the minutes of the Junta Patriótica de Los Ángeles, in which the members took turns criticizing Vega for his assault on Ramírez. The remarks of Jesús Silva were typical: "I am filled with indignation that a man who is a general, governor, and commissioner of the Mexican government would be so low as to brutally attack in public one of the purest patriots California has ever known." After each member vented his anger, they supposedly exclaimed in unison: "We protest with all our might!" This dramatic version of the junta's meeting was published in several editions of El Nuevo Mundo.

Before Ramírez could fully react to the Confederate surrender, he received the devastating news of Lincoln's assassination. His April 17 issue was blocked out in thick black margins as a demonstration of mourning. The occasion called for appropriate expressions of sorrow, but even beyond that, Ramírez seemed genuinely affected. He may have revered Lincoln as much as he did Benito Juárez. He wrote that the president was a giant whose death had caused "the Republic's greatest and most venerable men to weep like children." Ramírez thought that Lincoln's name "would forever remain immortal alongside those of Franklin and Washington."

The unsettled conditions brought about by Lincoln's death did not prevent Ramírez from pursuing his obsessive hatreds. The April 21 issue once again reprinted a detailed account of his month-old affray with Vega. A few days later, on April 26, Ramírez reported that Antonio Mancillas had lost a lawsuit brought against him by Manuel E. Rodriguez. The suit was based on an article in La Voz de Méjico, charging Rodriguez with embezzling money from the Junta Central while acting as the general treasurer. Rodriguez brought a suit for libel in San Francisco, where a jury awarded a judgment of $2,000 in his favor. In a transparent move to avoid the seizure of his newspaper under the judgment, Mancillas transferred it to Luis A. Tostado. Ramírez published news of his rival's apparent downfall with obvious pleasure.

Mancillas also figured in an article written by Felipe Fierro, the Chilean editor of El Nuevo Mundo and a close associate of Ramírez. The article was presented in response to an accusation in Mancillas's newspaper that Fierro was an American citizen and therefore not the true Chilean patriot he pretended to be. Fierro's answer, published on May 1, 1865, made it clear that he was, in fact, a citizen of Chile. Nevertheless, he wrote, "Anyone who understands the energy, learning, patriotism, and civic spirit of this great nation with its democratic principles established for the good of humanity would be honored to be a citizen of the United States."

Earlier, as a radical young editor in Los Angeles, Ramírez had learned not to publish unqualified praise of Americans. Such pronouncements were often followed by reports of American atrocities against Latins. He found that, despite proclaiming principles of equality, Americans brutally discriminated against ordinary Mexican people. At that time he had been driven to angrily protest American racism. Now, at the age of twenty-eight, more than five years after closing *El Clamor Público*, he rarely mentioned racial or social issues in his newspaper. Ramírez was completely focused on his personal ambitions. As a member of the Union Party who aspired to a place of prominence, he had little to say that was politically inexpedient.

Plácido Vega nearly made an exit from Ramírez's life during May 1865. At great sacrifice, including the pawning of jewelry belonging to his family, Vega chartered the sailing ship *Brontes* to transport 400 volunteers and armaments to Mexico. Unhappily for Vega, the ship was seized by the U.S. Coast Guard on May 20, just as it was about to put to sea. The pretext for blocking Vega's departure was an order prohibiting the export of munitions, although it had been revoked by President Andrew Johnson. The U.S. Customs Office feigned ignorance of Johnson's rescission of the order, which had been heavily influenced by Charles de Cazotte, the French consul in San Francisco, who allegedly bribed various officials to stop Vega.[21] The incident was reported by *El Nuevo Mundo* in a May 26 article that harshly concluded, "The failure of this expedition once again manifests the complete ineptitude of Mr. Vega."

The first anniversary of *El Nuevo Mundo* was observed in an article on June 26, 1865, that contended that the newspaper's circulation was "more than two times greater" than that of its rival, *La Voz de Méjico*. A few days later Ramírez left for Los Angeles to take part in a Fourth of July celebration sponsored by the Union Party. The event was described in the local July 8, 1865, *Tri-Weekly News* as "deranged by rain and mud." Nevertheless, the Declaration of Independence was read in English and Spanish, followed by several orations and a band playing the Star-Spangled Banner. Filomeno Ibarra, president of the junta patriótica, made a speech in Spanish with "feeling and patriotic remarks, connecting the struggle for liberty in Mexico with that of the United States." His comments reflected the tendency of most junta members throughout the state to support the Union Party for its opposition to the French presence in Mexico. Ramírez was scheduled to speak, but his address and those of "other prominent native Californians" were omitted because of an unusual summer rain. During the celebration the French vice-consul in Los Angeles refused to be seated beside Ramírez and his Mexican colleagues on the speakers' platform.

The trip to Los Angeles lasted nearly two weeks. During his visit Ramírez wrote several stories about local conditions, which were mailed to Felipe

[132]   A Clamor for Equality

Fierro for publication in *El Nuevo Mundo*. One dramatic event he described was a famous gunfight on July 6, 1865, at the Bella Union Hotel in Los Angeles between Robert Carlisle and the brothers Frank and Houston King. Carlisle and Frank King were killed, while several others, including Houston King, were wounded. Most of the injured were bystanders hit by stray bullets.[22] Ramírez sent a report of the episode to his newspaper; it appeared in a July 12 article called "Carnival of Blood." The combatants were popular men whose deaths stunned the editors of the Los Angeles *Tri-Weekly News*. Their July 8 edition agonized, "We are unable to describe fully the horrors which have been conferred upon the public mind. We shrink from the subject."

Ramírez's visit was largely spent with members of the local junta patriótica, his most devoted supporters for the office of general treasurer. He attended a special meeting of the group on Sunday, July 11, to honor three Mexican army officers who had been prisoners of war in France. These men—José María Herrera, Francisco Rivera, and Modesto Medina—caused an enormous stir in the Mexican community when they unexpectedly arrived by steamer. Their amazing story was soon verified by dumbfounded local residents. The three officers had been captured by French forces during the second battle at Puebla, south of Mexico City, then taken to France, where they were confined in prison camps at Tours, Blois, and Bourges. After a year they were released at the Spanish border. Having made their way to San Sebastian, the men worked in northern Spain long enough to obtain passage to New York. From there they went by steamship to Acapulco but found Mexico's west coast blockaded by the French navy. Finally, they landed in California, hoping to return to the war against Maximilian by traveling overland from Los Angeles to Juárez's headquarters in Chihuahua. The situation of the former prisoners aroused both curiosity and patriotic fervor among local Mexicans. The Los Angeles junta patriótica sponsored a banquet and dance to raise funds for the officers. A total of $398 was contributed to finance their return to the battle zone. Several individuals gave them clothing, horses, rifles, and pistols.

Once back in San Francisco, Ramírez published a full account of the odyssey of the liberated Mexican officers. The July 17, 1865, edition of *El Nuevo Mundo* recorded the many toasts and speeches in tribute to them, together with a list of those who had donated money for their journey home. Ramírez, who gave ten dollars, was one of the largest contributors. The affair of the Mexican prisoners ended with the August 28 publication of a letter from them, written at Fort Yuma, Arizona. They eloquently thanked those in Los Angeles for their generosity, then headed into the great Sonoran desert to whatever fate awaited them in Mexico.

The Mexican consul in San Francisco, José A. Godoy, inadvertently set off another wave of controversy in late July by announcing that Julio Valade, general treasurer of the juntas, was returning to Mexico. Godoy sent a letter dated July 31, 1865, to the Junta Patriótica de Los Ángeles, inviting it to nominate a replacement for the office of general treasurer. The letter appeared in *El Nuevo Mundo* on August 21, along with a reply from Los Angeles urging Ramírez's election. Every junta ultimately received a communication from Godoy asking for suggestions on naming a new general treasurer, but the question of who should succeed Valade was never settled.

During this time Ramírez seemed more concerned with improving the circulation of his newspaper than with renewing his campaign for general treasurer. Throughout the next few months he devoted most of the contents of *El Nuevo Mundo* to items about countries other than Mexico. Whole pages of the newspaper were suddenly filled with news from Spanish-speaking republics throughout South America. Ramírez placed great emphasis on the celebration of Chile's Independence Day, held on September 18. His entire front page on September 29 was taken up with a speech given by Augusto D. Splivato, a Chilean lawyer and politician, at his country's Independence Day celebration, which was attended by hundreds of his compatriots. The leading Chilean social organization, La Sociedad Patriótica de Beneficencia Mutua, began to receive detailed coverage of its meetings.

The increased attention to points beyond Mexico was an effort to attract more subscribers. One edition, on October 23, contained a small item concerning a meeting of the Junta Patriótica Mexicana de Wilmington, which had again nominated Ramírez as general treasurer. However, the bulk of the paper consisted of articles on Chile, Peru, Argentina, Columbia, and Venezuela. Ramírez now wrote fewer controversial items relating to his own ambitions. *El Nuevo Mundo* was becoming a lively pan-American journal.

Occasional signs of a new struggle over the office of general treasurer emerged in the form of letters to the newspaper from various juntas. One of these letters, from a group in Nevada called El Club Patriótico Mexicano de Virginia City, observed that the office was "now vacant" and urged "all the patriotic societies of California and Nevada to elect Ramírez as general treasurer." Remarkably, this endorsement was barely acknowledged by Ramírez. He was more interested in the war that had erupted between Chile and Spain. Ramírez realized that the conflict would be of intense interest to San Francisco's Chilean community. In a bid for new subscribers, his November 15 issue was almost completely given over to dramatic descriptions of the warfare in that country.

In the absence of a new election, several juntas recognized Ramírez as the *de facto* general treasurer. The November 22 issue of *El Nuevo Mundo* printed a letter to Ramírez from the junta in Virginia City, which had enclosed $168 in cash raised at a dance. The group wrote that it would send more money in the future. Similarly, another junta at Austin, Nevada, sent $66 to Ramírez, according to a December 11 item in his newspaper. A response was published both times, acknowledging receipt of the money and thanking the juntas for their recognition of Ramírez as general treasurer. An open letter from Francisco G. Ramonet of the Junta Patriótica de Sacramento was placed in *El Nuevo Mundo* on December 22, 1865, at the request of the writer. It was directed to "All Clubs and Juntas Patrióticas in California and Nevada." The message suggested a complete reorganization of the junta movement. It lamented that "the juntas have been inactive for some time because of difficulties in naming a general treasurer." Ramonet argued that Ramírez should be named as a unanimous choice for the office and directed to resuscitate the junta movement.

This letter coincided with a general decline of the juntas. The observation that many organizations were inactive was undoubtedly true. Many California Mexicans began to suspect that a French withdrawal from Mexico was inevitable and consequently that their efforts to aid the Juáristas were not needed. This view was supported by a story in the November 15 edition of *El Nuevo Mundo*. According to the item, the Paris correspondent of the *London Times* had learned that the French would depart from Mexico within a few months. He claimed that Napoleon III feared that the United States, no longer distracted by the Civil War, would enforce the Monroe Doctrine by driving the French from Mexico. Another compelling reason for the French to leave was the ruinous expense of maintaining a large military presence in such a hostile and impoverished country. Napoleon III had originally believed that his venture in the New World would be a profitable one, but Mexico offered little to justify the cost of its occupation.

In early 1866 rumors of France's impending evacuation of Mexico were confirmed. Emperor Napoleon III addressed his parliament on January 22, declaring his intent to remove all French forces there. A week before he had sent a letter to his commander in Mexico City, Marshal François Achille

Bazaine, ordering him to return his men to France by the beginning of 1867. Plans were made for an orderly departure in three separate embarkations from the port of Veracruz.

A personal note from Napoleon III, dated January 15, 1866, was delivered to Maximilian, advising him of a planned gradual withdrawal of French troops.[23] This unwelcome news was a fatal blow to the Austrian archduke. His brief reign had proved to be much more difficult than expected. Ultraconservative Mexicans had made solemn assurances that the country's people desired him as their emperor, but the falsity of these representations soon became apparent to the distraught Austrian. Without French military support his position was untenable. Only a small part of Mexico was actually under French control.[24] Elements of the Juárista army were often encamped just two hours from Mexico City. The Mexican treasury was empty, and Maximilian could not count on support from the enlisted troops of his imperial army, a sullen group of Indians and mestizos who constantly deserted.[25]

Reports of an irrevocable French decision to retreat from Mexico began to appear in the San Francisco press during the first part of 1866. Since a triumph of the Juáristas seemed certain, most local juntas saw no reason to continue making sacrifices on their behalf. Patriotic groups throughout California began to rapidly disintegrate as members abandoned them in the belief that Mexico's crisis was over.

However, despite a widespread collapse of the juntas, the members of some groups were not prepared to dissolve until the French had actually left Mexico. A few such diehards turned to Ramírez for leadership. The February 14, 1866, edition of *El Nuevo Mundo* published a letter from the Junta Patriótica Mejicana de Marysville, advising Ramírez that he had been selected to receive their contributions for transmission to the Juáristas. The next issue, on February 19, contained an open letter from the Junta Patriótica de San Andrés, appealing for Ramírez to become general treasurer and promising to send him regular donations.

The fact that various organizations looked to Ramírez for guidance in the waning days of the junta movement is not strange. His work as editor of *El Nuevo Mundo* had made him a highly visible public figure. The reach of his reputation as a Mexican patriot was shown in a letter published on November 22, 1865, from distant Cabo San Lucas at the tip of the Baja California peninsula. The writer, a leader of armed resistance to Maximilian, described a failed attempt to make local residents swear allegiance to the emperor. The letter, which had been directed to a friend in San Francisco, concluded by giving regards to "the Mexican consul and Mr. Ramírez."

During January 1866 Ramírez rejoined the Club Patriótico Mejicano de San Francisco. His renewed association with the group was a result of Plácido Vega's failure to attend its meetings. With the French about to withdraw, Vega was under pressure to complete the organization of an armed force to take back to Mexico. Unless he soon returned with weapons and recruits, his mission would be considered a failure. With Vega no longer present to disturb him, Ramírez's January 29, 1866, issue of the newspaper gave notice that he had accepted a seat on the club's board of directors.

Although deeply involved in Mexican affairs, Ramírez remained connected with Americans in the Union Party. The political implications of the junta movement were obvious to him. They may have accounted in large part for his struggle to attain prominence among his countrymen. Ramírez was aware that his future in American politics would be assured if he could arrange to deliver the Mexican vote. Meantime, his advocacy of the Union Party placed him among those eligible for employment based on political considerations. The February 14, 1866, issue of *El Nuevo Mundo* reported Ramírez's appointment by the legislature as one of California's official Spanish translators.

Before Ramírez was named to the office, Thomas R. Eldredge had acted as the official state translator by himself for over ten years. Now he and Ramírez shared the responsibility of rendering the state's laws into Spanish. Ramírez was already acquainted with his new colleague, whom he praised in the announcement of his own appointment: "Our dear friend and companion, Mr. Eldredge, combines constant practice translating English to Spanish with linguistic skills of the highest order." The two men collaborated on the translation of statutes and state publications for over a year. Some of their work, such as the preparation of fiscal reports and budgets in Spanish, would involve considerable drudgery.[26] Nevertheless, Ramírez seemed pleased with his appointment. He probably needed the modest income it produced.

One of Ramírez's other language skills, the ability to read and write French, greatly contributed to his newspaper at this time. Throughout March 1866 translations of articles from the French press regularly appeared in *El Nuevo Mundo*. They described popular discontent in France with the army's involvement in Mexico and the slow progress made by officials in effecting a withdrawal. Such articles helped accelerate a massive falling off in membership of local juntas. However, despite a decline in organizations formed to channel money to the liberal government, almost all Mexicans in California remained completely devoted to President Benito Juárez. This was demonstrated when he issued a decree from his temporary capital in Chihuahua, extending his term of office until the French left Mexico. The legality of Juárez's decision to prolong his presidency was extremely doubtful. The Constitution of 1857 strictly prohibited federal officials from serving beyond the term for which they were elected. Consequently, Juárez asked the Mexican people to override the constitution because of the crisis created by the French intervention.

When Juárez's appeal for additional time in office reached José A. Godoy in San Francisco, he convened a special meeting of the Club Patriótico Mejicano. The group unanimously resolved to support Juárez's request to remain as president. A written statement to this effect signed by all the members, including Ramírez, was forwarded to Mexico.

The April 2, 1866, issue of *El Nuevo Mundo* noted that Antonio Mancillas had written an article in *La Voz de Méjico* opposing an extension of Juárez's presidency. Although he had allegedly sold his newspaper to Luis A. Tostado, Mancillas stayed on as the editor, a fact that disgusted Ramírez. Already handicapped by a poor reputation in the Mexican community because of his obnoxious personality, Mancillas's precarious position in San Francisco was totally destroyed when he published his opinion that Juárez should not continue in office. The Mexican president, a living symbol of national independence, was idolized by most of his people. In a frenzied demonstration of rage against Mancillas, nearly all Mexican residents in San Francisco canceled their subscriptions to his newspaper. The April 18 edition of *El Nuevo Mundo* contained a protest against Mancillas signed by more than 100 people. Within a few weeks *La Voz de Méjico* was forced to shut down its printing press forever.

Unfortunately, Ramírez's career in San Francisco cannot be followed through his newspaper for a two-year period from April 1866 to May 1868. Nearly every copy of *El Nuevo Mundo* during that time has been lost, presumably in the San Francisco earthquake and fire of 1906. Only a few scattered editions exist for June and July of 1867. Of course, several events occurred during Ramírez's final two years of editing *El Nuevo Mundo* that would have been covered in the missing editions of his newspaper. One of these was the return of Plácido Vega to Mexico in July 1866. Vega chartered the bark *Keoka* and the brig *Josephine* to carry about forty Americans and thirty Mexicans to the war against Maximilian. He picked up a number of other recruits at Ensenada and La Paz. The ships left San Francisco with 7,000 rifles, as well as enough equipment and uniforms for 3,000 soldiers.

Vega's expedition landed at Topolobampo on the west coast of Mexico, then marched to Chihuahua, where it linked up with Juárista forces in November 1866. Vega received a surprisingly hostile reception since liberal officials suspected that he was disloyal to Juárez. Like his friend Antonio Mancillas, he had publicly expressed the opinion that the Constitution of 1857 barred an extension of Juárez's presidency. This view angered those who wanted Juárez in office when he triumphantly entered Mexico City after the French were gone.

The Juáristas demanded that Vega fully account for his expenditures in San Francisco. He prepared a small booklet for this purpose, which was summarily rejected. Juárez's cabinet then ordered Vega to personally appear before it, but he refused, and the minister of war issued a warrant for his arrest. Vega had left all his records and correspondence with Mariano Vallejo in Sonoma, California. They were later given to the historian Hubert Howe Bancroft for safekeeping, with the proviso that he return them to Vega when requested to do so. These documents might have vindicated Vega from charges of financial impropriety, but he never sent for them, a fact that puzzled Bancroft in later years.[27]

Vega ultimately went to Sinaloa and Nayarit, where he joined dissident liberals in a conspiracy to replace Juárez as president. He frequently allied himself with Porfirio Díaz, who eventually succeeded Juárez. Strangely, Vega once took refuge in Tepic with his former enemy, the conservative warlord Manuel Lozada, "El Tigre de Alica." Because of his resistance to Juárez, Mexican historians have not treated Vega's memory kindly. An imperious and complex man, he died of tuberculosis in Acapulco in 1878, at the age of forty-seven.

The news from Mexico that would have most absorbed Ramírez was the fate of Maximilian. This naive member of the Hapsburg dynasty allowed his conservative Mexican generals to persuade him that they could defeat Juárez without the forces of Napoleon III. The last of the French military had embarked from Veracruz in March 1867. As the French army with its colorful Foreign Legion and North African units departed, a horde of peasant soldiers advanced to take Mexico City for Juárez. Only three months later Maximilian was captured in Querétaro with his leading Mexican generals, Miguel Miramón and Tomás Mejía. A court martial was convened that sentenced the men to death. Despite international appeals to spare Maximilian, clemency was out of the question. The unyielding attitude of the Juáristas was partly the result of a "black decree" that Maximilian had imprudently signed, which ordered his soldiers to shoot all Mexican prisoners of any kind, without exception. Under the circumstances, Maximilian could hardly expect mercy from Juárez. On June 19, 1867, he was led to the top of a small hill in Querétaro and shot by a firing squad. Generals Miramón and Mejía were executed with him. Those in attendance were deeply moved by the serenity of Maximilian at the moment of his death.

Ramírez thought it was wrong to kill Maximilian. He once told an investigator for the historian Hubert Howe Bancroft that the execution was a "disgrace to Mexico." He probably published a similar opinion in the pages of *El Nuevo Mundo*. A year after Maximilian's life ended at Querétaro, Ramírez's newspaper career in San Francisco came to a close. The junta movement had vanished as suddenly as it had appeared. The last extant editions of *El Nuevo Mundo*, printed during June and July of 1867, contain no reference to patriotic organizations.

The end of the junta movement brought about by the French withdrawal from Mexico severely diminished prospects for the survival of Ramírez's newspaper. He could no longer attract Mexican subscribers outside San Francisco by providing news of the French intervention to scattered patriotic organizations. His ambition to control a voting bloc created from the junta movement was never realized. Beyond that, Ramírez could not call on the Union Party for assistance in finding alternative employment. The coalition that formed the Union Party was dissolving into its original Republican and Democratic components. During 1866, with the Civil War over, many Democrats abandoned the Union Party to resume their original political affiliation. The Democrats took issue with vengeful Republican policies in the reconstruction of the South, as well as in attempts by Congress to extend voting rights to blacks. By 1867 a resurgent Democratic Party defeated the Republicans and installed Henry H. Haight as governor. Ramírez's connection with the Union Party and its Republican leaders now counted for little.

Ramírez may have considered remaining in San Francisco as a journalist, but his former Chilean editor, Felipe Fierro, had opened a competing newspaper in 1866 called *La Voz de Chile y Las Repúblicas Américas*. As a result of Fierro's defection, Ramírez lost many of his Chilean readers, as well as subscribers from other South American countries. He began to experience a financial decline, as evidenced by the appearance of his name on a list of delinquent taxpayers published on September 21, 1867, in the San Francisco

Daily Morning Call. To cut his losses, he sold *El Nuevo Mundo* to Fierro just before May 27, 1868. On that date Fierro changed the name of his journal to *La Voz de Chile y El Nuevo Mundo*.

By the middle of 1868, most of Ramírez's friends and acquaintances had returned to Mexico, but he had no inclination to join them. He was a California Mexican whose roots were in Los Angeles. Ramírez now turned to his native city as he thought about the future. At the age of thirty-one, he decided it was time to go home.

CHAPTER EIGHT
A Lawyer in Los Angeles

The June 13, 1868, edition of the *Los Angeles Star* reported Ramírez's return to his hometown. The notice was extremely cordial, probably based on the editor's having encountered Ramírez in the street:

> We had, also, the pleasure of meeting, this week, another of Los Angeles' native sons, Don Francisco P. Ramírez, a Gentleman long connected with the newspaper press of this city, and until lately editor and proprietor of *El Nuevo Mundo*, San Francisco, decidedly the best and most ably conducted Spanish paper on the coast. We understand Mr. Ramírez returns to make his home with his parents and friends. He has our best wishes for his success in whatever branch of business he may engage.

The item was remarkable since it was written by Henry Hamilton, who, as we have seen, left Los Angeles in 1864 at about the same time Ramírez departed for San Francisco. Now, coincidentally, both men reappeared in Los Angeles within a few weeks of each other. Hamilton was the first to arrive. He had resumed publication of the *Star* on May 16, 1868, less than a month before Ramírez's homecoming.

During his four-year absence, Hamilton first went to Tucson, where he entered the 1865 election as an unsuccessful candidate for county recorder.[1] He next surfaced in Honolulu, where he associated with James J. Ayers in running a newspaper called the *Daily Hawaiian Herald*. The little sheet was "directed to spreading and intensifying the pro-American sentiment" that the editors believed existed in Hawaii.[2] The enterprise only lasted from September 4 to December 21, 1866. Its demise was not related to opposition by the government of King Kamehameha V or a lack of subscribers. Instead, an employee inadvertently left a water tap running overnight in the *Herald*'s printing plant on the second floor of a large brick building; it flooded a men's clothing store below. The storekeeper's extensive damages were paid by the editors, leaving no money to continue the paper.³ Discouraged, both Ayers and Hamilton returned to California.

Less than two months after his Hawaiian venture, Hamilton started anew in San Bernardino. He opened another newspaper, the *Guardian*, publishing its maiden edition on February 16, 1867.⁴ After living more than a year in the little backwater of San Bernardino, Hamilton sold the *Guardian* and returned to Los Angeles, where he met Ramírez on his return from San Francisco.

Ramírez could not have expected the *Star*'s warm and complimentary notice of his return. Five years before, during 1863, he and Hamilton had been involved in a rancorous contest for a seat in the state senate. Prior to that, as editors of rival newspapers and political enemies, each had frequently published insulting remarks about the other. The *Star*'s friendly reception of Ramírez signaled an end to their feud. Hamilton seemed considerably changed after his experiences outside California. His political editorials in the *Star* were more moderate and conciliatory. Within a few years he would retire to raise oranges on a ranch he bought near Mission San Gabriel.

During the spring of 1868, Ramírez found that Los Angeles was no longer the little adobe settlement he had known since childhood. It was being transformed by a large influx of settlers from the eastern half of the United States. The end of the Civil War caused an unprecedented movement toward the Pacific slope. California was one of the most publicized places in the world. Since the end of the Gold Rush, it had constantly been the subject of popular books and articles depicting it as a kind of Eden. Just before the completion of a transcontinental railroad in 1869, numerous wagon trains entered the state on the same trails used by the pioneers before them. Unlike earlier immigrants, most Civil War veterans intended to stay permanently, and they brought their families with them.

The December 19, 1868, *Los Angeles Star* commented on a sight becoming familiar to local residents: "Not a day passes but long trains of emigrant wagons pass through town." The same issue reported the arrival of so many settlers that "their camps looked like a tented field, so numerous are they, where people halt to look them out a location." The *Star* noted that great numbers of those arriving were Southerners fleeing from the devastation of the Confederacy's defeat. The paper's remarks on these refugees reflected a pro-Southern feeling common among Los Angeles residents: "While we are sorry that they are broken up and ruined at home, we extend to them a welcome, and can assure them that there are thousands here who will do everything in their power to aid them."

Nearly all the newcomers were farmers who wanted a place where they could put in a crop. Some had enough money for a down payment on a piece of land but needed an arrangement to pay the balance in installments. As early as 1867, one of the wealthiest men in Los Angeles, former Governor John G. Downey, advertised a subdivision of 20,000 acres sixteen miles south of the city. He was prepared to accommodate settlers by selling fifty-acre parcels at $500 each with at least part of the purchase price deferred at ten percent annual interest.[5]

A truly monumental subdivision was proposed by a group of San Francisco investors known as the Robinson Trust during May 1868. This was the idea of Alfred Robinson, an old California hand who came as a merchant during 1829. His friend Abel Stearns, whose residence in Los Angeles also predated the American conquest, owned 177,796 acres of ranch land extending into present-day San Bernardino, Orange, and Riverside counties. Robinson knew that Stearns was nearly bankrupt after the drought of 1862–1864. Stearns was persuaded by Robinson to accept a payment from investors large enough to liquidate his debts. In exchange a trust became responsible for the subdivision and sale of the ranches, with Stearns taking part of the profits. This remarkably successful enterprise began to dispose of Stearns's properties by an aggressive promotional campaign offering favorable terms to purchasers.[6] A young Los Angeles attorney named Robert M. Widney was appointed as a local sales agent. From his office in the Stearns Building on Main Street, he advertised land for sale "in quantities to suit purchasers on easy terms of payment."[7] When Stearns died on August 23, 1871, he left his much younger Mexican wife, Arcadia Bandini de Stearns, with the colossal amount of $1 million in cash.[8]

Almost every large landowner in Los Angeles County followed the example of Downey and Stearns. Local newspapers were suddenly filled with advertisements of farm-sized subdivisions at ten to fifteen dollars an acre. Lawyers in Los Angeles announced themselves as "attorneys and real estate brokers." Most of those offering land to settlers had only recently acquired it. The drought that ended a few years before had destroyed nearly all vestiges of original Mexican ownership. The native ranchero elite, holders of vast Mexican land grants, had been heavily in debt to American moneylenders when the drought struck. Before the disastrous dry spell they raised money by selling livestock to the San Francisco market. As the drought killed off their herds, they had nothing to sell and could not repay their loans. American lenders secured by mortgages began a wave of foreclosures that dispossessed nearly all Mexican owners.[9]

The rigidly traditional ranchero elite that Ramírez had earlier criticized in *El Clamor Público* for its support of the pro-slavery Chivalry Democrats now began to disappear. They gradually faded from their ranches and town houses on the plaza into genteel poverty. Harris Newmark's memoirs recalled one such member of the fallen: "In his later years, he used to sit on the curb stone near the Plaza a character quite forlorn utterly dejected in appearance and despondently recalling the by-gone days of his prosperity."[10] A few embittered aristocrats returned to Mexico. José Andrés Sepúlveda left California to die in Caborca, Sonora.[11] Juan Bandini, remorseful for his initial support of the Americans, devoted more time to his land in Baja California's Valle de Guadalupe.[12]

The breakup of the old ranchos made way for a new agricultural era. American settlers discovered that promoters touting the fertility of the land were right. Nearly anything could be grown with enough water. The greatest challenge faced by farmers was how to irrigate a harshly arid country where most native vegetation was chaparral, yucca, and cactus. The first Mexican settlers had addressed this problem by cutting a trench from the Los Angeles River to the pueblo. This source of water, called a *zanja*, was expanded into several channels by Americans who created an irrigation system that made Los Angeles a complex geometry of gardens. Grapes and citrus were grown in huge quantities not far from the Los Angeles Plaza.

During 1868 only three farming communities existed outside the reach of the Los Angeles River irrigation. San Bernardino and Anaheim were situated near the Santa Ana River in order to drain its erratic flow into fields and vineyards. El Monte, an early settlement of Texas immigrants, grew corn along the bottom of the San Gabriel River. Those buying land in the subdivided ranches had to find their own source of water. Some were able to tap the Los Angeles or San Gabriel rivers, while others relied on digging wells. During August 1868 an artesian well was successfully drilled near Compton. The water gushed over four feet high, provoking so much astonishment that stage coaches "turned aside from the road to give passengers a sight of it."[13] This was the first evidence of a vast aquifer under Los Angeles County that would soon give rise to other artesian wells and hundreds more pumped by windmills.

An artesian well in Riverside County, circa 1900. Such wells were common from an early date on farms in Los Angeles County. Reprinted by permission of the University of Southern California Special Collections.

The industrious and sometimes ingenious farmers in Los Angeles County were surprisingly productive. Corn and barley were popular crops since they did not require a great deal of water and could be grown in a wet year without irrigation. It was possible to sow barley with the first rains, harvest it in the spring, and then plant a second crop of corn. The *Los Angeles Star* reported on September 5, 1868, that 154,000 bushels of barley and 238,500 bushels of corn were raised in 1867. In addition to citrus and grapes, the variety of other crops mentioned in the *Star* attest to the land's wondrous fertility: several hundred thousand bushels of beans, potatoes, onions, peanuts, hops, pumpkins, squash, and turnips. Over 700,000 gallons of wine and 77,000 gallons of brandy were made, most of it for San Francisco. Much of this abundance, especially the fruit and vegetables, was wasted because it could not be sold. The May 30, 1868, Los Angeles *Republican* lamented that there were tons of figs "rotting under the trees, for the reason that they were too perishable for transportation to a distant market."

The shift from ranching to agriculture intensified the problem of the region's isolation. Without a railroad connection the best way to ship crops to the San Francisco market was by one of the regular coastal steamers such as the *Orizaba*. However, sea transport was not satisfactory since space aboard the steamers was too limited to accommodate the region's massive output. The only way to fully realize southern California's potential wealth was to move its agricultural production by railway. A factor in the rising value of land in Los Angeles County was an expectation that a railroad connection would eventually open distant markets beyond the Pacific slope. By the end of 1867, the Central Pacific Railroad Company had completed tracks across the Sierra Nevada eastward from Sacramento, but there was no assurance that it would extend its system to southern California.

Several influential men in Los Angeles were impatient with the lack of progress in obtaining a rail link with the rest of the country. They decided to hasten matters by constructing a local railroad from Los Angeles to the port of San Pedro. It was believed that the existence of this short, twenty-one-mile line would encourage the Central Pacific to make a connection with Los Angeles. A corporation called the Los Angeles and San Pedro Railroad Company was formed in 1868 with John G. Downey as its titular president. The actual leader of the local railroad movement was Phineas Banning, owner of a freight company in San Pedro, who controlled a wharf where steamers from San Francisco landed. An election was held on March 24, 1868, to determine whether the city of Los Angeles would issue bonds totaling $225,000 to help finance construction of the railroad. Largely through Banning's efforts the measure passed by a majority of only thirty-nine votes.[14]

The editor of the *Los Angeles Star*, Henry Hamilton, envisioned the little line someday extending to San Bernardino and beyond. The December 19, 1868, edition of his newspaper grandly declared that such railroads "bring us into close proximity with the great markets of the continent; they will change our locality from being an isolated spot of the earth to a prominent land mark in the great highway of the world." The local railway was completed in November 1869, when it began moving passengers and freight to San Pedro from a depot on Alameda and Commercial streets. Meantime, Los Angeles continued to agitate for a rail connection to markets outside California.

Among the first customers of the new railroad to San Pedro were the operators of the Cerro Gordo silver mines in Inyo County. Beginning in 1868, thousands of silver ingots were hauled by wagon some 240 miles due south to Los Angeles. With the advent of a local railroad, they were transferred from the wagons for a short trip by rail to Banning's wharf. Local haulers such as Remi Nadeau became wealthy by moving ingots across the desert on wagons pulled by mules and horses. The same wagons returned to Cerro Gordo filled with merchandise supplied by Los Angeles merchants. Local farmers shared in the prosperity since freight haulers with animals to feed bought all the extra hay and barley they could produce.[15] Silver mining at Cerro Gordo buoyed the economy of Los Angeles until the middle of the 1870s.

Ramírez came home aboard a coastal steamer running between San Francisco and San Pedro. Since the local railroad was not yet completed, he took a stage coach to Los Angeles across a twenty-one-mile expanse known to early residents as "the plains." There were two competing stage companies, one owned by Phineas Banning and the other by John J. Tomlinson. The stages raced each other on the way to Los Angeles with passengers placing bets on which would arrive first. After an hour's ride they lurched to a dusty stop on Main Street near the Lafayette and Bella Union hotels. On his way to Los Angeles, Ramírez would have occasionally seen signs of increasing agricultural activity. Fields of corn, barley, and other crops appeared where none had been before. Scattered American barns and farmhouses now stood where Mexican cattle once grazed, but only a small portion of the land was actually under cultivation. The rural transformation of southern California by American settlers was just beginning.

The most obvious evidence that the region was entering a new era was found in Los Angeles itself. Old Mexican adobes were being torn down and replaced with American buildings. There was little nostalgia associated with their destruction. The June 6, 1868, *Star* noticed that an adobe next to the Bella Union Hotel was being destroyed to make way for a two-story brick bank. The paper commented, "Another of the old adobes is going the way of all mud piles, to fill up the streets." New structures were being put up so fast that another newspaper, the Los Angeles *Republican*, observed on November 14, 1868, that the town was experiencing a "building mania." It was nearly impossible to keep up with the demand for lumber, according to the *Republican*: "At no period in our history have there been more buildings in the course of erection than at present, and less lumber on hand with which to build them." The December 5 *Star* agreed: "On every hand we hear complaints of the want of lumber for building purposes. We know of many projected improvements which cannot be entered upon for the want of the main portion of the material."

A wholesale district for the sale and distribution of the region's agricultural output arose on Los Angeles Street south of the plaza. Buyers from San Francisco made frequent visits to purchase shiploads of citrus, grapes, and grain crops. Such transactions often required letters of credit and access to local bank deposits. In February 1868 John G. Downey opened the first bank in the city on Main Street. It was followed by another in the same year owned by Isaias W. Hellman and Francis Pliny Fisk Temple, known as Hellman, Temple & Co. As the population increased and commercial activity quickened, merchants on Main Street expanded their operations and inventory. The area around the plaza was converted to a business center that soon spread toward the southwest. By the late 1860s a growing number of American buildings were scattered in that direction.

An earlier movement of Mexicans to their own section of town north of the plaza separated Los Angeles racially. Nearly all ordinary Spanish-speaking people found homes in the district known as Sonoratown. James J. Ayers, once the partner of Henry Hamilton, depicted Sonoratown as a kind of exotic native quarter:

> It was Mexican all over. The adobe house flourished there in its most formidable, as well as its most contracted shape, from the great rectangular building, with its ample patio in the center, to the hut of one or two rooms with the evidence apparent of an indefinite amount of filth and squalor. To cross the Plaza and enter this ancient part of Los Angeles was like stepping from an American town into a small pueblo in Guadalajara or Sinaloa. English was as foreign from the speech that one would hear in its streets as it would be in Culiacán or Jalapa.[16]

Over 2,000 Mexicans were living in Los Angeles at the end of the 1860s, about thirty-seven percent of the total population.[17] Beyond the loss of social and political influence caused by the decline of the ranchero elite, Mexicans were now outnumbered nearly two to one. Most were unskilled laborers who turned to American landowners and entrepreneurs for employment.

A telling remark on the American attitude toward Mexicans appeared in the August 1, 1868, *Republican*. The editor, John H. Worth, blamed Mexico's political and economic problems on "the absence of education and general intelligence among the people." This deprecating remark followed an article he had written on April 18, 1868, criticizing an editorial in the Los Angeles *News*, which advocated denying blacks and other people of color a right to vote in the forthcoming presidential election. Worth noted that the editor of the *News*, Andrew J. King, was a Southern pro-slavery Democrat and white supremacist who nevertheless encouraged Mexicans to vote because they supported the Chivalry. Worth accused King of hypocrisy and called Mexicans "an extraordinary type of the white man." He described Mexican voters as people who "neither read nor write, sleep on beds or wear shoes but part their hair in the middle and speak the language of the aborigines about as fluently as either Spanish or English, and would in a new country, be killed and scalped for Indians."

Worth's comments were more than an expression of his frustration with Democratic control of Mexican voters. His disdainful portrayal was typical of the way many Americans saw common Spanish-speaking people. An American belief in their own superiority was reinforced by the introduction of modern agriculture, commerce, a local railroad, new construction methods, the telegraph, and banking—all innovations in which Mexican participation was generally limited to providing labor.

After returning to Los Angeles, Ramírez once again found himself at a crucial point in his life. His most recent failure running a Spanish-language newspaper convinced him not to continue in journalism. He had to find a way to make a living compatible with his self-esteem and ambition. At this time it was natural for Ramírez to think of becoming a lawyer. A few years before as a notary public, land register, U.S. commissioner, and deputy clerk of the federal court in Los Angeles, he had acquired a fair amount of legal knowledge. While editor of *El Nuevo Mundo*, he used this to advantage by drafting legal instruments to supplement his income. Besides advertising himself as a translator in San Francisco, Ramírez had offered his services in preparing contracts, mortgages, deeds, and other documents.[18]

As Ramírez knew, admission to the bar was obtained by making an application to the judge of the district court. It was advisable for the applicant to obtain the support of an experienced lawyer who could vouch for his qualifications. Those who aspired to the bar usually read law under the direction of such a lawyer.[19] When the applicant was considered ready, the lawyer under whom he studied made a motion to the court for his admission. This process might take years, but such applications were seldom denied. Few lawyers actually attended law school.

Occasionally admission was requested without the benefit of a sponsoring lawyer. In such instances the court appointed a committee of three bar members who subjected the candidate to a test of his legal knowledge. This was a challenging approach that could lead to rejection. Ramírez was in a hurry to become a lawyer since he chose to hazard an application without a lawyer to sponsor him. To prepare for an examination by a committee, he undertook an autodidactic course of study, just as he had educated himself as a child. For nine months after his arrival in Los Angeles, he was immersed in law books.

Ramírez remained secluded while reading law, a marked contrast with his homecoming in 1862, when he returned from Sonora. At that time he rapidly obtained several public offices, ran as a Republican candidate for the state senate, and was frequently mentioned in the local press. Within nine months he had regained his standing as a public figure. Now, six years later, his presence in Los Angeles was hardly noticed.

If Ramírez had been so inclined, he could have immediately taken up politics again. One of the principal issues in Los Angeles during the last half of 1868 was a contest between Ulysses S. Grant and Horatio Seymore for the presidency of the United States. The local Republican organization made every effort to gather support for Grant. Part of its strategy was to take the Mexican vote away from the Democrats. Toward this end it formed an organization called the Spanish Republican Club to campaign for Grant in the Mexican community.[20] This endeavor was perfectly suited to Ramírez's background, but he was too occupied with his legal studies to participate.

Most public offices continued to be held by conservative Southern Democrats. This group, until very recently known as the Chivalry, continued its dominance despite the influx of new settlers. Southern newcomers outnumbered those from other parts of the country and tended to vote for their brethren already established in Los Angeles. During municipal elections in 1868, the Republicans managed to elect five out of ten municipal common council members, but they lost every other office. They had no chance in the presidential election. The nomination of Grant by the Republican Party was especially offensive to Southerners. He was a hated figure for his role in defeating the Confederacy. Los Angeles Southerners backed the Democratic candidate, Horatio Seymore, a former governor of New York. Seymore was regarded as a copperhead since he had opposed the emancipation of slaves and encouraged riots in New York to protest the drafting of civilians into the Union army. The November 14, 1868, *Los Angeles Republican* unhappily acknowledged the power of the Southern majority when it reported that Seymore had carried the city by a vote of 1,236 to 748.

Some nine months after arriving in Los Angeles, Ramírez filed a petition with Judge Murray Morrison of the Seventeenth District Court requesting that he be allowed to practice law. The March 11, 1869, *Republican* announced that Charles Hathaway Larrabee, Andrew J. King, and William McPherson "were appointed a committee to examine and report concerning the qualifications of Francisco P. Ramirez to be admitted a member of the bar." Of these three lawyers Ramírez was best acquainted with Andrew J. King. At this time King was both editor of the *Los Angeles News* and a commissioner of the district court. He had obtained the position of court commissioner from Judge Murray Morrison since the two had been law partners before Morrison's elevation to the bench on May 25, 1868.

Ramírez may have felt some concern about King's presence on the committee to examine him. King was a native of Georgia and a devoted member of the Chivalry. His family had settled in El Monte during 1852. He became a lawyer in 1860 after studying with Benjamin I. Hayes, a pioneer judge in Los Angeles. As a conservative Chivalry Democrat he was elected to several offices including city attorney.[21] The thirty-five-year-old King was well aware of Ramírez's previous career eight years before as editor of *El Clamor Público*. At that time the young Mexican had adopted an antagonistic posture toward Southerners like King. Now, in his own newspaper, King espoused a purely Southern view, attacking the extension of voting rights to blacks and bitterly criticizing "radicals" in Congress, whose reconstruction programs aimed to punish the South for its rebellion. However disguised, there must have been some degree of tension between King and Ramírez.

The other committee members, William McPherson and Charles Hathaway Larrabee, had little cause to oppose Ramírez. McPherson, a man of moderate political views, would be chosen as city attorney at the next election. Although corresponding secretary of the Los Angeles Democratic Club, McPherson was not a dogmatic member of the party. His wide acceptance in the community was demonstrated by an editorial endorsing his candidacy for city attorney that was published in the *Republican* on November 11, 1868.

Ramírez had little difficulty convincing the committee that he was qualified to practice law. The March 18, 1869, issue of the *Republican* announced that he was officially admitted to the bar. Perhaps by previous arrangement, as soon as Ramírez became a lawyer he began to work for Charles Hathaway Larrabee, a member of the committee that had recommended his admission. This was an advantageous relationship for both men. Besides an income, Ramírez needed a period of apprenticeship, which Larrabee was eminently qualified to provide. Newspaper advertisements, such as one in the May 23, 1868, *Star*, described Larrabee's practice as a "Southern California land agency" specializing in real-estate litigation. Ramírez would be invaluable in such work since he understood Spanish and Mexican land records. He could also interview Mexican witnesses in their own language concerning memories of important events affecting title to land. Ramírez was not Larrabee's partner. He was more of an associate paid on the basis of work performed.

Larrabee had appeared in Los Angeles about a year before he met Ramírez. He was a man of considerable distinction. Born in Rome, New York, in 1820, he was educated in Ohio as a civil engineer. After helping to design the Little Miami railroad in Ohio, Larrabee moved to Mississippi, where he was admitted to the bar. Surprisingly, in 1846 he was the city attorney of Chicago, Illinois. His most impressive achievements took place in Wisconsin, where he was a circuit judge and justice of the Wisconsin Supreme Court from 1848 to 1858. He resigned from the court to successfully run for the U.S. Congress in 1859, where he was known as a fine orator. At the outbreak of the Civil War, Larrabee raised a company for the First Wisconsin Regiment. Thereafter he served with General Winfield S. Hancock, rising to the rank of colonel. Larrabee was allowed to resign his army commission on August 27, 1863, because of ill health.[22]

Although a Democrat, Larrabee had little sympathy for the Southern branch of the party. Like other Northern "War Democrats," his main preoccupation was to preserve the Union. Larrabee's lack of concern for Southern interests made him a highly unusual figure in local Democratic circles. Most of the party's adherents in southern California remained strongly pro-Southern, still resentful over the defeat of the Confederacy and the abolition of slavery. The editor of the *Republican* noted on September 19, 1868, that Larrabee's political orientation was foreign to most members of his party in Los Angeles:

> Thursday evening last, Col. Larrabee orated in the district courtroom much to the delight of the war Democracy and to the great disgust of the rebel wing of the same party. The Colonel's Democracy is suited to a more northern latitude; it is almost Unionism here.

Larrabee found little acceptance among Los Angeles Democrats. He therefore turned to the state Democratic organization in Sacramento, which had a greater appreciation for his views. The Democratic Central Committee sent him on a speaking tour throughout California during the 1868 presidential campaign. However, stumping the state did not give Larrabee greater local popularity. He presented himself to Los Angeles voters as a candidate for judge of the Seventeenth District Court in 1869 but withdrew after failing to gain much support.

Ramírez's position as a lawyer working alongside Larrabee was unusual. He was just the third Mexican admitted to the bar in Los Angeles. The first was Agustín Olvera who acted as judge of the county court during the early 1850s. Olvera's admission was probably more of a courtesy based on his status as a judge than a recognition of his qualifications. With a limited knowledge of American law, he usually held court in Spanish since he possessed an imperfect command of English. The only other Mexican to precede Ramírez as a lawyer was Ignacio Sepúlveda, who had been admitted on September 6, 1862.

One California Mexican, although not a lawyer, was nevertheless important in the Los Angeles courts beginning in 1863. He was Pablo de la Guerra, a politician who operated out of a family stronghold in Santa Barbara. Prior to 1863 he had a remarkably successful political career, rising to the office of president pro tem of the state senate, a rank equivalent to that of lieutenant governor. Together with his brothers, Antonio and Francisco, he had a regular Spanish-speaking political machine in Santa Barbara to promote his aspirations.[23] Before district court judges were required to be lawyers, de la Guerra defeated the Los Angeles incumbent, Benjamin I. Hayes, for the office, becoming judge during 1863. Judge de la Guerra was the most powerful figure in the Los Angeles courts until 1868, when he was assigned to another judicial district near his home. De la Guerra came to Los Angeles to hold court periodically but was never a resident of the city. The only native Mexican residents of Los Angeles involved in the local judicial system were Francisco P. Ramírez and Ignacio Sepúlveda.

The careers of Ramírez and Ignacio Sepúlveda unfolded at roughly the same time but were quite dissimilar. Beyond being born in Los Angeles and the only Mexicans admitted to the practice of law, they had little in common. Ramírez was a liberal who sympathized with ordinary Mexican people and insisted on greater equality for them. His upbringing had made him a kind of discontented social and cultural hybrid. Although he functioned well in an American environment, much of his time was spent in Sonoratown, where he was recognized as a Mexican patriot and a devoted follower of Benito Juárez. Ramírez usually worked for the minority Republican Party since he believed it stood in opposition to reactionary and racist white Southerners who dominated Los Angeles. He almost instinctively opposed the status quo, often finding himself at the forefront of movements for political and social reform.

Ignacio Sepúlveda rejected Ramírez's liberalism and desire for change. He was a profoundly conservative person who resisted social innovation. Born on July 1, 1842, he was the son of José Antonio Andrés Sepúlveda, an aristocratic landowner famous for reckless spending and betting large amounts of money on horse races. His family sent him to Massachusetts during 1854, at the age of twelve, to learn English and receive an American education. His later career as a prominent jurist in Los Angeles has caused some writers to speculate that he attended one of the great universities on the east coast. In reality, he was enrolled in a small boarding school for boys in Kingston, Massachusetts, run by a Williams College graduate named Wylie R. Ellis.[24] Sepúlveda's education was limited to this experience since he never attended college.

By 1858 Sepúlveda was back in Los Angeles. As a sixteen-year-old he began a kind of apprenticeship with the lawyer Joseph Lancaster Brent, the undisputed leader of the Chivalry Democrats. A native of Maryland, Brent was a masterful exponent of Southern conservative politics. He imparted such views to Sepúlveda while providing him with considerable legal training. After Brent left California in 1862 to join the Confederate Army and ultimately become a brigadier general, Sepúlveda continued reading law under the direction of Volney E. Howard, successor to Brent as chief of the Chivalry.

Howard sponsored Sepúlveda's admission to the bar on September 6, 1862, just two months after his twenty-first birthday.[25] The next year he was elected as a Chivalry Democrat to the state assembly, where he represented Henry Hamilton in the election contest brought by Ramírez for the office of state senator from Los Angeles.

Sepúlveda next took a course of action that Ramírez would find appalling. While Ramírez was in San Francisco during 1865, denouncing the Emperor Maximilian in the pages of *El Nuevo Mundo*, Sepúlveda went to Mexico City, where he offered his services to the court of the Austrian archduke. The twenty-three-year-old lawyer from Los Angeles was well received by imperial officials. He was appointed to judicial office as a military magistrate and given a commission as a major in the imperial army.[26]

When Maximilian was captured—and subsequently executed in Querétaro by the Juáristas—Sepúlveda was among those who had accompanied him. Along with some fifty other field grade imperial officers, he was taken prisoner and subjected to an agonizing week-long march on foot to Morelia, where he was locked up in the public jail.[27] He was later sentenced to serve four years in Mexico City's Santiago Tlatelolco Penitentiary for his involvement with the imperial government.[28] When word of Sepúlveda's incarceration reached Los Angeles, Volney E. Howard and Phineas Banning made extraordinary efforts to obtain his release. They were able to procure the intervention of the U.S. State Department, which persuaded the Mexican government on October 28, 1865, to commute Sepúlveda's sentence to "banishment from the Republic."[29]

Sepúlveda was allowed to sail from Veracruz with memorabilia of his adventures, including a medal of the Order of Guadalupe awarded him by Maximilian and an oil portrait of the emperor. He must have also had some money since he was able to visit Joseph Lancaster Brent in Baltimore before returning home. Through a bizarre coincidence an announcement of his arrival in the June 13, 1868, *Los Angeles Star* appeared in the same column that noted Ramírez's homecoming from San Francisco. Henry Hamilton, Sepúlveda, and Ramírez had all returned at about the same time.

Only six weeks after his return, Sepúlveda married Ora Anderson in a July 30 high-status ceremony at St. Mary's Cathedral in San Francisco, conducted by Archbishop Joseph S. Alemany. The *Alta California* printed an announcement of the event with the comment "London and Philadelphia papers please copy."[30] Antonio Coronel of Los Angeles, then California's state treasurer, acted as best man. The bride was a resident of Sacramento, where the couple probably met while Sepúlveda was an assemblyman during 1864. The marriage was too sudden for them not to have had a previous relationship. The 1860 census showed Ora Anderson as a nineteen-year-old teacher during that year residing, with her sister Elizabeth and her brother-in-law, William English.[31] She was born during 1842 in Worcester County, Maryland, where her parents kept a small tavern and hotel.[32]

Three weeks after his marriage, Sepúlveda was back in Los Angeles with his bride. His union with an American woman was uncommon. While large numbers of American men took Mexican wives, there were few marriages the other way around.[33] The local press warmly congratulated the young couple, politely ignoring the unusual nature of their match. Sepúlveda was immediately invited by Volney E. Howard to become his law partner. The new firm of Howard & Sepúlveda was first announced in the *Star* on August 22, 1868. This was a flattering arrangement for the young Mexican since Howard was fifty-six years old, nearly twice Sepúlveda's age, and one of the most successful attorneys in southern California.

While Sepúlveda enjoyed a partnership with the highly regarded Volney E. Howard, Ramírez worked as a kind of assistant to Larrabee. They filed several lawsuits during 1869 on behalf of Mexican landowners. Ramírez appeared in each instance on the same side as Larrabee and acting under his direction. Most of their cases were of slight consequence. One involved an injunction to prevent a tenant farmer from harvesting a crop until he paid his landlord $300 in back rent. Another was a demand for $786 by a Mexican rancher against an American who drove away a few head of cattle.[34] Such suits were generally settled out of court. Larrabee used Ramírez exclusively for Mexican clients. He hired other lawyers to help him represent Americans. On June 16, 1870, the *Star* announced that Larrabee had formed a law partnership with Frank Ganahl and E. H. McDaniel. Even so, Ramírez continued to work for Larrabee on Mexican cases.

During the first six months after his admission to the bar, Ramírez was too busy with Larrabee to indulge in politics. He would have noticed, however, that the solidarity of Southern Democrats was temporarily broken in the election held on September 1, 1869, after the county Democratic convention selected Andrew J. King as its candidate for state senator. This nomination was opposed by Benjamin Davis Wilson, a popular Democrat from Tennessee, because he feared King was not a strong advocate for bringing a railroad to Los Angeles. Wilson was the owner of Lake Vineyard, a magnificent estate in what is now the city of San Marino. He was a grape grower, one of those most in need of rail transportation. In addition to being one of the first mayors of Los Angeles under American rule, he served two terms as a state senator, beginning in 1856. Rather than attempt to reverse his party's nomination of King, Wilson announced his own candidacy on an Independent ticket. Several other office seekers, mainly Republicans, joined Wilson. Seeing a chance to defeat the Democrats, the Independent ticket was endorsed by the Republican Party without Wilson's approval. Although most of the Independent ticket was unsuccessful, Wilson's popularity assured his victory over the regular Democratic candidate.

Andrew J. King's defeat by Wilson was only the first of his disappoint-

Portrait of Judge Ignacio Sepúlveda as a young man, date unknown. Reprinted by permission of the Los Angeles Public Library.

ments in 1869. The county court judge William G. Dryden died at his residence on September 10 of that year. Three days later King was appointed to succeed Dryden. However, being named to the county court at that time was of slight benefit since Dryden's term was about to expire. In order to keep his new judgeship, King would have to face a judicial election on October 20, just five weeks after taking office.

Ignacio Sepúlveda was the first to declare his candidacy for judge of the county court in opposition to King. A justice of the peace, O. H. Allen, also announced that he would run for the office. In the Seventeenth District Court, Judge Murray Morrison was challenged by Ramírez's associate, Charles Hathaway Larrabee, as well as Cameron E. Thom.

The October 16, 1869, edition of the *Star* correctly predicted that King would withdraw as a candidate. The newspaper reported, "It is generally conceded by Mr. King's friends that his cause is hopeless." His lukewarm support of a railroad connection had alienated his own party. Without organized support King was obliged to abandon the election. Meantime, finding few backers, Larrabee retired as a candidate for judge of the Seventeenth District Court, leaving Cameron E. Thom to face Judge Murray Morrison.

The *Star* printed election results for judges on October 23, 1869, showing that Sepúlveda and Morrison had enjoyed decisive victories. Sepúlveda, at the age of twenty-seven, had won the second most important judicial office in Los Angeles. Since he had to rely on American voters to attain the office, his election proved that during this period a few exceptional Mexicans were not subject to the same degree of discrimination as other Spanish-speaking people.

Sepúlveda's term as county judge began on January 1, 1870, forcing Ramírez to occasionally present cases before a man whose social and political views were repugnant to him. The other judge, Murray Morrison of the Seventeenth District Court, also lacked Ramírez's confidence. Not long before the judicial election of July 22, 1869, the *Republican* had published a list of local attorneys endorsing Andrew Glassell to replace Murray Morrison. Ramírez's name figured among those opposed to Morrison. This fact would not be helpful when appearing in Morrison's court after he won the election. In any event, Glassell was an odd choice for Ramírez's endorsement. He was a conservative Virginian and a staunch Southern Democrat. Glassell could not obtain his party's backing because he had only recently arrived in Los Angeles. Sepúlveda and Morrison were veteran Democratic loyalists who took precedence over newcomers. After he understood the situation, Glassell used the August 26 *Republican* to announce the withdrawal of his candidacy. Ramírez and other lawyers who had publicly rejected Morrison were left to make amends with him as best they could.

During most of 1870, Ramírez continued to work with Charles Hathaway Larrabee and his partners, Frank Ganahl and E. H. McDaniel. Apparently he shared office space on an informal basis with them. Unlike Ramírez, the firm was on good terms with the district court. The June 28, 1870, *Star* mentioned a "hunting excursion in which Judge Morrison was accompanied by Messrs. Ganahl and McDaniel, of the firm of Larrabee & Co."

Larrabee's firm would have turned out with the rest of Los Angeles for the funeral of Judge Sepúlveda's wife, the former Ora Anderson. The cause of her death on June 5, 1870, at the age of twenty-eight, was not announced, but it was the result of childbirth gone tragically wrong. Ignacio Sepúlveda lost his wife after she delivered a healthy girl he named Ora Anita Sepúlveda.

The June 9, 1870, *Los Angeles News* reported: "The funeral cortège was nearly one mile in length evincing the public respect both for the dead and living of the family." The couple had been married less than two years.

Ramírez's arrangements with Larrabee ended when his partnership dissolved. The *Star* announced on November 30, 1870, that the firm was disbanded by "mutual consent." Ganahl and McDaniel opened another firm as partners at the corner of Spring and Temple streets. They had been in practice with Larrabee only five months. The fact that Ramírez shared office space with Larrabee's partnership is shown by his use of printed legal forms with the firm's name on them. When he borrowed such forms to file in court, Ramírez crossed out the name of the partnership and wrote in his own. Larrabee left for San Francisco but kept in touch with his Los Angeles affairs through a local attorney, John Bicknell. Much later, on September 16, 1891, Larrabee would die in a famous fiery train wreck at Tehachapi Pass, which was reported by the *Los Angeles Times* as having burned the passengers "to a perfect crisp."

Ganahl and McDaniel might have asked Ramírez to join them in their new office. While not a partner, Ramírez could share some of the expenses. The year 1870 had been a quiet one for Ramírez. He did not get politically involved, and his name seldom appeared in the press. However, during the next year, all this would change. Ramírez would once again become a prominent figure among Americans and Mexicans in Los Angeles. His energy and ambition made this result inevitable.

The first opportunity for Ramírez to assert himself in local politics took place on June 6, 1871. On that date the Los Angeles precinct of the local Republican Party organization met at the courthouse to select nine delegates to the county convention on June 17. At the same time five other precincts throughout the county held meetings for the same purpose. Those sent to the county convention would decide who would represent local Republicans at the state convention in Sacramento. The names of twenty men from the Los Angeles precinct were placed in nomination as delegates. Among them was "Frank Ramirez."

The *Evening Express*, a Republican newspaper recently begun by George A. Tiffany, reported the Los Angeles precinct meeting in the June 12, 1871, edition. Ramírez received ninety-six votes, a number that put him in tenth place. He just missed being among the nine named as delegates to the county convention. His disappointment must have disappeared a week later when Ramírez learned that the county convention had appointed him as a member of the local Republican Central Committee. This important sixteen-member group was the executive arm of the party. During the election campaign in the months ahead, every issue of the *Evening Express* carried Ramírez's name printed on the masthead along with those of other committee members.

While maneuvering for a position of leadership in the Republican Party, Ramírez was also involved in a kind of political uprising led by Max Strobel, a former mayor of Anaheim. Only a few days after Ramírez took his place on the Republican Central Committee, Strobel organized a June 25, 1871, meeting in Anaheim, which he called a "people's convention." A resolution signed by "prominent citizens irrespective of party" accused Los Angeles County politicians of running a corrupt "ring" that monopolized public office in order to collect exorbitant fees and salaries.[35]

Strobel was influenced in drafting the resolution by the desire of Anaheim to break away from Los Angeles County. During the 1869–70 legislative session he was in Sacramento to promote a bill creating a new county southeast of Los Angeles with its seat at Anaheim. The assembly actually passed such a measure, but aroused Los Angeles County officials managed to prevent it from being approved by the senate.

Beyond the problem of being situated so far away from Los Angeles, a frugal and sober colony of German farmers in Anaheim objected to the free-wheeling Southern-style politics of their dominant neighbor. Despite steep taxes they saw no public improvements to justify them. It was assumed that funds were wasted and sometimes misappropriated by local officials. This was also the opinion of Ramírez, who had protested fiscal mismanagement by county officers since the days of *El Clamor Público*.

While in northern California, Strobel observed that city and county officials in San Francisco were often elected based on people's and taxpayer's tickets originated by popular organizations that promoted the candidacy of certain individuals regardless of party affiliation. In handling municipal tax money, it was thought that an individual's reputation for honesty and integrity superseded political considerations. An editorial speaking of city government in San Francisco's *Alta California* observed, "Every strongly-partisan administration has been corrupt and every People's or Tax-payer's administration has been, in general, pure."[36]

The *Los Angeles Evening Express* published a paid advertisement on June 27, 1871, that must have surprised members of both regular political parties. Entitled "People's Ticket," it contained the names of candidates recommended by Strobel's convention for city and government offices in the September 6, 1871, Los Angeles elections. At the head of the list were Max Strobel and Francisco P. Ramírez as candidates for the assembly. The other men nominated for office were a strange admixture from both political parties. Some, like Cameron E. Thom, endorsed for the position of district attorney, were conservative Southern Democrats.

The advertisement set out several reforms advocated by its sponsors. It demanded a reduction of fees charged by county officers and cuts in local taxes. The concerns of farmers like those in Anaheim were emphasized. A law to protect their fields from marauding cattle was urged, together with the construction of bridges to help take crops to market. It also objected to the government's providing subsidies for the construction of railroads unless it took ownership of them in the interest of the public. The advertisement concluded: "*It is an honest ballot.* Will you use it, or will you, under the lash of party discipline, and at the command of party politicians, vote a straight party ticket, against your own judgment and interest?"

Most of those supported for office by the People's Ticket would later be nominated by their own parties. The names on the People's Ticket, other than Strobel and Ramírez, represented men who were almost certain to be selected as candidates by one regular party or the other. The most radical feature of the People's Ticket was its eclectic nonpartisan nature. The call for protection of crops from livestock was already being addressed by the legislature. A "no-fence" law for farmers would soon be enacted, requiring ranchers and owners of animals to fence their property to keep livestock away from crops. The law allowed farmers to cultivate without the expense of putting up fences as a protection against cattle, an idea that was already recognized as necessary for Los Angeles agricultural interests. The People's Ticket presented opposition to railroad subsidies, but this was not novel. Both parties had earlier incorporated a rejection of such subsidies in their official state platforms. If the People's Ticket was designed to reform politics and control spending, few of the candidates it endorsed were known to have propensities in that direction. They were mainly local politicians who would not support sudden change.

A highly unusual feature of the People's Ticket was the presence of Strobel and Ramírez at the top of the slate as candidates for the assembly. Of all those named on the ticket, they were among the least likely to be nominated by their own parties. Strobel was an unpopular Democrat identified with a movement to break up Los Angeles County. Ramírez was just reentering local politics after a long absence. He was not yet a major figure among Republicans.

The People's Ticket had some financial backing from Strobel's constituents in Anaheim. The *Evening Express* and the *Los Angeles Star* both accepted paid advertisements promoting the People's Ticket. Its list of candidates was published daily for several weeks. These same newspapers, however, presented editorials opposing Strobel and his ticket. On July 27 the Republican editor of the *Evening Express* rejected the People's Ticket, saying, "While it professes to be the people's movement, it was done in the dark, and the people know nothing about it." Referring to Strobel and Ramírez, the editor concluded that the People's Ticket was "a combination of those gentlemen whose names are on the ticket, to assist toward their own election."

Henry Hamilton's July 20 *Star* regarded the People's Ticket as a ploy to elect Strobel to the legislature:

> We are decidedly opposed to the division of the county. Major Strobel, whose name heads the ticket, is known as the champion of division. He made a contest on this subject before the last Legislature, and it is not to be supposed that, should he be elected, he would prove untrue to his record.

The editorial noticed "a few names of Democrats on this ticket," but Hamilton added, "We have no idea that they were consulted in the matter."

The regular Republican county convention met in the Temple Block on Main Street on July 29 to select candidates for county offices. Twenty-seven delegates from different precincts were present. By this time Ramírez's name had appeared for over a month in every daily edition of the *Evening Express*, both as a member of the Republican Central Committee and as a candidate for the assembly on the People's Ticket. He hoped the Republican convention would ratify the People's Ticket by selecting him as one of the party's two candidates for the assembly. He needed fourteen votes to win the nomination.

Five names were placed in nomination for the assembly, including that of Ramírez. On the first ballot Edward Evey of Anaheim was elected as one of the party's assembly candidates. Evey received twenty-two votes, while the lawyer Anson Brunson got one vote and Ramírez only two. In balloting for a second assembly seat, Brunson had fourteen votes with Ramírez receiving six. After being declared the winner, Brunson refused the nomination.

Instead of turning back to Ramírez, the convention ignored him and made Oscar Macy the other assembly candidate.[37]

The nominations for the assembly were the only ones truly contested. The party's candidates for other offices had already been informally determined before the convention. The certainty of their nominations was well known and quickly confirmed by acclamation. Two of them had already been listed as candidates on the People's Ticket for over a month.

Ramírez's failure to obtain a Republican nomination for the assembly put him in a difficult position. If he stayed on the People's Ticket, he would have to run against his own party's candidates. The standing of Ramírez among Republicans was already compromised to some extent by his presence on the competing People's Ticket. The editor of the *Evening Express*, a Republican spokesman, observed that the People's Ticket "has on it the names of Democratic candidates for the more important offices." His editorial regarded the ticket as an adversary. He wrote that it would receive little support, "especially not by the Republican Party, against whom it seems to be principally directed."[38]

Republicans who disapproved of the People's Ticket doubtlessly communicated this fact to Ramírez. They likely put him under considerable pressure to renounce his candidacy. In the meantime, as if to demonstrate his loyalty to the party, Ramírez began to actively campaign on behalf of Republican candidates for statewide offices.

The Republican state convention in Sacramento on July 29, 1871, nominated Newton Booth for governor. In an unexpected move Romualdo Pacheco, a California Mexican, was selected for the office of lieutenant governor. It was announced that Pacheco planned to undertake a speaking tour of the state that would include Los Angeles on August 15. Ramírez saw Pacheco's visit as an opportunity to regain some of his credibility among Republicans. He quickly assumed a leading role in preparing for Pacheco's arrival.

Ramírez was in a unique position to militate on behalf of the Republican state ticket. When he reemerged on the local political scene in 1871, he did not limit his involvement to the American community. Following a pattern that characterized his entire life, Ramírez was also engaged in the affairs of his own people. He was a familiar figure both among Americans below the plaza and Mexicans north of it in Sonoratown. The August 11 *Evening Express* noted that Ramírez had been elected president of the Spanish-American Republican Club. In that capacity he was part of a committee to arrange a reception for Romualdo Pacheco when he came to speak in

Los Angeles. Ramírez helped organize a grand August 15 mass meeting of Republicans on Pacheco's behalf in front of the Lafayette Hotel. Several distinguished Republican politicians from northern California shared the platform with Pacheco. One of them was Augusto D. Splivato, a Chilean lawyer from San Francisco, whom Ramírez knew from his days as editor of *El Nuevo Mundo*. By taking on the role of host and publicly exchanging amenities with Pacheco and Splivato, Ramírez was able to make a highly visible expression of solidarity with state Republican leaders.

Less than two weeks after Pacheco's appearance in Los Angeles, Ramírez decided to withdraw from the People's Ticket. The *Evening Express* of August 28 announced this development:

> We have received a communication asking whether Mr. Ramirez is a candidate for the Assembly. We are requested by Mr. Ramirez to say he is not a candidate; that he hopes to see the Republican party successful in the coming election and therefore will not be a candidate as there is a Republican ticket before the people. Mr. Ramirez is President of the Spanish-American Republican Club, one of the largest political organizations in the county; and one that will do good work from now till the close of the polls on election day, for the State and county ticket.

The next edition of the *Evening Express* dropped Ramírez's name from the People's Ticket. The August 29 advertisement of the People's Ticket, appearing one day after Ramírez withdrew, was the last ever published. Strobel now abandoned his nonpartisan movement. If he printed any ballots for his ticket, few were distributed. The People's Ticket vanished by the time of the election on September 6.

Ramírez now focused his energies on the Republican campaign. The September 2, 1871, *Evening Express* noticed that Ramírez and other officers of the Spanish-American Republican Club "have been very active in the work of this campaign." The newspaper reported plans for a torchlight procession by the club through the plaza area and "the upper part of the city." It was understood that Mexicans in Sonoratown were the target of this demonstration directed by Ramírez. The editor of the *Evening Express* enthused, "We shall have a good report from this Club at the election Wednesday as they are at work in earnest."

The final Republican rally was on the evening of September 3, once again in front of the Lafayette Hotel. Ramírez was announced as the principal speaker. The September 4 *Evening Express* described his speech as "a very able argument to the Spanish-Americans present in their own language." Ramírez evoked past offenses of the Southern Democrats against working class Mexicans. He accused them of racism in terms that could have been taken from *El Clamor Público*: "The Democrats ridicule Pacheco, pass laws in which they call the Spanish people 'greasers' then ask for their votes at elections." Besides his speech, Ramírez contributed to the mass meeting by providing the Spanish-American Republican Club for another march through the streets. According to the *Evening Express*, "The Spanish-American Club had a large number of torches and transparencies and with the band of music presented a fine appearance."

The election of September 6, 1871, conformed to the usual pattern of Los Angeles politics. The Democrats, controlled by Southern conservatives, rolled over the Republicans by a vote of nearly two to one. Although the Republican candidate for governor, Newton Booth, won the election against the Democratic incumbent, Henry H. Haight, elsewhere in the state, he lost in Los Angeles by 2,177 to 1,421.[39] Despite the efforts of Ramírez and others, the Mexican vote, as always, came down on the side of the Democrats.

The City of Los Angeles was organized for election purposes at that time into three wards. The first ward embraced Sonoratown, representing an almost purely Mexican vote. The official results appearing in the September 13, 1871, *Star* show that Mexicans in the first ward voted against Romualdo Pacheco, the Republican candidate for lieutenant governor, by 201 to 128. Even when presented with a Republican candidate from their own people, the majority of Mexicans continued to vote for conservative white Democrats.

Although it was customary for both parties to buy votes, the 1871 election was particularly corrupt. Five days after the election, on September 11, Judge Ignacio Sepúlveda made a stirring statement to the county grand jury, charging it to investigate "the buying and selling of votes, and the corruptions attending our elections." The entire text of his eloquent denunciation of election practices in Los Angeles was printed in the September 12 *Star* and repeated on September 14 by San Francisco's *Alta California*. The *Star* acknowledged the existence of election fraud by stating, "It is very well known that in this county the traffic in voters is a regular business; that agents will contract for a batch of votes at so much a head, just as an agent will for the delivery of any other commodity at a stipulated price." Despite the well-publicized scandal involved, Judge Sepúlveda's thoughtful address to the grand jury had little effect, and no action was taken to remedy the problem.

Ramírez's efforts to attract Mexican voters during the Republican campaign had largely failed, but he was nevertheless considered a notable figure in the Spanish-speaking community. This is evident from the fact that he was chosen to be the main speaker at the celebration of Mexican independence on September 16. The organization Ramírez had helped establish in 1862, now known as the Junta Patriótica de Juárez, made elaborate arrangements for the festivities. The September 16 *Star* reported that a parade of "handsomely decorated cars" passed through the city streets, then returned to a stand near the junta's rooms on Main Street north of the plaza. After fireworks and singing of the Mexican national anthem, Ramírez and others "gave orations worthy of the distinguished speakers who delivered them."

Ramírez was now thirty-four, but his youthful opposition to racism was unabated. This was made clear in his recent speech at the September 3 mass meeting of Republican voters. As we have seen, on that occasion he once again attacked the Democrats for referring to Mexicans as "greasers." As a young editor sensitive to racial issues, his defense of minorities had extended to the Chinese. A January 19, 1856, editorial in *El Clamor Público* protested a movement to exclude Chinese from the United States, saying, "It would not be just to deny them entry merely because their customs are different from ours and they have another color." Ramírez must have been horrified only a few weeks after his speech on Mexican Independence Day when a famous incident occurred in Los Angeles, often referred to as the "Chinese massacre."

During 1870 some 236 Chinese were present in Los Angeles County, compared to only eleven a decade before.[40] Their numbers continued to increase as they drifted south after completion of the transcontinental railroad in 1869, which had been built mainly by their labor. Some were accepted in American households as cooks and domestic servants. Others were forced into a highly segregated part of Nigger Alley. This area, now given the more acceptable name "Negro Alley" by the local press, was a string of derelict adobes reserved for saloons, prostitutes, and social outcasts. The appearance and behavior of the Chinese were completely alien. They embodied everything that triggered xenophobic hatred among Americans toward people of color.

The Los Angeles press constantly encouraged hostility toward the Chinese. Little concerning them appeared in local newspapers except gross misrepresentations and vicious ridicule. When the editor of the *Los Angeles Republican* discovered that California's governor had accepted an invitation

Crowded Chinese tenements near the southeast corner of the Los Angeles Plaza, circa 1885. Reprinted by permission of the University of Southern California Special Collections.

to dine with the Chinese ambassador in San Francisco, he wrote on May 23, 1868, that the menu probably consisted of "fricasseed rats and tom cat salad." A year later, on May 20, 1869, he quoted an article in the *New York Tribune* describing Chinese people as "utter heathens, treacherous, sensual, cowardly, and cruel." Since Chinese folklore held that the emperor was appointed to rule by heaven, China was sometimes called the Celestial Empire. The American press seized on this to mock Chinese by calling them "celestials." A deliberate effort was made to degrade and dehumanize them. A simple Christian-style wedding between an ordinary Chinese couple before an American justice of the peace was treated in the October 3, 1871, *Star* as follows: "In Justice Gray's office, yesterday, the lovely moon-eyed Si Chu, was united in the bonds of barbarian matrimony to the celestial Ah Chung." The same edition described an accident much the same way: "A Celestial vegetable peddler in attempting to jump from a wagon, on Main Street, yesterday, got his gracefully pendant queue caught in a rail and sustained a compound fracture of that 'fifth wheel' to his heavenly locomotion." The July 19, 1871,

Star published a rumor that a Chinese in Negro Alley planned to kill his wife. The sinister item suggested he might do so with impunity: "We venture the assertion that many a dark and terrible deed has been perpetrated by these heathen in their secret dens, which will never come to the knowledge of the Christians whose places they are usurping."

Tension between the people of Los Angeles and the small colony of Chinese in Negro Alley erupted into an incredibly violent incident on October 24, 1871. At about 5:00 p.m. that day, the police attempted to interfere in a fight between rival Chinese gangs after they heard a shot. According to Americans and Mexicans present, the Chinese began to fire indiscriminately at the police and the crowd that had gathered. Officer Jesús Bilderrain was struck in the shoulder. A reporter for the October 25 *Star*, who claimed to be a witness, wrote, "The citizens armed themselves hastily and ran to the rescue of the police." At this point, "the people closed in on the accursed pagans and forced them to seek shelter in the adobe dens of the Coronel Block with a loss of one killed outright and four wounded." An American named Robert Thomson approached the door of the adobe where the Chinese had hidden and was shot in the chest, dying within minutes. A Mexican boy standing in the street was hit in the leg and another bystander received a bullet in the hip.

A few Chinese attempted to escape from the adobe but drew fire from the crowd and were instantly killed. A mob had now collected, which forced its way into the building, pulling eight Chinese into the street. All those removed were immediately hanged. It was later shown that they were not involved in the shooting that had infuriated the mob. Other Chinese were seized in the street and lynched on a corral gate or hung from an upended wagon. At least nineteen Chinese lost their lives. Most of those who died were cooks or domestic servants. One was a medical doctor. Ironically, the Chinese who provoked the incident were thugs from San Francisco. They managed to escape, leaving local residents to the wrath of the mob.

Judge Ignacio Sepúlveda convened a grand jury to investigate the massacre, but nothing of any significance resulted. The Chinese massacre would long remain in the collective memory of Los Angeles. It may have reminded Ramírez of the Mexican lynchings he had condemned in *El Clamor Público* some thirteen years before. This time, however, Mexicans were members of the lynch mob, not its victims.

The Chinese were the latest addition to a diverse Los Angeles population. Despite the rejection and cruelty they suffered, a sullen and detached group

Scene of the Chinese massacre in a photograph taken about 1875, facing north. The adobe in the center is where the Chinese took refuge. To the right, extending to the eastern boundary of the plaza, is the center of vice called Negro Alley by racist Americans. Reprinted by permission of the University of Southern California Special Collections.

of them persisted in Negro Alley. Their isolation from the larger community was the natural consequence of a widely accepted racial hierarchy in Los Angeles. Americans of Anglo-Saxon descent born in the United States stood at the top of the structure. They were a numerous conquering race that had imposed its own culture, institutions, and language on the region. They constituted most of the landowners. At nearly the same level were white immigrants from Europe who adopted American customs and the English language.

Mexicans were below Americans and Europeans on the social scale, but their status was equivocal. They were an intermediate group in most respects. A few were indistinguishable in appearance from Europeans. Others—the majority—were of a more Indian type and clearly people of color. California Mexicans were generally seen as an inferior people whose lack of status was only mitigated by the fact that after the Mexican-American War the United States felt obliged to placate world opinion by granting them citizenship and the right to vote. Some of them were the only nonwhite people in Los Angeles to exercise that right. The social position of certain Mexicans was often difficult to define because of the interaction between the races over the period of more than twenty years since statehood. Many Ameri-

An American neighborhood south of the plaza, about 1880. Reprinted by permission of the University of Southern California Special Collections.

A hardware store south of the plaza offering an abundance of goods to American patrons, circa 1880. Reprinted by permission of the University of Southern California Special Collections.

cans, including prestigious individuals like ex-governor John G. Downey, had married Mexican women. There were instances of close friendships, family ties, and warm personal relations between old-time American and Mexican residents. Rare individuals like Ramírez and Ignacio Sepúlveda were accepted on terms amounting to complete equality.

The Chinese joined blacks and Indians in the depths of the social order. There was no question about the abased position of these groups. During 1870 the U.S. census counted 134 blacks in Los Angeles County. They were usually ignored by the press unless arrested for some crime. Robert Owens and his wife, Winney, were among the best-known blacks. Like other members of their race, they were not accorded much respect. They were patronizingly called "Uncle Bob" and "Aunt Winney" by the whites. The general attitude toward blacks was demonstrated by the August 14, 1871, *Evening Express*, which announced, "The men and brethren of our city who boast the 'rich tropical blood' of Africa, have formed unto themselves a Republican club." The Republican newspaper rejected an association with the blacks. It suggested they join the pro-slavery Democrats instead. The editor sarcastically wrote: "If the Africans wished to form an alliance with the Democracy all that is necessary is for old Aunt Winney to provide a free lunch, as she did two or three years ago and the unterrified will be on hand."[41]

A black woman named Biddy Mason was one of the most generous and admirable citizens of Los Angeles. She arrived during 1851 as a slave. After Judge Benjamin I. Hayes ordered her freedom, she worked as a midwife and managed to invest in real estate. She became wealthy as her holdings increased in value, and she used much of her money to found a church, a rest home, and a nursery school. Although she was constantly involved in altruistic activities like visiting jail inmates to cheer them up, little attention was paid to her by whites.[42] The press preferred to satirize and ridicule blacks, ignoring the decency and charitable instincts of a person like Biddy Mason.

The most mysterious race in Los Angeles occupied the absolute bottom of the social order. They were the Indians known as Gabrielinos because of their association with the Mission San Gabriel. What they actually called themselves is uncertain. The word "Tongva" has been suggested as a generalized name for these people, but that term was only used in the Tejon area by a small group, while far more numerous Indians in the Los Angeles basin had an array of other names to describe themselves, depending on the area where they lived.[43] At the time of first contact with the Spanish in 1771, there were about 5,000 members of this indigenous race in Los Angeles County.

Sonoratown north of the plaza, about 1885. Most houses are Mexican adobes with American-style wooden roofs. Reprinted by permission of the University of Southern California Special Collections.

A typical adobe made for two families in Sonoratown, about 1875. Reprinted by permission of the University of Southern California Special Collections.

Mexicans in front of a small dilapidated store on Aliso Street between 1880 and 1882. Reprinted by permission of the University of Southern California Special Collections.

Their encounter with Europeans was devastating since they had no immunity to the diseases of white men. The U.S. census found 2,014 of them in 1860, but only 219 were left ten years later. Their inability to resist infectious disease was made worse by a powerful and fatal addiction to alcohol. Instead of working for a semblance of healthy sustenance, they labored in local vineyards for a few coins to buy cheap liquor. The editor of the *Republican* published an article on April 1, 1869, that contemptuously described Los Angeles Indians: "Sunday is the day they usually celebrate by a most beastly 'drunk' celebrated alike by both sexes in such an abandoned, filthy, naked state of intoxication as to cause one to disgust the human species for having any connection with such outcasts." The article correctly predicted their extinction in a casual manner: "But the number of Indians is diminishing so rapidly that they will soon cease to be a source of much annoyance."

Within a few decades every full-blooded Indian was dead, their race wiped out. The effects of brutal labor, white exploitation, alcoholism, and disease liquidated an entire people. A small number of mostly Mexican American families claim partial descent from them today. Some can iden-

Indian shelters in front of the Mission San Gabriel, date unknown. To the left is a conical hut made in the ancient style. Reprinted by permission of the Huntington Library, San Marino, California.

tify distant ancestors in Spanish mission records. However, there are no descendants with more than a tiny fraction of Indian blood. The last burial of a full-blooded Indian at the Mission San Gabriel took place in 1921, when José de los Santos Juncos, age 101, was placed in the cemetery without the rites of his own people since no one living knew what they were.[44] Although academics are laudably attempting to resurrect fragments of their language, no one speaks it fluently or possesses any significant cultural traits acquired directly from Gabrielino ancestors. There is little in the historical record offering insight into their individual lives and personalities. Newspapers of the time mention them in dismissive terms more befitting animals than human beings. Sadly, without much more information about these extinct people than has so far been discovered, an understanding of who they really were is closed to us, unknowably and perhaps forever.

Ramírez opposed American racism and the hierarchy it created. The mistreatment of nonwhites had long been a source of concern. His sympathy for the Indians was expressed in a June 4, 1859, edition of *El Clamor Público* that protested acts of violence against them: "In California, Indians are killed by whites as if they were birds or wild animals. The Indian race is not seen as part of the human family. It is generally believed that they ought to disappear." While in San Francisco, Ramírez learned that blacks had been refused permission to participate in a march celebrating the Fourth of July. He reacted by publishing an editorial in *El Nuevo Mundo* on July 7, 1865, criticizing such discrimination. He regarded blacks in the same way that he saw all people of color: "A dark skin may harbor beneath it a noble and generous heart as well as a profound intelligence."

Ramírez's admission to the bar probably stretched the limits of American tolerance. Not only was he a Mexican, but his social and political views conflicted with those of most Americans. After the election of Ignacio Sepúlveda as judge of the county court, Ramírez was the only Mexican lawyer in southern California. To protect his privileged status, he had to exercise discretion in dealing with Americans. For example, it is not likely that he would have vehemently expressed his opinions about race to his first employer, Charles Hathaway Larrabee.

This 1905 photograph in Eagle Rock depicts the new order brought by the American conquest. The owner of the Shumacher Ranch, which was created from land taken from the Mexican Rancho San Vicente, poses with his property, elegant carriages, and family. Four Mexican laborers stand subserviently behind him, representing a displaced people. Reprinted by permission of the University of Southern California Special Collections.

In 1859, while a member of Congress from Wisconsin, Larrabee had delivered a speech on the floor of the House of Representatives, declaring that blacks were "not created with equal political rights, nor was it ever so intended."[45] The editor of the *Los Angeles Star*, Henry Hamilton, heard a speech given by Larrabee on September 17, 1868, at a Democratic meeting in the Los Angeles courthouse. Hamilton, a profoundly racist person, admired it as "one of the most effective addresses we have heard on any similar occasion." Larrabee's remarks echoed overwhelming white opinion when, according to Hamilton, "he denounced the dogma of manhood suffrage, that is, negro equality and Chinese equality and their inherent right, as human beings, to be admitted to the privileges of American citizenship." Despite Larrabee's undisguised bigotry, however, Ramírez worked surprisingly well with him.

During the last part of 1871, Ramírez had very little in the nature of a law practice. After the departure of Larrabee, he shared office space with a series of attorneys and was occasionally hired to perform minor services for them. He appeared in one matter during this time which illustrates his activity. The case was *José Francisco Rivas v. Andrew Glassell*, an action for ejectment from real property on Eternity Street.[46] The plaintiff's lawyer, Henry T. Hazard, associated Ramírez as "of counsel." The reason for Ramírez's involvement is made clear by the presence of a long chain of title for the property translated from Spanish to English. After the initial pleadings, Ramírez was no longer involved in the case. Apparently, a translation of the chain of title was all that Hazard wanted.

The November 8, 1871, *Star* announced that on the previous day Frederick A. Stanford had been admitted to the Los Angeles bar. He was a New York lawyer who had recently arrived via Texas with his wife and children. Stanford formed a friendship with Ramírez almost immediately. The two men soon joined with Volney E. Howard in defending the case of *José Dolores Guerrero v. Bartola Ballerino*, filed on December 26, 1871.[47] It was the first case of any importance that Ramírez had worked on since Larrabee left. Stanford persuaded Howard to give Ramírez a place on the defense beyond doing research and translating documents. In any event, the meeting of Stanford and Ramírez would soon alter the lives of both men. At the close of 1871, Ramírez's career was about to undergo a dramatic change.

CHAPTER NINE
Stanford and Ramírez

Only four months after arriving in Los Angeles, Frederick A. Stanford joined Ramírez in forming a law partnership. Their association was formally announced in the March 28, 1872, *Los Angeles Star*, which ran an advertisement for "Stanford & Ramirez, Attorneys, Office—Temple Block, Room 6."

Ramírez had little to lose by joining Stanford. He had already been a lawyer in Los Angeles for three years without much success. After the departure of Charles Hathaway Larrabee during November 1870, Ramírez experienced a long period in which he had few clients. His name seldom appeared in court records throughout 1871.

Stanford's personal history is unusually obscure. Nothing can be found describing his life before he appeared in Los Angeles. In noting his admission to the local bar, the November 8, 1871, *Star* reported that he had arrived from Texas. Later census records show that he was born in New York about 1835. Most of his life must have been spent in the east. His wife, Mary Elizabeth, née Olcott, some five years younger, was also a native of New York. Their two children, Cornelia and Frederick, Jr., had been born there in 1862 and 1865. The *Star*'s account of Stanford's coming from Texas meant he had traveled to Los Angeles during the fall of 1871. The difficult trip would have been by stage or wagon train through the desert, along the Southern Route taken by so many Los Angeles immigrants.

Stanford possessed proof that he was a Texas lawyer. The minutes of the Los Angeles District Court for November 7, 1871, recited that Stanford showed the court a certificate of admission as an attorney to the district court of the Eleventh Judicial District in Houston, Texas. Judge Murray Morrison admitted him to the Los Angeles bar immediately upon presentation of the certificate. The newcomer had a further claim in that the first references to him in the local press were as "Colonel Stanford," a title he used throughout his life. The source of this military rank is unknown. Civil War records disclose no one with his name serving as a colonel on either side. Stanford

Portrait of Volney E. Howard, date unknown. Reprinted by permission of the Los Angeles Public Library.

had probably displayed some form of entitlement to his military rank since he was known by it at once. In the Southern tradition, a few Los Angeles residents, like E. J. C. Kewen and J. J. Warner, were popularly addressed as "colonel" although they had no legitimate military background. The title was honorary, the result of prestige gained over many years. However, Stanford was accepted as a colonel and a high-status individual from the moment he appeared in the city.

Since the *Los Angeles Star* mentioned that Stanford had arrived by way of Texas, perhaps he had held some office there in the reconstruction government imposed by the U.S. Congress after the Civil War. More than one New Yorker was recruited to serve as a carpetbagger in the defeated Southern states. It may be speculated that Stanford acquired the title of colonel as a member of one of the militias organized by the federal government to control a hostile ex-Confederate population. If Stanford was involved with one of the reconstruction governments in Texas, he might have departed because it was an unpleasant experience.

During the four months between Stanford's arrival and his partnership with Ramírez, the two men discovered their compatibility in several areas, including politics. Stanford was a Republican whose views largely coincided with those of Ramírez. On a practical level Stanford probably recognized that Ramírez had not sufficiently used his lifelong connection with the Mexican and French communities in recruiting clients. For his part Ramírez had not yet operated out of his own office or acted alone on many cases. He was still more or less a legal novice. Stanford was experienced and willing to help Ramírez. The two men now confronted the practice of law as it existed in Los Angeles during 1872.

Nearly all prominent lawyers were Southerners and fervent partisans of the Chivalry. As repeatedly seen, this pro-slavery faction of the Democratic Party was brought to Los Angeles by immigrants from the Deep South. The Chivalry's belief in white supremacy was repugnant to Ramírez, but the majority of American voters were Southerners who naturally held such views. Los Angeles remained a bastion of Confederate sentiment throughout the Civil War. To Ramírez's disgust a fair number of wealthy Mexicans were attracted to the Chivalry and helped maintain its dominance in Los Angeles.

Although not a Southerner, Volney E. Howard was a leading attorney for reasons beyond his legal talent. He was also a great exponent of antebellum values. Born in Maine on October 29, 1809, he studied law there and was admitted to the bar. At age twenty-two, Howard left to join an uncle's law practice in Mississippi. His experiences in the Deep South caused him to become "southernized."[1] He eventually moved to New Orleans and later Brownsville, Texas.[2] Howard had a distinguished career in Texas, where he was elected to the U.S. Congress. In 1849 he voted against the admission of California into the Union because its new constitution prohibited slavery. Howard County in west Texas was named in his honor, and it retains the name today. During 1853 Howard accepted a position in San Francisco as law agent for the U.S. Land Commission. He soon acquired a certain renown as a political leader. Governor J. Neely Johnson appointed him to command the California state militia in 1856 with the rank of major general. In that capacity Governor Johnson ordered him to suppress a vigilante movement occurring in San Francisco. Howard failed in this assignment and was forced to leave the city.[3] Nevertheless, he was always known afterward as General Howard since it was the custom of the time to address lawyers who were former commissioned officers by their erstwhile military rank.

The August 24, 1861, *Star* announced that the general had come to reside in Los Angeles. The Southern qualities he had acquired during his long stay in Mississippi, Louisiana, and Texas aided his law practice. After Joseph Lancaster Brent left California in 1862 to join the Confederate Army, Howard succeeded him as chief of the Chivalry Democrats. In 1865 the Los Angeles county clerk, John W. Shore, wrote a letter to Brent, then residing in Baltimore, advising him of Howard's political ascendancy and stating that he had obtained "the greater portion of the legal business of the county."[4]

Among Howard's competitors for legal preeminence was Edward John Cage Kewen, whose unwieldy name was usually reduced to E. J. C. Kewen. A neighbor at his residence near San Gabriel described Kewen as "somewhat undersized but every ounce of his anatomy filled with Southern fire."[5] He was a brilliant orator, the greatest in southern California and perhaps the entire state. The Chivalry often called upon him to speak at political meetings, where his audiences were enraptured by poetic flights of eloquence describing the world from a Southern perspective.

Kewen, born on November 2, 1825, in Columbus, Mississippi, was an orphan at the age of eight and raised by a guardian. His restless nature led him to briefly practice law in Missouri, then to cross the plains to California during 1849 in a wagon train led by Dr. Thomas J. White. Upon their arrival in Sacramento, Kewen married one of White's daughters. Impressed by his oratorical abilities, the California legislature appointed him as the state's first attorney general in 1850, when he was just twenty-five years old. Although prestigious, the position was poorly paid. Kewen abandoned this office, and later a more lucrative law practice in San Francisco, to join William Walker's filibustering expedition to Nicaragua during 1855. On the collapse of this adventure, he joined his wife's family in Los Angeles during 1858, where he resumed practicing law.[6] Kewen was a combative Southern spirit who attracted numerous like-minded clients. As earlier noted, he was arrested by the Union army and briefly sent to Alcatraz in 1862 for making public pronouncements in favor of the Confederacy. Kewen's open resistance to Union authority enhanced his standing in Los Angeles. It helped his election to several public offices, including two terms as state assemblyman.

Kewen's Southern background was typical of most lawyers in Los Angeles during the 1870s. Cameron E. Thom, a leader of the Democratic Chivalry, was a native of Richmond, Virginia, who had fought for the Confederacy, attaining the rank of captain. He was elected as the Los Angeles district attorney in 1870 and later served as mayor.[7] His nephew, Erskine M. Ross, was a Confederate veteran who became a longtime federal judge.[8] Both men were close to Aurelius W. Hutton, a popular lawyer who had attended the University of Virginia and seen action in the Confederate Army. Hutton wound up his law career as a judge in the Los Angeles Superior Court.[9]

One of the most flamboyant trial lawyers, Frank Ganahl, was a Georgia-born activist in Chivalry politics.[10] Next to E. J. C. Kewen he was the most popular orator in Los Angeles. Ganahl was often joined in political affairs by Andrew J. King, an extremely conservative Southerner, also from Georgia.[11] Nearly all election campaigns during the 1870s included old-fashioned mass meetings with torch-lit speeches by Volney E. Howard, E. J. C. Kewen, Frank Ganahl, and A. J. King on behalf of Chivalry candidates.

Three Southern attorneys were less inclined to public demonstrations but highly influential nevertheless. They were Andrew Glassell, Alfred Beck Chapman, and George Hugh Smith. Their partnership of Glassell, Chapman, and Smith had a greater volume of business by 1870 than any other law firm. Local courts processed so many documents from them that the clerks eventually took to referencing the firm's name on files and records as simply "G.C. and S."

Andrew Glassell was born in Virginia in 1827 but raised in Alabama. He and Alfred Beck Chapman were boyhood friends in Alabama; they formed a law partnership when they encountered each other in Los Angeles during 1865. They were joined by George H. Smith in 1868. Smith was from an old Virginia family, a twice-wounded Confederate colonel noted for an exceptionally heroic war record. He married Andrew Glassell's younger sister, Sue, the widow of George S. Patton. A first cousin of Smith, Patton was killed commanding a Confederate regiment in 1864. Smith became the stepfather of Sue Patton's children, then a surrogate grandfather to George S. Patton, Jr., the celebrated World War II general. Smith would become a state senator, and much later in life, a justice of the California Court of Appeals.[12]

The Southern lawyers formed a fraternity that dominated the local judicial system and had an enormous influence on Los Angeles politics. During the first few decades after statehood in 1850, they monopolized legal business involving the city and county governments. At election time the offices of city attorney and district attorney were passed around among members of the inner Southern circle. The success of these Southern lawyers was so great that they attracted even clients who were political enemies. Pío Pico, a loyal Republican, used Glassell, Chapman, and Smith as his attorneys for several years. When the wealthy Republican landowner John Forster faced litigation, he turned to Volney E. Howard for help although the two men despised each other's politics.[13]

A few Republican attorneys enjoyed success within the Southern ambience of the Los Angeles bar, but they were initially prevented by the Chivalry from gaining public office. All were immigrants from points outside the South, unaffected by the antebellum culture of their colleagues. One of the most prominent was Anson Brunson, an Ohio-born attorney who graduated from the University of Michigan in 1857. He formed a partnership with James G. Eastman, a Republican whose reputation as a dramatic speaker nearly equaled that of stellar Chivalry members. Henry T. Hazard, a well-regarded young lawyer, was brought to Los Angeles by way of Illinois in 1853 as a nine-year-old. A more recent arrival, Robert M. Widney, born in Ohio, appeared in Los Angeles in 1868. Widney was not dependent on his law practice for a living. He spent most of his time working as an agent for the Robinson Trust, selling off ranch lands of Abel Stearns.[14]

There was little outward animosity between Southern lawyers and their less numerous Republican colleagues. Professional courtesies tended to overcome regional and political differences. This tolerance extended only to matters of personal civility, however. None but Chivalry lawyers would be admitted to intimate late-night meetings in the Bella Union or Montgomery House saloons, where the course of Los Angeles politics was plotted over bourbon and cigars.

Ramírez would not have been well liked by Chivalry lawyers. Some Southern attorneys, such as E. J. C. Kewen and A. J. King, were present in Los Angeles when *El Clamor Público* was published. They were aware that Ramírez's hatred of slavery caused him to circulate articles attacking the South and insulting those who came from there. Ramírez had used his newspaper to contemptuously denounce the most cherished ideals of the Chivalry. Moreover, during the twelve years since he had closed *El Clamor Público*, there was no indication that he had moderated his views. Since returning from San Francisco, Ramírez expended much of his time and energy on behalf of the Republican Party, trying to overthrow the Chivalry's control of Los Angeles.

It might be supposed that Ramírez's position in American society was prejudiced because he was Mexican, but this was not always true. A few Mexicans like Ramírez managed to avoid the worst effects of American racism. This phenomenon was limited to rare individuals who clearly manifested characteristics that the Americans considered desirable. A nearly white appearance was indispensable. Only those resembling Americans would qualify for treatment approaching equality. Some Mexicans, including Ramírez, had no Indian characteristics. This was an advantage in dealing with Americans, but visible evidence of European ancestry was not in itself enough to gain acceptance.

Besides broadly conforming to a certain physical type, Mexicans seeking a place within the American community had to show a high degree of acculturation. This necessarily required a mastery of English. It also meant a willingness to participate in American society on terms dictated by its members, together with an understanding of its customs, law, and politics. The handful of individuals who clearly manifested such attainments were often immune from the discrimination experienced by other Mexicans in Los Angeles.

Ignacio Sepúlveda was the most spectacular example of integration. Aside from his name and slightly dark complexion, there was almost nothing that would identify him as Mexican. After his childhood experience at the Ellis School for Boys in Kingston, Massachusetts, he returned to Los Angeles with a good command of English. While studying law with Joseph Lancaster Brent, he unconditionally adopted the Chivalry's conservatism and racial views. Sepúlveda never protested American treatment of Mexicans. His reactionary tendencies were demonstrated in 1864 when he volunteered his services to the Emperor Maximilian. Soon after his return from Mexico, Sepúlveda's 1869 election as county judge was promoted by conservative Democrats. They believed Sepúlveda was a man of superior abilities, whose intelligence and loyalty to American interests qualified him for the office. In effect, Sepúlveda crossed over the racial divide and became the equivalent of a white American. As noted earlier, he even married an American woman.

Sepúlveda was embraced by nearly everyone, including his political opponents. The June 20, 1872, *Los Angeles Express*, a Republican newspaper, praised Sepúlveda's work as a judge, calling him "a credit to the bench of California." In that same year the Americans awarded Sepúlveda the greatest honor they could give him. He was chosen to be the principal orator at the July Fourth celebration. Sepúlveda delivered a patriotic speech in English to an appreciative American audience.[15] He was the first Mexican to ever do so.

Ramírez would never be as popular as Sepúlveda. His liberal political views and his insistence on Mexican equality ensured him a place just outside the American mainstream. He was nevertheless accepted in American circles about as well as any other radically Republican lawyer. In fact, he had a privileged position among Americans and could have spent more time among them had he chosen to do so. However, he was seldom found at social functions outside the Mexican quarter in Sonoratown. Stanford would eventually discover that, while Ramírez felt obliged to engage in business and politics with Americans, the core of his existence was Mexican.

Just before his partnership with Ramírez, Stanford was benefited by a change of judges in the district court. Judge Murray Morrison died on December 18, 1871, less than six weeks after admitting Stanford to local practice. He was replaced by Robert M. Widney, a Republican who maneuvered himself into office by racing to Sacramento as soon as he heard of Morrison's death. Once in the capital, Widney was the first to petition Governor Newton Booth for an appointment to succeed Morrison in the Los Angeles District Court.[16] Governor Booth, a Republican, had no hesitation in naming his fellow party member to the position.

Widney was the first Republican to serve as a judge in Los Angeles. His appointment circumvented the Chivalry, which was accustomed to electing judges they had chosen to run for office. To everyone's surprise Judge Widney assumed office on January 1, 1872. One of his first acts was to appoint a committee of ten lawyers to revise the local court rules. Three Republican lawyers were among those selected for the honor: Anson Brunson, Frederick A. Stanford, and Francisco P. Ramírez.[17]

Judge Widney had apparently developed a friendship with Stanford before he took the bench. The two men were close to the same age, with common political outlooks. Widney used his position as judge to aid Stanford in beginning his law practice. The *Los Angeles Star*, on January 24, 1872, reported that when E. J. C. Kewen withdrew as defense counsel in a criminal case, the court appointed Stanford to replace him. The *Star* noted a week later that Stanford was in court assisting the district attorney, C. E. Thom, in prosecuting a criminal case. This too was likely brought about by the court.

Apart from any question of friendship, Judge Widney had a high opinion of Stanford's legal abilities. The sincerest expression of this occurred when he chose Stanford as his personal attorney. In a lawsuit filed on March 7, 1872, Stanford successfully ejected one Fredric Foyal from real property owned by Judge Widney.[18] Whatever his background and legal training, Stanford was soon recognized in Los Angeles as an excellent lawyer.

About three weeks after announcing their partnership, Stanford and Ramírez appeared in a jury trial together, representing Teodoro Verdugo in an action to eject Nicolas Urías from the Rancho San Rafael.[19] The defense was handled by the redoubtable Volney E. Howard. Stanford took advantage of the occasion to instruct Ramírez on the art of conducting a jury trial. The men took turns examining witnesses and presenting final arguments. The jury returned a verdict in their client's favor, which no doubt helped to educate Ramírez and raise his level of confidence in the courtroom.

One day after winning the jury trial for Verdugo, they were hired by Mariano Santacruz, on April 19, 1872, to foreclose a mortgage.[20] Other cases were brought to the new partnership as well. Teresa Lastra hired them to partition a parcel of land on Main Street in an action filed on April 25, 1872.[21] Four days later they began a lawsuit for Andrea Elizalde de Davila, a lady once married to Bernardo Yorba, owner of the Rancho Cañón de Santa Ana in present-day Orange County.[22] Yorba had died on November 20, 1858, leaving the ranch to his wife and several children. His widow, now married to someone else, wished to formally divide the ranch between her children and herself by a legal partition, a complicated and expensive proceeding since the services of referees, surveyors, and appraisers were required. The lawsuit, involving large fees, was exactly the kind of case that Stanford and Ramírez had hoped to attract.

Legal documents drafted by Stanford and Ramírez, as well as other attorneys, were learned, uniformly well written, and sometimes even elegant. It seems impossible that early Los Angeles lawyers, often men of dubious learning, could have produced them. The reason for their apparent erudition becomes clear when it is realized that the papers they filed in court were not original. Instead, legal documents were copied from books containing forms of every kind. Spaces for names, dates, and a few indispensable facts were left blank, to be filled in by the attorney. Lawyers could produce almost any kind of pleading or motion needed by copying from a form book. Such books also contained hundreds of transactional documents like sample contracts, deeds, and mortgages. One of the most popular of these books was a 1,166-page volume published in San Francisco called *Forms and Use of Blanks, Being Over 1,000 Forms*.[23] In 1866 it cost $300, a huge expense at the time, but few lawyers could function without one.

The bulk of legal work done by Stanford and Ramírez took place outside the district court. Most of the cases they litigated were heard in justice courts and the county court. The organization of these courts in Los Angeles was based on a statutory plan imposed throughout California. It tended to favor the employment of lawyers and helped to keep Stanford and Ramírez busy.[24]

The lowest rung of the judicial system was that of the justice courts. There were about six such courts in Los Angeles County during most of the 1870s. They were presided over by justices of the peace, men elected for a term of two years, who did not have to be lawyers. Their brief terms required them to frequently run for reelection, a reality that helped to moderate their behavior and caused them to avoid unpopular decisions. Justices of the peace were paid no salaries but were authorized by law to collect fees for their services from the parties in the civil and criminal cases appearing before them. The fines they assessed in minor criminal matters often exactly matched their fees. Positions as justice of the peace were desirable enough to attract candidates at every election. A certain dignity was attached to the office since justices of the peace were addressed as "judge"—a title customarily retained for the rest of their lives.

In 1872 the justice courts had jurisdiction of civil cases where the amount demanded was less than $300. To meet this limit many cases were filed asking for $299. This was not a small sum of money at the time. It was about ten months of wages for an ordinary laborer at the prevailing rate of one dollar a day. A few highly skilled workers earned as much as five dollars a day, but even at that rate it would take three months to accumulate $299. A fairly good adobe house could be bought in Los Angeles for around $300. Ex-governor John G. Downey would sell twenty acres of ranch land for $300 at fifteen dollars per acre. Based on the value of money in the 1870s, the potential stakes in justice court proceedings were not necessarily inconsequential.

Justice courts in the 1870s were an essential part of the judicial system. They operated in the same way as courts on a higher level. Lawyers filed lawsuits in them, and cases were conducted in the same manner as in the higher courts, even to the point of having jury trials. A criminal side also existed in the justice courts, which had jurisdiction over minor charges such as petty theft and breaches of the peace. Punishments were limited to fines not exceeding $500 or six months in jail. A part-time deputy marshal was retained by each justice of the peace to control criminal defendants in custody. The wages of the deputy were not a public charge since they were paid from fees collected by the justice courts. No one found guilty was spared from jail without paying a fine that the justice of the peace used for his own fee and the cost of a deputy marshal.[25]

The only courts with less standing than the justice courts were those that the legislature identified as "inferior municipal courts." They had no role other than to process the most minor criminal offenses, such as public drunkenness. Los Angeles had a single court in this category, alternately known as a police court or city court. It was presided over for several years by Bryant Lorenzo Peel, a commission merchant with no legal training. The local press gave this court much coverage, seemingly amused by the embarrassment of intoxicated citizens picked up by the police. The city's newspapers constantly contained wry, somewhat comical descriptions of remorseful hungover defendants appearing before Judge B. L. Peel.

The next level in the judicial hierarchy was the county court, which was presided over by a judge who was required to be a lawyer. Judges of the county court were elected for a four-year term. The court had no original jurisdiction respecting claims for money. Those with complaints alleging $300 or more in damages had to bypass it and proceed directly to the next level, the district court. Rather than hear original demands for money, the county court was mandated by the legislature to hear and decide appeals taken from the justice courts. Except in rare cases where a special writ was possible, decisions on appeal from the justice courts were final.

Stanford and Ramírez participated in scores of appeals from the justice courts to the county court. Appeals could be decided by reviewing the record from the lower court, but usually there was a trial *de novo*, meaning that the case appealed from was tried all over again in the county court. This practice tended to create strange results when both courts held jury trials. Sometimes the same case was heard by two different juries with opposite verdicts.[26] This created a strain on litigants, facing uncertain outcomes, who had to pay attorney fees and costs for two separate trials when they could never recover more than $299, the limit of the justice courts' jurisdiction. Nevertheless, appeals to the county court were often little deterred by economic or practical considerations.

The practice of having a second trial on appeal to the county court sometimes ended up disastrously. In one case Ramírez represented an impecunious artist against Antonio Coronel, a famous and wealthy Los Angeles resident, once the state treasurer. The artist claimed that Coronel had brought him from San Francisco to give his wife art lessons in exchange for a large sum of money. After three and one-half months of lessons, the artist was paid only twenty-five dollars. Ramírez sued in the justice court for $299 on behalf of the artist. After a full-fledged jury trial the artist was given a judgment for fifty dollars. Coronel's attorney, Volney E. Howard, appealed to the county court, where yet another jury trial was conducted. This time the artist lost and was awarded nothing. Worse, the court assessed $51.15 in costs against him, which he was ordered to pay.[27]

Attorneys were sometimes willing to file complaints in the justice courts for such small amounts that no favorable result was possible after the inevitable appeal to the county court. Stanford and Ramírez were guilty of doing so more than once. Incredibly, in one case they represented a client in the El Monte Justice Court, where they demanded a mere twenty dollars for unpaid wages. There was actually a jury trial over this small amount, with a verdict for their client of only five dollars. They appealed to the county court, where they were given a new trial and finally awarded the requested twenty dollars. Their client paid $56.65 in court costs to attain the judgment![28] Although the court ordered the defendant to reimburse the costs, he may not have done so. The attorney fees must have been substantial, since they included several hours of buggy rides from downtown Los Angeles to El Monte in pursuit of a trifling judgment.

Stanford and Ramírez usually appeared before justices of the peace in downtown Los Angeles such as John Trafford, William H. Gray, and Pedro C. Carrillo. Civil and criminal appeals to the county court were handled first by Judge Ignacio Sepúlveda, then later by Judge Harvey K. S. O'Melveny. As noted, the county court was confined to hearing appeals from the justice courts on money matters, but it had original jurisdiction in other areas. One of the county court's most important functions was to adjudicate probate cases, the process of distributing the estates of decedents to their heirs. It was the only court authorized to do so, sometimes ruling on cases involving huge amounts of wealth. It was the basic criminal court for felony offenses other than treason, murder, and manslaughter. The county court judge also presided over the grand jury, something we have seen Judge Ignacio Sepúlveda do with respect to the Chinese massacre and the investigations into the selling of votes in Los Angeles.

The highest judicial authority in Los Angeles County was the district court. Its jurisdiction embraced any money claim for $300 and above. It was the only court that could determine title to real property. The district court was also given exclusive jurisdiction to deal with equity cases, those involving the adjustment of disputes by ordering the parties to behave in some manner that the court felt fair. Such orders were discretionary with the judge, enforceable by contempt, and gave the district court great power. Both civil and criminal cases were appealed directly to the California Supreme Court since there were no district courts of appeal established in California until much later. District court judges were lawyers elected for a term of six years. Stanford and Ramírez had most of their business before Judge Robert M. Widney, then his successor, Judge Ignacio Sepúlveda.

Throughout the partnership of Stanford and Ramírez, their trials were held in the old Clocktower Courthouse between Main and Spring streets, just south of the Temple Block. This unusual two-story building, perhaps modeled on Boston's Faneuil Hall, was built in 1859 by John Temple, a native of Massachusetts. The twenty-nine-year-old Temple arrived in Los Angeles during 1827, married into a Mexican family, and became one of the wealthiest entrepreneurs in Los Angeles. His building was originally intended to be a market on the first floor with an assembly hall and theatre above. It was 120 feet long by 45 feet wide, built of brick, and surmounted by a cupola containing a clock with four faces, one in each direction.[29] Los Angeles County acquired the building for use as a courthouse in 1861, installing public offices below and the district and county courts on the second floor.[30] The courts were accessed by interior stairways on the east and west entries, but the second floor was too crowded and uncomfortable to accommodate those awaiting trial. Lawyers and clients tended to congregate outside the building, usually on the northern side to avoid the sun. If they had the time, some might drift north a couple of dozen yards to the Temple Block for an interlude in one of its three saloons, a practice condoned at the time regardless of the hour. It was customary for the bailiff to call parties and witnesses when their cases were ready by shouting from one of the upper windows.[31] Lawyers were identified by yelling "Esquire" after their names. If it was known that an attorney was once a commissioned military officer, his rank would be used as a kind of honorific title. The partners often heard "Colonel Stanford" and "Francisco Ramírez, Esquire" bellowed from atop the courthouse during the anxious moments before trial.

The office of Stanford and Ramírez was in the Temple Block, the location of so many law firms in its upper floors that it was sometimes referred to as the "Lawyers Block." Besides having conveniences such as gas lights and running water, it was almost adjacent to the north side of the Clocktower Courthouse. From a stairway on the south side, lawyers could reach the courthouse within a minute or two.[32] The building was the work of Francis Pliny Fisk Temple, the younger brother of John Temple. Only a little more than five feet tall, he was called "Templito" by Mexican residents. He had come from Massachusetts to join his brother in Los Angeles during 1841. Templito soon married Antonia Margarita, the half-Mexican daughter of William Workman, a principal figure in the famous 1841 Workman-Rowland Party that arrived in Los Angeles from New Mexico. After the death of John Temple in 1866, Templito acquired his brother's adobe just north of the Clocktower Courthouse. Now wealthy, Templito ambitiously erected the three-story Temple Block on the site, a splendid brick example of

A view of the lower plaza area looking east, about 1870. The largest building is the Pico House Hotel on Main Street. Sonoratown is northward, on the left, outside the picture. The nascent American downtown area is partially seen toward the south, on the right. Reprinted by permission of the University of Southern California Special Collections.

Looking south on Main Street a little past the Pico House Hotel in 1880. In the middle is the Temple Block where most lawyers, including Ramírez, had their offices. Reprinted by permission of the University of Southern California Special Collections.

The Clocktower Courthouse in 1872. The Temple Block is partly visible immediately to the north of it on the left. Reprinted by permission of the University of Southern California Special Collections.

Italianate architecture. He also formed a bank with his father-in-law, called the Temple-Workman Bank, which he installed in the northwest corner of the Temple Block lobby.[33] The rest of the ground floor was occupied by various commercial tenants who paid a high premium for their privileged locations. The building was completed in November 1871, about the time that Stanford appeared in Los Angeles. The rent for an office in the pretentious Temple Block may have been excessive for either Stanford or Ramírez alone. The benefit of sharing office expenses was likely a factor in their decision to form a partnership.

At some point near the beginning of the new partnership, Ramírez received a proposition from an unusual source. An Italian acquaintance, Eduardo F. Teodoli, asked him to be the editor of a proposed Spanish-language newspaper in Los Angeles to be called *La Crónica*. Teodoli, born and educated in Rome, had only been in the United States for three years. For the first two years he was a typesetter in Santa Barbara, although he had not yet learned English. He was especially popular in the Mexican community of Santa Barbara, where he learned a fair amount of Spanish and entertained at parties with a pleasant singing voice.[34] Teodoli needed Ramírez since his imperfect knowledge of Spanish would not allow him to edit the newspaper himself. Ramírez was ideal for the position. Although a novice lawyer, he had more than a decade of newspaper experience. The problem with the offer was that Ramírez was already committed to a law practice with Stanford. There would not be enough time to function both as a newspaper editor and a lawyer.

It seems that a compromise was worked out—with the assistance of Stanford—allowing Ramírez to help Teodoli. Based on their behavior, it was probably agreed that Ramírez would only act as editor of the weekly newspaper for about two months. During that time he would do what he could for the law practice. After the first eight issues or so, Ramírez would return full time to working with Stanford. To divide Ramírez's time more efficiently, the editorial office of *La Crónica* was placed in Room 16 of the Temple Block, very near Rooms 9 and 10, the new suite recently occupied by Stanford and Ramírez in the same building.

This temporary arrangement was no doubt seen as beneficial to the law partnership. Stanford's brief association with Ramírez had already proved capable of attracting Mexican clients with land and money. Part of their success was based on Spanish-speaking clients' being able to express every nuance and subtlety of their problems to Ramírez in their native language, backed by Stanford's ability to win cases. By Ramírez's acting as editor of *La Crónica* for a short time, the partnership would gain publicity among the newspaper's Mexican readers. Teodoli was an entrepreneur with the support of several investors. Ramírez was paid for his services, no doubt contributing the money to his partnership with Stanford.

The first edition of *La Crónica* appeared on May 4, 1872. Ramírez was not named on the masthead as editor. Instead, the newspaper stated that it was owned and managed by "Teodoli and Co." The next week's edition reprinted articles from other newspapers commenting on the appearance of *La Crónica*. Nearly all mentioned that the new publication was under the editorial direction of Ramírez. The May 11 issue of the *Southern Californian* of Anaheim reported, "The 'Co.' after the name of Teodoli we believe, is F. P. Ramírez, one of the most sophisticated and popular men in Los Angeles, a talented writer and experienced journalist." The *Los Angeles Evening Express* of May 7 recognized Ramírez's editorship, calling him "a gentleman of ability and culture."

Several items were published in *La Crónica* that Ramírez thought would interest his Mexican readers. When "Colonel J. J. Warner" showed him a copy of a census from 1781 listing the names, ages, and racial classifications of Los Angeles's first settlers, Ramírez printed it in the May 18, 1872, edition. It was the first public acknowledgment that most early "Spanish" settlers from Mexico were actually hispanicized blacks and Indians. Almost no white men were involved. The content of this document is now preserved on a bronze tablet in the plaza next to Olvera Street, a revelation to residents and tourists ignorant of the city's past.

The July 20, 1872, issue of *La Crónica* announced that Eulogio de Celis had become the new editor-in-chief. As likely planned, Ramírez withdrew to continue his law partnership with Stanford. While editor, Ramírez had received a fair amount of public attention. One reader in Arizona sent a letter published July 6, which remembered Ramírez's days as editor of *El Clamor Público*. The letter praised Ramírez as a kind of genius and defender of the Mexican people. It even included a few lines of poetry in his honor. Throughout his time with *La Crónica*, every issue of the newspaper contained prominent advertisements for the law firm of Stanford and Ramírez.

After departing *La Crónica*, Ramírez retained a connection with the newspaper through his friendship with Eduardo F. Teodoli and Eulogio de Celis. He contributed occasional articles to *La Crónica* for several years. The newspaper survived in the Mexican community for nearly three decades. During most of its history, *La Crónica* was under the editorial supervision of Eulogio de Celis. Both Ramírez and de Celis were militant Republicans. As editor of *La Crónica*, de Celis was an advocate of equality for Spanish-speaking people. He quickly responded to insults directed at Mexicans with sarcastic editorials attacking American racism.

In one respect de Celis was absolutely unique. Although born in Los Angeles, he was educated in Europe, where his intellectual development was shaped in the classic Spanish tradition. No other local Mexican had a similar background. His father, also called Eulogio de Celis, was a native of Spain who had come to California as a merchant during 1836. The elder de Celis became wealthy, returning to Spain in 1853 with his California-born wife, Josefa Arguello, and their children. Young Eulogio received a privileged

Portrait of Eulogio de Celis, editor of *La Crónica*, date unknown. Reprinted by permission of the University of Southern California Special Collections.

education in Spain, France, and England, where he studied the languages of all three countries. Sometime around 1870 de Celis's father sent him back to Los Angeles with a power of attorney to administer the family's remaining real property.[35] Despite his European appearance and ability to speak English, de Celis apparently felt some degree of bias against him. He was joined by his brother, Pastor de Celis, in forming the nucleus of a Latin social circle with Mexican, French, and Italian components. One of the oddest members of the group was a French nobleman named Frédéric François, Vicomte Cazeaux de Mondran, which was usually abbreviated to F. V. C. de Mondran. Claiming a place in local Latin society, he was a sometime journalist who occasionally contributed to *La Crónica* since Spanish was among his repertoire of languages.[36] The dissatisfaction of the de Celis brothers and their friends with the American treatment of Latins provoked occasional protests in the pages of *La Crónica*.

While Ramírez was editor of *La Crónica*, the May 11, 1872, edition printed a circular calling for a public meeting in the courthouse to discuss some means to link Los Angeles with a transcontinental railroad. A short article written by Ramírez accompanied a Spanish version of the circular. It urged readers to attend the meeting scheduled for May 18 at 2:30 p.m., since a railroad was "of the highest importance for our prosperity, progress, and well-being."

Los Angeles residents avidly followed the development of a continuous rail line between northern California and the east coast, which was completed on May 10, 1869. On that day, tracks laid by the Central Pacific Railroad out of Sacramento officially met those of the Union Pacific from Omaha, Nebraska. The event was celebrated by a ceremonial meeting of locomotives from different ends of the continent at a desolate place called Promontory Point, Utah. But this realization of a long-held dream to connect the Pacific and Atlantic oceans did not benefit southern California. Its agricultural production still had to be transported by coastal steamers with limited cargo space to a distant northern railhead. Los Angeles needed a direct line to the north. Once there, it could join the intercontinental railway in order to forward local fruit and produce to markets in St. Louis, Chicago, and New York before they spoiled.

It was assumed that Los Angeles would someday be part of a national railroad system. This was a factor in setting the price of farm-sized subdivisions after the Civil War. Most residents believed that rail transport to distant markets would cause an enormous increase in land values and agricultural sales. It would also bring more people to the underpopulated region, accelerating Los Angeles's development as an urban center. Farmers, ranchers, land speculators, merchants, bankers, and business entrepreneurs envisioned spectacular opportunities with the coming of a railroad. There was a virtual mania for bringing rail transportation to the city.

The meeting of May 18 attracted 400 enthusiastic citizens. Harvey K. S. O'Melveny, a former judge from Illinois, was elected chairman. Several prominent persons were chosen to address the crowd. Democrats John G. Downey, E. J. C. Kewen, Volney E. Howard, and Benjamin D. Wilson joined the Republican, Phineas Banning, in speeches proclaiming the necessity of bringing a railway to Los Angeles. It was unanimously decided by those assembled to organize a Committee of Thirty to locate a railroad company that might be induced to run a line to Los Angeles.[37]

The most likely candidate to bring a rail line to Los Angeles was the Southern Pacific Railroad, headquartered in San Francisco. The company was an entity formed by the owners of the Central Pacific Railroad, which had already constructed the western part of the intercontinental line. The controlling interest in both the Central Pacific and the Southern Pacific was held by the so-called Big Four: Collis Huntington, Leland Stanford, Charles Crocker, and Mark Hopkins. These men, who had begun their careers as modest merchants in Sacramento, were inspired by a visionary engineer, Theodore H. Judah, to invest relatively small amounts in a dangerously speculative corporation called the Central Pacific Company of California. The idea was to survey a route from Sacramento over the Sierra Nevada and build a railroad toward the east, financed by federal subsidies. Judah unwisely allowed control of the corporation to devolve on Huntington, Stanford, Crocker, and Hopkins in exchange for their purchases of stock. These investors became president, vice president, secretary, treasurer, and directors of the enterprise.

An indispensable part of Judah's scheme was to obtain government financing. The construction of the proposed railroad called for greater expenditures than any group of private investors was able to make. Judah left for Washington, D.C. in 1861, just as he had earlier done, to lobby Congress for funding to build a railroad. He could not have expected the success he encountered on this occasion. Aided by Aaron Sargent, a congressman from California, his efforts led to the passage of a bill that authorized the Central Pacific to construct a line eastward from Sacramento, aided by federal subsidies ranging from $16,000 to $48,000 per mile depending on whether the terrain was flat or mountainous. In addition, the Central Pacific was given an enormous boon in the form of ten square miles of public land for every linear mile of track it laid. This award, ostensibly to help finance railroad construction, would make the Big Four and their railroad the largest landowners in California.

When Judah returned to California bearing the details of Congress's largesse, he was stunned by the cynical reaction of the Big Four. They proposed to falsely certify before Congress that the route for their tracks from Sacramento met the Sierra Nevada twenty miles sooner than it actually did. By this deceit they would receive an extra twenty miles of subsidies at the mountainous rate of $48,000 per mile, instead of the $16,000 designated for level areas. This fraud would net the Big Four a windfall of something like $640,000.[38]

When Judah refused to participate in the Big Four's misrepresentations to Congress, they used their controlling interest in the Central Pacific to shut him out of further involvement with the company. In October 1863 Judah sailed for New York on a search for investors to buy out the interests of the Big Four. It was a desperate attempt to get rid of his former partners, who had demonstrated greed and indifference toward the public welfare. Judah's mission was never completed since he caught yellow fever in Panama, dying within a few days of landing in New York. Any immediate hope of a railroad in California that would operate for the common good disappeared with him.

In the absence of Judah, the Big Four pressed forward with construction of the Central Pacific railway. They were challenged by a condition imposed by Congress that forty miles of track be completed before any subsidies were paid out. Since they had not yet attained much personal wealth, the requirement that they build the initial stretch of track on their own seemed an impossible barrier. Stanford, one of the Big Four, was elected governor of California in 1862. Using his political influence, he was able to rescue his colleagues. He induced the state government and several counties to buy Central Pacific stock to finance the first forty miles of track.

It was soon discovered that federal subsidies exceeded the actual cost of laying track, but the Big Four had no intention of sharing this surplus money with shareholders of the Central Pacific. Instead, they formed the Charles Crocker Company, making contracts with it for construction of the railroad. Most subsidies received by the Central Pacific were immediately transferred to the Charles Crocker Company for alleged construction costs. Ostensibly a separate company, it was exclusively owned by the Big Four, who divided its profits among themselves. In this way each of the Big Four drew excess subsidy money from the dummy corporation, and they quickly became millionaires. The Central Pacific was left with little money. Its shareholders eventually realized that they were the victims of a legally permissible swindle.[39]

Regardless of their rapacious and socially irresponsible behavior, the Big Four were highly effective individuals. Seemingly ordinary merchants from Sacramento with no special skills, they somehow managed to oversee the creation of a spectacular railway across the Sierra Nevada. During their association each drifted into a specialty at which he was particularly adept. Huntington moved to New York and Washington, D.C., where he assumed Judah's role as a corporate fund-raiser and lobbyist in Congress. Stanford remained in California, becoming president of the Central Pacific and an expert in obtaining state and county subsidies. Hopkins administered the corporation and its paperwork. Crocker, strangely enough, turned out to be a born engineer. He personally supervised the actual construction, eventually bringing 15,000 Chinese to labor on the ever-expanding railroad for miserably low wages.

Almost as soon as the Central Pacific began operation, small farmers and merchants complained that the Big Four charged unjustifiably high shipping rates. The cost of moving goods on the western end of the transcontinental railway depended on their whims. Rates were often fixed to gouge small shippers and maximize profits. The public was shocked by a realization that the railroad had no interest in their welfare. Huntington, Stanford, Hopkins, and Crocker were seen as greedy, ruthless men, devoid of any social conscience. It was apparent that they had used the Central Pacific to enrich themselves at public expense.

A popular wave of resentment and anger arose against the Big Four.[40] These negative feelings increased as the Central Pacific bought up the few existing independent lines in California, such as the Pacific Railroad Company, running from Sacramento to Vallejo. The Big Four began to encircle San Francisco's harbor with train tracks and moved to take control of the Pacific Mail Steamship Company. The people of California awoke to find that by 1871 the Big Four's railroad monopoly, together with its enormous landholdings, made it the greatest economic force in the state.

Movements to convert the railroad to a public utility or subject it to government regulation had no success. Political upheavals demanding public control of the railroad would last for decades, at least until 1910. Meantime, the Big Four perpetuated their freewheeling monopoly by bribing government officials and suborning the court system. It was well known that many members of the governor's office, legislature, and judiciary were on the railroad payroll. Both the Democratic and Republican platforms in California criticized the railroad and opposed further subsidies, but high officials in both parties secretly accepted money to protect the Big Four's monopoly. In 1871 the Republican candidate, Newton Booth, was elected governor on an antirailroad platform. Nevertheless, Booth's administration and those that followed were nearly paralyzed by railroad corruption. So many elected officials covertly sold themselves to the Big Four that the railroad's power became greater than the pathetically corrupt state government. A distinguished historian has aptly described this bizarre situation: "The fundamental contention of the critics that transportation rates should be subject to regulation is taken for granted today, but in the California wonderland of the seventies, it was inverted: state government was regulated by the railroad."[41]

As it did elsewhere in the state, the behavior of the Big Four created hostility and distrust among Los Angeles residents. The apparent need for a meeting on May 18, 1872, to discuss a railroad connection showed a lack of confidence in the Big Four's monopoly. Only the year before Congress had passed an act granting the Southern Pacific Railroad the right to build a line to Yuma on the Colorado River, provided that it proceed "by way of Los Angeles." When news of Congress's decision was published in the *Los Angeles Star* on February 4, 1871, the city went on a celebratory spree in the belief that a railroad connection was certain.

By early 1872 local railroad proponents were losing faith in Congress's directive. They realized that the Big Four's lobbyist in Washington D.C.— Collis Huntington—had enough influence in Congress to cancel the provision that the Southern Pacific pass through Los Angeles. The Big Four had good reason to do so. If track was laid thirty miles east of Los Angeles proceeding directly to the Cajon Pass, the Southern Pacific would acquire more subsidies in the form of federal public land. The route via Los Angeles mandated by Congress would necessarily cross huge areas of privately owned property that the railroad could not take.

Fearful that Congress would be induced to strike Los Angeles from the Southern Pacific's line to Yuma, the Committee of Thirty decided to make its own arrangements with the Big Four. John G. Downey and Harris Newmark were sent to meet with Leland Stanford and Collis Huntington in San Francisco. Downey and Newmark were instructed to make a deal to bring the railroad to Los Angeles even if the county had to subsidize its construction. State law limited the amount of subsidies that counties could provide a railroad to five percent of their assessed tax valuation. This amount represented approximately $602,000 that Los Angeles County would have to raise by the sale of bonds. But this was not sufficient for Stanford and Huntington. They also demanded a controlling interest in the Los Angeles & San Pedro Railroad owned by the city and county of Los Angeles. This local twenty-one-mile railroad had cost $225,000 to complete in 1869. It was now a successful enterprise and worth considerably more. The Big Four made it clear that the little railroad would be an unconditional gift. Downey dispatched a report from San Francisco, published in the July 8, 1872, *Los Angeles Evening Express*. He apologetically stated, "I confess the conditions are pretty hard . . ."

Another delegation headed by B. D. Wilson went north within a few days to see Stanford and Huntington.[42] Ironically, Wilson was credited with convincing Congress to place the words "by way of Los Angeles" in its act authorizing the Southern Pacific's line to Yuma. He had paid his own way to Washington, D.C. in 1871, where he enlisted California's congressional delegation to help put Los Angeles in the path of the Southern Pacific Railroad. Wilson later became aware of the Big Four's apparent ability to reverse his efforts in Congress. With a sense of resignation, he confirmed the earlier negotiations with Downey. Wilson then returned to Los Angeles to promote a $602,000 bond issue and a gift of the Los Angeles & San Pedro Railroad.[43] However, approval of the Big Four's price for a railroad line had to await a vote by the people of Los Angeles County since it would be paid with public money.

Ramírez did not favor giving a subsidy to the Big Four. The People's Ticket movement of 1871, which Ramírez had supported as one of its candidates for the state assembly, advocated a ban on subsidies to private railroad corporations. Those behind the People's Ticket believed that federal and local tax money should only be used to create a railroad operated as a public utility. After the meeting of Los Angeles residents on May 18, 1872, endorsed the railroad subsidy, Ramírez boycotted further such gatherings. Instead, he was involved in a statewide political movement directed against the railroad monopoly that would have an explosive effect on the coming election of 1873. Ramírez was helpless to prevent Los Angeles from giving a subsidy to the Southern Pacific, but he was becoming a leading figure in a political uprising designed to control the railroad and combat the corruption it spawned.

Resistance to the Southern Pacific was not limited to men like Ramírez and advocates of the aborted 1871 People's Ticket. Rejection of the Southern Pacific was widespread and greatly increased when an alternative presented itself. The *Star* of August 26, 1872, reported the arrival in Los Angeles of Thomas A. Scott, president of the Pennsylvania Railroad. Scott had obtained a promise of subsidies from Congress in order to build a rail connection from Texas to San Diego along the thirty-second parallel. The railroad magnate was conveyed to the Bella Union Hotel where local luminaries, including B. D. Wilson, gave Scott and his party a regal banquet. The outcome of the affair was a proposition by Scott to connect Los Angeles via San Diego with his proposed Texas Pacific Railroad. This would place Los Angeles on a transcontinental route to the east. The offer was entirely credible since Scott was an experienced railroad builder. In exchange, he wanted the same subsidy offered the Southern Pacific.

The question of whether to give the proceeds from a $602,000 bond issue and ownership of the Los Angeles & San Pedro Railroad to the Big Four's Southern Pacific or to Thomas A. Scott's Texas Pacific Railroad was also a matter that had to be decided by an election. There was a possibility that, despite the desperation of railroad proponents, the majority of voters in Los Angeles County would decide against giving a subsidy to anyone. To force a resolution, a massive petition was presented to the county board of supervisors, requesting that the railroad question be placed on the ballot during the regular election set for November 5, 1872. The petition was unanimously granted.

A presidential election was scheduled for November 1872, but in Los Angeles the people's interest was almost entirely focused on the railroad subsidy issue. There was little excitement when the Republicans nominated President Ulysses S. Grant for another term. However, local Democrats were surprised by their party's nomination in Baltimore of Horace Greely for president since he had always been a Republican. From the beginning of the Republican Party in 1856, the sixty-one-year-old editor of the *New York Tribune* had been one of its most devoted members. He was famous for his editorials opposing slavery. But unlike many Northerners, Greely strongly believed in reconciliation after the Civil War. He denounced vengeful Republican policies to punish the rebellious Southern states. In the hope of reunifying the country in a spirit of forgiveness, Greely bolted from the Republican Party to accept the Democratic nomination.

A minority of Democratic loyalists in Los Angeles supported Greely, overlooking his Republican antecedents. The *Los Angeles Star* of August 13, 1872, reported the formation of a Greely Club led by a contingent of the Southern Chivalry. Greely's plans to ease the suffering of the South through reconciliation appealed to those with friends and family there. The new editor of the *Star*, George Washington Barter, a conservative Democrat, wrote a September 18 editorial in favor of Greely, expressing the sentiments of many local Southerners: "Let us be friends again—let us have peace—let us be reconciled . . ."

The majority of Los Angeles Democrats could not accept Greely's uncertain conciliatory notions or his newly found allegiance to their party. It was the first time in Los Angeles that the Chivalry could not rally a majority of Democrats to their presidential candidate. However, Greely's long history of advocating liberal causes also attracted a fair number of supporters from the local Republican Party. An odd mix of people in favor of Greely wore special hats from Desmond's Store on Main Street to demonstrate their presidential preference. One of them was Ramírez's partner. The September 30 *Los Angeles Star* observed, "We are pleased to note that Mr. Stanford, of the firm of Stanford and Ramirez, has donned one of Desmond's best Greely hats."

Stanford's wearing of a Greely hat was probably intended as an amusing prank. There were few passionate advocates for either candidate, and most residents would see a touch of humor in his appropriating a symbol of the opposition. Stanford's true political leanings were shown in the *Los Angeles Evening Express* on August 9, 1872, when he went to hear a campaign speech for Grant and the Republican ticket given by a touring congressman from Pennsylvania. It was the custom, even at one-time political gatherings, to elect a president and several vice presidents to conduct the proceedings. Stanford was chosen as one of the vice presidents on that occasion, a gesture of respect and a recognition of his adherence to the Republican cause.

CHAPTER TEN
The Independent Movement and Prosperity

The presidential campaign of 1872 did not preoccupy Ramírez. He was already engaged in a developing political revolt that would not be fully revealed until the elections of 1873. Ramírez's opposition to railroad subsidies and his penchant for unconventional politics increasingly led him into a movement that rejected both Democratic and Republican leadership. It was based on a popular swelling of antirailroad feeling. Ordinary people throughout the state were becoming aware that the railroad monopoly of the Big Four had corrupted politicians from both parties, inducing them to promote railroad interests over those of the people who had elected them. Proof that public officials were secretly on the railroad payroll was seldom discovered because of the extraordinary discretion used by those involved. However, enough evidence existed to create a sense of outrage and betrayal on the part of small businessmen, farmers, and working people.

The reaction to the railroad-sponsored corruption was a statewide attempt to form an organization of independent voters who would put forth candidates of any political persuasion as long as they were honest. The character of a candidate would be more important than adhesion to the sophistries of party ideology. Those campaigning for political office would not have to conform to party discipline to avoid being cut off from money and support. Their needs would be met by what became known as the Independent movement. The basic qualifications necessary for a candidate would be proven personal integrity and the strength to resist railroad bribery. It was thought that if enough Independent candidates of good character were elected, the railroad monopoly could be brought to heel.

The strategy of backing Independent candidates was similar to the People's Ticket organized in 1871 by Max Strobel. As previously seen, nonpartisan tickets in local elections had long been popular in San Francisco. Strobel probably got his idea for the People's Ticket while visiting there. His efforts had died in Los Angeles County since Independent tickets like those in the Bay Area seldom spread beyond it. However, during 1872 the idea of independent voters promoting nonpartisan candidates spread rampantly throughout California. At first there was no agreement on what to call the movement. Eventually it became known as the People's Independent Party. In Los Angeles during the election of 1873, it was referred to as the People's Reform Party. But the most popular name for it among both friends and enemies was the Dolly Varden Party. It was so styled from a character in Charles Dickens's novel, *Barnaby Rudge*, a flirtatious young girl who liked to wear dresses of shockingly different colors. The novel's description of her wardrobe set off a fashion craze for gaudy dresses called Dolly Vardens. The unusual contrast in colors on the dresses suggested to some the extreme variations of political opinion among supporters of the Independent movement.[1] Men with normally antagonistic views and party orientations united under the umbrella of the Independent movement as a protest to the railroad's monopoly and promotion of political corruption.

Beginning about the middle of 1872, the Dolly Varden Party became like an unseen subterranean river, gathering momentum as its agents went from one part of the state to another. Its existence was not mentioned in Los Angeles newspapers until the August 16, 1872, *Evening Express* reported a local Republican meeting at which a San Diego lawyer named Charles P. Taggart described the degree of support for President Grant in his city. Taggart told the group that the Republican Party there was free of outside influences since "the Dolly Varden element had gone over to the real Dolly Varden party." The *Express* did not explain Taggart's reference to the Dolly Varden Party, assuming that its readers were already acquainted with it. Obviously, knowledge of political affairs did not entirely depend on the press. Taggart's audience already knew something about the Dolly Vardens.

During 1872 Ramírez was absorbed in promoting the Independent movement. This accounts for the failure of the local press to mention his presence at Republican Party meetings and gatherings on the railroad question. His political activities escaped public notice since there was almost no newspaper coverage of Dolly Varden activities. Likewise, San Francisco newspapers such as the *Alta California*, usually attuned to all political developments, made no reference in 1872 to the Dolly Vardens. The best evidence that Ramírez was an early exponent of the Independent movement appeared in the press later. In 1873, when the Independents overwhelmed local elections, Ramírez was a spokesman for the movement. He could not have instantly assumed a leadership position. A period of involvement on behalf of the Independents in 1872 necessarily preceded the prominent role he played the next year.

Ramírez enjoyed an advantage in working for the Independent movement that he did not have as a candidate for the state assembly on the 1871 People's Ticket. Since local Republicans were inclined to support the Dolly Vardens, they did not regard Ramírez's activism as a betrayal. As will be seen, Los Angeles Republicans were willing to surrender their organization to the Independent movement during the 1873 elections. Unlike the situation in 1871, there was no pressure on Ramírez to choose between being a loyal Republican or a candidate on an upstart People's Ticket. At this time, he was free to engage in radical politics without endangering his position in the Republican Party.

After Ramírez stepped down as editor of *La Crónica*, he and Stanford renewed their efforts to build a lucrative law practice. The *Star* of June 28, 1872, announced the publication of a Los Angeles city and county directory, the first ever produced. A quarter-page advertisement was bought by the partners to announce their location at "No. 6, Temple Block." They regularly spent money on publicity in the local press. Moreover, whenever their names appeared as part of a legitimate newspaper story, their law practice was promoted a little. Stanford got more mention in the press than Ramírez in 1872 because he attended Republican meetings and even looked in on rallies for a railroad subsidy. Like many other lawyers Stanford recognized the value of joining civic organizations to recruit clients. He soon enrolled in the International Order of Odd Fellows, becoming an officer of the group.[2]

Throughout the second half of 1872, Ramírez and his partner were kept busy by a good number of clients seeking their services. Neither of them received much notice in the press for involvement in local public affairs. Stanford was a newcomer whose place in Los Angeles was yet to be defined. Ramírez refrained from attending Republican Party functions while quietly working for the Independent movement.

The election of 1872 occurred without the active participation of Stanford and Ramírez. The railroad question, the most important issue for Los Angeles voters, was decided in favor of the Big Four's Southern Pacific.[3] The defeat of Thomas A. Scott's Texas Pacific Railroad was caused in large part by a pamphlet written by Judge Robert M. Widney, entitled "Which Subsidy Should I Vote for, or Shall I Vote Against Both?" This little tract, published by the *Los Angeles Star* printing plant, was mailed to every voter in the city. It argued that a Texas railroad connection, with its terminus in San

Diego, would make Los Angeles an inferior backwater. San Diego would be the principal depot of the railroad and emporium of Southern California, while Los Angeles would be nothing but a dead-end northern spur on a railroad whose circuitous southern route would never deliver fruit to eastern markets before it spoiled. The result of the election incorporated Los Angeles into a railroad monopoly that was the greatest political and social problem of the day. In comparison, the presidential election was of slight consequence. Grant defeated Greely in Los Angeles with an 82-vote majority, mainly by default, since most Democrats refused to support their party's nominee, regarding Greely as a member of the enemy Republican camp. In another contest—this one for a congressional seat—E. J. C. Kewen was defeated in a quest to extend his influence outside Los Angeles County.[4]

Toward the end of 1872, Ramírez was distracted by a scandal involving his older brother, Juan Bernardo, the family's first born. This person, not the same as Juan de la Resurrección, a younger brother who had accompanied Ramírez to Sonora in 1860, was sued for divorce by his wife, Francisca, on December 17, 1872.[5] The wife's allegations against Juan Bernardo were particularly nasty, accusing him of beating her and the children, as well as being a "common drunk." The court appointed an attorney, George C. Gibbs, to hear the case as a referee. A daughter, Petra, age 17, testified against her father by confirming his mistreatment of the family. The couple and their children lived in the Ramírez family homestead on Aliso Road, making Ramírez and his mother witnesses to their discord. Juan Bernardo claimed that his violent behavior was provoked by his wife allowing their fourteen-year-old daughter, Juana, to have sex with her cousin, Ramon Dominguez. Midway through the proceedings, Juana was found to be pregnant and married Ramon. But this did not prevent a judgment of divorce. Stanford intervened by representing Juan Bernardo, thereby sparing his partner from direct involvement in the family's legal turmoil.

By this and other interactions with the Mexican community, it appears that Stanford, a New York and Texas lawyer, was becoming acclimated to the local environment. The *Los Angeles Star* of December 28, 1872, published an item describing Stanford's representation of one David de la Osa, jailed on a larceny arrest warrant from Inyo County. Stanford noticed that the warrant was invalid because it had not been certified by a judge. He filed for a writ of habeas corpus before Judge Ignacio Sepúlveda, who had no choice but to order the prisoner's release. However, Sepúlveda wrote out a new arrest warrant in chambers, which he was about to sign, but "Col. Stanford was equal to the emergency." According to the *Star*, "He turned to his client, and told him in very understandable Castilian that he better *vamos* the ranch pretty damned quick, or he would be in the calaboose again before he could say 'Jack Robinson.'" Hearing Stanford's whispered exclamation, or something like what the *Star* claimed, the prisoner made a sudden exit from the court. The *Star* thought Stanford's action was "getting out of a pretty tight spot gracefully and effectively." Like many other American lawyers, Stanford had perforce acquired a certain knowledge of Spanish.

The presence of an Independent movement in Los Angeles was finally recognized in the press at the beginning of 1873. Newspaper editors could sense a coming disturbance in local politics. George Washington Barter, the Democratic editor of the *Los Angeles Star*, published an item on January 7, 1873, expressing early concern about the Los Angeles County elections scheduled for eight months away, on September 3. The elections would select a new state senator, two assemblymen, and a host of county officers. Barter made explicit reference to the Independents and predicted a breakdown of control over the elections by the regular Democratic and Republican parties: "The main strength of two parties will be arrayed in battle, and with sufficient splits and independents to make the chances of many individual candidates doubtful."

Barter, a Democratic loyalist, regarded the growing Independent movement as a threat to his party. He would no doubt have mounted a campaign in the *Los Angeles Star* against the Independents, but a scandal soon drove him from the city. The relatively young editor was a handsome man regarded as one of the region's prime bachelors, a belief he helped encourage. It was therefore an enormous shock when a woman from the state of Washington appeared in Los Angeles with two small daughters, claiming that Barter was her husband and the children's father. The January 15, 1873, *Evening Express*, a Republican newspaper, published a detailed account of the woman's suit for divorce in Los Angeles against Barter, which alleged desertion and failure to support his family. The answer filed by Barter's attorneys must have been mortifying. It denied that Barter had the ability to support his family and admitted that his newspaper was "hopelessly insolvent." His published claims of the *Star*'s success and his status as a bachelor were revealed as lies. Under these embarrassing circumstances Barter fled Los Angeles on a steamer for San Francisco on Saturday morning, March 29, 1873. This most unfortunate man, regarded as merely eccentric in Los Angeles, continued as a journalist in the state of Washington, where he eventually developed symptoms of severe mental instability. He died in a Seattle insane asylum on April 24, 1891.[6]

Henry Hamilton lost the most from the Barter debacle. He had sold Barter the *Star* under a promise of full payment, which was never made. Hamilton took back possession of the *Star* two days after Barter's flight from Los Angeles. The masthead of the March 31, 1873, edition of the *Star* once again showed Hamilton as its proprietor. This assertion of ownership did not mean that Hamilton wanted to resume the duties of an editor. He asked his old friend and one-time partner in Hawaii, James J. Ayers, to temporarily run the newspaper. Hamilton had lost interest in politics. He passively allowed Ayers a free hand in writing editorials. The emerging Independent movement appealed to Ayers who wrote in the April 9, 1873, *Star* that a "selfish clique" controlled Los Angeles politics, with the result that "private fortunes have been built up by nefarious practices." He cautioned his readers that the power of a "ring" dominating Los Angeles could not be broken unless "people of good political prejudices will refuse to commit themselves to the acts of their political managers."

Just as dissatisfaction with local politics was becoming more noticeable, the legislature in Sacramento enacted a pair of laws that had a profound effect on Los Angeles. One was a statewide ban on gambling after January 1, 1873. The other was a Sabbath law, requiring saloons and most other businesses to shut down on Sundays. The law against gambling permanently dampened vice operations in Negro Alley, forcing games of chance to go underground.[7] Thereafter, the streets were more or less quiet on Sundays, starkly contrasting with the drunkenness and violence of previous years. In general, Los Angeles took on a more placid aspect.

The legislature's attempt to regulate public morals had the support of those who favored temperance. A substantial number of Los Angeles citizens opposed the consumption of alcohol. Two of them, Jesse Yarnell and Thomas Caystile, issued the first edition of a newspaper called the *Weekly Mirror*—an advocate of temperance—on February 1, 1873. The newspaper's editorial stand against drinking did not get in the way of its commercial success. The owners had a radical approach to making money through journalism. Their little publication, about half the size of a regular newspaper, began by being distributed in the streets for free. Most of its content consisted of advertisements sold at lower than normal rates. The tiny paper became a popular advertising medium that made money without the need for subscribers. Stanford and Ramírez never failed to buy publicity in its pages at bargain prices. From these unpretentious origins, the *Weekly Mirror* gradually increased in size until it merged a decade later into the Times-Mirror Co., under the direction of Harrison Gray Otis, publisher of the *Los Angeles Times*.

Ramírez, who had been working almost surreptitiously for the Independent movement, was made a focus of attention at the Mexican community's 1873 Cinco de Mayo celebration. He was chosen by the Junta Patriótica de Juárez as the leading speaker of the day, a comfortable role for him. He had been the orator at the first Cinco de Mayo celebration eleven years before. The May 7, 1873, edition of *La Crónica* contained an account of the festivities written by Eulogio de Celis. It said that Ramírez's patriotic speech "was listened to attentively and warmly applauded." Afterward, a dance was held in Sonoratown that de Celis described in appreciative terms, including a narrative about the beautiful women he had admired there. He wandered out into the night seeing the "magical effect" of lights symmetrically strung across the rooftops. "From time to time a musical murmur of Spanish voices arrived at my distant and solitary place in the moonlight and I could hear the notes of violins and guitars from afar." It was a moment that de Celis thought "would be a sweet memory engraved in my soul." The pleasure of de Celis in such Mexican affairs must have been shared by Ramírez. The local press never mentioned Ramírez's presence at American social functions. He seems to have deliberately avoided them. His private and social life was entirely Mexican.

The coming of the Republican county convention, set for July 12, 1873, triggered an outburst of support for the Independent movement. The July 3 *Evening Express*, a Republican newspaper, ran an editorial entitled "People's Ticket," suggesting that the convention refrain from nominating its members to run for office. Instead, the Republicans were urged to send representatives among the voters to ascertain who they wanted to run for office, regardless of political party, on a People's Ticket. The editorial concluded, "The masses of this county are ripe for a local people's movement. Let abstention from nomination be the policy of the Republican convention, on Saturday; and place trusty sentinels on the outposts with power to accelerate and turn to practical account the sentiment that is rife in our midst."

The Republican county convention adopted a course of action much like that proposed by the *Evening Express*. A portion of its first resolution stated:

> WHEREAS, It is manifestly evident that the people of Los Angeles County and city desire and insist on having good and reliable men, irrespective of political faith, to fill the respective county offices, RESOLVED, That we deem it inexpedient to make party nominations as such nominations would tend to defeat the will of the people.

The convention appointed a committee of nine persons, including the editor of *La Crónica*, Eulogio de Celis, to meet with delegates "from the people" for the purpose of nominating a People's Ticket.

The willingness of the local Republican Party to subordinate itself to the Independent movement resulted to some extent from the influence of Governor Newton Booth, elected on an antirailroad platform. Booth had stumped the state, attacking the Big Four's Central Pacific Railroad, accusing it of setting unfair rates and abusing its position as the greatest economic force in California.

Booth publicly aspired to become a U.S. senator from California during 1873. The Republican Party opposed this ambition since it had elected him governor expecting that he would complete his full term of office. Booth's becoming a senator would require his resignation as head of the state government, an act considered adverse to his party's interests. United States senators were still elected by the state legislatures, not by a popular vote. Booth realized that most regular Republican members of the legislature would not vote for him as senator. He therefore determined to use the 1873 elections to pack the legislature with as many Independents as possible in the expectation that they would put him in the U.S. Senate.

Booth did not campaign for the Republican Party during the 1873 election. He devoted all his energies to the Independent movement. In the political terms of the day, he "bolted" from the Republican party. The *Alta California*, a staunchly Republican newspaper in San Francisco, bitterly commented on Booth's quest for the Senate: "Having been defeated at the primaries, he has bolted; and his organs are now trying to persuade the people that he must be elected [senator] to save California from the Central Pacific Railroad Co."[8]

An enormous wave of antirailroad sentiment aided Booth's political efforts. Outrage by farmers against the railroad monopoly resulted in the organization of statewide Grange and farmers' unions. A farmers' union met in San Francisco with the prestigious pioneer John Bidwell as its president on April 9, 1873.[9] The meeting produced resolutions against the Big Four's railroad that typified the protests of the time:

> That the rates charged for freights over the railroads in this state are ruinous to our agriculture interests. That if we find it impracticable under present management of such railroads to obtain a fair reduction on such freights, we will agitate the subject, and insist that the railroads built by money of the government shall be operated by the government in the interest of the people, rather than by private persons for personal aggrandizement. That as these matters are political, we will so far make this a political body as to cast our votes and use our influence for such men for our state Legislature as will carry our views into effect.

Booth appeared before such groups, denouncing railroad greed and corruption. The *Alta California* of September 2, 1873, ran an article about one of Booth's speeches, entitled "Dolly Varden Gathering," noting that the governor "had entirely cast his lot with the Independents." Booth made a speech on that occasion, criticizing railroad corruption and bribery of public officials. Booth swore to his audience that he "would bow down to no one and never wear the collar of a corporation."

An almost invisible organization led by Booth promoted the Independent movement. He sent agents throughout the state to encourage local People's Tickets. The July 12 *Los Angeles Star* listed several counties where the Independents suddenly seemed to be in control: Santa Barbara, Ventura, Yuba, Sacramento, Mendocino, Butte, Sutter, and Merced. The reach of Booth's campaign extended to Los Angeles as well. Representatives of Governor Booth in communication with the local Republican Party were a factor in persuading it to declare for a People's Ticket. The August 27 *Evening Express* recognized that this was the case, saying: "The so-called People's Movement here is, if not a part of, in sympathy with the movement in other portions of the State led by Governor Booth."

Los Angeles voters, having recently approved a subsidy to the Southern Pacific, were not as embittered toward the railroad as Independents in the north. Still, there was anxiety about the coming of a railroad monopoly, based on its behavior elsewhere. This was reflected in a resolution made at the July 19 meeting of the Farmer's Clubs of Los Angeles County in Gallatin, which stated the group's demands on legislative candidates: "That our Representatives to the Legislature will use every exertion in asserting the undoubted rights of the people in checking the rapacious encroachments of existing railroad companies on the rights of the people."[10]

Along with antirailroad pronouncements, the Independent movement in Los Angeles tended to focus on reforming local politics. There was a widely held belief that the city and county governments were controlled by a corrupt clique of politicians who exploited public office for financial gain. This opinion was held by all Los Angeles newspaper editors, among the closest observers of the political scene. In the weeks prior to the elections of September 3, 1873, the local press came out in favor of the Independent movement and a radical change in public officials. This was noticed in a July 20 article in the *Los Angeles Star*: "But the most imposing aspect of this whole affair is exhibited in the fact that the entire press of Los Angeles—the *Express*, *Crónica*, *Mirror*, and *Star*—are opposed to the longer continuation of party lines, at least during the coming election."

At the July 12, 1873, Republican Party convention, the delegates decided to sponsor a People's convention to select independent candidates. They set the convention for Saturday, July 26 at the county courthouse. The *Evening Express* of July 22 praised Republican support of the People's convention and rendered an opinion on their motives: "They intend that officials shall come from the people, and not from a maneuvering clique, who determine in a back room the candidates they shall permit the people to vote for."

The Spanish-language newspaper, *La Crónica*, agreed with the *Evening Express*. It published a special supplement on the People's convention, written by F. V. C. Mondran, a French member from the Latin social circle of the editor Eulogio de Celis. Mondran called for the newspaper's readers to support the People's convention and its "noble purpose of choosing honorable men from all parties to be candidates for office." He hoped that the People's ticket would destroy a ring that he alleged monopolized political offices in Los Angeles.

The *Los Angeles Star* was in favor of the Independent movement, but it did not have the support of Henry Hamilton. Beginning on July 1, 1873, Benjamin C. Truman took over the *Star* by purchasing it from Hamilton for $6,000 cash.[11] From that point forward, the *Star* was never again the voice of hard-line Southern Democrats. Truman was a political moderate, a sociable man with conciliatory instincts, who had been a reporter for the *New York Times* during the Civil War. He had served as private secretary to President Andrew Johnson until 1866, when he was sent to California as a high official of the U.S. Postal Department. When his federal assignment ended, he worked for Wells Fargo and was later a San Diego newspaperman.[12] Although he supported the Independents, Truman asked in the July 26 *Star* whether the movement in Los Angeles was truly "a virtuous uprising of the *people*, who are opposed to *cliques, rings, trades [of votes]*, and all the nefarious practices of professional politicians." He had a cynical opinion of how the Independent convention would be conducted. On the morning of the convention, he wrote, "If there isn't more trading and selling out done today by these same *indignant masses* than was ever done by the *ring* as it is called, then our head may be taken as a football."

Curiously, despite all the talk in the newspapers about a political ring in Los Angeles, no individual was identified as being a member of it. The editors openly stated that leading politicians belonged to such a ring, using their positions for personal financial gain, but they did not describe how this was done or give any instance of its having occurred.

The much vaunted People's convention met on Saturday afternoon, July 26, in the district court building. A Republican committee of seven met with an equal number of dissident Democrats who took leave from their party to help choose candidates for the "People's Reform Ticket."

The men they nominated were not likely to disturb the status quo. They selected a forty-seven-year-old physician from Pennsylvania, Charles W. Bush, as candidate for state senator, about whom the August 9 issue of *La Crónica* said, "Although a man of integrity, he has the misfortune of being unknown." The two nominees for the assembly were A. Higbie and James Miller Guinn, the first a Democrat and the other a Republican, but neither a political leader of standing.

Higbie's full name was never stated in the press. He was known only by his initial and last name. Two other candidates were similarly treated: Dr. N. P. Richardson for coroner and W. M. Osborne for road commissioner. Their anonymity was such that they cannot now be found in any public records.

Three other persons advanced for office were less obscure at the time. A young deputy county clerk with an odd first name, Jery W. Gillette, was nominated for county recorder. Lathar Seebold, a Prussian civil engineer, was selected for surveyor. The editor of *La Crónica*, Eulogio de Celis, was named for public administrator.

The most notable independent candidate was Volney E. Howard for district attorney. Once regarded as a principal figure among the Chivalry Democrats in Los Angeles, he had become something of a political rogue. Howard was disillusioned by the Democratic Party's nomination of Horace Greeley for the U.S. presidency, believing that the old newspaper editor inwardly remained a Republican.[13] His discontent extended to the Democratic

Party on a local level. In a debate with C. E. Thom, the Democratic candidate for district attorney, Howard complained that Democrats in Los Angeles were controlled by a small ring but that he never played a part in it.[14]

Howard's political bitterness aside, a fundamental cause of his adhesion to the Independent movement was his animosity toward the Big Four's Southern Pacific Railroad. Unlike the majority of Democrats, he favored a connection to the east coast along the southern route proposed by Thomas A. Scott's Texas Pacific Railroad. Several diehard Southerners, such as A. J. King, seconded Howard's advocacy of a rail line straight to Dixie. With the election's defeat of the southern route, Howard turned his energies toward undermining the Big Four's monopoly. An astute politician, Howard recognized the potential of the Independents to impose controls on the railroad. In his unhappiness over the Southern Pacific, he temporarily left the Democratic Party.

Besides Volney E. Howard, the best-known candidates on the People's Reform ticket were Francis Pliny Fisk Temple for county treasurer and William R. Rowland, the incumbent sheriff. Both were connected to survivors of the Workman-Rowland Party of 1841 who had come to Los Angeles from New Mexico. They were well-liked in the Mexican community, in part because they were associated with Spanish-speaking families. Temple was married to Antonia Margarita, the half-Mexican daughter of William Workman.[15] They lived a luxurious Mexican lifestyle on the Rancho La Merced, adjacent to Workman's Rancho La Puente in eastern Los Angeles County. Temple was prominent for his ownership of the Temple Block and a half-interest in the Temple-Workman Bank.

William R. Rowland was the son of John Rowland, the other leader of the pioneering Workman-Rowland expedition. Born in 1846 on the Rancho La Puente, Rowland was half Mexican, with the distinction of being the youngest person to ever occupy the office of sheriff. His mother was a Spanish-speaking native of New Mexico. Rowland's wife, Manuela, had a Mexican mother named Jesús Villanueva de Williams. Her father was an early American settler, Isaac Williams, owner of the Rancho Santa Ana del Chino.[16]

Members of the Los Angeles press, once enthusiastic advocates of the Independent movement, were generally disappointed by candidates on the People's Reform ticket. The editor of the *Evening Express*, Henry C. Austin, published a negative reaction to the ticket on July 29, 1873: "Individually the nominees are respectable, but without that normal strength which should characterize the leading champions in a cause of reform."

Benjamin C. Truman, editor of the *Los Angeles Star*, was also dissatisfied with the People's Reform ticket. He wrote in his July 29 edition that the Independent ticket "is weak in parts, a fact transparent to all." Truman prepared his own "independent ticket," which he published on his masthead. It consisted of a few names from the People's Reform ticket, but most of Truman's endorsements were taken from the regular Democratic Party ticket. It was an unauthorized amalgam of candidates of both factions, a virtual third ticket based on Truman's caprice.

The most dramatic protest to the political situation came from Eulogio de Celis, editor of *La Crónica*. His July 30 issue carried an editorial entitled "La Bofetada"—"The Slap in the Face." De Celis indignantly complained that both the Independent and Democratic conventions had insulted the Mexican people of Los Angeles by ignoring them in nominating their candidates. There was no genuine Mexican placed on either ballot, according to de Celis. He thought the omission of true Latin candidates was a deliberate affront to the Spanish-speaking community. De Celis pointed out that he had been nominated by the People's Reform ticket for the office of public administrator but had refused to accept the nomination. He believed that the office was too minor to be of value to himself or the Mexican community.

De Celis emotionally urged a redoubling of political effort by Latinos to ensure a presence on the ballot during the next election. To illustrate the potential of Spanish-speaking voters in elections, de Celis consulted the Great Register, the official record of those entitled to vote in Los Angeles County. The August 3, 1873, issue of *La Crónica* claimed that approximately 3,600 voters in the county were members of the "Latin race," enough for a significant impact on political contests.

The negative assessment of the People's Reform ticket by the Los Angeles press and its absence of Mexican candidates did not deter Ramírez. He appeared as a speaker on behalf of the ticket on September 2, 1873, at what the *Los Angeles Star* called "a monster meeting." It was held in front of the Pico House, "pronounced by all present the largest gathering of the campaign, and by far, the most enthusiastic."

Ramírez was chosen to address the rally since he was a major figure in the Independent movement, although barely noticed in the press. The *Star* reported that Ramírez "felicitously held his audience for nearly an hour, during which time he made a multiplicity of excellent points." The *Evening Express*, which had gone from disapproval of the People's Reform ticket to actual opposition, was not kind to Ramírez. The next day it took advantage of the occasion to denigrate him as a spokesman for the ticket: "He has a tearful voice and an emotional temperament, and recited a speech replete with sarcasm and very eulogistic of the Fusion ticket."

The September 3, 1873, election put Ramírez on the winning side for the first time in his life. Eight of the twelve candidates on the People's Reform ticket were elected. Only three from the Democratic Party eked out a win. One setback for the Independents was Francis Pliny Fisk Temple's loss for the position of treasurer. However, the other well-known candidates, including Volney E. Howard, running for district attorney, won by respectable margins. Ramírez must have understood that most of the People's Reform ticket did not consist of men who shared his liberal views. Nevertheless, the Independent victory at last removed old-line Southern Democrats from office, something Ramírez had wanted since his battles with the Chivalry as editor of *El Clamor Público*.

Two weeks after the election, the Spanish-speaking community held an unusually spectacular celebration of Mexican Independence Day on September 16, 1873. A parade took place that impressed the *Star*: "The procession was one of the largest that we ever saw in Los Angeles, being nearly two-thirds of a mile in length." The most interested newspaper, *La Crónica*, printed a detailed description in its September 20 edition. Behind dignitaries, members of La Junta Patriótica de Juárez marched two by two ahead of allegorical cars representing various regions of Mexico. A marching band marked the cadence with military music, followed by a mounted military company called Los Rifleros de Los Angeles, composed of four officers and fifty-two soldiers wearing smart blue-and-maroon uniforms in the style of the Mexican army. A long line of festively decorated carriages and over two hundred horsemen completed the procession. There was a pause at the Temple Block for the photographer, Henry T. Payne, to take a picture of the colorful assemblage.

Of course, this was Ramírez's element. He spent much of his time in Sonoratown where he was a respected figure. Over the years he had participated in numerous Mexican celebrations. As usual, he was in demand as the main patriotic orator. Ramírez complied with an appropriate speech in Spanish, but this time he brought Stanford with him and arranged for his partner to make some remarks in English. The New York lawyer may have felt out of place speaking before a group of Mexican patriots, but it was good public relations for the partnership. That night Sonoratown was illuminated by lanterns strung across rooftops and torches closely aligned in the streets. Their light revealed masses of Mexican flags and banners with the national colors. The usually cynical editor of the *Evening Express* was struck with admiration. The next day he wrote, "We never saw a more beautiful or picturesque scene than that which the Spanish-American quarter of our city presented last night." The final event was a spectacular fireworks display that concluded with a pyrotechnic Mexican flag on a hill ablaze with the date of independence: 16 de septiembre, 1810.

About a week before Mexican Independence Day, Ignacio Sepúlveda announced in the September 8 *Evening Express* that he intended to run for election as judge of the district court. The incumbent, Robert M. Widney, had earlier been appointed by Governor Newton Booth to fill the unexpired term of Murray Morrison, who had died in 1871. Widney expressed no interest in being a candidate to succeed himself, leaving the judgeship open for a contest in the election set for October 15, 1873. In those days the California constitution required a separate judicial election after the one for political offices. It usually occurred about six weeks later, presumably less affected by party politics.

Ramírez's reaction to Sepúlveda's candidacy has not been recorded, but he must have disapproved. The two men were so strongly opposed to one another on social and political issues that little warmth could exist between them. Ramírez's liberal views starkly contrasted with Sepúlveda's conservative, even reactionary politics. Instead of advocating the rights of ordinary Mexicans, as Ramírez had done while editor of *El Clamor Público*, Sepúlveda accepted the Chivalry and its rejection of common Mexican people. The life of Sepúlveda was spent entirely in the American community, where he was deeply involved in social and political affairs. Unlike Ramírez, he seldom spent time in Sonoratown. Sepúlveda preferred to avoid contact with the Mexican working class.

When the French invaded Mexico and installed Maximilian as emperor, Sepúlveda had volunteered his services to the imperial army. His reactionary tendencies were thus revealed. At that time Ramírez was editor of *El Nuevo Mundo* in San Francisco, struggling to raise money for the resistance against the French by the liberal government of Benito Juárez. He would have seen Sepúlveda's joining the imperial forces as a monstrous betrayal of his people and their ancestral homeland. In the pages of *El Nuevo Mundo*, Ramírez had constantly referred to Mexicans on Maximilian's side as traitors.

A minority of Americans saw Sepúlveda's imperial antecedents as a disqualification for judicial office. The October 4, 1873, *Daily Express* carried a letter signed by "anti-monarchists" who argued that only those who supported democratic political institutions should hold judicial office. The paper's correspondents thought that Sepúlveda had little allegiance to American ideals: "The gorgeous tinsel of the invading monarch had more charms for don Ignacio than the cause of Republican liberty."

If successful, Sepúlveda's efforts to raise himself from the county court to the district court would make him head of the entire county judicial system. It also involved a pay increase of at least $500 per year. The other contender for the office, Andrew Glassell, was a partner in the leading law firm of Glassell, Chapman, and Smith. Glassell would ordinarily have been considered an ideal choice for judge. He was a Southerner, a preeminent lawyer, and a reliably conservative Democrat. These qualifications were of little value, however, compared to Sepúlveda's enormous popularity. The October 28, 1873, *Los Angeles Star* announced the official voting tally, showing that Sepúlveda had overwhelmed Glassell by 2,320 votes to 772.

Despite Sepúlveda's lack of involvement with the Spanish-speaking community, many of its members felt a sense of pride in his election. He was one of the few Latinos in Los Angeles holding a position of genuine authority. Mexican enthusiasm over his success led to an ironic celebration on the evening of October 20, 1873. La Junta Patriótica de Juárez, originally organized to combat the French intervention in Mexico, gave a ball in Sepúlveda's honor at the Merced Theatre. This group, devoted to Mexico's independence and liberal government, was the antithesis of Sepúlveda's reactionary inclinations. Although just six years before the junta members had anguished over the Mexican empire, wishing to destroy it, they now feted Sepúlveda's election, overlooking his past support of Maximilian and his service as an officer in the imperial army. It was one of the rare instances of Sepúlveda's having close contact with a group basically composed of ordinary workingmen.

At the beginning of Sepúlveda's term of office in the district court on January 1, 1874, Stanford and Ramírez were fully occupied with their law practice. They had handled several notable cases during their brief partnership, which had led to an ever increasing number of Mexican and French clients. The great majority of their cases, scores of them, took place in the justice courts with appeals to the county court. However, some cases were tried in the district court, with four of them going to the California Supreme Court on appeal. Stanford and Ramírez joined Volney E. Howard to represent Bartolo Ballerino in a supreme court case heard during the 1874 April term in Sacramento.[17] Their client, the administrator of an estate, lost the case. The opposing attorneys were Glassell, Chapman, and Smith.

During the 1874 October term Stanford and Ramírez argued three other cases before the California Supreme Court. They won one of them for their client, Jacob Strelitz, a prosperous tailor and clothing merchant from Prussia.[18] The court reversed an injunction issued by Judge Widney in Los Angeles preventing Strelitz from selling land he had mortgaged. This time Volney E. Howard was on the other side.

Two cases appealed by Stanford and Ramírez in 1874 did not succeed. Francisco Ruiz de Ocana lost an ejectment against Matthew Keller.[19] In their final appeal of 1874, a Los Angeles merchant, José María Davila, failed in an effort to reverse an order for a new trial given by Judge Sepúlveda.[20] Stanford and Ramírez were intimately acquainted with lawyers like Volney E. Howard and Andrew Glassell. This would be an important consideration later in Ramírez's life.

Throughout 1874 Los Angeles was quiescent politically. There were no major elections to disturb a relatively tranquil time in Los Angeles. As many predicted, the officeholders elected on the People's Reform ticket the year before did nothing of a radical nature.

The celebration of Mexican independence in 1874 once again demonstrated Ramírez's stellar position in the Spanish-speaking community. He reprised his role as the fiesta's principal patriotic speaker. The September 19 issue of *La Crónica* noted his performance with approval:

> The celebration's president, Loreto Benavides, introduced the orator of the day, Francisco P. Ramirez, who began his patriotic speech. He traced the great themes of Mexico's history, celebrated its glories, mentioned its misfortunes, and gave hope for the happy future of his beloved country. After half an hour he retired from the podium amid an ovation from the crowd that had repeatedly interrupted his speech with applause. As he stepped down, the military company saluted him with several volleys fired in his honor.

The dormant state of American politics did not remove Ramírez from the public eye. As usual, he remained active in the affairs of Sonoratown, where he continued to be a leader.

The busy law practice of Stanford and Ramírez produced an abundance of money for both of them. The *Los Angeles Star* of September 27, 1874, observed that Stanford could afford to ship a luxurious new buggy from the East, which it described as "a model of elegance, lightness, and strength." This remarkable acquisition reflected the prosperity that he and Ramírez were enjoying. The year 1874 was the best that Stanford and Ramírez would have in Los Angeles.

CHAPTER ELEVEN
Panic, Death, and Dissolution

The *Los Angeles Star*'s January 1, 1875, edition contained a column headed "New Year's Receptions," listing the names and locations of prominent American families holding open house to celebrate the holiday. The paper's editor, Benjamin C. Truman, included his own residence, where his wife would receive guests from 11:00 a.m. to 9:00 p.m., assisted by several young girls. Among them was "Cornie" Stanford, the nickname used for Cornelia, the daughter of Ramírez's partner. Her presence in Truman's home that day was evidence of the Stanford family's acceptance among the city's elite.

The first part of 1875 was little disturbed by economic or social turmoil. Harris Newmark, a successful merchant well attuned to business conditions, wrote about early 1875 in his memoirs:

> Southern California was now prospering; in fact, the whole State was enjoying wonderful advantages. The great Comstock mines were at the height of their prosperity; the natural resources of this part of the country were being developed, land once hard to sell at even five dollars an acre, was being cut up into small tracts, new hamlets and towns were starting up; money was plentiful and everybody was happy.[1]

Popular support for political revolts like the Independent movement was beginning to wane. It was felt that after the great struggle to achieve power the Independents had done little to curb the railroad or reform state politics. The January 19, 1875, *Los Angeles Herald* articulated a sense of disillusionment felt by many voters after the first session of the legislature dominated by an Independent majority: "While the shouts of victory were echoing from one end of the State to the other, the Independents laid down their arms, trailed in the dust the flag that had never known defeat, and surrendered body and boots to corporations and office seekers." The article suggested that instead of resisting railroad corruption the Independents had succumbed to it, "defeated by the skirmishers of the Central Pacific Railroad corporation."

The controversy over the advent of the Southern Pacific Railroad was ignored by land developers such as the Los Angeles Immigration and Land Cooperative Association. It used the railroad as a selling point in auctioning off land in Artesia for agricultural purposes. The *Star*, on February 10, 1875, contained the association's announcement that 3,500 acres would be "cut up into small farms and homesteads" just south of the Norwalk station of the Southern Pacific Railroad. In addition to easy access to rail transportation, it advertised that "strong flowing Artesian Wells can be had on every acre of the Tract." Similar advertisements for auctions of land at Santa Gertrudes near Downey and Centinela in west Los Angeles County appeared regularly in the *Star*, beginning on March 12, 1875.

The expansion of land sales and auctions throughout the county provoked much enthusiasm on the part of the *Star*:

> It is very certain that at no time has the legitimate growth of the county, in all that pertains to permanent growth and prosperity, been of a better assured character than at present. With good crops in prospect, the old settlers are liberal in the measures they are taking for improvement and beautifying of their homes, and new-comers, inspired by the manifold evidence which they see around them of thrift and prosperity, are putting their hands to the plough with a vim and energy which foretokens success.[2]

The same column cited rapid population growth, as shown by an increase of 1,400 names in the book of voters, the Great Register, within the preceding eighteen months.

The impulse toward development accelerated in 1875 when John T. Jones, a U.S. senator from Nevada, proposed to build a railroad from Santa Monica to Independence, a settlement in Inyo County. After earlier purchasing two-thirds of the Rancho San Vicente from Robert S. Baker, the senator began to lay out the beach town of Santa Monica as a port and starting point for his railroad. It was thought that the rail line would pass through Los Angeles to Inyo County's silver mines at Cerro Gordo. From there it would return with silver bullion to a deep-water harbor in Santa Monica. The enterprise would be called the Los Angeles & Independence Railroad.[3]

There was great excitement over the projected railroad. A public meeting in Los Angeles on March 3, 1875, to raise stock subscriptions resulted in several of the city's wealthiest men pledging a total of $31,000 toward purchasing the initial issue of shares. The entire subscription requested by Jones was

$300,000, to be shared by investors in Los Angeles, Kern, and Inyo counties. Many stock subscribers envisioned the railroad extending far north beyond Inyo County to join the transcontinental rail line, thereby undercutting the Southern Pacific Railroad. This was particularly the hope of Volney E. Howard, always an antagonist of the Big Four. He went to Anaheim accompanied by some Los Angeles investors to drum up additional stock subscriptions. His persuasive oratory and that of his colleagues brought promises of over $7,000 in additional subscriptions.[4] The Los Angeles & Independence Railroad was in fact partially constructed but not beyond a line extending between Santa Monica and Los Angeles. Beginning service in December 1875, it would eventually cause an increase in building construction and land values from Los Angeles to the Pacific Ocean.

A surge in the population of Los Angeles exacerbated some of the city's long-standing preoccupations. One of them was the slowly growing number of Chinese homes crossing over Alameda Street into the plaza area. The *Star* of February 17, 1875, complained that Sanchez Street, between Arcadia Street and the plaza, was made a cesspool every day by the Chinese dumping the contents of their slop buckets on it. The newspaper reported on February 28 that the grand jury believed the majority of Chinese women in Los Angeles had come for immoral purposes. It accused American landlords renting to Chinese of rendering themselves "obnoxious to the public good." It claimed that virtually every dwelling occupied by a Chinese woman was a place of prostitution, although no reasons were cited to support the grand jury's pronouncement. Such official proceedings denigrating the Chinese reflected the enormous hatred and resentment toward them in Los Angeles.

In early 1875 the law practice of Stanford and Ramírez was unchanged from the previous year. It remained active, with the majority of its clients coming from the Mexican and French communities. However, the volume of cases did not approach that of the most successful lawyers in town. The partnership of Glassell, Chapman, and Smith, together with the firm of Volney E. Howard, accounted for most of the important cases filed on behalf of wealthy Americans. They were usually chosen by public officials to handle matters involving the city and county. These firms also attracted Mexican and French clients who were better able to communicate with Ramírez but who sought instead the reassurance of consulting with the best-known lawyers. This was true even though Stanford and Ramírez not only held their own against notable adversaries but frequently defeated them.

The trial of one such case, *Simon Levy v. Jacob Strelitz*, began on February 25, 1875, with Volney E. Howard representing the plaintiff.[5] Stanford and Ramírez undertook the defense of Jacob Strelitz, a prosperous tailor from Prussia, who was charged with the defamation of Simon Levy, a Los Angeles merchant. Levy was the agent of François Breón for collecting a loan of $10,000 made to Strelitz the previous year. Since Breón lived in Paris, Levy was empowered to act on the Frenchman's behalf locally.

Strelitz wrote a letter to Breón in Paris with the help of local French residents, advising him that Levy was behaving suspiciously, pressing for payment of the debt to Breón before it was due, and that he might intend to embezzle the money he collected from Strelitz. When Levy learned of the letter suggesting that he could be planning a theft, his outrage took the form of a lawsuit against Strelitz; he probably paid Volney E. Howard a sizeable retainer to bring it.

The defense of Stanford and Ramírez was quite sophisticated, showing a good understanding of the law. They said that the letter was an ordinary business communication, made without malice, subject to a privilege against defamation. They brought an amalgam of French, Italian, and Mexican witnesses before the court, each testifying in his own language to state that Levy was strangely aggressive about collecting the loan prematurely and that he had a bad reputation for honesty. Stanford and Ramírez argued that, under the circumstances, the letter was merely a warning to Breón, justifiably made, without malicious intent to further injure Levy's standing in the community.

The jury agreed with the case presented by the defense. They awarded nothing to Levy. The court assessed costs against him of $308.60 as the losing party. Stanford and Ramírez were awarded $100 as attorney fees by Judge Ignacio Sepúlveda under a special statute governing defamation cases. This amount was typical of court-awarded attorney fees after trial, regardless of the difficulty or length of the case.

The contest with Volney E. Howard was immediately followed by a divorce case between a well-to-do Basque sheep raiser named Baptiste Amestoy and his wife, Francisca, which demonstrated the ordeal imposed by the law in such proceedings.[6] To obtain a decree dissolving their marriage, the plaintiff husband had to show some misconduct by his wife as grounds for the divorce. The fact that neither desired to be married any longer was not enough. The kind of misconduct required was set out by statute: desertion, adultery, or cruelty. This also affected the division of community property since the spouse guilty of misconduct had to receive less than the "innocent" one. The attorneys for the husband—Glassell, Chapman and Smith—accused the wife of adultery since she had allowed another Basque, a shepherd named Jean Pierre de la Bord, to live and sleep with her in the house she occupied separately from her husband. The wife, represented by Stanford and Ramírez, could not refute the extramarital affair but countered with charges that her husband frequented brothels in Los Angeles and maintained a continuing sexual relationship with an American prostitute known as Eliza. She also claimed that he betrayed her by paying for the favors of Indian women in the street. These allegations were explicitly stated in her answer written by Ramírez.

The lawyers were forced to place these scandalous allegations in the court record to prosecute and defend the divorce action, but they had tragic results. The accusatory contest had no effect on the division of community property. Finding that the property had already been divided by agreement, Judge Sepúlveda made no ruling on that point. Instead, he focused on the custody of their ten-year-old child, Margarita. The conduct of her parents might have been worse than disclosed in the court file since Sepúlveda decided that neither party was fit to raise the child. Despite Ramírez's arguments on behalf of the mother and those of the opposition for the father, the child was sent to be cared for by the Los Angeles Sisters of Charity for the rest of her minority, a harsh result when viewed from a modern perspective.

Other cases handled by Stanford and Ramírez about this time were less dramatic. In one of them, a typical case of the time, they filed a lawsuit on January 1, 1875, on behalf of Bernard Dubordieu, described by Harris Newmark as "a corpulent little French baker."[7] He had a shop in Sonoratown and wanted to collect a $400 loan through foreclosure on property owned by his debtor, one Gregorio Gonzalez. A default judgment in Dubordieu's favor led to the sale of a lot on Eternity Street and an award of $60.24 in attorney fees to Stanford and Ramírez. In another collection case, filed on March 17, 1875, they unsuccessfully defended Manuel Dominguez, not a member of the famous family, on a debt of $225 owed to Romain Grand.[8]

Throughout 1875 and somewhat later, Ramírez was strangely aloof from the politics and social affairs that had once engaged him. This might have been related to the demands of his law practice, but it is still difficult to understand. For example, the May 9, 1875, issue of the *Star* announced the advent of the Union Club, a purely social organization with Judge Ignacio Sepúlveda as president. Its membership spread across the political and ethnic divisions of Los Angeles. Besides archly conservative Democrats such as

Sepúlveda and Frank Ganahl, the membership included liberal Republicans like Ramírez's old friend from the days of Fremont's 1856 presidential campaign, John O. Wheeler, as well as C. C. Lips and Henry Hazard. There was even a Latin contingent including Manuel Arevalo, Eulogio de Celis, and Eduardo F. Teodoli.

Joining such an organization would be normal for an attorney trying to promote his law practice, yet Ramírez did not do so. Stanford was a member of the Odd Fellows, but Ramírez eschewed contact with American social groups. He also failed to take part in the affairs of La Junta Patriótica de Juárez in Sonoratown. When new junta officers were elected on July 9, 1875, Ramírez was absent, although he had been a founding member and the junta's secretary for several years.[9]

The May 15, 1875, *Star* reported the proceedings of the Republican county convention, which in the past had usually attracted Ramírez's interest. On this occasion he did not appear as a delegate or nominee for office. However, several other Mexicans were present, such as Eulogio de Celis, J. J. Carrillo, and Ramon Sotello. With a lessening of Ramírez's involvement in Republican Party affairs, the half-Spanish, half-Mexican editor of *La Crónica*, Eulogio de Celis, temporarily assumed Ramírez's place as the leading Latino Republican in the city.

Anticipation of the elections scheduled for September 1, 1875, stirred a wave of political agitation during the preceding months. It began with a declaration by the local Republican Party that it would defer to the Independents, just as it had done in 1873. The *Star* of July 22 announced, "It is generally understood that the Republicans will make no county nominations, but will allow the Independents to select a People's Ticket, which they will support." More than a month earlier, on June 5, a group called the Los Angeles County Committee of the People's Independent Party had met and determined to run a slate of candidates for local office that they called the county reform ticket. The committee also chose eight delegates to attend an Independent state convention in Sacramento where candidates for governor, a congressional seat, and statewide offices would be selected.

The state Independent convention nominated John Bidwell as its gubernatorial candidate on June 25, 1875. A native of New York, Bidwell was an early California pioneer who had arrived in 1841 by way of Missouri. Bidwell was celebrated for his rectitude and honesty. He owned a plush estate in Butte County, where the mansion in which he resided still stands. Even though rich, Bidwell had once labored in his fields and liked to call himself a farmer. An advocate of agricultural interests, he was an opponent of the Southern Pacific Railroad's transportation monopoly.

The choice of the Independent convention for lieutenant governor was none other than Romualdo Pacheco, who at the time was actually serving as the state's governor. Newton Booth was elected to the United States Senate in 1873 by loading the state legislature with Independents. He was required to take his seat in Washington, D.C., by early March 1875, and he had therefore resigned as governor on February 27, 1875, to travel east. Pacheco, the lieutenant governor, finished Booth's term of office, which expired nine months later, on December 9, 1875. Pacheco remains the only Mexican to occupy the governor's chair during the American era.

As in the case of Judge Ignacio Sepúlveda, it could be argued that, at forty-four years of age, Romualdo Pacheco had become more American than Mexican. His father, a Mexican army officer of the same name, was killed in 1831 near Los Angeles during one of the region's frequent armed revolts. Pacheco's American stepfather, John Wilson, sent him to Honolulu for several years, where he received an education from New England missionaries. He returned home so well acclimated to American society that he was comfortable taking an Anglo wife, Mary McIntire, from outside the Mexican community.[10]

Apart from being completely at ease in English, Pacheco was a handsome man with fair skin and Caucasian features that assisted his entry into American politics. Before becoming Newton Booth's lieutenant governor, he had lived in San Luis Obispo where he was an assemblyman and county judge, eventually being elected to the office of state treasurer.[11] Although a Republican since the party's emergence in 1856, he now felt that there was a better chance of election as an Independent. This was recognized as a risky change of loyalty by the June 24 *Los Angeles Herald*, in an article referring to Pacheco's nomination: "His sudden conversion to the new faith may somewhat affect his popularity. He is open to the suspicion of having left the Republican Party because it would not give him office, and going into the Independent faction because it would."

As announced, the Republican Party held no county convention in Los Angeles, throwing all its support to the Independents. E. J. C. Kewen, a fanatically Southern Democrat, was reported in the *Star* as saying, "The Independent Party is but another name for the Republican organization; it is the lion's skin over the animal that brays."[12]

An Independent county convention met in the Los Angeles district court building on July 28, 1875, to put up a slate of local candidates that included few notable personalities. One of the best known was Henry T. Hazard for assemblyman, a lawyer who would someday become mayor. The other assemblyman candidate was Alexander Bailey, a justice of the peace in Anaheim. F. P. F. Temple, who had lost in the last election, was once again asked by the Independents to stand for county treasurer.[13] The candidate for district attorney was Steven M. White, a gifted young attorney whom the Democrats would elect as a U.S. senator fourteen years later.

Ramírez had helped organize the Independent movement in Los Angeles two years before and campaigned for its candidates. The success of the Independents at local and state levels was unquestionably gratifying for him. They replaced the Southern Democrats in city and county offices, men whom Ramírez had always despised. Like others working for the Independents, Ramírez's hopes were raised when they took over the state legislature. The great issues were the railroad monopoly and the pervasive corruption it spawned. The new Independent legislature was given a popular mandate to bring the railroad under state control.

Ramírez was soon disillusioned by the Independents, however. He made no effort to assist their campaign. After the Independents ousted the old Southern guard from city and county governments, they undertook no significant reforms. In the state legislature railroad influence and bribery were undiminished. The Independents had achieved nothing to distinguish them from political parties of the past.

Outside Los Angeles the Republicans did not surrender to the Independent Party. They put up a full statewide ticket in opposition to the Independents and Democrats; it was headed by their nominee for governor, Timothy G. Phelps, and their choice for Congress, the incumbent Samuel O. Houghton.

Meantime, the state Democratic Party advanced William Irwin as its candidate for governor and Peter D. Wigginton for a congressional seat. At a Democratic county convention held in the Los Angeles courthouse on August 4, 1875, John R. McConnell and Fred Lanbourn were nominated by local Democrats for the two seats in the state assembly. These men were unlikely candidates, neither being prominent in local politics. McConnell was a lawyer who had briefly acted in 1853 as California's attorney general and later was a Civil War brigadier general in the Fifth Illinois Cavalry. The other candidate, Fred Lanbourn, was an English-born foreman on

F. P. F. Temple's ranch.[14] He later opened a grocery store where his presence generally went unnoticed.

By acclamation, the Democratic county convention put forth Thomas E. Rowan to succeed himself as county treasurer. After a close and rancorous contest Cameron E. Thom was rejected as a candidate to serve another term in the district attorney's office because he admitted to soliciting votes from the Independents. Instead, a young lawyer named Rodney J. Hudson was selected. David W. Alexander, an old but robust pioneer, was named for the office of sheriff.

Each of the statewide candidates denounced the Big Four's railroad monopoly and accused the others of being controlled by it. The Democratic candidate for Congress, Peter D. Wigginton, gave a speech in Los Angeles on August 7, stating that the incumbent Republican congressman, Samuel O. Houghton, was elected to office "backed up by the influence of the Central Pacific Railroad."[15] On the other hand Volney E. Howard, now claiming to be an Independent, attracted a large audience at one of his speeches in front of the Temple Block on August 14, when he claimed that Wigginton was a tool of the railroad and that "there will always be an unseen power behind the throne controlling his actions."[16]

Pacheco intended to arrive in Los Angeles by steamer to deliver a speech on behalf of the Independents on August 20, but he took ill in Santa Barbara a few days before and did not come. A banquet to celebrate his visit had been scheduled on that day and paid for by several prominent Mexicans at the French restaurant Hotel des Princes on Main Street in the Downey Block. Since arrangements had already been made, it was decided to go forward with the banquet in Pacheco's absence. About twenty-five people attended, including Ramírez and Judge Sepúlveda. Both men made speeches praising Pacheco. It is likely that the bitterness that Ramírez felt toward Sepúlveda because of his youthful adhesion to the Mexican empire had diminished. *La Crónica*, on August 21, described their remarks and those of others on the occasion as eloquent expressions of Mexican unity.

The election results of September 1, 1875, confirmed the almost unanimous predictions of the local press. The Democrats easily defeated the Independents in state and local contests. William Irwin won the governorship for the Democrats, and Peter D. Wigginton took the congressional seat for the same party. In Los Angeles Democratic candidates swept the Independents aside. The only Independent to win was F. P. F. Temple, who gained the office of county treasurer. There was little talk of rings controlling city politics in the Los Angeles press, as there had been two years before. The crusade for reform had died. No candidate of either party accused the other of corruption. The election confirmed the general feeling that the Independent movement had failed. The *Star* of September 8 asserted that "the result of the late election is accepted as a coup de grace to the so-called Independent Party." Based on his refusal to work for the Independents, Ramírez had apparently lost faith in popular reform movements. In the future he would drift back toward the Republican fold, never to leave it again.

Just four days before the election, the *Star*'s August 27, 1875, headlines stunned Los Angeles: "A Terrible Calamity" and "The Most Dreadful Financial Crash of the Age." The event referred to was the sudden collapse of the Bank of California in San Francisco, the most important financial institution in the state. The cause of the bank's failure was not clearly explained in the press at first, but it was later evident that William C. Ralston, president of the Bank of California, had ruined it through silver speculation.[17] He had invested most of the bank's deposits in shares of corporations operating silver mines at the Comstock Lode in Virginia City, Nevada. When silver production fell off, mining shares suffered an enormous decline in value. The bank's huge holdings of such shares caused losses exceeding the amount owed to depositors. Their money, which had been spent by the bank on speculative mining shares, simply disappeared when the stock's value dramatically dropped. Word of the bank's distress caused a mob of depositors to make a run on it to withdraw their money, but most were turned away and the doors were locked. Hours after the bank's closure was announced, the body of William C. Ralston was retrieved from the waters of North Beach, the victim of drowning under mysterious circumstances that some believed was suicide.[18]

When the debacle at the Bank of California was reported in the Los Angeles press, depositors in the city's only two commercial banks feared that they would also collapse and rushed to get their money out the same day. The Farmers and Merchants Bank, headed by ex-governor John G. Downey and Isaias W. Hellman, had long lines of depositors withdrawing their gold coin, causing a depletion of the bank's reserves. A few doors south, the Temple and Workman Bank experienced the same phenomenon. The Panic of 1875 was on.

The situation was made worse since Isaias W. Hellman was on vacation in Europe when the panic struck. In his absence John G. Downey was left to make decisions concerning the Farmers and Merchants Bank. Downey met with F. P. F. Temple of the Temple and Workman Bank to figure out how to deal with the emergency. The men agreed to temporarily close both banks. Depositors calling on the morning of September 1 found cards on each of the banks' doors, announcing that operations had been suspended for thirty days.[19]

The *Star* of September 30, 1875, noticed the hurried return of Hellman from Europe. The next day the Farmers and Merchants Bank reopened with a lavish display of solvency. The *Los Angeles Herald* of October 2 reported, "The tables were covered with trays filled with twenty-dollar pieces, piles of gold notes were lying about, on the floor were a score or more of boxes filled with silver, and a peep into the vault disclosed a number of large bags puffed out with coin." Hellman was irate over Downey's suspension of the bank while he was gone. He knew that a large part of the money needed to meet depositors' demands was on hand and that with some sacrifice the bank could quickly get the rest. There was no reason to close the bank except for Downey's panic. Downey lost Hellman's confidence and was forced to resign as the bank's president. Hellman would eventually oust Downey from the bank entirely by purchasing all his shares.[20]

In San Francisco Ralston's bank was quickly revived by several wealthy businessmen who regarded it as essential to their economic success. A headline in the *Star* on October 3, 1875, proclaimed, "Great Rejoicing over the Opening of the Bank of California."

Meantime, the Temple and Workman Bank did not reopen because it was in a genuine financial crisis. F. P. F. Temple and his cashier, Henry S. Ledyard, were guilty of disastrous mismanagement by violating fundamental banking rules. They threw away depositors' money by making unsecured loans, based on sympathy and friendship, to some of the least creditworthy people in Los Angeles. When the panic caused depositors to make a run to withdraw their money from the Temple and Workman Bank, they could not get it. Their money was gone, dissipated all over Los Angeles in the form of loans that could never be collected. Temple's reputation for poor business judgment spread to San Francisco, a handicap in seeking money to refinance his bank. Strangely, despite his problems, he was elected on September 1, 1875, as county treasurer, the only Independent candidate to gain public office.[21]

Temple spent much of November 1875 in San Francisco, searching for a loan to restart his bank. After being rebuffed by several experienced financiers, he found an exceedingly wealthy man, Elias J. Baldwin, who was will-

[232] A Clamor for Equality

ing to lend him $310,225. Known as "Lucky Baldwin" because he had sold his stock in the Comstock Lode for millions prior to its collapse, he was a ruthless man with little sympathy for Temple's plight. He was interested in making investments in southern California, having earlier purchased the Rancho Santa Anita from Harris Newmark for the unprecedented price of $220,000, paid in cash from a box of money that Baldwin carried around with him.[22]

The loan that Baldwin made to Temple had harsh terms and a high interest rate. It was secured on December 2, 1875, by a blanket mortgage covering everything that Temple and his father-in-law, William Workman, owned: the Ranchos Potrero Chico, Potrero Grande, La Puente, Potrero de Felipe Lugo, and La Merced, together with an interest in the Centinela subdivision, and three large parcels in downtown Los Angeles, including the Temple Block.[23] A partner of Temple in the Ranchos La Merced and Potrero Grande, Juan Matías Sánchez, was induced by friendship to put up his property for security as well.

With money provided by Baldwin, the Temple and Workman Bank reopened on Monday, December 6, 1875. That night a banquet was held in the first-floor dining room of the Pico House to celebrate the bank's new beginning. The *Star*'s editor, Benjamin C. Truman, attended the banquet. He reported on December 7 that the scene was viewed "by hundreds of spectators through the windows." Baldwin was called by the *Star* "the banker's friend" and "the most solid and solvent millionaire upon the Pacific Coast." Continuous congratulatory speeches and toasts were made by various luminaries, including Truman, to honor the bank's resurrection. "The supper kept up until about 1 o'clock this morning, when the party dispersed with three cheers for Messrs. Temple and Baldwin."

Ramírez and his partner were witnesses to the drama surrounding the Workman and Temple Bank, but they had little contact with it. About June 22, 1875, they were hired by Temple to collect a debt of $467 owed by E. W. Squires and J. J. Bullis, the only recorded instance of their representing the bank.[24] The case resulted in a default judgment in the bank's favor on September 7, while operations were suspended. Consequently, Stanford and Ramírez may not have been paid for their services.

As was the custom of La Junta Patriótica de Juárez, it invited Ramírez to be the principal speaker at its celebration of Mexican independence on September 16, 1875. At eleven o'clock that morning a large procession marched through the center of Los Angeles, accompanied by allegorical cars, carriages, horsemen, Los Rifleros de Los Angeles, and two brass bands. Returning to a point on Eternity Street near Sonoratown, the crowd heard Ramírez make one of his customary speeches on Mexican patriotism from a large platform surrounded by booths offering drinks and barbecue. The September 18 edition of *La Crónica* gave an admiring account of Ramírez's Spanish oration:

> The speeches were begun by the lawyer, Francisco P. Ramirez, with one of those patriotic presentations he knows so well how to make. He deeply moved his audience with sincere and noble sentiments straight from the heart. He was frequently interrupted by prolonged and well-deserved applause.

As he had done the year before, Ramírez arranged for Stanford to be on the podium to address the crowd in English, a gesture toward promoting their partnership. Another American, Henry T. Hazard, a lawyer who had lived in Los Angeles since early childhood, also spoke after Ramírez. Completely at home among the assemblage of Mexicans, he gave a speech in Spanish with no difficulty.

Fewer new clients consulted with Stanford and Ramírez during the latter part of 1875, a sign of increasing financial stress partly brought on by the closure of the city's two commercial banks. The limited number of cases received at this time were somewhat interesting but not lucrative. One of them was *Andrea Lopez v. Mateo Garbalini*, where Stanford and Ramírez represented the plaintiff, an impecunious woman who claimed to be a cook and housekeeper.[25] She sued Mateo Garabalini, identified as her former employer, for $540 in back wages that had not been paid since 1872. Because of the poverty of their client, Stanford and Ramírez probably accepted the case on a contingency fee basis, meaning that payment of their fees would depend on collecting money from the defendant if they won. Otherwise, they would not be paid, an arrangement still common among personal-injury lawyers and others who represent clients without money against solvent defendants and insurance companies. Mateo Garabalini was represented by the partnership of James G. Howard and Henry T. Hazard, the latter the speaker at the recent Mexican Independence Day celebration. They lodged an answer alleging that the lady was never a cook or housekeeper for the defendant since other people did that work. Instead, Garbalini kept her for sexual purposes, as his "mistress and concubine." Besides, she had waited over two years to file a lawsuit so that her claim was barred by the statute of limitations. Judge Sepúlveda agreed that the case was brought too late, ordering it dismissed. Stanford and Ramírez probably received no fees.

A highly unusual case, filed on December 20, 1875, was captioned *Marcel Daguerre v. Bernardo Errecca*.[26] The plaintiff's attorney was Volney E. Howard. His claim was that the defendant, represented by Stanford and Ramírez, had thrown the plaintiff over a ten-foot cliff in a fight on the Rancho Trabuco. The fall had paralyzed the plaintiff's legs and "crippled him for life." The defendant was from the area of San Juan Capistrano, a Basque sheep raiser on his way to market in San Francisco. The case was settled for an undisclosed amount, probably obtained from the sale of sheep, and dismissed. The plaintiff had asked for $10,000, a huge amount at the time, but must have received much less. The resolution of the case suggests that Stanford and Ramírez were not paid a great deal for their services.

On January 13, 1876, just five weeks after its reopening, a card appeared on the door of the Temple and Workman Bank, announcing that it was closed forever. The massive loan from Baldwin had not sustained it. Depositors, hearing of Temple's lack of business acumen and mindful of Baldwin's unfavorable loan, had quietly withdrawn their money. There was no wild run on the bank as before but rather a gradual daily bleeding for over a month until the bank no longer had funds.

Temple surrendered control of the bank to two assignees, Edward F. Spence and Daniel Freeman. They would attempt to settle the bank's affairs and pay as many debts as they could. At the same time Temple and William Workman tried to establish homesteads on their residences to make them exempt from the claims of creditors, but they were not permitted to do so because it was too late. Temple was left with a small, insignificant part of his ranch only because it was in his wife's name.[27] Both Temple and Workman were ruined. They had thrown the dice with Baldwin and lost. A remorseless foreclosure on the mortgages they had given would ensue.

Ramírez's family was altered by the death of his mother on January 22, 1876. An item in the *Star* about her demise appeared the next day:

> We are pained to announce the death, after a brief illness, of doña Petra Ávila de Ramírez, the mother of Mr. F. P. Ramírez, one of the leading lawyers of our city. Her funeral will take place from the old family residence on Aliso Street, this afternoon at 2 o'clock.

Ramírez had lived with her at the Aliso Road homestead and vineyard most of his life. It appears that he stayed away from his law practice for several weeks during a period of mourning and was unavailable to help Stanford. More than a month after Ramírez's mother had died, Stanford began a trial in a wrongful attachment case entitled *Seriah Perpich v. Jose Redona*.[28] On March 4, 1876, in Ramírez's absence, Stanford presented the highly experienced Cameron E. Thom and his nephew, Erskine M. Ross, to the court as co-counsel to assist him at trial. Not long afterward, Ramírez rejoined his partner.

A trial in the district court on March 14, 1876, in the matter of *T. J. Askins v. John Wilson*, once again placed Volney E. Howard in opposition to Stanford and Ramírez.[29] Howard represented the plaintiff, who had a judgment for $2,000 against one Joshua Hewitt. Howard attempted to show that John Wilson took ownership of a business from Hewitt without paying him anything in order to prevent the plaintiff from selling the business to satisfy his judgment. He claimed that there was a fraud against creditors and demanded the return of the business or $2,000.

Ramírez's client, John Wilson, took the stand and conceded that he had not paid Hewitt directly when he bought the business. Instead, Hewitt had asked him to pay someone else to whom he owed money. Ramírez argued that this was as good as paying the money to Hewitt himself. His client did not know of the plaintiff's judgment and was innocent of any wrongdoing. Sepúlveda accepted Ramírez's view of the case by rendering judgment in favor of Wilson. This trial, and others like it, demonstrate that Stanford and Ramírez could successfully oppose the best lawyers in the city.

The day of May 15, 1876, was extraordinary for Stanford and Ramírez. It was the first and only time they monopolized the second floor of the Clocktower Courthouse, which was divided between the district court and the county court. Stanford spent the day in the district court before Judge Ignacio Sepúlveda, successfully defending M. D. Hare, a Los Angeles deputy marshal, from a claim that he had wrongfully sold a horse worth $700 under a writ of execution.[30]

At the same time, next door in the county court Ramírez was arguing an unusual case involving a woman named Eulalia Pérez Guillen. It was claimed that Mission San Gabriel records proved that she was 138 years old. Although this was never established, she undoubtedly had lived more than a century. Her daughter Mariana was persuaded by a group of speculators, who would pay for the trip, to take her mother to Philadelphia and exhibit her at the 1876 Centennial Celebration, where admission would be charged to see "the world's oldest person." Another daughter of the ancient lady opposed the trip, petitioning the county judge, H. K. S. O'Melveny, to make her the guardian of her mother so that she could prevent her from going. Ramírez was hired by Mariana, with money from the speculators, to oppose the guardianship. Steven M. White, a rising young attorney, was retained by members of the family who were against the trip to Philadelphia. Judge O'Melveny rejected Ramírez's side, ordering Mariana not to take her mother out of Los Angeles County and to post a $500 bond as a guarantee that she would not do so. The case was reported by the local press in detail.[31]

While Stanford and Ramírez were occupied with these cases in the courthouse, the horrendous consequences of F. P. F. Temple's defaulted loan with Lucky Baldwin began to unfold. Before noon on May 17, 1876, one of Baldwin's agents, Richard Garvey, went to Workman's ranch to announce that he was taking possession of the property under the foreclosed mortgage. Between 5:00 and 6:00 p.m. that day, Workman went into the parlor of his house, placed a revolver under his right ear, and pulled the trigger.[32] The suicide of the seventy-six-year-old pioneer caused enormous consternation. The *Herald* of May 19, 1876, naturally attributed his death to the sudden loss of a great fortune. It said that Workman feared that "he would be swallowed in the vortex and himself thrown upon the world without means. This drove the old gentleman to desperation, and in a moment of wild despair, he sent a bullet crashing through his brain." The *Los Angeles Daily Republican* was in accord: "Of late the deceased has been impressed with the morbid fear that the assignees would turn him penniless from his homestead and to save himself from the disgrace took his own life." The paper added a comment on the ultimate cause of the tragedy: "He was driven to his death by the scoundrels who managed the bank and they are responsible before God for his death."

Workman's suicide occurred at the beginning of a decline in southern California's economy. The Panic of 1875 reversed a boom in the region that had begun soon after the Civil War. A distinguished historian has described the phenomenon:

> All over the county the panic brought a sudden collapse of the boom. Land sales fell off abruptly and prices of unimproved land in the south-county region dropped from a high of $100 an acre to between $30 and $65. Los Angeles county's assessed valuation, which had risen two to three million dollars since 1868, retreated for the first time in 1876. The

promoters of Downey, Orange and practically every new community along the railroad soon found the influx of settlers dwindling off.[33]

Hard times in 1876 were aggravated by a drought, which became markedly worse in 1877. Los Angeles County was no longer inviting to immigrants. For the first time the population actually declined. Instead of receiving new arrivals there was a movement to leave Los Angeles County. This loss of people demonstrated the severe financial distress of newcomers who could not find work or afford to buy land. The exodus retarding the county's development is verified by official records:

> During the late 1870's this downward trend in population continued, so that by 1880 the city's census figure had fallen to 11,183 from an estimated 16,000 persons in 1876. In these same years the number of county votes cast in Presidential elections dropped from 6,656 to 6,086. School attendance, which had been 9,239 in 1876, stood at only 6,022 three years later. So deadening was the effect that even the first Los Angeles Chamber of Commerce passed out of existence.[34]

Depressed economic conditions continuing beyond 1877 had a negative effect on Stanford and Ramírez. From the middle of 1876 until the end of their partnership about a year and a half later, they experienced a discouraging reduction in legal business. This must have caused them both to contemplate the future of their partnership.

A curious feature of Ramírez's life at this time was his continued lack of participation in organized Mexican civic affairs. While his advocacy of Mexican people in the pages of *El Clamor Público* might be remembered, the militancy of that period was nearly two decades distant. During his editorship of *El Nuevo Mundo* in San Francisco, he had enjoyed the unanimous, unyielding support of the Los Angeles Junta Patriótica in his efforts to become treasurer of the state Junta Central. Now he had no role in the junta's leadership. Ramírez had become a kind of elder statesman, a notable figure invited to make speeches for Mexican celebrations, but he took little part in the daily concerns of his people.

His disengagement is exemplified by an organization called the Sociedad Hispano-Americana de Beneficencia Mutua—the Hispano-American Society of Mutual Beneficence—also known as the Mexican Benevolent Society. The group's first meeting was mentioned in *La Crónica* on May 12, 1875, the culmination of efforts since 1874 by the paper's editor, Eulogio de Celis, to

[238]   A Clamor for Equality

organize it. The cost of membership was two and a half dollars a year, with dues employed to retain a doctor for sick members, to bury the dead, and to assist widows and children. Several other ethnic groups, such as the French Benevolent Society, the Turnverein-Germania, the Hebrew Benevolent Society, and the Sons of St. Patrick, had already formed similar associations.

A Mexican Benevolent Society would have strongly appealed to Ramírez in his youth. It was a step toward Mexican organization and unity, exactly as he had espoused in *El Clamor Público*. There was even a kind of pan-Latin aspect that Ramírez had favored while editor of *El Nuevo Mundo* in San Francisco. A Frenchman, F. V. C. Mondran, was on the board of directors, as well as an Italian, E. F. Teodoli. Several members were partly Mexican, such as Andrés Warner and James Kays. A picnic in the Arroyo Seco given by the Mexican organization was heavily attended by members of the French Benevolent Society, with the French consul, J. A. Moerenhout, proposing toasts in honor of the greater Latin community of Los Angeles.[35] This gesture toward Latin unity was in part a reflection of Eulogio de Celis's social circle, which consisted of Mexican, Spanish, French, and Italian members. There is no record of Ramírez's being involved with the Mexican Benevolent Society. He did not attend the picnic in the Arroyo Seco or spend much time with de Celis and his friends.

Ramírez's apathy toward social and civic events among his friends in Sonoratown developed slowly. He had previously enjoyed Mexican fiestas and celebrations. His negative attitude respecting similar matters among Americans was of much longer standing. He was seldom involved in American activities outside of business and politics. While Ramírez always observed Mexican Independence Day with impassioned oratory, he never once had the slightest role in the Fourth of July, ignoring it entirely. Unlike Judge Ignacio Sepúlveda, the principal Fourth of July orator in 1872, Ramírez avoided the American holiday.

As was his custom, Ramírez had nothing to do with the 1876 Fourth of July, a centennial celebration of the Declaration of Independence. The most spectacular event of its kind ever held in Los Angeles, the whole city was decorated with flags and the national colors. An enormous parade of allegorical cars, carriages, and marching men carrying banners passed through the streets. Except for Chinese, blacks, and Indians, every ethnic group and organization in the city was represented, including the French Benevolent Society and the Junta Patriótica de Juárez. The local press carried long descriptions of the festivities and those who participated, but none made mention of Ramírez.[36] He probably confined himself to looking down on the excitement in the street from the window of his office in the Temple Block.

A sign that Ramírez was being drawn back into politics occurred on July 31, 1876. He went to what the *Star* called on the next day "a monster meeting" of Republicans in support of the national convention's choice of Rutherford B. Hayes as its presidential candidate. A large skating rink hired by the local Republican Party was the scene of a speech by George L. Woods, a former governor of Oregon, who praised his party and its nominee. Ramírez's old friend John O. Wheeler presided over the meeting attended by several hundred persons. As it began, he called Ramírez to the podium as a vice president to sit with the speaker.[37] About twenty of the most prominent Republicans present were likewise asked to ascend the platform. This was a public honor, confirming that Ramírez was still well regarded among the Republicans.

A monumental event in the history of Los Angeles took place on September 5, 1876. On that day a railroad connection between Los Angeles and San Francisco was declared officially completed. A trainload of leading Los Angeles citizens departed at 9:00 a.m. from the Southern Pacific's downtown depot, heading north toward Soledad Canyon for a great celebration at a point where the tracks from San Francisco at last met those of Los Angeles by passing through the San Fernando Tunnel. There they would meet a train from San Francisco carrying politicians and railroad dignitaries.[38]

A rail line between the two cities had waited for over a year while more than a thousand Chinese coolies dug the San Fernando Tunnel through 7,684 feet of granite.[39] This colossal project resulted in the third largest railroad tunnel in the United States. The lives of a large, but unknown number of Chinese and other workers were sacrificed boring the giant hole through the San Fernando mountain. The tunnel cost more than $2 million, over three times the $602,000 subsidy put up by the city of Los Angeles.

Accompanied by a brass band and the blasts of locomotive whistles, the president of the Southern Pacific Railroad, Charles Crocker, deftly drove a ceremonial golden spike into the last section of track. By 2:00 p.m. the parties from north and south were traveling together toward Los Angeles, where a sumptuous banquet awaited them. The struggle of Los Angeles to get a railroad had ended successfully. The city was connected to an intercontinental rail system and all the markets that beckoned beyond. It was a transcendent moment when everyone understood that Los Angeles would never be the same again.

This curious photograph shows a train encountering covered wagons in 1869 near Promontory Point, Utah. The first transcontinental railroad connection was celebrated here in that year. Los Angeles joined this line in 1876, when it was linked by rail to the Bay Area. Reprinted by permission of the University of Southern California Special Collections.

The next day, September 6, the huge list of guests invited to attend the golden-spike ceremony was published in the *Star*. Hundreds of names appeared—practically everyone in Los Angeles County with the slightest claim to prominence. The list included politicians, civic leaders, merchants, bankers, lawyers, judges, and old pioneers. It is not known who prepared the invitations, but the railroad must have controlled the guest selection. The name of Volney E. Howard, an implacable enemy of the Southern Pacific Railroad, was omitted. The railroad did not care to entertain an influential antagonist capable of causing it trouble in the future. Another name that did not appear among the guests was Francisco P. Ramírez. His early opposition to railroad subsidies and his leadership in the Independent movement to bring the railroad under state control put him on a par with Howard. Fred Stanford accepted an invitation to the ceremony and banquet, but Ramírez spent the day elsewhere.

Just two weeks after ignoring the hubbub over the direct rail line connection between Los Angeles and San Francisco, Ramírez was again called upon as the principal orator at the celebration of Mexican Independence Day. This time he had a rival for the public's adulation in the form of ex-governor Romualdo Pacheco, a candidate for the fourth congressional district. At first Ramírez's speech was interrupted by loud applause and volleys fired by a ceremonial Mexican honor guard, Los Rifleros de Los Angeles, to underscore patriotic crescendos in his speech. However, the audience soon became restive, calling for Ramírez to conclude so that Pacheco could speak. The September 20, 1876, *La Crónica* complained that Ramírez had held forth too long in view of the audience's impatience to hear the former governor.

Ramírez's partner was absent on this occasion, the only American speaker being the lawyer Henry T. Hazard, who *La Crónica* said, "amazed the public with an extremely well-delivered speech in the Spanish language." Other non-Hispanics and people of mixed ancestry were an integral part of the celebration, demonstrating a significant amount of intermarriage and acculturation between Mexicans and other elements of the population. An example was the presence of twenty girls on an allegorical cart adorned with flowers during a parade in this purely Mexican fiesta. Each girl symbolized one of the Mexican states, although five of them had names demonstrating that their backgrounds were not entirely Hispanic. Nevertheless, these girls were strongly identified with the Mexican community: Fanny Richards, Adelaida Faine, Dolores Daums, Isabel Foster, and Ana Alexander.[40]

The presidential contest between the Republican candidate, Rutherford B. Hayes, and his Democratic opponent, Samuel J. Tilden, was carried out in Los Angeles through a series of rallies organized by each party in support of its candidate prior to the November 6, 1876, election. Ramírez did not participate in these except for one appearance at an early Republican rally for Hayes on July 31. At the same time Romualdo Pacheco, running for a seat in Congress, campaigned hard in Los Angeles, but there is no evidence that Ramírez attempted to help him.

Toward the end of 1876, Ramírez was preoccupied with the status of his partnership. Fred Stanford's wife, Mary, was ill with an undiagnosed disease beyond the understanding of the era's limited medical knowledge. She was probably suffering from some form of internal cancer. Stanford's availability to practice law with Ramírez was necessarily affected.

The illness of Stanford's wife ended with her death on December 16, 1876. The next day, a public notice of her demise in the *Star* stated that she was only thirty-eight years old. It announced her funeral at the family residence near the corner of Jail and New High streets.

The family's social standing required more than a mere public death notice. The *Star* published a special item of sympathy:

Mexican riders in an 1897 Los Angeles parade. Ramírez saw many such events as a frequent orator at Mexican celebrations. Reprinted by permission of the University of Southern California Special Collections.

A Mexican crowd at a Los Angeles fiesta in 1890. These were Ramírez's people and his favorite audience, although he could never quite capture all their votes. Reprinted by permission of the University of Southern California Special Collections.

> We are pained to be obliged to chronicle the death of Mrs. Mary E. Stanford, wife of Col. Stanford, of this city, who leaves many relatives and friends to mourn. Mrs. Stanford was peculiarly noted for her Christian Virtues and her great goodness of heart, and her death is a sad loss to our community.

Stanford's grief, however great, did not prevent him from quickly returning to his law practice, perhaps as an antidote to his family's tragedy.

Only ten days after burying his wife, Stanford defended the case of *John McFadden v. Wilson Beach* in the district court on December 27, 1876.[41] The plaintiff was a Los Angeles policeman represented by E. J. C. Kewen and Stephen M. White. The case was one for defamation, based on Beach's having told a police commissioner during some idle moments in a saloon that he took an "Indian squaw" behind a brass foundry on Requeña Street around 1:00 a.m. on July 1 and was having sex with her when McFadden appeared and threatened to arrest him for public indecency. Beach said he gave the policeman ten dollars to go away, which he did. McFadden was indignant over the story that he had accepted a bribe, asking the court for money to compensate him for Beach's false accusation of official dishonesty. Beach admitted that the story was untrue but said he had told it only as a joke. He invented the false anecdote to amuse his friends, not meaning to harm McFadden. A jury of only nine men saw no levity in Beach's lie and awarded McFadden $50.

The year 1876 ended at a low point with Stanford's representation of Wilson Beach in a minor trial about a lie concerning impunity for public sex with an Indian street woman. The number and quality of cases coming to Stanford and Ramírez had diminished as economic conditions deteriorated following the panic of 1875. Benjamin C. Truman, the *Star*'s editor and an optimistic booster of Southern California, seldom made negative statements about the region, but the September 7, 1876, edition of his paper finally conceded that Los Angeles was in the midst of a severe business depression. To compound the misery, a continuing drought had bankrupted many local farmers, the foundation of the county's economy. In the city, commercial transactions were nearly halted by a scarcity of money. This downturn adversely affected Stanford and Ramírez through a great reduction in business. Problems that the partnership faced were especially difficult for Stanford since he also had to cope with his wife's early death.

The survival of their partnership was increasingly doubtful during 1877.

They filed only two new cases during the first 60 days of that year; one on January 3 and another on February 27. Afterward, no one hired them until July 3, a period of over four months. Without new retainers or some other form of income, their practice was becoming untenable. Between March 6 and 19, 1877, Stanford and Ramírez tried five cases in the district court, but those coming to trial had been filed before 1877 and the initial retainers used up. Based on the dwindling number of new clients in 1877, they could not have been optimistic about the future. However, despite their worsening financial condition and reduced prospects, neither Stanford nor Ramírez was yet prepared to abandon the partnership.

In early 1877 the declining economic situation in Los Angeles nearly brought the Spanish-language newspaper *La Crónica* into bankruptcy. A year before, the newspaper's owner, E. F. Teodoli, had organized a group of investors—La Compañía Publicista de la Crónica de Los Angeles—to resuscitate the failing newspaper.[42] The wealthy political conservative Antonio Coronel, a major investor, was installed as president of the company, but by early 1877 it was clear that there would be practically no return on the money put into the paper. Investors began to withdraw from the enterprise, and *La Crónica* would have disappeared had not Pastor de Celis and M. J. Varela volunteered to continue publishing it. Both men recognized that they were assuming a great risk. In the first edition under their direction, March 7, 1877, they wrote, "We understand that we take control of our newspaper in a moment of crisis for the whole country and every kind of business, and we will therefore redouble our efforts." Eulogio de Celis resigned as editor in favor of his brother, Pastor de Celis. The original Italian publisher of *La Crónica*, E. F. Teodoli, walked away from the newspaper. He was thereafter seldom subject to public notice.

La Crónica was revitalized under its new management. The paper gave precedence to issues affecting Mexican people, just as Ramírez had done in the days of *El Clamor Público*. The May 16, 1877, edition criticized the municipal government for failing to maintain Sonoratown in as good a condition as the rest of the city. Soon after, a theme that had long preoccupied the de Celis brothers appeared in a May 19 article. It concerned a proposed Latin Club to unite the Mexican, French, and Italian elements of Los Angeles. A meeting was announced at the home of Felix Signoret, a leader in the French community, to organize the club. Pastor de Celis believed that a unified Latin organization would serve as a counterweight to a sometimes abusive Anglo-Saxon dominance. He urged his readers to attend Signoret's meeting in force.

Another step in the direction of Latin unity took place on July 15, 1877, when an Italian benevolent society with about seventy-five members was formed at a meeting in the home of Lorenzo Garibaldi .[43] It was announced that in anticipation of the meeting, an arrangement had been made with the French Benevolent Society so that sick members of the Italian organization could receive care at the newly dedicated French hospital. This exchange between the groups was reminiscent of the interplay of such organizations already seen in San Francisco's Latin Quarter when Ramírez was a resident there during the 1860s.

By July 28, 1877, Stanford and Ramírez had filed only five new cases, although nearly eight months had elapsed in the year. On that date Ramírez attended the Republican county convention, having been elected as a delegate some two weeks before. The slump in Ramírez's law practice allowed him the time to address politics again.

The convention's purpose was to select Republican candidates for local elections scheduled on September 5, 1877. The convention also formulated a platform setting forth the position it took on various issues, including condemnation of the Southern Pacific Railroad Company by name for acquiring ocean steamship companies in an attempt to monopolize every form of transportation in the state. The railroad had thereafter announced increases in fares and freight charges by sea to and from Los Angeles. The convention called this tactic "uncalled for, unjustifiable, and oppressive," noting that it was especially egregious since the railroad was "generously subsidized by Federal and local capital."[44] Reflecting a common belief that the railroad was subverting political institutions to its own ends, the convention called on voters to be vigilant against "the aggressive movements of railroads and other moneyed monopolies to secure control of Federal, State, and local governments."

Ramírez would have agreed with the convention's negative view of the Southern Pacific Railroad, but the platform also contained an attack on Chinese immigration that he did not approve. As shown in Ramírez's denunciations of racism in the newspapers he had edited, he believed in equality for all minorities without distinction. The convention, however, adopted the popular view that the Chinese presence "undermined civilization, republicanism, patriotism, liberty, and Christianity." It protested further Chinese immigration by saying that it would convert America into a land of pagan coolies who brought "mental, moral, and physical leprosy."

The convention also took up a new and distressing phenomenon that it had not dealt with before. It mentioned violence by underpaid and unemployed workers in the eastern states and San Francisco who were protesting their miserable living conditions. The platform's authors were surprisingly sensitive to the plight of the workingmen and tolerant of the disorders they were creating:

> Resolved, That while we deprecate violence and bloodshed, and believe that the law should extend its protecting arm over persons and property and punish its violators, we yet sympathize with the laboring poor, who are now in this manner asserting their rights to their daily bread against the parsimony of combined capital, which seeks to oppress them ...

The Republican convention's concern over destructive acts of workingmen protesting their lack of decent employment arose out of newspaper reports published shortly before it convened.

Just three days prior to the Republican convention, readers of the Los Angeles press were surprised on July 25, 1877, with alarming news of rioting by railroad workers in the eastern half of the United States. Nearly all the railroads, acting in concert, had suddenly reduced the wages of their workers by ten percent for no perceptible reason other than a desire to pay them less. In response a general strike occurred among railroad employees that soon went out of control when outraged workers began tearing up tracks and setting fire to railroad facilities. Several were killed by the police and hastily called-up military units. A startled *Los Angeles Star* reported great destruction in Reading, Pennsylvania, as well as riots in other cities such as New York, St. Louis, Buffalo, Chicago, Cincinnati, and Cleveland. It called the widely spread disturbances and consequent fatalities "the most dreadful and stupendous riot that has ever taken place in this, or, probably, any other country." The newspaper's sympathies were with "the unfortunate men who have been driven to such a degree of desperation by the iron hand of greed and gain that directs the grinding of the faces of the poor." The *Los Angeles Herald* and the *Republican* also thought that the greed of railroad directors had caused the conflagration. Remarkably, the pro-labor opinions of the local press were little affected by reports that some German workers in Cincinnati had displayed a Communist flag.

Word of rampages by railroad workers in distant parts of the country was not enough to induce much fear in Los Angeles. However, stories about eastern disturbances appearing in the local press on July 25, 1877, were accompanied by a separate article describing riots and the burning of Chinese buildings in San Francisco following a workingmen's meeting. This was the first mention of a workingmen's organization in California associated with violence. As subsequent events showed, news of violent demonstrations in the relatively nearby city of San Francisco caused great alarm in Los Angeles.

Rioting in San Francisco was one of the unintended consequences of joining the city to the intercontinental railroad. Between 1873 and 1875 some 154,300 immigrants arrived in California via the Central Pacific Railroad from points throughout the United States in search of employment. Many were laborers who had lost their jobs during the depression that struck the Atlantic states during 1873.[45] Most ended up in San Francisco, where they discovered that there was little work for them. Thousands of hungry, desperate men wandered the streets trying to find a way to make a living, while sleeping in improvised shelters and enduring the city's well-known freezing winds and fog. Their miserable situation was made worse by having to compete for scarce jobs with numerous Irish and Chinese workers released by the railroad after completing the intercontinental line.

This vast army of unemployed vagrants blamed the Chinese for their condition. They believed that they had been displaced from employment by Chinese who were willing to work for wages that no white man would accept. They cursed the Chinese and the men who employed them.

When a fairly innocuous organization in San Francisco, called the Workingmen's Party of the United States, announced a public meeting on July 23, 1877, in support of the striking railroad workers in the east, some 8,000 unemployed workers showed up. The meeting's organizers presented moderate speakers expressing sympathy for the eastern strikers, with no mention of the Chinese. Some of the audience rebelled, demanding that the speakers address the Chinese question. When they refused, a mob separated from the meeting and marched on Chinatown, where they destroyed several laundries with rocks and brickbats, then set fire to a building, causing at least $20,000 in damages.[46]

The next day a committee of safety, supplied with arms and ammunition by U.S. authorities, was set up to control the rioters. Three gun boats were sent to protect the waterfront. San Francisco was patrolled by 252 policemen, 1,200 militia volunteers, and 4,000 men hired by the committee of safety armed with pick handles.[47] Within forty-eight hours a mob of unemployed workers made another attack, this time burning docks of the Pacific Mail Steamship Company, accused of transporting Chinese to California. The authorities subdued the mob at a cost of four men killed, fourteen wounded, and property loss amounting to over $80,000.[48]

The Los Angeles press kept its readers well informed about events in San Francisco. Reports of death and destruction shocked the city. It was therefore a cause of near hysteria when a "labor meeting" was announced for 8:00 p.m. on the evening of August 4, 1877, in front of the courthouse. In the early afternoon of that day, a very large number of citizens met to discuss whether the projected meeting at 8:00 p.m. meant that the violence in San Francisco was about to spill over into Los Angeles. The attorney and Republican leader James Eastman told those assembled that he had heard that "a hundred of the roughs who had lately been concerned in the San Francisco riots" were coming to Los Angeles. The chief of police thought that a group of citizens to assist him in guarding against labor violence would be appropriate. A Committee of One Hundred was therefore selected to prevent any violence similar to that in San Francisco. Four taps on the fire bells would summon them in case they were needed. The *Star* of August 4 published the names of those on the committee, men who ranged across the entire spectrum of political divisions in the city.

That night the feared labor meeting, attended by an "immense throng", proceeded in an orderly fashion without the slightest difficulty. It was presided over by Alfred Moore, an old resident and auctioneer, who had earlier promised the Committee of One Hundred that there would be no violence. Several speakers denounced the presence of Chinese in the city, but made no suggestion to march on their settlement. As if to emphasize their respectability, a number of men stayed after the meeting to select candidates to run for office on a workingmen's ticket in the upcoming September 5 election.

Ramírez was an early advocate of the Mexican working class while editor of *El Clamor Público*, but he did not favor the rebellious unemployed Americans in San Francisco or their more passive offshoot headed by Alfred Moore in Los Angeles. This was shown on August 14, 1877, when the *Star* published a notice of a series of Republican election campaign meetings scheduled for fifteen cities in Los Angeles County between August 16 and September 3. Each of the meetings would be attended by the Republican candidates and twelve leading members of the party to speak on their behalf. Both Ramírez and Fred Stanford were chosen to be among the twelve speakers.

The Republican tour would be grueling. There was an appearance each day in a different town beginning at 7:30 p.m. The first part swept the southern county with stops at Norwalk, Anaheim, Westminster, Santa Ana, and Orange. Then came a tour of the more central section encompassisng Downey, Los Angeles, Pasadena, El Monte, and Pomona. Finally, visits were scheduled to scattered locations at Azusa, Santa Monica, Wilmington, Compton, Andrew Station (Newhall), and a last push in Los Angeles on September 3, just before the election.

The preference of Ramírez for the Republican Party was made clear by his commitment to the grand tour. Both he and his partner had time for such an excursion since they had little legal business pending. Although their selection was an honor for both, they may also have considered it a kind of effort to generate publicity for their failing law practice.

The Republican candidates they would tout were H. D. Barrows for state senator; E. Hilton and J. E. McComas for the assembly; H. C. Wiley for sheriff; and Anson Brunson for district attorney. The Democratic opposition consisted of George H. Smith for state senator; Asa Ellis and J. B. Holloway for the assembly; H. M. Mitchell for sheriff; and Cameron E. Thom for district attorney.

To the surprise of most residents, a Labor Organization ticket appeared to challenge the regular political parties. It was an outgrowth of labor meetings held by Alfred Moore and a forerunner of the California Workingmen's Party that would persist in Los Angeles over the next two years. Its candidates were W. C. Wiseman for state senator; Edward Evy and James Thompson for the assembly; P. Higgins for sheriff; and George C. Gibbs for district attorney.

The result of the September 5, 1877, election was an across-the-board victory for the Democrats. The Labor Organization ticket did not qualify to be counted because it had been filed too late for official recognition. Nevertheless, the labor movement would overcome this setback and continue to grow in Los Angeles.

Eleven days after the election, Ramírez gave his customary patriotic speech on Mexican Independence Day. He was joined on the podium by Fred Stanford, who made some appropriate remarks in English. For a third time Henry T. Hazard made a speech in Spanish, once again gratifying the audience with his mastery of the language. It was the last time that Stanford and Ramírez would make a joint public appearance.

The depression that racked Los Angeles found a new victim on October 1, 1877, in the form of Benjamin C. Truman, editor of the *Los Angeles Star*. On that date he published an announcement of having sold the *Star* to Rome G. Vickers and John W. Paynter. Truman's farewell editorial proudly claimed that "the *Star* does not owe a dollar in the world." Yet, he did not mention the profitability of the paper, which must have been in steady decline since the Panic of 1875. Proof that the paper could not support its proprietors is shown by the fact that within three months the new owners transferred the *Star* to A. M. Campbell. This new editor was also unable to derive a living from the *Star* in Los Angeles's harsh business climate. Within two years of Truman's having disposed of the newspaper, the *Los Angeles Star* would be bankrupt and seized by creditors, disappearing forever.

The difficult financial circumstances in which Ramírez found himself led to his taking a $1,000 loan from E. W. Burr and J. M. Shotwell of the San Francisco Savings and Loan Society on April 12, 1877. As security he gave them a deed of trust on a lot he owned at the northeast corner of Alameda and Aliso streets. This lot was originally a gift to him by his godfather, Jean Louis Vignes.[49] Another loan was made to Ramírez by the same firm on August 1, 1877, for $1,000, but this time Ramírez gave a deed of trust for his land on the San Rafael Ranch.[50] Ramírez was aware that many Mexicans had lost their homesteads in similar transactions through their inability to repay loans. His conduct as a debtor was impeccable. The principal and interest on both loans were paid off within twelve months, exactly as promised, with the deeds of trust cancelled by the lenders on April 18, 1878.[51]

By the end of 1877, the partnership of Stanford and Ramírez had become another casualty of the depression. The income they received was reduced to a point where it could no longer support them both. Stanford, a widower, was free to begin elsewhere. He chose to try his fortune in Arizona, a place that other Los Angeles residents were beginning to find attractive. The *Los Angeles Star* of January 18, 1878, reported Stanford's arrival in Florence, Arizona, where he traveled in the luxurious buggy he had purchased in 1874. The next month, on February 13, 1878, the paper announced that he had opened a law office in Florence, Arizona. In later years word would arrive in Los Angeles that Stanford was residing in Tucson, then the more lawless town of Tombstone, Arizona. He returned to Los Angeles during the middle 1880s, forming another law partnership and residing on Maple Street, where he died in 1889. Stanford left few traces of his life. Not even a photo of him can be found. He is buried in Los Angeles at Rosedale Cemetery.

Notice of an amicable dissolution of partnership between Stanford and Ramírez was published in the *Star* on February 5, 1878. Up to the time of the depression, their partnership had been generally successful. Most of the eighty-two civil cases filed in the district court by Stanford and Ramírez terminated in favor of their clients. Forty-seven of such cases went to trial, where they won thirty-two, thereby prevailing in sixty-eight percent of the contested cases. They won fifteen other district court trial matters because the opposition failed to defend, losing by default. Finally, twenty other cases were settled by agreement so that their clients gained at least some advantage in the outcome.

Ramírez attracted most of their clients by his high standing in the Mexican and French communities, together with his ability to speak the language of both nationalities. Out of the eighty-two cases of all kinds that they filed in the district court, thirty-four of their clients were Mexican and nineteen were French. The two groups accounted for fifty-three clients, about seventy-eight percent of all litigants they represented in the district court. Stanford probably realized that between the two of them Ramírez was better able to practice alone in Los Angeles because of a lifetime spent among the Mexican and French communities.

When Stanford left Los Angeles, it had been eighteen years since Ramírez stopped publishing *El Clamor Público*. Editor of that newspaper between the ages of eighteen to twenty-three, he had manifested an incredibly precocious intelligence. Ramírez's editorials are still studied by scholars for his analysis of social issues and his commentary on the world from a Mexican perspective. The scope of his knowledge and the depth of his intellectual powers continue to surprise the reader. His editorials in *El Clamor Público* present the image of a sympathetic, earnest young man with a social conscience, whose views were far ahead of his time. They have earned him posthumous honors by modern journalists.[52]

Ramírez's career as a lawyer removed him from journalism, the field in which he truly excelled. From the celebrity of being a crusading editor, he went to the relative anonymity of a law practice. In some mysterious way Ramírez receded from the brilliance of his youth. Now, with the departure of Stanford, he would inexplicably fall into an abyss of his own creation.

CLAMOR PUBLICO

Periódico Independiente y Literario.

LOS ANGELES, CALIFORNIA, MARTES, JUNIO 19 DE 1855.

COMISION DE LOS ESTADOS UNIDOS
PARA LA APROBACION DE LOS TITULOS DE TERRENOS.

[Sesion de 22 de mayo de 1855.]

Opinion del Comisionado Farwell.

APROBADOS.

N.° 250.—El título del Sr. M. G. Vallejo por 10 leguas cuadradas y 5 mas en el condado de Petluma.

N.° 291.—Otro del mismo, por un terreno en el condado de Solano.

N.° 291.—El título de John Rose, seis leguas cuadradas en el condado de Yuba.

N.° 462.—El título de los herederos de Juan B. Alvarado, por el Rincon del Diablo en el condado de San Diego.

N.° 550.—El título de Jno P. Davison, cuatro leguas cuadradas en Santa Paula y Santicoy, cudado de Sta. Barbara.

N.° 461.—El título de Juan Foster ocho leguas cuadradas en el valle de S. Felipe, condado de San Diego.

N.° 664.—El título de los herederos de David Littlejohn, una legua cuadrada en Los Carneos, condado de Monterey.

N.° 502—El título de Samuel G. Reid, tres leguas cuadradas en el rancho del Puerto, condado de San Joaquin.

N.° 248—El título de Chas Convilland, parte de 1 leguas concedidas primero á J. A. Sutter, Concesion por recompensa y con condiciones en 1841. El terreno esta situado en Feather River.

DESAPROBADO.

N.° 68.—El título de Temple y Alexander, por 100 varas cuadradas en el condado de Los Angeles. Concedidas provisionalmente en 1854.

Mexico.

El General Alvarez ha espedido el siguiente decreto para favorecer á las personas que deseen emigrar á Mexico para esplotar los ricos placeres de oro que se han descubierto en Ajutechlan, cerca de Acapulco:

El Capitan Juan Alvarez, General de Division de la República Mexicana y en Gefe del ejército restaurador de la Libertad á los habitantes de la República, sabed:

Que haciendo uso de las amplias facultades que me concede el "Plan de Ayutla," para promover por cuantos medios me sean posibles la prosperidad y engrandecimiento de la nacion, he tenido á bien decretar:

ART. 1. El laboreo de los placeres de San Francisco del Oro, situados en el distrito de Ajutechlan del departamento de Guerrero, se declara libre para mexicanos y estrajeros desde la publicacion de este decreto.

ART. 2. Todo individuo, ya sea nacional ó estranjero, que se dirija al distrito mencionado con objeto de trabajar los placeres, se presentará á las autoridades políticas para obtener de ellas "gratis," sus correspondientes resguardos.

ART. 3. Es libre de todo derecho la introduccion que se haga por el puerto de Acapulco, de maquinaria, instrumentos y provisiones para el trabajo de las minas.

ART. 4. Los metales preciosos del distrito mineral, que se estraigan fuera de la república, solo pagarán al erario el 1 por 100, sujeando en pena de comiso los que contravengan á esta disposicion.

ART. 5. Todo trabajador de placeres referidos, ya sea nacional ó estranjero, que desee adquirir terrenos para fabricar ó dedicarse á la agricultura, ocurrirá á la autoridad política, que facilitará de los terrenos valdios el que se le pidiere, á precios convencionales y equitativos.

ART. 6. Las diferencias que ocurran entre los mineros, se resolverán por quien corresponda con sujecion á la ordenanza del ramo.

Por tanto, etc. Dado en cuartel general del Ejército Restaurador en Texca, á 20 de Abril de 1855.   JUAN ALVAREZ.

Sud America.

CHILE.—Segun las últimas noticias continúa su marcha pacifica y progresiva. Las elecciones para miembros del Congreso han pasado sin ocurrencia alguna notable. Entre los Senadores electos vemos con suma satisfaccion el nombre del ilustre colombiano D. Andrés Bello.

PERU.—El general Flores habia llegado á Lima, y protestado contra el tratado que celebró Echenique con el gobierno del Ecuador, por el cual se le niega á aquel el asilo en el Perú. Parece que el gobierno provisional tiene por ominoso el tratado, y le concidera humillante para el honor nacional. Pero el ministro del Ecuador protestó, y le han seguido los demas Ministros de la América septentrional residentes en Lima. Piden que Flores salga del Perú inmediatamente. "Si Flores (dice un diario del Sur) ha sido siempre una amenaza para los Estados Colombianos, hoy es mayor esa amenaza, mediante la expedicion que se quedaba formando en los Estados Unidos por él, con el fin de tomar las islas de los Galápagos."

Es un hecho imposible que salga de aqui expedicion contra el Ecuador, por mas que hagan Flores y su edecan Clemens.

BOLIVIA.—No son menores las inquietudes en Bolivia con motivo del anunciado regreso del general Santa Cruz. El Presidente Belzu ha dictado un decreto, ordenando el secuestro de los bienes de todo el que tome parte en alguna sedicion, invasion etc. etc. Uno de los articulos de ese decreto manda concidrar sin efecto las transacciones que se hubieren celebrado sobre dichos bienes, desde seis meses antes de cometido el delito, en cuando fueren aquellos necesarios para indemnizar el Gobierno y á los particulares de los perjuicios causados por los perturbadores. Se ha dado á luz una carta que se dice dirigida por el general Santa Cruz al coronel Puch, fechada en Bruselas á 15 de noviembre del año próximo pasado, y en la cual manifiesta el Protector su determinacion de "regresar á America y oponerse á la reeleccion en que está empeñado Belzu, adoptando al efecto el sistema de Rosas."

BRASIL Y PARAGUAY.—Por los extractos que ofrecen los diarios del Istmo de Panamá sabemos que la guerra del imperio del Brasil contra el Uruguay se está haciendo, y segun parece, sin una declaratoria que la precediera, "siendo lo mas extraño (dice el Panameño) ver que la marina de guerra de los Estados Unidos ayude á S. M. I; en su agrecion contra los paraguayos. Estos, empero, oponen fuerzas considerables á sus adversarios, y hasta ahora alcanzan el triunfo en los combates habidos."—He aqui lo que dice el Constitucional de Mendoza, en el asunto: "Se hacia serio nos informa uno de los pasajeros llegados en la mensajeria, el conflicto del Paraguay, atacado por una fuerte escuadra brasilera y un vapor norteamericano; dos potencias poderosas han llevado la guerra contra esta naciente y pequeña república; el Almirante del Paraguay, hijo del Presidente Lopez, de dos vapores que habian comprado en Europa, no habia conseguido introducir sino uno antes que la escuadra brasilera ocupase los rios. Habia tenido lugar un combate entre el vapor norteamericano que hemos mencionado y una bateria paraguaya, la que causó con sus fuegos algunas averias en el vapor matándole dos hombres ademas. Este desmontó algunas piezas de aquella. En la frontera con el Brasil, en las guardias ó fuertes se trataban encuentros parciales entre paraguayos y brasileros, en los que aquellos habian salido vencedores."

Los periódicos de Buenos Ayres dan la noticia de que una fuerza paraguaya de 8,000 hombres habia obtenido á inmediaciones de Villarreal un triunfo sobre las fuerzas brasileras invasoras. Sobre el Paraná tenian los paraguayos 20,000 hombres estacionados, habian tapado de las tres bocas del rio Paraguay, echando á pique piraguas cargadas de piedras y están formados...

FRANCIA.—Un decreto del Emperador aumenta al ejército en 90,000 hombres.—Cada regimiento de línea tendrá un refuerzo de 900.

Esperando la visita de la Reina Victoria á Paris, el Emperador ha mandado poner el Liceo Imperial en un pié de espléndida magnificencia.

Por decreto de 31 de marzo, Mr. de Thouanevel Ministro Plenipotenciario de primera clase y director de los asuntos politicos, se encargará durante la audiencia del Ministro Secretario de Estado de Negocios Estranjeros, Mr. Drouyn de Lhuys, de la direccion de los trabajos de ese departamento y de la correspondencia diplomática.

El gobierno frances se ha quejado oficialmente al belga, ó instancias del Príncipe Napoleon, por un opúsculo publicado contra el Emperador sobre la guerra y que se atribuyó al Príncipe.

EL PROXIMO CONGRESO.—Hasta hoy los miembros electos para el próximo Congreso son como sigue: Administracion 31; Oposicion 129. Todavia resta que elejir 37 miembros en los Estados donde las elecciones congregacionales aun no han tenido lugar.

INTERESANTE.—Un astrónomo Aleman dice que en veinte millones de años la tierra será destruida por una cometa!

LA MEDALLA RUSA.—En los cuerpos de algunos soldados rusos que cayéron en Eupatoria se encontró la medalla de plata de la decoracion de San Jorge. En un lado está grabada el águila rusa, con dos cabezas, teniendo en los piés del globo terrestre y el cetro del soberano; sobre el águila esta la corona imperial y una paloma iluminada. Sobre estas figuras tiene las siguientes palabras en lengua rusa: "Arrodillense, idolatras, porque Dios es con nosotros."

En el otro lado tiene la siguiente divisa tambien en rusa:

"Para la sumision de Hungria y Transilvania."

☞ Dícese que casi todo el vino de la Moselle ha sido comprado por el gobierno Francés para mandarlo al ejército de Crimea.

☞ La Union de Sacramento hablando del San Francisco Chronicle dice: "No se encuentra dentro de los límites de este Estado otro periódico mas cortéz, independiente y elegante."

☞ Los soldados heridos y enfermos que han muerto en Liverpool, (Inglaterra) serán enterrados en un mismo lugar, sobre el cual se erijirá un monumento por suscricion publica.

PISCATORIO.—Mr. Joseph S. McIntyre, de la armada de los E. U. estacionada en Benicia, publica una carta en el Herald de San Francisco, anunciando que sacó un pescado y abriéndolo encontro un látigo de veinte pulgadas y media de largo y montado en plata. Se ha dudado mucho la veracidad de esta historieta.

POZO ARTESIANO.—Se ha cavado un nuevo pozo artesiano en San José, y segun el Tribune es una curiosidad.

CONVENCION DEMOCRATICA.—El dia 27 de Junio tendrá lugar una convencion democratica en Sacramento con el objeto de nombrar oficiales para la eleccion general en Setiembre próximo.

EL CENSO.—La Constitucion del Estado previene que se tome el censo este año, pero como la legislatura no dispuso nada sobre esto, se tomara el año de 1860.

PELEGRINOS PARA PALESTINA.—Una caravana de pelegrinos se embarcó recientemente en Marsella para la Tierra Santa.—Antes de su salida fueron invitados al palacio por el Obispo y cada uno recibió una crucesita de plata, con la fecha de su par...

La ley del Dom...

SECCION 1. Toda diver... belliciosa será en lo suce... dias domingos.

SEC. 2. Todo individuo ayudase á abrir un establecimiento público, tal como juego, cuarto ó salon, juego... lugares propios para carre... combate de osos, de toros, diversiones bárbaras y l... prendido por un delito est... ley, y despues de convicto, á una multa cuyo minimo cuenta pesos y el maximum... cuenta.

SEC. 3. Todo individuo... billete de entrada á una... de las diversiones enumer... gunda seccion de esta acta... te castigado con una mult... al minimum, y de cincuen...

SEC. 4. Los jueces de... en todos casos de infracciones de esta ley.

SEC. 5. Esta ley estará... desde Junio de 1855.

PAPEL DE TULE.—El Ex-Bigler en su último mensa... los terrenos inundados y... presa como sigue:

"Y ya que estoy tocan... acaso no sea fuera de luga... llegan á tener buen éxito lo que ahora se están hacien... del Atlántico, no tan solo s... sino que aumentará necesa... lor. Nadie ignora que un... los terrenos adquiridos p... virtud de la ley de Sept... está cubierta de lozano T... este suelo, y que por térmi... toneladas por acre.

"Durante el último oto... sido cuidadosamente ecsa... bricantes experimentados, presado que, en su opinion... con él un papel de calida... perior.

"Puesto que el tallo del... está maduro y antes que... la lluvia, es casi blanco, s... to del blanqueo seria co... pequeño. Estando cubierto... y compacta fibra, é interio... un tejido ceelular con nu... fibras longitudinales, se... todas las cualidades reque...

"Se han remitido var... Tule á algunos fabricantes... Estados del Atlántico, y p... hagan ensayos con él, y p... el resultado de estos imp... mentos.

"A fin de poder aprecia... la importancia de este esper... que tenga feliz éxito, a... explicacion de algunos he... rentes.

"El precio medio, en l... Atlántico, del material en... fabrica el papel es de une... la libra. A dos centavos t... tercera parte del precio de... los trapos, cada acre prod... ochenta pesos ($80) ó can... cientos pesos ($12,800) cad... acres, y esto, sin mas gas... se orijinen al tiempo de la... ño despues que haya com... durado.

"Sin embargo, cualquie... sultado de los esperiment... haciendo acerca de la pri... papel de cartas ó de ma... duda han los hombres en... han cogido de estas orillas el Tule se puede fabricar... na calidad.

CHAPTER TWELVE
Politics and Crime

Not long after Stanford's departure, Ramírez moved his office to Room 72 in the Temple Block, a smaller place that cost less but required a longer walk up the stairs. He showed his determination to continue as a lawyer by advertising in each of the daily newspapers, something he could probably ill afford. A few cases pending when Stanford left became the responsibility of Ramírez. One of them, *Ybarra v. Lorenzana*, was tried and lost by Ramírez alone on January 16, 1878.[1] The first case he handled entirely by himself as a sole practitioner was *A. B. Peltier v. J. P. Jordan*, filed on February 24, 1878.[2] Ramírez was hired by the plaintiff to enforce a contract promising to convey him real property on Vine and First streets. Ramírez settled this case within a month, obtaining a deed for his client.

Ramírez's law practice was far from prosperous in 1878. From February to June, he had only two new cases. In one of them, filed on April 24, 1878, *Giuseppi Massabo v. Guiseppi Amillo*, the plaintiff's attorney was Horace Bell, a contentious man later known for being the editor of the satirical newspaper *The Porcupine* and author of a book on Southern California history filled with semi-humorous exaggeration called *Reminiscences of a Ranger*.[3] Bell's client filed suit to collect a $1,600 promissory note, which he won. Ramírez engaged in procedural delays to postpone his client's payment of the debt as long as possible. The only other case that Ramírez handled during the first half of 1878 was *Joseph Bonino v. Juan Garibaldi*, in which Ramírez successfully represented the plaintiff in collecting a debt of $2,419.50.[4] He allowed the trial to proceed before Judge Ignacio Sepúlveda without a jury. Despite previous tensions between the men, Ramírez had confidence in Sepúlveda's ability to be impartial.

While Ramírez was struggling to keep his law practice alive during the first half of 1878, he witnessed a new social and political phenomenon in Los Angeles. Its first public manifestation was in the January 5, 1878, edition of the *Star*, which announced the formation of the Workingmen's Club,

No. 1 of Los Angeles. This novel organization was in frank imitation of similar clubs that had sprung up all over San Francisco within the preceding three months. They were the core of a rapidly growing political movement called the Workingmen's Party of California.

The advent of the Workingmen's Party was a direct result of frustration among San Francisco's unemployed masses. They attributed their miserable condition to the presence of low-paid Chinese, who, they believed, took their jobs, and to the great corporations, including the railroad, who employed them. The workingmen felt excluded from California's economy, the victims of giant monopolies with aristocratic pretensions supported by cheap Chinese labor, virtual serfs of their corporate masters. As already noted, the outrage of unemployed whites in San Francisco led to destructive riots in July 1877 that were feared and abhorred in Los Angeles.

The first popular leader of the unemployed in San Francisco was Denis Kearney, a poorly educated Irish immigrant who owned a small drayage company. After initially opposing demonstrations by unemployed workingmen as a member of a pick handle brigade hired by city officials to batter rioters, Kearney shifted sides, becoming an advocate of the unemployed. In this new role he called for the first of many famous sandlot meetings on September 16, 1877. Held near San Francisco's city hall, these gatherings allowed angry unemployed workingmen to release some of their frustration by loudly cheering speeches demanding labor reform and calls for the expulsion of the Chinese from California.

Kearney's first turn as a sandlot speaker before some 200 people was a surprise, probably even to him. He turned out to be a captivating speaker, a charismatic figure with a gift for arousing a highly emotional response in his audience. After presenting some theatrical declarations about driving out the Chinese, the need for soup kitchens, and demands that the city provide jobs, the relatively small gathering responded to Kearney with nearly hysterical approval. At the next sandlot meeting on September 21, over 700 men appeared, having heard of Kearney's remarkable talent as a voice of the unemployed.[5] His oratorical abilities were most effective before large masses of people. Like other rare individuals similarly gifted, Kearney could not resist becoming a demagogue.

The desperate unemployed reacted most favorably to Kearney's threats of violence against corporations employing the Chinese. At his second sandlot meeting Kearney told those assembled that "a little judicious hanging would be the best course to pursue with the capitalists." It was on this occasion that

Kearney called out the words that were repeated countless times and became the war cry of the workingmen: "The Chinese must go!"[6]

At another meeting, on October 29, Kearney spoke before several thousand workingmen near the Nob Hill mansion of Charles Crocker to protest his imperious behavior toward a neighbor, which typified the oppression by the railroad oligarchy. A small proprietor named Jung had refused to sell Crocker a little house adjacent to his mansion for the price offered, so Crocker built a huge fence to block the offending property from view and reduce its value. Looking up Nob Hill where the Central Pacific Railroad magnates Charles Crocker, Leland Stanford, and Mark Hopkins owned residences amounting to private palaces, Kearney told the vast crowd of unemployed workingmen:

> The Central Pacific Railroad men are thieves and will soon feel the power of the workingmen. When I have thoroughly organized my party, we will march through the city and compel the thieves to give up their plunder. I will lead you to the City Hall, clean out the police force, hang the Prosecuting Attorney, burn every book that has a particle of law in it, and then enact new laws for the workingmen. I will give the Central Pacific just three months to discharge their Chinamen, and if that is not done, Stanford and his crowd will have to take the consequences. I will give Crocker until November 29 to take down the fence around Jung's house, and if he does not do it, I will lead the workingmen up there and tear it down, and give Crocker the worst beating with sticks that a man ever got.[7]

Not surprisingly, such statements were seen as inciting violence. Kearney was arrested along with some of his companions on November 3, 1877, on a charge of using language "having a tendency to cause a breach of the peace." After signing a rather humiliating letter to the mayor promising not to use incendiary language in the future, Kearney was released and his speeches became more subdued.[8] This submissive behavior was irreconcilable with his defiant public posturing. It somewhat diminished his reputation among the unemployed as a courageous leader and spokesman.

Early rhetorical calls by Kearney for armed insurrection and organized violence were largely intended to excite his sandlot audiences so that he could create the notoriety needed to maintain his leadership. Despite all of Kearney's bombast, the unemployed workingmen in San Francisco never repeated the riots of July 1877. Nevertheless, city officials and wealthy residents sensed that a revolution was afoot. Some nineteenth-century historians such as Hubert Howe Bancroft mistakenly regarded the workingmen's movement as inspired by communism and necessarily tending toward revolution.[9] The May 1878 platform of the Workingmen's Party of California refuted such notions, stating in the second paragraph that the party "utterly repudiates all spirit of Communism."[10]

In reality, the workingmen's movement supported capitalism but felt that it had evolved into a monstrous form in California that needed changing. They recognized that most of the state's land had been concentrated into very few hands through the abuse of federal programs and fraud. Of 23,637 farms in California during 1870, a mere 122, mostly owned by corporations, occupied more land than all the rest combined.[11] Huge principalities were owned by land barons like Isaac Friedlander, Hugh Glenn, Henry Miller, and Charles Lux. Other near monopolies existed but none greater than the Central Pacific Railroad, which owned enormous areas of the state's land surface, thanks to gifts from an incredibly benevolent U.S. Congress. The workingmen perceived the development of an aristocracy of monopolistic corporations that undermined the American republic.

The Workingmen's Party of California was formed at a meeting in San Francisco attended by 150 persons on October 5, 1877. Denis Kearney was elected president, John G. Day vice president, and H. L. Knight secretary. A statement of the party's principles, written by H. L. Knight, was issued, which clearly set forth what it wanted to do if it took control of the legislature: "We propose to destroy land monopoly in our state by such laws as will make it impossible." The statement went straight to the question of how the workingmen would deal with monopolistic concentrations of wealth: "We propose to destroy the great money power of the rich by a system of taxation that will make great wealth impossible in the future."[12]

San Francisco witnessed the stunning rate at which the Workingmen's Party of California spread. The city was organized into various wards, each with workingmen's clubs that were the basic units of the party. Kearney often visited the clubs, removing officers he did not like and shouting down opposition to his authority with a gang of thugs that he brought for the purpose. Within two months of establishing the party, Kearney and his lieutenants decided to stage a parade in San Francisco on Thanksgiving Day. Thousands took to the streets, making a tremendous demonstration of the workingmen's strength. In a well-organized event they carried pictures of George Washington and other founders of the republic with slogans such as "Workingmen to the Front! In Your Hands Rests the Future." Most alarming to city officials were several military companies organized by the workingmen with uniforms and rifles, although some of the poorest carried nothing but broomsticks. Kearney was designated as commander-in-chief of these militias with the title "lieutenant general," a pretension that was mocked in the press.[13]

As already seen, it took less than three months after its founding in San Francisco for the Workingmen's Party of California to arrive in Los Angeles. The first sign of its presence was an announcement of the founding of the Workingmen's Club, No. 1, of Los Angeles, published in the *Star* on January 5, 1878, which cited the Chinese question as the reason for its formation:

> The Workingmen's Club, No. 1, of Los Angeles, respectfully submits the following facts: First—That hundreds of our own people, white and colored, citizens of this country, male and female, are suffering for the need of labor to earn an honest livelihood; some, from necessity, becoming tramps, and others from the same cause, consigned to our jails; and all this as a consequence of the substitution of the labor of the Chinaman (who is invariably a non-settler) and takes all that is paid to him and sends it out of the country and out of our circulation forever. Secondly—If this Chinese population had been replaced from the beginning by citizen workmen, our [state] population might have been to-day two millions instead of half a million, thereby developing the unequaled resources of our State, increasing its trade in every department beyond all computation, and adding to the individual wealth and welfare of our nation.

The announcement was signed by "Jesse H. Butler, Secretary," a little-known watchmaker and jeweler who would suddenly rise to a place of prominence in Los Angeles.

The Workingmen's Club, No. 1, of Los Angeles held its first general meeting in front of the Temple Block on Saturday evening, February 1, 1878. L. E. Page acted as president, with Jesse Butler as secretary. Various resolutions were read "amid great applause." Their bitterest resentment, found in the eighth resolution, was directed toward the railroad:

> Eighth—That in our opinion the greatest injury to the workingmen of this State and to the public welfare is the great monopoly under the control of Crocker, Stanford & Co., who, in combining their railroad power with the Pacific Mail Steamship Company are endeavoring by the continuing introduction and the employment of Coolie labor to compel white men, through want, to accept Chinese wages.

Just as their brethren in San Francisco had done, the Los Angeles workingmen expressed a profound loathing of monopolistic corporations. One of the resolutions declared in part, "The monopoly of public lands as well as all means of transit, the concentration of capital in the hands of a few to the great detriment of the laboring class, and the introduction of cheap Coolie labor into this country, threatens the extinction of the great middle class of our people, and to reduce us to a nation of a few arrogant capitalists to tyrannize over a multitude of serfs."[14]

Toward the end of February 1878, another club was organized called the Second Ward Workingmen's Club of Los Angeles. Its first meeting, held in the office of city judge B. L. Peel, was attended by some two dozen men who had never before joined in local politics.[15] They were soon followed by the Central Workingmen's Club of Los Angeles, which grew to over 400 members. Several groups were organized along national and ethnic lines. By the middle of 1878, the Workingmen's Party of California had German, Spanish, French, and Irish clubs in Los Angeles. A widespread sense that excessive corporate wealth and power was at the heart of their economic problems caused a huge increase in the Workingmen's Party. For a brief time it would become the most powerful political force in Los Angeles.

Just after the Workingmen's Party of California was established, it saw an almost providential chance to intervene in state politics.[16] This came in the form of a special election to choose delegates to a constitutional convention, the second in the state's history. On September 5, 1877, a majority of voters approved of such a convention, based on a common belief that a new political and legal structure was necessary to control land monopolies, corruption, and railroad abuses, which were somehow behind the state's economic distress. A statewide election of delegates to the convention was scheduled for June 19, 1878. Although the Workingmen's Party of California came into existence too late to have a part in organizing the convention, it seized the opportunity to send as many delegates to it as possible.

The Workingmen's Party of California in San Francisco began a feverish voter registration drive, urging foreign-born members to become naturalized so they could vote. Membership soared, increasing so much that the state's regular political parties thought they would be overwhelmed by the phenomenal Workingmen's Party of California in selecting delegates to the constitutional convention. Out of desperation the Democratic and Republican parties joined to form a nonpartisan slate of delegates to oppose the workingmen. By an act of the legislature, there would be 152 delegates, three from each of the forty state senatorial districts and eight from each of the four congressional districts. When the June 19, 1878, election results came in, the Workingmen's Party of California had won an astounding fifty-one delegates. The nonpartisan effort obtained seventy-seven, while Republicans who refused to merge elected eleven, and similarly recalcitrant Democrats got ten delegates. There were also three Independents.[17] In Los Angeles the ever-active Volney E. Howard was elected as a delegate on the nonpartisan slate, along with J. J. Ayers, editor of the *Evening Express*. Howard was a dedicated opponent of the railroad, who wanted to curb its monopoly by creating a competing line running to California out of Texas. At the age of sixty-nine, he was a major figure in the convention, even a contender to preside over it.[18] The convention would be in session from September 28, 1878 to March 3, 1879. The new constitution it drafted could only be adopted after it was approved by the voters in a general election. The Los Angeles press continuously published articles describing the convention's progress and discord.

Ramírez ignored manifestations of the Workingmen's Party of California in Los Angeles. He had no taste for the utter racism that the workingmen directed toward the Chinese people. He would have agreed with a rare editorial in the *Star* of October 6, 1878, which for once presented a well-reasoned, dispassionate treatment of the Chinese:

> If the Chinese are a dangerous element, demoralizing to the Citizens and inimical to the Republic, then the government should immediately prevent their influx; and, as early a day as practical, remove those already here. The question is then, do they constitute such an element? The whole argument hinges on the answer. If they do, they must go; if they do not, their rights here are the same as our own, and our efforts to prevent their coming are simply a crime against humanity.

Ramírez did not think that the Chinese were a dangerous element. The Chinese enclave on the east side of Alameda Street nearly abutted parts of Ramírez's family homestead on Aliso Street. He passed by it daily on his way to his Temple Block office, but apparently it did not engender in him the same revulsion that the Americans claimed to feel. Within two years he would once again become a Republican candidate for the state assembly, but he would not campaign on a policy of Chinese exclusion, however much voters and members of his party demanded it.

Two themes running throughout Ramírez's life were his rejection of racism and his opposition to political corruption. He tried, during 1873, to resist the abusive railroad monopoly as a leader of the Independent movement in Los Angeles. He might have campaigned for the Workingmen's Party of California if it dealt solely with releasing the chokehold of the railroad and corporate monopolies, but he would not participate in a movement so highly charged with racism that violent rejection of the Chinese was written into the public declarations of party principles.

The last half of 1878 was disastrous for Ramírez's law practice. He filed only one new lawsuit in the district court during the six-month period between June and December. His advertisements in the local press were modified beginning June 25, 1878, so that, in addition to publicizing himself as a lawyer, he also held himself out as "interpreter and translator of English, French, and Spanish."

For the first time in several years, the 1878 celebration of Mexican Independence Day did not feature Ramírez as the principal speaker. He refused an invitation to be the orator because he was offended by his audience's behavior the year before. On that occasion Ramírez had preceded another speaker, Romualdo Pacheco, the ex-governor who was an 1877 candidate for Congress. The crowd was eager to hear Pacheco. It showed rude signs of impatience with Ramírez, urging him to step down so Pacheco could take the podium. This affront probably accounts for his refusal to appear the next year.

Instead of Ramírez, the main speaker of the day was Reginaldo del Valle, a young man who was becoming a leader in both the Mexican and American communities. Del Valle had been admitted to the bar just the year before at the age of only twenty-three, after studying in the noted law firm of Winans & Belknap in San Francisco. Prior to that he had attended St. Vincent's College in Los Angeles, then graduated with a bachelor of science degree from Santa Clara College in 1873.[19] He was the son of Ignacio del Valle, owner of the Rancho Camulos and a conservative Democrat, one of the first converts to the pro-slavery Chivalry wing of the party led by Joseph Lancaster Brent during the 1850s. Brent was Reginaldo's godfather and a compadre of his father, who had resided in the home of the del Valle family in Los Angeles before they moved to Rancho Camulos. For years after Brent's departure to join the Confederate Army in 1862, he maintained a correspondence in Spanish with the elder del Valle.

Reginaldo del Valle became actively involved in Democratic Party affairs after becoming a lawyer. He was accepted without reservation by white Dem-

Portrait of Reginaldo del Valle in middle age, date unknown. Reprinted by permission of the Huntington Library, San Marino, California.

ocrats, much like Ignacio Sepúlveda had been a decade before. Although Mexican, he was thoroughly imbued with an American outlook. Moreover, English was as much his native language as Spanish. He seldom complained about prejudice toward ordinary Mexicans or challenged conventional American racism. Del Valle had no difficulty advocating the exclusion of the Chinese. He was considered a rising young star, pro-American, and a loyal Democrat. Del Valle became Ramírez's main rival for prominence in Sonoratown. They would soon oppose one another for public office, as will be seen. Unlike the ultraconservative Ignacio Sepúlveda, young del Valle easily interacted with the Mexican working class.

Eulogio de Celis, who had resumed editorship of *La Crónica*, was another speaker at the 1878 Mexican Independence Day celebration. His proclivity for uniting the Latin population of Los Angeles was probably the reason for an unusual feature of the parade that day. In addition to the usual Mexican participants, elements of the French and Italian benevolent societies took part in the line of march.[20]

It is a curious fact that, despite being a wealthy social and political figure at this time, de Celis eventually lost his land, dying in poverty, without friends or influence in the city. The *Los Angeles Times* of May 26, 1903, contained an article describing his "pathetic little funeral" at the plaza church. There were no flowers or even pallbearers. The few women present were only able to move his casket by asking some men passing by on the street to do so. De Celis had long since given up his editorship of *La Crónica* and eked out a small living as an occasional Spanish interpreter in the local courts.

The last part of 1878 saw an explosive increase in the membership of the Workingmen's Party of California in Los Angeles. The *Star* was now controlled by George W. Brown, a dedicated exponent of the workingmen's movement. The newspaper's masthead proclaimed its new mission: "Devoted to the organization and emancipation of the working people." The October 1, 1878, edition called agitation by workingmen "the great reform movement," which the *Star* supported because "its principles are right and the revolt against the rule of monopoly with all its consequent corruption is necessary to the existence of the Republic itself." Every issue contained a burgeoning list of workingmen's clubs in Los Angeles, along with the names of their officers. Many anti-Chinese advertisements appeared in the *Star*, designed to attract members of the Workingmen's Party of California: The October 15, 1878, ad for the Ocean House, a hotel in Santa Monica, announced, "No Chinese About the House!"

A convention of the Workingmen's Party of California was held in Los Angeles on the evening of November 16, 1878, to select a slate of candidates for the December 2 municipal elections. They chose James R. Toberman as their candidate for mayor. He was not a workingman, but he had already been mayor once before, acquiring a reputation for frugality with city money. Toberman came to Los Angeles as a federal tax collector, then became an agent for Wells Fargo. He later acquired considerable wealth as a land developer.[21] The second most important candidate, selected for city attorney, was a lawyer named John F. Godfrey, who would launch a political career based on the workingmen's movement.

The Workingmen's Party of California had grown so large and powerful in Los Angeles that members of both the Republican and Democratic parties believed that they would have to unite on a single ticket in order to defeat it. Neither party thought it could win the municipal elections alone. In a highly unusual proceeding they joined in a "people's convention" on November 16 to cobble together a slate of candidates in opposition to the Workingmen's Party of California.[22] Their candidate for mayor was Bernard Cohn, a well-known merchant and moneylender. In fact, Cohn was already acting as mayor since he had been appointed to complete the short time left in Mayor Frederick A. MacDougal's term when that gentleman died just fifteen days before the December 2, 1878, election.

The vote was a complete victory for the Workingmen's Party of California in Los Angeles. Toberman won the office of mayor by 1,422 votes to Cohn's 562. The contest for city attorney went to the workingmen's candidate, John F. Godfrey, by a vote of 1,308 to 671. Every candidate offered by the Workingmen's Party of California was elected to office.[23] The *Star* of December 3 published an image of a rooster blowing a horn above the words "Workingmen Triumphant!" and "A Redeemed City!" Jesse H. Butler, a leader of the local Workingmen's Party of California, was elected to the city council along with enough others of his party to form a new majority. On the morning after the election, Butler sent a telegram to Denis Kearney, informing him of the election results in Los Angeles. By noon of that day, Kearney replied: "We glory in your success. People are awake for reform."[24]

The great majority in Los Angeles voted for the Workingmen's Party of California as a protest against the depressed economy and corporate abuses. Many voters were not actually committed to it. This was demonstrated when the *Los Angeles Star* suspended publication on December 5, 1878, three days after the municipal elections. Its editor, George W. Brown, had turned the paper into an organ of the Workingmen's Party of California, but the newspaper was generally rejected by the public.

The editorship of the *Star* was transferred to Isaac McKinley just prior to January 1, 1879, when publication was started anew. The newspaper resumed its enthusiastic advocacy of the Workingmen's Party of California, reducing its subscription rate to only two dollars a year. Even so, lack of support for the *Star* induced it to make periodic appeals for additional subscriptions, which were ignored. In contrast, the *Los Angeles Herald* under Joseph D. Lynch, a moderately conservative Democratic newspaper, was far more popular, even though a subscription at ten dollars a year cost five times more than the *Star*.

The *Herald*'s editor was a witty cynic who opposed the constitutional convention that was intended to create organic laws to control the railroad. His treatment of the railroad was so favorable that the *Herald* was occasionally accused of being in the pay of the Southern Pacific Railroad. Volney E. Howard, a proponent of railroad reform and a leading delegate to the constitutional convention, was a natural target of the newspaper. The *Herald* of February 5, 1879, accused Howard and a large number of convention delegates of neglecting their duties after they were seen at a risqué performance of dancing girls in a Sacramento theater, where they had gone "to see a leg show." When Volney E. Howard entered the place, according to the *Herald*, he was given a tumultuous reception by his admiring fellow delegates. "His face was one vast expanse of smiles, and as he walked down the aisle and took a very prominent front seat, the cheers and applause fairly shook the building." The newspaper accused Howard and the other delegates of not working as they were elected to do. Instead, they were "really absorbed in critical reveries as to the niceties of the ankles of the ladies of the ballet."

Denis Kearney arrived in Los Angeles to give a speech in front of the courthouse on the evening of March 18, 1879, to promote adoption of the new constitution.[25] His visit was part of a speaking tour of Southern California. By this time Kearny had lost control of the Workingmen's Party of California. The party's executive committee had deposed him earlier as president, based on various criticisms, the most truthful of which was that "he assumed the role of the dictator who would brook no opposition to his will, suspecting everybody of treason who dared to differ with him in opinion."[26]

Although Kearney appeared in Los Angeles without the official sponsorship of the Workingmen's Party of California, his immense celebrity was unabated. The *Star* of March 19, 1879, claimed that 4,000 to 5,000 people came to hear him. Taking his cues from local activists, he attacked the burdensome taxes paid by workingmen and small farmers in Los Angeles, where great landowners paid little in comparison. He asked why there were no decent roads or other improvements in the county to justify the high taxes. This question had long vexed Los Angeles taxpayers. It had been one of the reasons for the rebellious People's ticket organized by Max Strobel some eight years before and the more recent Independent movement alleging that a ring of elected officials was misappropriating public money.

The use of biased local informants in delivering his speeches got Kearney into trouble at Santa Ana. He made derogatory comments about several of the town's wealthiest citizens, relying on what he had heard from some of the workingmen residing there. After his speech he was approached by a group of friends and employees of the men he had insulted, demanding to know the basis for his demeaning remarks. When Kearney refused to state the source of his information, he was struck in the face. Kearney was chased into a drugstore, where he was disarmed, and an employee of a man he had denigrated "wound his hand into his hair, drew his head down onto the counter of the store and gave the agitator a terrible beating."[27]

The *Los Angeles Herald*, a newspaper opposed to the new constitution and the workingmen's movement, approved of Kearney's treatment in Santa Ana. A March 22, 1879, article describing the assault on Kearney was entitled "Old Fashioned American Thrashing" and stated, "The wonder is that he did not get it long and long ago." The *Star*, voice of the workingmen, accused enemies of the new constitution and labor reform of responsibility for the attack on Kearney. Angry workingmen were unable to procure any action by law enforcement officials against the assailants. When Kearney finished his speaking tour in San Diego, "his face was still considerably disfigured from the effects of the attack on him in Santa Ana."[28]

The controversy over whether to adopt the new constitution divided Los Angeles and resulted in mass meetings by both its proponents and its enemies. Volney E. Howard, one of the principal authors of the new constitution, was often called upon to address rallies of those in favor. On May 6 the *Los Angeles Herald*, although opposed to ratification, begrudgingly acknowledged Howard's efforts on behalf of the new constitution, stating, "Gen. Howard is always forcible and eloquent." The *Star* no longer favored adoption of the new constitution after April 9, 1879. On that date Isaac Kinley resigned as editor, surrendering possession of the paper's printing press to a hurriedly formed entity called the Star Publishing Company. The paper's new management, never publicly identified, rejected Kinley's advocacy of the workingmen's movement. The May 6 edition denounced the new constitution as an "abortion." This sudden conservative turn in the *Star*'s orientation was extremely brief. The newspaper became bankrupt, going out of existence after its final edition on May 27, 1879, another victim of the depression in Los Angeles.

At a special election on May 7, 1879, the new constitution was adopted by a statewide vote of 77,959 to 67,154. It was approved in Los Angeles County by 6,124 to 4,201. The May 14 *Herald* noted a huge celebratory parade by workingmen and conceded that the election was a signal victory for them. One of the objectives of the Workingmen's Party of California was met in article XIX of the constitution, which prohibited private corporations and governmental entities from employing Chinese workers. Another provision limited the normal work day to eight hours. Two major constitutional reforms especially supported by farmers included a system for taxing land uniformly and the establishment of control over the railroad's charges for transportation. The new constitution set up a board of equalization to fairly apportion taxes and a railroad commission to regulate freight costs, but the elation of the workingmen and farmers over the new constitution was tempered by a cynical belief that politicians and judges in the pay of the railroad would subvert its reforms.

To overcome the railroad's malignant influence, a political movement called the New Constitution Party arose in San Francisco to elect public officials immune from railroad graft who would carry out the desired reforms. This new political phenomenon quickly extended to Los Angeles where ex-governor John M. Downey presided over the party's local organization.[29]

For the first time in the city's history, the regular election for county and state offices in Los Angeles on September 5, 1879, had four competing political parties. The usual contest between the Democrats and the Republicans was now joined by the California Workingmen's Party and the New Constitution Party. Each had separate conventions during July 1879 to nominate candidates. The divisions between the parties resulted in a jumble of issues and candidates that prevented any one of them from being dominant.

One of the reforms brought by the new constitution was a restructuring of the judicial system. The county court was abolished and the district court replaced with a superior court. Under the new regime, justice court decisions would be appealed directly to the superior court. Judges of the superior court would handle everything once done by the county and district courts. Los Angeles was allocated two judges for the new superior court. Judicial elections were eliminated, with candidates for judgeships standing among those for political office at regular elections. These innovations required voters to choose two judges. Both the New Constitution and Workingmen's Party of California had conventions that nominated Volney E. Howard for the superior court. Ignacio Sepúlveda was picked by the Democrats. Each was elected, defeating a field of four other candidates, with Howard getting more votes than any of the others, including Sepúlveda.[30] Howard had become one of the most popular men in Los Angeles. As chairman of the judiciary committee of the state constitutional convention, he was largely responsible for the court reorganization.

The results of the election for political offices generally favored the Democrats but were scattered across party lines. The New Constitution Party's nominee, J. P. West, was elected state senator. Successful Democratic candidates were Reginaldo del Valle, assemblyman; Thomas B. Brown, district attorney; A. W. Potts, county clerk; and William R. Rowland, sheriff. The Republicans only managed to elect P. M. Green as one of the two Los Angeles assemblymen. The Workingmen's Party of California was shut out, except for Walter Lindley, elected as county treasurer.[31] The election of Reginaldo del Valle to the assembly at the age of twenty-five gave the young Mexican Democrat a great advantage in his future rivalry with Ramírez.

Elections for statewide offices held at the same time were disastrous for proponents of the new constitution and political change. The most ardent proponents of reform, the Workingmen's Party of California and the New Constitution Party, each with a different ticket, failed to unite their votes for the same candidates. The old Democrats, competing against the two new parties with yet another ticket, saw votes taken away and support for their candidates drain away. The Republicans prevailed over their split opposition, electing George C. Perkins as governor. Perkins was a conservative businessman opposed to the spirit of reform in the new constitution. He was noted for his alignment with railroad interests and large corporations. Tolerance of railroad monopoly and corruption by men like Perkins delayed reform for more than three decades. Members of the legislature and judiciary continued to sell themselves by secretly accepting railroad money. In 1885 and again in 1890, Leland Stanford bought a seat in the U. S. Senate by showering gold on those in the legislature who elected him.[32] Only after Hiram Johnson was elected governor in 1910 would the Progressive movement put an end to the domination of California by the railroads. A great many advocates of the 1879 constitution would not live long enough to see its reforms carried out.

Throughout 1879 and the first half of the next year, Ramírez was absent from public affairs. The successful Democratic candidate for the state assembly, Reginaldo del Valle, largely supplanted Ramírez as a leader in the Mexican community. For the second consecutive year Ramírez did not participate in the 1879 celebration of Mexican Independence Day. His place as the main orator of the day was once again taken by Reginaldo del Valle.[33] The 1879 constitution eliminated the requirement that laws be published in the Spanish language. This would have provoked an outraged response by Ramírez in his younger days, but now he merely tended to his law practice in silence. A Spanish-language newspaper in San Francisco, *La Sociedad*, listed Ramírez as its Los Angeles correspondent on the masthead in 1879, but nothing he contributed to it has survived.

The hard times that had characterized the past few years were still continuing. Ramírez had only seven new cases in 1879. The most difficult, filed on January 18, 1879, was *Maybury v. Ruiz*, where Ramírez attempted to defend a married woman against foreclosure of her home, on the ground that she had recorded a homestead before her husband incurred a mortgage. The law did not yet clearly establish a wife's homestead as an exemption from a mortgage foreclosure. Ultimately, the dispute went to the California Supreme Court, where Ramírez's view of the case prevailed, but since he had earlier lost in Judge Sepúlveda's court, he probably did not receive fees commensurate with his efforts.[34]

In early 1879 Ramírez defended two other cases against foreclosure, *Garvey v. Labory* and *Friedman v. Rogers*.[35] However, there was little money in having debtors as clients. Finally, on April 8, 1879, he successfully represented a creditor in a foreclosure and was awarded $150 in attorney fees by Judge Sepúlveda. He had three other district court cases with small amounts of money involved. The only notable case, *Alexandre v. Aillard*, was made so because Ramírez won a $600 judgment against Volney E. Howard through a clever argument that invalidated the defenses in the prominent lawyer's answer to the complaint.[36]

At the beginning of 1880, an editorial in the Los Angeles *Evening Express* described the struggle to survive the previous year's depressed economy as "a long fight of deep dejection."[37] The article called on public officials to refrain from plunder and on farmers to be content with small profits. Exhibiting the optimism typical of hometown newspapers, it predicted a better day, when Los Angeles would control the flow of mineral wealth from Arizona and farmers would profit from reduced shipping rates imposed by the new constitution's railroad commission.

One group of people had no future in Los Angeles regardless of how much the economy improved. The Los Angeles Indians were rapidly dying off. Shunned and abused by whites, the Indians were left to die in the streets like stray dogs and cats. The February 24, 1880, edition of the *Evening Express* published the following item without reproach to local residents:

> The dead body of an old Indian woman was found Sunday morning last, lying inside a fence on Aliso street. Her only shelter in her last hours had been a few boards placed at an angle against the fence, and it is evident

she died from exposure and the infirmities of age. About two months ago, the old woman's husband was found dead under a hedge on Washington Street.

Unconscious Indians were commonly found in the streets of Los Angeles. They were usually ignored or carried off to work on a chain gang, based on the assumption that they were drunk in public. The item in the *Evening Express* was an unusual instance of a newspaper's noticing the death of an Indian outcast. No one knows how many others died the same way in the midst of white indifference.

The year 1880 proved to be the most eventful and tragic in Ramírez's life. A presidential election was set for November 2, with congressional seats and other federal offices in dispute. The contest in California was widened since the recently approved constitution required a new beginning in the state assembly. Every member was forced to stand for election, even those whose terms under the old order had not yet expired. State senators were not so obligated.

In these circumstances Ramírez made an effort to resurrect his political career. He attended the Republican county convention on August 5, 1880, where he was suddenly projected into politics again by being nominated as one of the two assemblymen from Los Angeles County. The other Republican candidate for the assembly was James F. Crank. The somewhat unexpected choice of Ramírez to head the local Republican ticket along with Crank necessarily involved some adroit campaigning. Ramírez must have approached Republican leaders in order to express his interest in running for office, setting forth the reasons why he should be elected. His successful reentry into politics could not have occurred without some prior planning and strategic maneuvering.

Calling on more than twenty years of fairly constant loyalty to the Republican Party, Ramírez privately buttonholed each of the delegates to ask for their votes. Although he had not taken part in official Republican business for several years, Ramírez was well known and considered a good party member. He worked the convention well enough to receive a unanimous vote for nomination as an assemblyman.

Many Republicans refused to run for public office because their party had declined in recent years. Potential candidates were aware that their status as Republicans was a disadvantage. The fame of men like Denis Kearney and Volney E. Howard far overshadowed them. The Workingmen's Party of

California, the New Constitution party, and the Democratic party attracted more adherents than Republicans in Los Angeles. Among other problems the Republicans at this time had no militant newspaper to publicize their cause. Consequently, there was little popular recognition of the party's most notable local figures. An item about Ramírez's acceptance speech published in the *Evening Express* on August 6, 1880, shows that he was conscious of the virtual anonymity of longtime Republican leaders:

> Mr. Ramirez, in his address before the Republican convention yesterday stated that he supported Fremont in 1856, and had been a consistent republican ever since, adding, "and that is the reason, probably, why you have never heard of me before." The statement was greeted with cheers and laughter, and Mr. Ramirez was nominated by acclamation.

Beginning on August 16, the local press was crowded with political advertisements, even though the election, set for November 3, 1880, was more than ten weeks away. Each day every newspaper in the city printed political advertisements that carried the name "Francisco P. Ramirez" in very large letters above the words, "One of the Republican Candidates for Member of the Assembly." It had been a long time since his name was so prominently held out for public notice.

Just a few days before Ramírez's nomination, the Democratic county convention was held on August 2 in the courthouse. Reginaldo del Valle and William F. Heathman were nominated for the assembly. Although del Valle had already been elected to the assembly the preceding year, he had to run again in 1880 because the new constitution demanded it. Ramírez faced a Mexican incumbent who had already undermined his position of leadership in Sonoratown. Del Valle had another special advantage over Ramírez. At only twenty-six years of age, del Valle was exceedingly popular with Americans. He was chosen to be the principal orator at the 1880 Fourth of July celebration, just a month before the Democratic Convention. The Superior Court judge, Ignacio Sepúlveda, was the only other Mexican so highly honored. The Americans could make no greater demonstration of esteem for del Valle.

An appreciation of del Valle was not confined to Americans. In addition to his address at the Fourth of July celebration, he was invited to be the principal speaker at the Mexican community's Independence Day fiesta on September 16, 1880. Both Americans and Mexicans regarded del Valle as one of their own and a leader of their respective communities.

Once again Ramírez was not a part of Mexican Independence Day, having in effect ceded the speaker's platform to del Valle. As the election approached he began to seriously campaign for a seat in the assembly. He had little to lose by devoting all his energies to promoting his candidacy. Only a small part remained of the law practice he had acquired after Stanford's departure. The October 6 edition of the *Evening Express* reported, "Francisco P. Ramirez, the republic candidate for the Assembly, is about to make a thorough canvas of the county."

While Reginaldo del Valle was a formidable opponent, at least Ramírez would not have to worry about candidates from other political parties. The Workingmen's Party of California had collapsed by the time of the election. Much of its strength was dissipated after the adoption of the new constitution. Many workingmen believed that they had accomplished what they had set out to do, and they lost interest in the party. Surprisingly, some leaders, including Kearney, opposed trade unions.[38] Their disputes with unionists within the party helped cause disarray in the organization. The misery of the workingmen that had originally fueled the movement was gradually reduced as the unemployed began to find work or leave the state. In Los Angeles the Workingmen's Party was discredited because the municipal officers it elected in 1879 did not live up to the expectations that they would reform the city government. Some Workingmen's Party of California members united with the Greenback Party, an east-coast movement with complicated notions of relieving debtors by the use of paper money instead of gold. They briefly formed an organization in Los Angeles in 1880 called the Greenback-Labor Party, which soon disappeared. The New Constitution party lasted only a few months. Both Democrats and Republicans felt that carrying out reforms of the new constitution could best be done by their own parties, but as already seen, this was not true.

Ramírez's desire for an assembly seat was obviously part of a plan to transition from his failing law practice to a career in Republican politics. Consequently, the results of the election would have been enormously disappointing. The other Republican, James F. Crank, won 3,070 votes, the most received by any candidate for the assembly. Del Valle came in second with 2,852. Both men were elected, shutting out Ramírez, who placed third with 2,747. Despite del Valle's popularity, he had defeated Ramírez by only 105 votes. Now, at the age of forty-three, Ramírez had to reassess his situation. It was the fourth time he had failed to gain public office. In 1858, when only twenty-one, and again in 1859, he unsuccessfully ran for the assembly. He tried for the state senate against Henry Hamilton in 1864, a disputed election that ended in a contest before the senate election committee, which Ramírez lost. Ramírez's moribund law practice and his failure to resurrect himself through politics must have been disheartening.

At this time Ramírez had another source of unhappiness. He had been courting a beautiful half-Basque, half-Mexican eighteen-year-old girl named Lastania Abarta during 1880. Their relationship progressed to the point where they were engaged to be married. Even though he was forty-three, social convention allowed romantic relations between older men and girls barely out of adolescence. Lastania's widowed mother favored the match and tried to bring about a marriage between her daughter and Ramírez. All things pointed toward a wedding between them until Lastania jilted Ramírez in favor of Francisco "Chico" Forster, the popular forty-two-year-old son of John Forster, a wealthy rancher married to the sister of Pío Pico. Chico was a handsome man with a reputation as a playboy. He liked to gamble and frequently brought horses from his father's Rancho Santa Margarita in San Diego County to race in Los Angeles. Lastania's rejection of Ramírez was likely painful since he was apparently sincere in his desire to marry her.

The relationship between Ramírez and Lastania Abarta was only brought to light by newspaper coverage of a tragic event. On the afternoon of March 15, 1881, Lastania shot and killed Forster because the night before in the Hotel Moiso she had surrendered her virginity to him in reliance on a promise that he would marry her the next day. When Forster evaded Lastania's attempts to get married in the morning, she realized his promise had only been a ploy to seduce her. During the afternoon, deeply ashamed of having lost her virginity in violation of the era's sexual mores, she avenged herself by buying a pistol and shooting Forster on the sidewalk of Commercial Street. Within minutes she went to the sheriff's office to give herself up.[39]

A trial was held on April 29, 1881, in which her lawyers presented a novel defense. They claimed that she was innocent by reason of temporary insanity because she had killed Forster while suffering from a menstrual disorder that affected her ability to reason and to control her behavior. This theory, backed by dubious medical testimony, resulted in a rapid acquittal by the all-male jury. The packed court applauded the verdict as she left the building. Victorian notions of avenging female honor were sustained.[40]

Lastania testified about her relationship with Forster, saying that he was jealous of Ramírez. Forster asked her to marry him weeks before his death, but Lastania said, "I told him no, I could not marry him, as I was engaged

Lastania Abarta at about eighteen years of age, in 1880. She was the fiancée of Ramírez until she jilted him for Chico Forster. Courtesy of Mike Abarta, Los Angeles.

to F. P. Ramírez." Forster replied, "Don't marry that black Indian!"[41] This remark, intended to be insulting, was strangely inaccurate since Ramírez's appearance was entirely European. It was ironic because Forster himself had a fair amount of Indian and African blood in his ancestry. Lastania's mother was opposed to the rakish Forster as a suitor. The girl testified that when Forster went to her house "my mother would not let him in because I was going to marry Mr. Ramírez." After the trial Lastania Abarta married a wealthy Frenchman living in Los Angeles named Auguste Maurice Cazaux. The couple eventually moved to Mexico City, where they had a respectable life and started a family that survives to this day.[42]

The trial of Lastania Abarta fortuitously contained the only public references to Ramírez having a romantic liaison. There must have been others, but they understandably remained private. His relationship with Lastania Abarta ended during the autumn of 1880, when Forster intervened in her life. Ramírez had no connection with Lastania at the time she shot Forster or during her trial. As will be seen, by then he was immersed in his own problems and absent from the city.

Sixteen days after the elections of 1880, an incident occurred that changed Ramírez's life forever. Articles in the November 20 *Evening Express* and *Herald* papers described what took place. Ramírez accompanied a man named Ramon Hidales to the Los Angeles County Bank on November 19 at about noon. Hidales wanted to cash a $2,100 certificate of deposit in his name from a San Francisco bank. Ramírez vouched for the identity of Hidales, telling bank officials that he was the party whose name was on the certificate. Relying on Ramírez's representation that Hidales was the rightful owner, the bank paid him $2,100 in cash. Earlier that day one of Sheriff William R. Rowland's informants had told him that the certificate was forged. It was originally owned by one S. P. Jones, but his name had been traced over in ink and changed to J. R. Hidales. Sheriff Rowland went to the bank to investigate. He quickly found Hidales had left the bank but was at a livery stable, ready to leave town on a horse he had just purchased. Only $1,050 was recovered since Hidales claimed that—in a remarkably short time—he had also bought a suit of clothes, an expensive watch, and a pair of pistols. Even after accounting for these purchases, the amount of $500 was missing. Sheriff Rowland put Hidales in the city jail on charges of forgery, with bail set at $5,000, after confirming with bank officials that the certificate had indeed been altered.

Ramírez's unfortunate connection with Hidales did not initially create suspicion that he was an accomplice of the forger. When the November 20 *Los Angeles Herald* reported the arrest of Hidales, it treated Ramírez's presence at the bank in a manner that assumed his innocence:

> Hidales went to the bank accompanied by F. P. Ramirez, Esq., one of our most reputable attorneys, who identified him in the usual manner. How he succeeded in palming himself off on Mr. Ramirez as a respectable man we have not learned, not having been able to see that gentleman.

Nevertheless, the newspaper recognized that Ramírez had helped to facilitate the fraud, even if unintentionally: "The forgery itself is not a very skilled one, and the bank officials were undoubtedly thrown off their guard by the respectable voucher Hidales had in the person of Mr. Ramírez."

Ramírez's relatives, friends, and circle of acquaintances were stunned on December 2, 1880, when the local press reported that he had been arrested the day before as an accessory to forgery. This development caused great consternation among those who cared about Ramírez, but for most Los Angeles residents it would be a deliciously entertaining scandal that they would savor and enjoy for months. The news of Ramírez's arrest created a wave of shock, gossip, and wonderment that went from person to person through the lawyers in the Temple Block and courthouse, down Main Street into stores, restaurants, saloons, and barber shops, then across the plaza to the Mexican quarter.

Sheriff Rowland had delayed arresting Ramírez for ten days after taking Hidales into custody. While in jail Hidales cooperated with the sheriff in building a case against Ramírez, in part through eavesdropping, as will be seen. There was every reason for Hidales to confess his crime and involve Ramírez in it. Sheriff Rowland undoubtedly told Hidales that he was facing a maximum of fourteen years in the penitentiary for forgery but that his sentence would be substantially reduced if he assisted in convicting Ramírez. Such an arrangement was denied by the sheriff and Hidales, but their conduct before and after Ramírez's arrest was obviously based on such an understanding.

After being processed in the city jail on December 1, Ramírez was taken for arraignment to the court of James A. Fisher, a justice of the peace in downtown Los Angeles who was well known by Ramírez. Bail was set at $1,000, and Ramírez was returned to jail until it was posted.[43] His sister Isabel intervened at this point by presenting the required bail bond. She was the widow of a wealthy Italian immigrant, Antonio Pelanconi, and better fixed financially than her brother. Giacomo Tononi also obligated himself on the bond. He was the deceased Pelanconi's business partner. Tononi and Isabel were married not long after Ramírez was released from jail.

Since Ramírez was charged with a felony, he would have to go through the established legal proceedings in such matters. He was subject to a preliminary examination in a justice court to determine whether enough evidence existed against him to justify sending his case for trial to either Judge Sepúlveda or Judge Howard in the Superior Court. The justice court preliminary hearing was held before James A. Fisher. Most preliminary hearings only lasted a few hours, just long enough to show that there was cause to believe that the defendant had probably committed a crime. No definite findings on guilt or innocence were made since that would be determined at trial in the Superior Court. Ramírez's preliminary hearing took over two weeks to complete. Justice Fisher, likely influenced by Ramírez's high status, patiently allowed the district attorney and Ramírez's counsel a wide latitude in presenting their cases.

Ramírez hired Henry T. Gage to defend him. An able lawyer, Gage was elected as city attorney in 1881, a few months after the termination of Ramírez's case. He was a masterful politician who would be elected governor of California in 1889, but his reputation was tainted by a slavish loyalty to the Southern Pacific Railroad, which financed his election to the governor's chair. When the preliminary examination began on December 14, 1880, Gage presented a written demurrer to the criminal complaint, challenging its validity and asking that the case be dismissed.[44] The demurrer was denied since it contained no factual matters pointing to Ramírez's innocence. At Gage's request the hearing was closed to the public. Local newspapers could only report on the dates when hearings took place. The details of testimony against Ramírez were kept secret until the case was over.

A series of witnesses were called, far more than would ordinarily be allowed in a preliminary examination. The hearing was so protracted by complicated testimony and Gage's delaying tactics that it almost resembled a trial. Ramon Hidales was taken from jail to testify against Ramírez.[45] He stated that he was born in Baja California, a resident of San Diego who spoke little English. On November 18, 1880, he had gone to Ramírez's office in the Temple Block after searching for a Spanish-speaking lawyer. Hidales showed Ramírez a certificate of deposit for $2,100, which he claimed he had found in the street. He confided to Ramírez that the original name on it was S. P. Jones but that he had traced his own name over that of the owner. After Ramírez examined the certificate, Hidales said he could not cash it because he was a stranger without any form of identification. Incredibly, he claimed that Ramírez then offered to become an accomplice to forgery in exchange for a share of the certificate, saying, "I will take you and introduce you to some bank, but you must go immediately after collecting the money."

According to Hidales, the two men negotiated the question of how to split the cash to be received. Ramírez at first demanded $1,000. When Hidales balked, it was agreed that Ramírez would get $500 for introducing Hidales as the owner of the certificate. At Hidales's request the penal code was consulted to see what punishment he would get if caught. Ramírez told him the penalty for forgery was one to fourteen years. Nevertheless, they decided to cash the certificate. Ramírez told Hidales to return to his office at ten the next morning. It was agreed that the certificate would be presented to the Los Angeles County Bank on the first floor of the Temple Block where Ramírez had his office.

Deputy Sheriff Adolfo Celis was another witness.[46] He explained to the court that he was a Spanish-speaking officer not known to work for the sheriff, assigned to surreptitiously patrol Sonoratown to detect any crimes that might be brewing. While performing his undercover duties, he had met Ramon Hidales drinking in a cantina. The two men had a long, amiable conversation at the bar. Hidales, while under the influence, told Celis that he enjoyed his company and that they should travel to Mexico together, never suspecting he was a deputy sheriff. Celis replied that he had no money for such a trip. Hidales then pulled the certificate for $2,100 from his pocket, showing it to Celis. He said that the next day about noon he would have plenty of money because the lawyer Ramírez would go to the Los Angeles County Bank with him to falsely represent that Hidales was the person entitled to cash the certificate. After that, Hidales planned to buy a horse so that he could flee the country, and there would be money to pay the expense of Celis going to Mexico with him. The next morning Celis reported his conversation with Hidales to Sheriff Rowland.

Sheriff William R. Rowland testified that after hearing Celis's report he went to the Los Angeles County Bank at about 12:00 noon.[47] When he arrived, the bank cashier, John M. Elliot, told him that Hidales had just cashed the certificate, based on Ramírez's identification of him as the owner. The bank was near Celestino's Stable. Rowland hurried there, remembering that Hidales had told Celis that he was going to buy a horse. He saw Ramírez at the stable, standing next to a man matching Hidales's description. After confirming Hidales's identity, the sheriff told him that he had to return the bank's money pending an investigation of the certificate with the institution in San Francisco that had issued it. After explaining that he had already bought a horse and other items with some of the money, Hidales gave the remaining cash to Rowland. All of it was accounted for except $500. Rowland put Hidales under arrest but did not charge Ramírez with a crime at that time.

Rowland went back to the bank to carefully examine the certificate of deposit. Both the sheriff and the bank's cashier could now clearly see that the name of the original owner had been altered. Afterward, walking down the sidewalk near his office with the bank's president, Jonathan S. Slauson, the sheriff met Ramírez heading toward the Temple Block. Rowland called Ramírez into his office, where Slauson heatedly accused him of being an accomplice to the theft and demanded a return of the missing $500. Although he denied criminal involvement or having the money, Ramírez admitted having used bad judgment in vouching for Hidales. He promised Slauson he would make the bank's loss good since it had been caused by his mistake. Despite Slauson's insistence, Rowland refused to search Ramírez for the missing money. A few days later, Ramírez met the sheriff on the street and gave him $500 in cash for delivery to the bank.

One of the witnesses for the people, Constable Thomas H. Botello, told a story at the preliminary examination that must have been devastating for Ramírez.[48] He was present at the jail on November 26, 1880, when Ramírez came to visit Hidales. He told the jailers that he wanted to interview Hidales in his capacity as a lawyer. Deputy Sheriff James C. Kays was quite obliging. He placed Ramírez in one of two rooms that made up the jail office, brought in Hidales, and locked the door.

While Ramírez thought his discussion with Hidales was private, Botello and Kays were eavesdropping. They put a blanket in front of the door and laid down with their ears to the bottom crack. Botello also peeked occasionally through two large key holes. Both men could hear what was being said and understood Spanish perfectly. Despite his name, Kays was a member of the Spanish-speaking community, the son of a Mexican woman. Hidales was no doubt part of the plan to elicit incriminating statements from Ramírez. He suggested that they sit near the door, close to the unseen listening officers.

Botello testified that he heard Hidales tell Ramírez, "Nobody knows that I gave you $500 to help me out." Ramírez replied, "Don't give me away for the sake of my family." Hidales told Ramírez that he needed money to hire a lawyer and to get outside food since the meals in jail were terrible. Ramírez promised to bring $200 that evening to accommodate Hidales. The two men discussed what would likely happen to Hidales in court. Ramírez said that he would get Henry T. Gage to represent him. He warned Hidales that he would get some prison time but not more than a year. Further, Ramírez said he would do all he could to help Hidales, suggesting that his efforts would be in exchange for silence about being paid $500. The prosecution contended that the conversation overheard by Constable Botello was both an admission of guilt by Ramírez and an attempt to cover it up.

Under cross-examination, Botello admitted that Hidales was receiving special treatment in jail. The sheriff's office had arranged for him to take some of his meals at Jerry Illich's Restaurant and Oyster House, the finest dining place in Los Angeles. Botello took Hidales there without restraints, even permitting him to enjoy its house wines. These special privileges were unquestionably provided to Hidales for helping in the prosecution of Ramírez. Of greater importance, he was promised a lenient prison sentence for his cooperation. After the entire case was over, Hidales pleaded guilty, receiving a prison sentence of two years from Judge Ignacio Sepúlveda, the crime of forgery being punishable by a term of one to fourteen years. His reduced sentence was no doubt given at the suggestion of the district attorney in exchange for Hidales's testimony against Ramírez, a tactic still used by prosecutors. These inducements also caused Hidales to reveal the source of the forged certificate of deposit. He told Los Angeles authorities that he had received it from J. W. McFatridge, an employee of the San Diego post office, who had found the certificate through his customary pilfering of the mail. As a result, McFatridge was arrested and brought from San Diego to the Los Angeles federal magistrate, B. C. Whiting, who set his bail at $8,000.

The long preliminary hearing before Justice Fisher ended on December 29, 1880. He ruled that there was enough evidence of guilt to justify a trial in the Superior Court. Ramírez was ordered to appear before Judge Volney E. Howard on March 22, 1881. Bail was increased by another $1,000, for a total of $2,000, which Ramírez's sister Isabel also paid.

When the day of the trial arrived, Ramírez was gone. He had arranged his affairs as much as possible, then left for Mexico by steamer. Before leaving, he gave his sister Isabel a deed to his part of the Aliso Road homestead to cover his forfeited bail. Ramírez also transferred his interest in the Rancho San Rafael to his sister for the amount of $2,683.88 in cash.[49] When Judge Howard opened court on March 22, 1881, he learned that Ramírez was missing. Howard again set bail at $2,000 and issued a permanent warrant for his arrest. Ramírez was now a fugitive from justice.

On the day set for Ramírez's trial, the *Los Angeles Herald* noticed that he had left for Mexico by a coastal steamer:

> We are assured, says *La Crónica*, that lawyer Francisco P. Ramirez has taken his portables and at this hour finds himself in the city of Hermosillo, Sonora. The county will gain by this movement the $2,000 bail given as the guarantee of his remaining here and avoid, besides, the expense of a probably costly trial.

A view of Aliso Street toward the east in 1885. The Ramírez homestead was near the end of it on the left, but the area was now greatly changed from the early days and had been for some time. Reprinted by permission of the University of Southern California Special Collections.

Part of downtown Los Angeles, circa 1880. The Temple Block is in the middle to the right. Main and Spring streets converge out of sight on the left. The place had taken on many attributes of a regular city. Reprinted by permission of the University of Southern California Special Collections.

Spring Street, looking north in 1880. Los Angeles was now possessed of nearly all the consumer goods and comforts of the age. In just this short block there was a giant emporium called the People's Store, as well as a grocery store, a liquor store, a music shop, a bakery, an oyster parlor, a dentist, and three real-estate offices. Reprinted by permission of the University of Southern California Special Collections.

The *Anaheim Gazette* used Ramírez's flight to make a comment on the era's politicians: "Ramirez always bore a fair reputation until he accepted a nomination for assemblyman."⁵⁰

Ramírez knew that an escape to Mexico would create the presumption that he was guilty. The high status he had acquired as an editor, lawyer, and public figure instantly vanished as he fled California in disgrace. He carried a fair amount of money on his person as the result of selling his interest in the Rancho San Rafael to his sister, enough to live for a long while in Mexico. Otherwise, he had lost everything. Ramírez's life was torn from its foundations in this dark moment. His anguish as the steamer he was aboard left San Diego and crossed into Mexican waters can only be imagined.

CLAMOR PUBLICO

Periódico Independiente y Literario.

LOS ANGELES, CALIFORNIA, MARTES, JUNIO 19 DE 1855.

COMISION DE LOS ESTADOS UNIDOS
PARA LA APROBACION DE LOS TITULOS DE TERRENOS.

[Sesion de 22 de mayo de 1855.]

Opinion del Comisionado Farwell.

APROBADOS.

N.° 250.—El título del Sr. M. G. Vallejo por 10 leguas cuadradas y 5 mas en el condado de Petaluma.

N.° 291.—Otro del mismo, por un terreno en el condado de Solano.

N.° 291.—El título de John Rose, seis leguas cuadradas en el condado de Yuba.

N.° 462.—El título de los herederos de Juan B. Alvarado, por el Rincon del Diablo en el condado de San Diego.

N.° 550.—El título de Jno P. Davison, cuatro leguas cuadradas en Santa Paula y Santicoy, condado de Sta. Barbara.

N.° 461.—El título de Juan Foster ocho leguas cuadradas en el valle de S. Felipe, condado de San Diego.

N.° 664.—El título de los herederos de David Littlejohn, una legua cuadrada en Los Carneros, condado de Monterey.

N.° 509.—El título de Samuel G. Reid, tres leguas cuadradas en el rancho del Puerto, condado de San Joaquin.

N.° 248.—El título de Chas Convilland, parte de 1 leguas concedidas primero a J. A. Sutter. Concesion por recompensa y con condiciones en 1841. El terreno esta situado en Feather River.

DESAPROBADO.

N.° 68.—El título de Temple y Alexander, por 105 varas cuadradas en el condado de Los Angeles. Concedidas provisionalmente en 1854.

Mexico.

El General Alvarez ha espedido el siguiente decreto para favorecer á las personas que deseen emigrar á Mexico para esplotar los ricos placeres de oro que se han descubierto en Ajutechlan, cerca de Acapulco:

El Capitan Juan Alvarez, General de Division de la República Mexicana y Gefe del ejército restaurador de la Libertad á los habitantes de la República, sabed:

Que usando de las amplias facultades que me concede el "Plan de Ayutla," para promover por cuantos medios me sean posibles la prosperidad y engrandecimiento de la nacion, he tenido á bien decretar:

Art. 1.° El laboreo de los placeres de San Francisco del Oro, situados en el distrito de Ajutechlan del departamento de Guerrero, se declara libre para mexicanos y extranjeros desde la publicacion de este decreto.

Art. 2. Todo individuo, ya sea nacional ó extranjero, que se dirija al distrito mencionado con objeto de trabajar los placeres, se presentará á las autoridades políticas para obtener de ellas "gratis," sus correspondientes resguardos.

Art. 3. Es libre de todo derecho la introduccion que se haga por el puerto de Acapulco, de maquinaria, instrumentos y provisiones para el trabajo de las minas.

Art. 4. Los metales preciosos del distrito mineral, que se extraigan fuera de la república, solo pagarán al erario el 1 por 100, cayendo en pena de comiso los que contravengan á esta disposicion.

Art. 5. Todo trabajador de placeres referidos, ya sea nacional ó extranjero, que desea adquirir terrenos para fabricar ó dedicarse á la agricultura, ocurrirá á la autoridad política, que facilitará de los terrenos valdíos el que se le pidiere, á precios convenciales y equitativos.

Art. 6. Las diferencias que ocurran entre los mineros, se resolverán por quien corresponda con sujecion á la ordenanza del ramo.

Por tanto, etc. Dado en cuartel general del Ejército Restaurador en Texca, á 20 de Abril de 1855. JUAN ALVAREZ.

Sud America.

CHILE.—Segun las últimas noticias continúa su marcha pacífica y progresiva. Las elecciones para miembros del Congreso han pasado sin ocurrencia alguna notable. Entre los Senadores electos vemos con suma satisfaccion el nombre del ilustre colombiano D. Andrés Bello.

PERÚ.—El general Flores habia llegado á Lima, y protestado contra el tratado que celebró Echenique con el gobierno del Ecuador, por el cual se le niega á aquel el asilo en el Perú. Parece que el gobierno provisional tiene por ominoso el tratado, y lo considera humillante para el honor nacional. Pero el ministro del Ecuador protestó, y le han seguido los demás Ministros de la América septentrional residentes en Lima. Piden que Flores salga del Perú inmediatamente. "Si Flores (dice un diario del Sur) ha sido siempre una amenaza para los Estados Colombianos, hoy es mayor esa amenaza, mediante la expedicion que se quedaba formando en los Estados Unidos por él, con el fin de tomar las islas de los Galápagos."

Es un hecho imposible que salga de aquí expedicion contra el Ecuador, por mas que haga Flores y su edecan Clemens.

BOLIVIA.—No son menores las inquietudes en Bolivia con motivo del anunciado regreso del general Santa Cruz. El Presidente Belzu ha dictado un decreto, ordenando el secuestro de los bienes de todo el que tome parte en alguna sedicion, invasion, etc. Uno de los artículos de ese decreto manda considerar sin efecto las transacciones que se hubieren celebrado sobre dichos bienes, desde seis meses antes de cometido el delito, en cuando fueren aquellos necesarios para indemnizar al Gobierno y a los particulares de los perjuicios causados por los perturbadores. Se ha dado á luz una carta que se dice dirijida por el general Santa Cruz al coronel Puch, fechada en Bruselas á 15 de noviembre del año próximo pasado, y en la cual manifiesta el Protector su determinacion de "regresar ó no á America á oponerse á la reeleccion en que está empeñado Belzu, adoptando al efecto el sistema de Rosas."

BRASIL Y PARAGUAY.—Por los extractos que ofrecen los diarios del Istmo de Panamá sabemos que la guerra del imperio del Brasil contra el Uruguay se está haciendo, y segun parece, sin una desaparicion que la precediera, "siendo lo mas extraño (dice el Panameño) ver que la marina de guerra de los Estados Unidos ayude á S. M. I; en su agresion contra los paraguayos. Estos, empero, oponen fuerzas considerables á sus adversarios, y hasta ahora alcanzan el triunfo en los combates habidos."—He aquí lo que dice el Constitucional de Mendoza, en el asunto: "Se hacia serio nos informa uno de los pasajeros llegados en la mensajería, el conflicto del Paraguay, atacado por una fuerte escuadra brasilera y un vapor norteamericano; dos potencias poderosas han llevado la guerra contra esa naciente y pequeña república; el Almirante del Paraguay, hijo del Presidente Lopez, de dos vapores que habian comprado en Europa, no habia conseguido introducir sino uno antes que la escuadra brasilera ocupase los rios. Habia tenido lugar un combate entre el vapor norteamericano que hemos mencionado y una batería paraguaya, la cual causó en sus fuegos algunas averías en el vapor matándole dos hombres ademas. Este desmontó algunas piezas de aquella. En la frontera con el Brasil, en las guardias ó fuertes se trataban encuentros parciales entre paraguayos y brasileros, en los que aquellos habian salido vencedores."

Los periódicos de Buenos Ayres dan la noticia de que una fuerza paraguaya de 8,000 hombres habia obtenido á inmediaciones de Villarreal un triunfo sobre las fuerzas brasileras invasoras. Sobre el Paraná tenian los paraguayos 20,000 hombres estacionados, habian tapado dos de las tres bocas del rio Paraguay, echando á pique

---

FRANCIA.—Un decreto del Emperador aumenta al ejército en 90,000 hombres.— Cada regimiento de línea tendrá un refuerzo de 900.

Esperando la visita de la Reina Victoria á Paris, el Emperador ha mandado poner el Liceo Imperial en un pie de esplendida magnificencia.

Por decreto de 31 de marzo, Mr. de Thounevel Ministro Plenipotenciario de primera clase y director de los asuntos políticos, se encargará durante la audiencia del Ministro Secretario de Estado de Negocios Extranjeros, Mr. Drouyn de Lhuys, de la direccion de los trabajos de ese departamento y de la correspondencia diplomática.

El gobierno francés ha quejado oficialmente al belga, á instancias del Príncipe Napoleon, por un opúsculo publicado contra el Emperador sobre la guerra y que se atribuyó al Príncipe.

EL PROXIMO CONGRESO.—Hasta hoy los miembros electos del próximo Congreso son como sigue: Administracion 31; Oposicion 129. Todavía resta que elejir 37 miembros en los Estados donde las elecciones congresionales aun no han tenido lugar.

INTERESANTE.—Un astrónomo Aleman dice que en veinte millones de años la tierra será destruida por una cometa!

LA MEDALLA RUSA.—En los cuerpos de algunos soldados rusos que cayeron en Eupatoria se encontró la medalla de plata de la decoracion de San Jorge. En un lado está grabada el águila rusa, con dos cabezas, teniendo en los pies el globo terrestre y el cetro del soberano; sobre el águila esta la corona imperial y una paloma iluminada. Sobre estas figuras tiene las siguientes palabras en lengua rusa:
"Arrodillense, idólatras, porque Dios es con nosotros."
En el otro lado tiene la siguiente divisa tambien en ruso:
"Para la sumision de Hungria y Transilvania."

Dícese que casi todo el vino de la Moselle ha sido comprado por el gobierno Francés para mandarlo al ejército de Crimea.

La Union de Sacramento hablando del San Francisco Chronicle dice: "No se encuentra dentro de los límites de este Estado otro periódico mas cortés, independiente y elegante."

Los soldados heridos y enfermos que han muerto en Liverpool, (Inglaterra) serán enterrados en un mismo lugar, sobre el cual se erijirá un monumento por suscricion pública.

PISCATORIO.—Mr. Joseph S. McIntyre, de la armada de los E. U. estacionada en Benicia, publica una carta en el Herald de San Francisco, anunciando que sacó un pescado y abriéndolo encontro un látigo de veinte pulgadas y media de largo y montado en plata. Se ha dudado mucho la veracidad de esta historieta.

POZO ARTESIANO.—Se ha cavado un nuevo pozo artesiano en San José, y segun el Tribune es una curiosidad.

CONVENCION DEMOCRATICA.—El día 27 de Junio tendrá lugar una convencion democrática en Sacramento con el objeto de nombrar oficiales para la eleccion general en Setiembre próximo.

EL CENSO.—La Constitucion del Estado previene que se tome el censo este año, pero como la legislatura no dispuso nada sobre esto, se tomara el año de 1860.

PELEGRINOS PARA PALESTINA.—Una caravana de pelegrinos se embarcó recientemente en Marsella para la Tierra Santa.— Antes de su salida fuéron invitados al palacio por el Obispo y cada uno recibió una crucesita de plata, con la fecha de su partida.

La ley del Dom[ingo]

SECCION 1. Toda diversion bulliciosa será en lo sucesivo [prohibida] los dias domingos.

SEC. 2. Todo individuo que ayudase á abrir en este dia [de descanso] juego, cuarto ó salon, juego [...] lugares propios para carreras, combate de osos, de toros, ó diversiones barbaras y bárbaras prendido por un delito esp[ecial] ley, y despues de convicto, á una multa cuyo mínimum [será de] cuenta pesos y el maximum [...] cuenta.

SEC. 3. Todo individuo [que venda] un billete de entrada en [cualquiera] de las diversiones enumeradas [en la se]gunda seccion de esta acta, [será] castigado con una multa [cuyo mínimo será] cuenta pesos y el máximo [de] cincuenta.

SEC. 4. Los jueces de [paz conocerán] en todos casos de infracciones de esta ley.

SEC. 5. Esta ley estará [en vigor] desde Junio 15 de 1855.

PAPEL DE TULE.—El Ex[-gobernador] BIGLER en su último mensaje [habla de] los terrenos inundados y [se ex]presa como sigue:

"Y ya que estoy tocan[do este punto] acaso no sea fuera de lugar [que se] lleguen á tener buen éxito los [ensayos] que ahora se están haciendo [en los Estados] del Atlántico, no tan solo [es util] sino muy numerosa necesa[ria] lo. Nadie ignora que una [gran parte de] los terrenos adquiridos por [nosotros en] virtud de la ley de Septi[embre...] está cubierta de lozano T[ule en] este suelo, y que por térmi[no medio] toneladas por acre.

"Durante el último oto[ño se han] sido cuidadosamente eesar[...] bricantes esperimentados, [y se ha com]probado que, en su opinion, [puede hacerse] con él un papel de calidad [su]perior.

"Puesto que el tallo de [esta planta] está maduro y antes que se [vea expuesto á] la lluvia, es casi blanco, con [el método] del blanqueo sería con [gasto] pequeño. Estando cubierto [de una] compacta fibra, y conten[iendo en su] un tejido cecular con nume[rosas] fibras longitudinales, se [reunen] todas las cualidades requer[idas]

"Se han remitido vari[as muestras de] Tule á algunos fabricantes [en los] Estados del Atlántico, con [el fin de que] hagan ensayos con él; y se [espera] el resultado de estos impo[rtantes experi]mentos.

"A fin de poder aprecia[r mejor] la importancia de este esper[imento y] que tenga feliz éxito, se ha[ce una] explicacion de algunos hec[hos e]videntes.

"El precio medio, en lo[s Estados del] Atlántico, del material con [que se] fabrica el papel es de unos [...] dos centavos la libra. De cada [...] tercera parte del precio ma[yor hay una] de los trapos, cada acre produ[ce unos] ochenta pesos ($80) ó sea [como ocho]cientos pesos ($12,800) cada [diez] acres, y esto, sin mas gasto [que los que] se orijinen al tiempo del co[rte, y sin] no despues que haya permi[tido se] durado.

"Sin embargo, cualquie[ra será el] sultado de los esperimentos [que se están] haciendo acerca de la prin[cipal] papel de cartas ó de impr[ension no ha]y duda hau los hombres ente[ndidos que] han ocupado de esta mate[ria de que el] Tule se puede fabricar [papel de bue]na calidad.

CHAPTER THIRTEEN
El Partido Norte

The Los Angeles press at first reported that Ramírez had fled to Hermosillo, capital of the Mexican state of Sonora. This was a logical surmise since Ramírez had formed some lasting friendships in Sonora while editor of the official newspaper, *La Estrella de Occidente*, nearly twenty years before. As already seen, while campaigning in San Francisco for the office of treasurer in the Junta Central during 1865, he had published in *El Nuevo Mundo* several letters from Sonoran friends attesting to his devotion to Mexico. Many of the same people who had corresponded with him were still living in Hermosillo and Ures. They might help Ramírez in his time of crisis.

Instead, Ramírez went to the port of Mazatlan in the state of Sinaloa, a regular stop for Pacific-coast steamers. Across from the tip of the Baja California peninsula on the mainland side, the place was verdant, almost tropical. It had a population of at least 10,000, with most of the usual urban amenities. Ramírez apparently intended to stay there indefinitely. In May 1881, less than sixty days after fleeing from Los Angeles, he opened a newspaper called *El Ferrocarril*—the Railroad—probably so named because of a local interest in bringing a railroad connection to the port.[1]

Ramírez's ability to pay the starting costs of a newspaper shows that he had brought money with him from the sale of his interest in the Rancho San Rafael near Los Angeles. However, his newspaper enterprise in Mazatlan was not successful. Only two months or so after beginning it, he left for Baja California. Abandoning *El Ferrocarril*, Ramírez took a steamer up to the Bay of Todos Santos, a natural harbor sixty-nine miles south of the United States border, where he could disembark. This place would someday be the site of Ensenada, a major city and the capital of northern Baja California. When Ramírez arrived, it was a barren expanse called Rancho de Ensenada de Todos Santos, with a solitary adobe house near the bay for the family of its owner, Pedro Gastélum.

Ramírez headed northeast toward Real del Castillo, thirty miles from the coast. It was the area's largest settlement, but it had fewer than 200 inhabitants at the time.[2] He found himself in an arid, vastly underpopulated country nearly free of governmental authority. The region's isolation was so complete that officials in Mexico City seemed scarcely aware that Baja California existed. The situation in which Ramírez found himself can only be understood in the context of northern Baja California's history. He would have to adapt to the conditions that had been created before he arrived. A review of the region's history before Ramírez entered Real del Castillo is necessary in order to appreciate his new environment and the hardships it presented.

In one of the central government's rare actions concerning the territory of Baja California, President José Joaquín de Herrera issued a decree on April 12, 1849, dividing the peninsula into two administrative districts. The principal one was called the Partido Sur—the Southern District—and the other the Partido Norte—the Northern District. The capital of the entire peninsula was placed near its southern end, at La Paz, a town on the east coast of Baja California about 100 miles above the peninsula's tip on the Sea of Cortez.[3]

The chief executive of the territory of Baja California operated from his capital in La Paz and was appointed by either the president of the republic or the minister of the interior. He was usually called the *jefe político*—the political chief—although he was also known as the *prefecto*—the prefect—and *gobernador*—the governor.

The jefe político of the Partido Sur in La Paz was the supreme authority over the entire peninsula, with the power to appoint an official to act on his behalf in the Partido Norte, called the *subjefe*. Due to geographical factors this subordinate in the north could be quite independent. The first capital of the Partido Norte to be occupied by the subjefe was San Vicente, a tiny crossroads about 110 miles from San Diego, but more than 1,000 miles from La Paz. Written communications between the jefe político in the south and his appointee in the north were never timely. Months could pass without either hearing from the other.

The precarious grip of Mexico's government over Baja California was challenged on November 3, 1853, by an American adventurer named William Walker. On that date a small group of men led by Walker arrived at La Paz by ship from San Francisco. They were piratical outlaws known as filibusters, men who acted on a popular belief that the United States should acquire parts of Mexico and Latin America by force. In the absence of a military invasion by the United States in such places, they would undertake it themselves in the hope that American annexation would soon follow. In the interim they would make their fortunes by looting the conquered areas.[4]

Mexico had neglected to provide Baja California with a military force to protect its territorial integrity. Walker's men entered La Paz without resistance, taking prisoner the jefe político, Rafael Espinosa, and placing him on board their ship. After three days they left for the northern harbor adjacent to the Rancho de Ensenada de Todos Santos. Upon arriving Walker used Pedro Gastélum's lone adobe as his headquarters.

There was no place in the underpopulated Partido Norte with urban pretensions, making it impossible to organize a large force to combat Walker. The only opposition to the invasion was a group of about forty ranchers, headed by a local leader named Antonio María Meléndrez. The number of filibusterers was increased at Ensenada by the overland arrival of additional fortune hunters from San Francisco and San Diego. Soon Walker was in charge of 600 men and two pieces of artillery. The subjefe of the Partido Norte, Francisco del Castillo Negrete, retreated to San Diego, the only place where he could request assistance from Mexico City by telegraph.

A disaster occurred for Walker when the jefe político, still a prisoner on board Walker's ship, bribed the captain to return him to La Paz. Without warning the ship weighed anchor, leaving Walker and his men stranded. The filibusterers eventually decided to march eastward toward Sonora, but on the road most of the cattle they used for food were driven away by Indians. Now they encountered their most formidable enemy, the hostile nature of Baja California itself. Passing through a country devoid of anything to sustain life, they suffered from grievous hunger and thirst. Most of Walker's men deserted, striking out on their own in search of food and water. After losing a large number of his men, Walker was attacked by local ranchers and their allies, some 300 Cucupá Indians. The only escape for Walker was a road leading north, deliberately left unblocked to encourage his departure. Half-starved and plagued by thirst, the surviving filibusterers staggered toward San Diego with no desire to return to the cruel aridity of Baja California.

A series of unpopular subjefes were sent to govern the Partido Norte after the expulsion of William Walker and his filibusterers. They were hated by the local ranchers because of their parasitic behavior. Both the central government in Mexico City and the jefe político in La Paz failed to send provisions to these distant officers or even pay their salaries. In order to sustain themselves, together with a small cadre of associates and soldiers, successive subjefes had no choice but to force the locals to supply them with food and housing. This was the cause of enormous resentment since the ranchers barely subsisted on their cattle, vegetable patches, and fruit trees raised with great difficulty by carefully hoarding water from rare springs and creeks. With few resources in a desolate environment, the seizure of what little the ranchers possessed put their survival at risk.

Some of the subjefes after Walker's defeat were virtual outlaws. One of them, José María Castro, a native of Alta California, was once the chief rival of Pío Pico for the office of governor of that province. He came to Baja California during the American conquest, preferring not to live under foreign domination in the north. After being named subjefe in 1856, he set himself up as a tyrant. Not only did Castro force the ranchers to give up much of their scant resources, he also illegally sold public land for cash in transactions later nullified by the central government. In the last of many drunken sprees, Castro was shot to death by a subordinate on April 14, 1860.[5]

With Castro removed from the scene, his second-in-command, Feliciano Ruiz de Esparza, appointed himself as the new subjefe without regard to the faraway jefe político in La Paz. One of his first acts was to execute fourteen men allegedly involved in killing Castro. A notorious bandit named Juan Mendoza, an aspirant to the office of subjefe himself, organized a large group of Mexicans in San Diego to attack Esparza, claiming he was motivated by a desire to avenge the men who had been shot. The border region fell into chaos, with constant warfare in which neither side could defeat the other. The followers of Esparza and Mendoza were often criminals wanted by United States authorities. Both groups sacked the ranches below the border, stealing whatever they could, and sometimes killing their owners. This caused an exodus from the Partido Norte to San Diego by people in search of safety. In late 1860 only twelve Mexican families remained in all of northern Baja California.[6]

The problem of criminal anarchy in the Partido Norte was so great that it was brought to the attention of Mexico's president, Benito Juárez. He ordered the new jefe político in La Paz, Teodoro Riveroll, to put an end to it. Juárez assisted Riveroll by sending two hundred troops from Sinaloa to suppress banditry in the Partido Norte. Orders were given to arrest or kill Esparza and Mendoza. The jefe político was fortunate to have a resident of the Partido Norte, José Matías Moreno, available for appointment as a legitimate subjefe. Moreno was in La Paz at the time, urging Riveroll to intervene in the north. When the troops sent by President Juárez arrived, Moreno accompanied them to the harbor of Ensenada, where they on landed March 11, 1861.

Most of the men led by Esparza were captured at a ranch called El Descanso. Their leader, however, escaped. Esparza took his family to the remote island of Guadalupe, 240 miles southwest of Ensenada, where he took refuge until he was forgotten.[7]

Juan Mendoza's men were also neutralized. Those not taken prisoner fled to San Diego. Mendoza himself reached San Diego County and procured a position as a foreman for a prominent American named Cave Couts on his Rancho Guajome near Oceanside. However, Mendoza made some drunken threats against Couts and his family, which lead to his demise. Couts took Mendoza's utterances quite seriously. One morning Couts waited for Mendoza to pass a point where he was hidden behind a butcher shop in San Diego's Old Town. As Mendoza went by, Couts emptied a shotgun in his back. A criminal indictment was filed against Couts, but he was a wealthy and highly influential citizen who got the charges dismissed.[8]

The Partido Norte was quiescent during the French intervention and the prolongation of foreign influence caused by the brief reign of the Austrian Archduke Maximilian as emperor of Mexico. With the defeat of Maximilian and his execution at Querétaro in 1867, President Benito Juárez triumphantly set about asserting his control over Mexico. At this time Bibiano Dávalos was appointed jefe político of Baja California. Dávalos in turn appointed Manuel Clemente Rojo to act as subjefe of the Partido Norte on October 29, 1868.

Rojo was one of the most intelligent and best-educated men in Baja California. Born in Peru about 1823, he was from a middle-class family that could afford to provide him with a legal education. In 1848 Rojo joined with an associate named Juan Lertora in a venture to take a chartered ship with a cargo of merchandise to San Francisco during the gold rush. The ship was wrecked near El Rosario, a point on Baja California's west coast about 300 miles below the border. Some of the cargo was saved, and Rojo stayed to care for it while his partner and the crew went north to find another ship. To pass the time awaiting rescue, Rojo undertook a detailed study of the area and the few people living there, which he recorded in the form of notes and drawings. In later years they were the basis for a popular book.[9]

Rojo eventually learned that his partner could not find a ship because the captains and crews of everything afloat, suffering from gold fever, had joined the rush to the placers in northern California. He therefore made his way to Los Angeles where he stayed until the middle of 1854. During the four or five years that Rojo resided in Los Angeles he was well regarded by both

Americans and Mexicans. At some point in his career, Rojo learned to speak the English language very well, something of great value in dealing with Americans. He became a partner of the pioneer lawyer Isaac S. K. Ogier, although Rojo's status as a foreigner prevented his formal admission to the bar.[10] Beginning in 1851 Rojo was also the editor of a Spanish-language section of the *Star*, Los Angeles's first newspaper. In that year he met Francisco P. Ramírez, only fourteen years old, who was hired as one of the newspaper's compositors.

Ramírez probably regarded Rojo as something of a mentor. Rojo's liberal views, intellectual attainments, and the worldliness acquired during his travels must have had an effect on the adolescent Ramírez. Neither could know that they would meet again some thirty years later as residents of Baja California.

Harris Newmark was present in Los Angeles during Rojo's long visit. He wrote that, while associated with a law practice, Rojo was "a clever, genial native of Peru." In addition to acting as a lawyer and newspaper editor, Rojo frequently appeared in the courts as a paid interpreter. Newmark criticized much court translation of testimony then as deliberately biased toward one party or the other. He singled out Sheriff George Thompson Burrill and Rojo as unusually good interpreters, saying that they were "officials I believe to have been honest and conscientious."[11]

Shortly after his law partner, Ogier, was appointed federal judge of the Southern California district, Rojo left Los Angeles to try his fortune in Mexico City. While there he joined a successful liberal conspiracy to remove the dictator Antonio López de Santa Anna from the presidency. In recognition of a certain degree of political prominence achieved by Rojo despite his foreign origin, the new president, Ignacio Comonfort, appointed him constitutional judge of Baja California in 1855, sending him to the capital of the territory at La Paz.

After Rojo had acted as a judge in La Paz for about ten years, he purchased a large parcel of government land in northern Baja California called the Rancho de San Vicente. His appointment as subjefe of the Partido Norte was probably influenced by his telling the jefe político, Bibiano Dávalos, that he had a desire to attend to his newly acquired property. After traveling to the northern part of the Baja California peninsula, Rojo found that it had hardly changed since he was stranded there twenty years before, in 1848. The vast Partido Norte was still desolate, abandoned, and practically unpopulated. As the subjefe, Rojo was required to reside in Santo Tomás, a tiny village recently designated as the capital of the Partido Norte. Although it had the largest population of any settlement in northern Baja California, the primitive and backward nature of the place can be inferred from Rojo's description of it in 1870. In that year, Santo Tomás had just eighty-nine inhabitants, living in eight adobes and a few brush huts.[12] Its one desirable feature was a rare source of water in the form of a little creek. For the sake of his office, Rojo was forced to endure the isolation and misery of the impoverished place.

After nearly two years in Santa Tomás, Rojo wrote a letter to the minister of the interior in Mexico City, on June 30, 1870, expressing his disappointment over the government's abandonment of Baja California. In the entire time that Rojo had acted as subjefe of the Partido Norte, he had never received his salary. This lack of support by the central government caused him to ask that he be allowed to resign. In his letter Rojo set forth the causes of his disillusionment, beyond not being paid. He called attention to the Partido Norte's extremely sparse population, economic prostration, lack of outside communication, and the nearly total absence of aid from the central government. Rojo wrote that the whole northern half of Baja California had only about 500 non-Indian inhabitants scattered among some twenty-five ranches.[13]

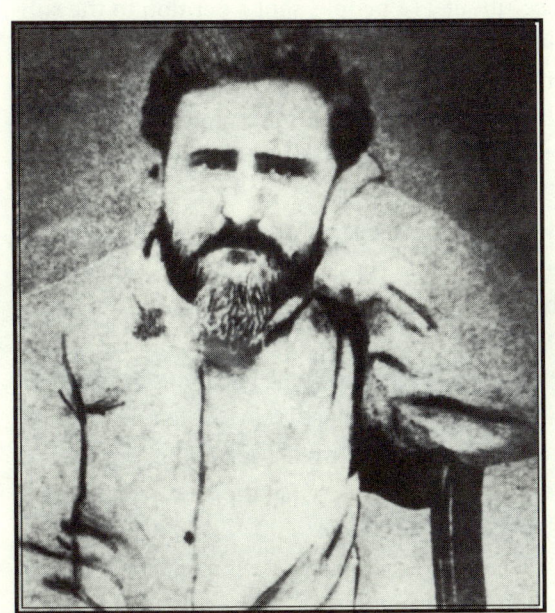

Portrait of Manuel Clemente Rojo, date unknown. Courtesy of Dr. Fernando Araujo, Ensenada.

Rojo recognized that the reduced number of people living there were more oriented toward the United States than Mexico. The small amount of money circulating in the Partido Norte was spent in San Diego for the necessities of life since there was only a trickle of commerce below the border. When provisions, clothing, or medical attention were needed, a wagon trip north was made to get them. San Diego was the source of everything, a refuge from criminals and the only place where those living in the harsh emptiness of the Partido Norte could occasionally find urban comforts.

Before Rojo could withdraw as subjefe of the Partido Norte, an astonishing development changed his mind. During June of 1870, two brothers, Ambrosio and Manuel del Castillo, discovered some small gold nuggets in the valley of San Rafael, about thirty miles northeast of the Ensenada harbor. News of what the del Castillos found was reported in the San Diego press on July 21, 1870, after Ambrosio del Castillo went there to sell some of his gold. The revelation of the gold's location in the valley of San Rafael set off a rush by Americans residing in San Diego. They were joined by nearly all the men from little settlements in the Partido Norte like Santo Tomás and even by highly experienced miners from the adjacent Mexican state of Sonora.

A village sprang up in the center of gold mining operations, called Real del Castillo in honor of the brothers who first found gold there. Those who took up residence in the place, about 112 people, sent a petition to the subjefe, Manuel Clemente Rojo, asking that the settlement be given official status as a township so that communal land could be set aside and legally distributed to those who had moved there. Rojo immediately consented and attended a ceremony on October 2, 1870, that marked the founding of Real del Castillo.

The influx of Americans and Mexicans searching for gold temporarily raised the population of Real del Castillo to roughly 400 people. Rojo requested that the capital of the Partido Norte be changed from the miserable and largely abandoned village of Santo Tomás to Real del Castillo. He wrote to the jefe político in La Paz that he had already begun living in Real del Castillo: "I am here because in Santo Tomás there is no one left to wash my clothes or even cook my food. It is a place lacking in everything."[14] Based on Rojo's recommendations, Real del Castillo was made the new capital of the Partido Norte during August of 1871.

The presence of gold and a relatively large concentration of people in Real del Castillo induced a few merchants from San Diego to open stores there. Among these men were Jacob Wagner, John Powers, and George Furlong.

Apart from selling general merchandise, they ran improvised saloons where liquor was sold twenty-four hours a day, attracting criminals and gamblers. The largest commercial house was begun in 1871 by Louis Mendelson, a Polish immigrant to the United States who made his way to Real del Castillo from Anaheim, California, after hearing reports of the gold strike. Also in 1871 William Sargent began a stagecoach line between San Diego and Real del Castillo.[15] He improved a primitive trail at his own expense in order to facilitate movement over it. Even so, it took three or four days to make the exhausting trip over rugged brush-covered hills.

Excitement over the gold strike and the movement toward it mostly resulted in disappointment. In the end no one truly struck it rich. The deposit found by the del Castillo brothers began to disappear almost as soon as Real del Castillo was organized as a township. In certain places pockets of gold remained trapped in quartz and rock, but it took expensive machinery to crush the ore so that the gold could be washed out of it. Whether mining was done by hand or machine, it required an abundant water supply, which simply did not exist. To aggravate the situation, the area suffered from a severe drought that had begun soon after gold was discovered.

At the beginning of 1873, Manuel Clemente Rojo was replaced as subjefe of the Partido Norte. Rojo was the subject of written complaints sent by residents to the jefe político in La Paz. Their grievances mostly concerned overly aggressive efforts by Rojo to collect money, even by forced loans, in order to create a national guard, an armed militia to control crime in the Partido Norte.[16] The gold strike brought a large number of outlaws from both sides of the border who were regularly holding up the stage from San Diego and robbing citizens on the roads. Sometimes the streets of Real del Castillo were not secure. Most people preferred to risk an encounter with criminals, however, rather than pay what they considered exorbitant amounts demanded by Rojo for public safety.

Rojo was succeeded by José María Villagrana, a stranger to the area, who had been sent from La Paz. At this time Real del Castillo's population was rapidly declining, as miners realized that the region's gold had played out. In 1874 more gold was found at a place called Japa, about thirty miles northeast of the San Rafael valley. A sudden movement toward Japa resulted in the desertion of Real del Castillo. It was reported that in August 1874 the little settlement consisted of only thirty families, thirty-five houses, four small stores, an adobe used as a hotel, and a tiny school.[17]

Beginning with Villagrana's term of office, the title of the Partido Norte's chief executive was changed from subjefe to subprefecto. Otherwise Villagrana's position was no different from that of his predecessors. He soon found that he was alone in a desolate place without support from his superiors. His greatest problem was uncontrollable crime throughout the Partido Norte. Perhaps he began to understand why Rojo had wanted to create an armed militia using local resources. Despite numerous unanswered appeals to the jefe político in La Paz and the authorities in Mexico City, Villagrana could not obtain a decent police force or military unit to maintain order. The only semblance of a jail was a structure more like a corral than a building. Unless constantly watched, the prisoners could escape whenever they wanted.[18]

Just a few months after taking office, Villagrana learned of a plot by several prisoners to take over Real del Castillo, rob whatever money was in the municipal treasury, and sack the few remaining commercial establishments. The assault was prevented, but Villagrana realized that he could have been killed if it had succeeded. Probably out of concern for his personal safety, Villagrana formed an alliance with a violent criminal gang leader named Pedro Badillo. Once known as Six-Toed Pete in Los Angeles, Badillo was a fugitive from American justice. While Villagrana presided over official affairs in Real del Castillo, the outlaw Badillo was allowed to rule the streets in exchange for keeping an eye out for the subprefecto's safety.[19]

Villagrana's protector, Pedro Badillo, had arrived in the Partido Norte during 1873, after jumping bail in Los Angeles on a charge of stealing two mules. Badillo was known to have committed several major crimes, but none could be adequately proven. Based on his criminal notoriety, even a conviction on the relatively minor charge of stealing the mules would have resulted in a long prison sentence. The *Los Angeles Express*, on April 7, 1873, noted his escape to Mexico and reported, "It is asserted that, at various times and places, he has killed a number of men. He has also been suspected of being the guiding spirit of a band of horse-thieves and law-breakers." The writer of the article in the *Express* had a high opinion of Six-Toed Pete's criminal abilities, calling him "a man of great cunning and sagacity, and of a fair degree of education, in his own tongue." With almost poetic prescience, he foresaw what Badillo would do when he arrived in Mexico: "He has always been a leader among his class; and in the fresh fields and pastures new to which he has gone he will no doubt continue to be a master spirit among those who live without the pale of the law." In 1874 Badillo made an application for Mexican citizenship, which Villagrana approved and forwarded to La Paz.

A western view of the San Rafael Valley, about 1886. The village of Real del Castillo lies below. Courtesy of Dr. Fernando Araujo, Ensenada.

The predicament of the Partido Norte as a forgotten corner of Mexico was dramatically illustrated when Villagrana was confronted with a possible Indian uprising.[20] Native people in the vicinity of Jacume had long complained about Americans crossing the border and killing members of their tribe. When a group of Americans carrying out attacks against the Indians were finally captured in 1876, a judge in Real del Castillo accepted a bribe to set them free. This flagrant disregard of justice for the Indians, one of a series of such incidents, caused them to convene a large war party that threatened to attack the Mexicans. An emissary sent by Villagrana to parlay with the Indians reported that there were approximately 600 of them gathered at Jacume and that 250 were armed with good rifles. Seminomadic and autonomous groups of Indians greatly outnumbered the Mexicans in the Partido Norte. A census in 1861 showed that the Indians made up over ninety percent of the region's population. Although generally peaceful, they had the power to annihilate the Mexicans.

Villagrana called for a meeting of Real del Castillo's residents on August 9, 1876, to discuss the Indian menace. After considering the need to arm the village, a search for rifles resulted in only twenty being found, most unserviceable. Without funds in the municipal treasury, Villagrana resolved to purchase weapons from San Diego with money taken from duties charged by a customhouse at Rancho Tijuana on the wagon road to Real del Castillo. The little customhouse, established in 1874 by the federal government, was a major aggravation to residents in the Partido Norte. The duties it imposed on merchandise brought from San Diego were often three or four times more than the original cost of the goods. Although no one passed by it if possible, it was a continuous problem for those living below the border.

Despite having no legal authority to do so, Villagrana appeared at the Tijuana customhouse on August 19, 1876, with a group of men. Over the objections of the person in charge, he broke open the cash box where the money from duties was kept. To everyone's surprise, it contained just $45, only enough to purchase two new rifles, nothing more. This disappointment revealed the precarious position of the Partido Norte. Enveloped in poverty and abandoned by Mexico, it was utterly defenseless. Fortunately, the Indian threat gradually subsided but not through any action taken by local Mexican authorities.

Villagrana continued his efforts to raise money for arms and ammunition by focusing on a small number of residents in Real del Castillo. He became extremely unpopular among the people who were forced to pay him money. His behavior was much like that of Manuel Clemente Rojo, his immediate predecessor. However, while Rojo was dismissed because of letters of complaint to the jefe político in La Paz, the inhabitants of Real del Castillo dealt with Villagrana on their own. While playing chess at Louis Mendelson's general store, Villagrana was taken prisoner at pistol point by a group of disgruntled residents.[21] Several of them volunteered to forcibly escort Villagrana eastward to the mouth of the Colorado River in the Gulf of California, where he might eventually find a steamer to take him to La Paz. Manuel Clemente Rojo was the leader of the movement against Villagrana, and he carefully documented the legal rationale for his actions, while counseling against violence. During the long ride to Villagrana's exile, a few of the party took pity on him and helped him escape. After an arduous trip over the desert, he showed up in San Diego where he got passage on a steamer to La Paz.

Meantime, José Moreno and José Valdez, men prominent in the coup against Villagrana, appointed themselves as leaders of the community. They took possession of the government house, formed a small group of armed men, and began a course of intolerably abusive conduct. Pedro Badillo, who considered himself a friend of Villagrana, met with several of the residents who desired to get rid of Moreno and Valdez. On the morning of

February 13, 1877, Badillo went to the government house, where he met Moreno and demanded that he surrender. When Moreno refused, Badillo shot and killed him.[22] Within a few hours Valdez suffered the same fate.

Although Badillo and other malcontents tried to form some kind of ad hoc government, nothing came of it. When Villagrana landed in La Paz after his expulsion from the Partido Norte, the new jefe político and military commander, Lieutenant Colonel Andrés L. Tapia, ordered him to return to Real del Castillo. On landing in San Diego, Villagrana announced his intent to become subprefecto again, which instigated a series of armed conflicts between his friends and enemies. Villagrana feared that if he left San Diego he would be killed on the road to Real del Castillo. He returned to La Paz directly from San Diego to inform the jefe político of the disorders in the Partido Norte.

The jefe político decided to personally visit the Partido Norte to end the anarchy. He was the first to ever do so.[23] He took one hundred soldiers with him and made a general tour after arriving at Ensenada on November 14, 1877. Tapia wanted to see more than just Real del Castillo. He visited Campo Juárez, Jacume, Valentín, Tecate, the Tijuana customhouse, and San Diego. He met with disaffected Indian leaders of the region, such as Necua and his twelve captains. When they expressed a desire to cease being nomadic, Tapia promised to grant them land so that they could attempt a sedentary way of life.

Before he left the Partido Norte, Tapia appointed Brigído Castrejón as the new subprefecto. To prevent further disturbances Tapia ordered certain individuals in the movement against Villagrana to be banished from the Partido Norte for periods of three to six months. The case of Manuel Clemente Rojo was special since he was considered the most important leader of those causing the disorders. Tapia exiled Rojo indefinitely. When told that Rojo was the most learned man in the Partido Norte and a great benefactor of education, having established the first public school in the Partido Norte at Santo Tomás in 1873, Tapia replied, "He can use his knowledge in some place other than the Partido." Rojo stayed away from the Partido Norte for three years while teaching school in San Diego from 1877 to 1880.

Tapia rounded up the most violent offenders against public order and took them back to La Paz with him where they were held in jail pending a determination of how they should be punished. About a year later there was a kind of general amnesty. All were released, including Pedro Badillo, who was guilty of homicide. Soon after returning to the Partido Norte, Badillo reverted to being the Six-Toed Pete of old. He led a band of outlaws to the customhouse in Tijuana on January 12, 1879, robbing it of $600 in gold and silver. According to several witnesses, he also raped an unfortunate woman who happened to be there. Badillo fled to Arizona, where he spent the rest of his life with impunity, not even bothering to change his name. The 1880 census for Luttrell, Arizona, now a ghost town on the border east of Nogales, shows him listed as a fifty-year-old farmer. In the 1900 Tucson census he is a miner, aged seventy-one, married to a twenty-eight-year-old woman named Estefania, the mother of Badillo's eleven-year-old daughter, Ernestina. Apparently Badillo died in Arizona untouched by his criminal past.

Brigído Castrejón, the subprefecto left by Tapia in the Partido Norte, was not long in office before he was driven out by a strange invasion. It began toward the end of 1879, when General Manuel Márquez de León, commander of the Mexican military's Pacific headquarters in Mazatlan, declared himself in a state of rebellion against President Porfirio Díaz.[24] Márquez landed in La Paz for the purpose of recruiting men and obtaining supplies by force. A small group of loyal soldiers, led by the jefe político, Andrés L. Tapia, resisted Márquez but were overrun. The rebel forces occupied La Paz for a brief time, then left for the Partido Norte. Led by Colonel José María Rangel, a battalion of 300 men sent to capture Márquez arrived in La Paz on February 7, 1880, but they found that the rebels had evacuated the place weeks before. After restoring Tapia to the office of jefe político, Colonel Rangel's battalion set off in pursuit of Márquez.

The rebel force led by Márquez entered Real del Castillo on February 9, 1880. They found that the subprefecto, Brigído Castrejón, had gone to San Diego, having realized that the capital of the Partido Norte had no means of defending itself. Although Márquez knew that he could not remain long in Real del Castillo because of a lack of resources and money, he nevertheless assumed control of the place, naming several persons to occupy official positions. Afterward Márquez went to San Diego, where he hoped to raise money from Americans in exchange for special privileges he would grant them after he succeeded in taking over the national government.

San Diego had always been the supply point for the Partido Norte and its window to the world. Everyone living below the border considered it an emporium for all the necessities of life and a safe harbor. Leaders of contending political factions in the Partido Norte might kill each other on their own soil, but San Diego had to be respected as neutral territory where lethal disputes were held in abeyance. It is quite possible that Márquez and Brigído

Castrejón met in San Diego on equal terms in one of the city's many comfortable saloons in order to discuss the surrender of the Partido Norte, as they were later accused of doing.

While in San Diego Márquez left his troops behind to garrison Real del Castillo. The lack of material well-being there was demonstrated when the soldiers ran out of food and could find nothing to eat. The place was deserted, all the residents having left to stay with relatives and friends on outlying ranches or gone to San Diego. Members of Márquez's force gradually slipped away from the inhospitable place in search of sustenance, much like William Walker's filibusterers had done more than twenty years before.[25]

When the battalion pursuing Márquez under the command of Colonel Rangel arrived in Real del Castillo, they found it totally abandoned. The public officials spuriously appointed by Márquez, realizing the illegality of their conduct in accepting office, left for San Diego to avoid prosecution. A representative of the Public Ministry in Mexico City, Luis B. Murillo, accompanied Colonel Rangel. He made an investigation of Márquez's short occupation of Real del Castillo, finding the subprefecto, Brigído Castrejón, culpable of abandoning his office and allowing the unobstructed entry of Márquez into the Partido Norte. Castrejón was also accused of misappropriating public money. He avoided difficulty with the government by remaining in San Diego.

At the beginning of 1881, Real del Castillo had regained some of its population. It was, however, in a frank state of decline since gold mining operations had ceased. There was no motive to stay in the absence of mining opportunities or wages. Most Americans, disillusioned with their search for gold, had left years before. Mexican families, faced with hardship and few means of subsistence, began to search for better prospects elsewhere.

A new subprefecto for the Partido Norte appeared in Real del Castillo during January 1881. He was an unusually sophisticated man named Ignacio Alas. He had lived for several years in Chicago and New York, where he learned excellent English. Alas was an enterprising and progressive figure who saw the Partido Norte as a backward area that needed to be developed. He had connections with American capitalists who proposed building a railroad from Sonora to integrate the Partido Norte with the rest of Mexico. It would bring freight, merchandise, and people.

Alas left the Partido Norte without asking permission so that he could discuss the Sonora railroad project with American investors in Mexico City. He sent a letter to Juan Bautista Verde, a former Mexican consul in San Di-

A group of residents, some mounted, pose on the main street of Real del Castillo in this view looking east, about 1886. Courtesy of Dr. Fernando Araujo, Ensenada.

A view of the main street of Real del Castillo toward the west, circa 1890. The last adobe on the left is where *El Fronterizo* was printed and where Ramírez probably lived. He may have had some difficulty adjusting to these rude surroundings. Compare this image with those in the preceding chapter showing the urban amenities that Ramírez was used to in Los Angeles. Courtesy of Dr. Fernando Araujo, Ensenada.

Two tourists stand on the main street of Real del Castillo in this northeastern view taken in 1903. The place was mostly abandoned by then. Reprinted by permission of the San Diego Historical Society.

ego, requesting that he take his place as interim subprefecto while he was gone. The letter sent by Alas was no legal basis for appointing an interim subprefecto. The law established that, in the absence of the subprefecto, his place would be taken by the president of the Ayuntamiento—the city council—of Real del Castillo. So it was that when Verde came to take his place in the government house as interim subprefecto on June 3, 1881, the president of the Ayuntamiento, Jorge Ryerson, told Verde that his orders would not be obeyed.[26] Ryerson said that he was the only person legally entitled to exercise the office of interim subprefecto because of his standing as president of the Ayuntamiento. Verde rejected this argument, but on June 6 Ryerson returned with an army captain, Lino Duran, as well as a group of municipal officials who removed Verde from the government house by force.

The jefe político in La Paz, José María Rangel, was disturbed by the manner of Verde's removal. He decided to visit the Partido Norte, a three-week voyage by sea, to make matters right. Rangel arrived in Real del Castillo on July 7, 1881.[27] Ryerson explained his position to the jefe político, who had to concede that it was correct under the law. To solve the problem, Rangel appointed Zeferino Castañeda as subprefecto, thereby eliminating the claims of Verde and Ryerson. This intervention of Jorge Ryerson in the politics of the Partido Norte would not be his last. Ryerson was one of the most fascinating characters in Baja California—and perhaps all of North America. More will be said about this remarkable man later.

It was during this time, about the middle of the summer of 1881, that Ramírez appeared in Real del Castillo. What he found was not impressive. The little settlement was nothing more than a central plaza of dried-out bare ground surrounded by perhaps three dozen or so small ill-kept adobes that were decaying after several periods of abandonment caused by crime and violent political upheavals. It was an unpleasant, dusty village with only about twenty-two families living there. This singularly backward and primitive place was devoid of any doctor, dentist, priest, or lawyer. Unlike Los Angeles, it had no civilized comforts. Ramírez was used to living where, among other things, there were fine restaurants, hotels, commercial establishments, bookstores, and theaters. The most prominent business in Real del Castillo was Louis Mendelson's half-empty little general store, where a limited selection of goods brought down from San Diego were sold at high prices. A look at the barren plaza and deteriorating adobes revealed no sign of prosperity or well-being. The poverty of the place was evident everywhere. The jefe político, Andrés L. Tapia, was disappointed when he first saw Real del Castillo. He wrote to his superiors on March 28, 1878, that he found the few people living there "immersed in absolute misery."[28]

The question is why Ramírez chose to stay in Real del Castillo. Why not go to Mexico City, the core of which presented a comfortable urban center comparable to San Francisco? It had wealth, a vibrant social life, professional services, and intellectual stimulation. The most probable answer is that there was no place closer to Los Angeles where he could live without the fear of being arrested. The cities of Ensenada, Tijuana, and Mexicali did not exist yet. As will be seen, he had unfinished business in his native city. On at least two occasions Ramírez would try to use the court system in Los Angeles while living in Baja California. He undoubtedly hoped to be vindicated from the criminal charges against him and to return home someday. From his position in Real del Castillo, Ramírez could communicate with Los Angeles. While mail service throughout Mexico was unreliable and frustrating, people from the Partido Norte were constantly going to San Diego. Ramírez could arrange to have them post his mail there for its safe arrival in Los Angeles.

The first record of Ramírez's presence in Real del Castillo was in the August 20, 1881, edition of a newspaper called *El Fronterizo*. Below the title, in Spanish, appeared the words "Editor in Chief, Lic. Francisco P. Ramírez." Only five months after leaving Los Angeles, Ramírez was back in the newspaper business for a second time. It is significant that he placed the abbreviation "Lic." before his name, a title that stood for *licenciado*—lawyer. He obviously planned to use his American profession in Mexico, if he could.

Ramírez was not the founder of the newspaper, *El Fronterizo*. Some believe it was begun by Manuel Clemente Rojo; however, for most of its existence, Jesús Ocaranza was its owner and editor. Besides printing his newspaper, Ocaranza was a judge in Real del Castillo who got into difficulty with the subprefecto, Ignacio Alas, during April 1881. A false charge of judicially approving corrupt grants of land resulted in Alas's having Ocaranza jailed in La Paz without a trial. Although he was fully exonerated, Ocaranza may not have returned to the Partido Norte.

Ramírez probably gave some consideration for Ocaranza's printing press as well as to obtain his permission to continue publishing *El Fronterizo*. His first edition stated in a small corner of the second page, "Municipal Printing Press in charge of F. P. Ramirez." Any documents generated in the adobe government house that needed to be printed would be done by Ramírez and paid for by the municipal treasury. The newspaper, published on Saturdays, was theoretically subsidized by Real del Castillo and the Partido Norte. Below its title appeared the words: "Official Newspaper of the Partido Norte of Baja California."

The content of the newspaper was consistent with its official character. Little was printed except edicts and notices from the jefe político, the subprefecto, and the municipal president. Ramírez's first edition had no news other than an item announcing horse races to be held on September 16, Mexican Independence Day. Just one commercial advertisement appeared—for a place called *Restaurante Universal*, owned by Isabel Andrade, that offered Mexican, American, French, and Spanish food. One senses that the advertisement, never repeated, was published by Ramírez as part of an arrangement for taking his meals there.

The first edition of the newspaper and several that followed contained an accounting of the municipal treasury's monthly income and expenses. On August 20, 1881, the paper reported that the treasury had an income for the month of $268.27, expenses of $159.68 and a balance of $108.59. The largest expense was a $30 monthly salary for the secretary of the Ayuntamiento. A schoolteacher received $25 a month, and the only paid policeman was given $24. The chronic shortage of money and the lack of support from either La Paz or the central government was demonstrated in a letter written by the

El Fronterizo.

Periodico Oficial del Partido Norte de la Baja California.

Redactor en Jefe, Lic. FRANCISCO P. RAMIREZ.

VOL. I.   REAL DEL CASTILLO, ENERO 14, DE 1882.   NUM. 21

EL FRONTERIZO.

Periódico Oficial del Partido Norte de Territorio de la Baja California.

LAS LEYES Y DEMÁS DISPOSICIONES DE LA AUTORIDAD SON OBLIGATORIAS CON EL MERO HECHO DE PUBLICARSE EN ESTE PERIÓDICO.

LA IGNORANCIA DE LAS LEYES NO SIRVE DE EXCUSA, Y Á NADIE APROVECHA.
Código Civil, Art.. 21.

GOBIERNO POLITICO Y COMANDANCIA MILITAR DE LA BAJA CALIFORNIA. N°. 1858.

Segun lo previene el Art. 3.° de la ley Orgánica de tribunales, debe procederse al nombramiento de Jueces de Paz en el Territorio, señalándoles su respectiva jurisdiccion. En consecuencia, y en atencion á que la distancia que separa esa cabecera de esta Capital hace imposible que con la debida oportunidad se expidan por este Gobierno esos nombramientos, y como por otra parte esa Sub Prefectura conoce perfectamente la localidad y los vecinos mas apropósito para tales cargos: el mismo Gobierno ha tenido á bien disponer en acuerdo de hoy que esa Sub Prefectura fije el número de jueces de Paz que deba haber en el Partido, su respectivo territorio jurisdiccional y el lugar de su residencia, con entera sujecion al art. 3.° ya citado. Tambien ordenará Vd.

al Ayuntamiento en vista de esa designacion, forme la terna ó ternas de que habla el art. 5.° de la propia ley para que por esa Sub Prefectura se dé cumplimiento á lo demás.

De todo lo que, así como del nombramiento de jurados que con arreglo al art. 372 del Código de procedimientos penales debe Vd. haber hecho y publicado, se servirá darme cuenta con la debida oportunidad.

Libertad y Constitucion. La Paz, Diciembre 17, 1881.—J. M. RANGEL.
F. CORTES. Secretario.

Al Sub Prefecto del Partido del Norte, Real del Castillo.

GOBIERNO POLITICO Y COMANDANCIA MILITAR DE LA BAJA CALIFORNIA—N°. 1772.

Con motivo del informe dado por el que suscribe al Supremo Gobierno, se me autorizó para formar el presupuesto para la construccion de una cárcel en esa cabecera. En consecuencia, ya se forma dicho presupuesto, para que, una vez aprobado, se proceda desde luego á la construccion de la obra; lo cual avisaré á V. oportunamente.

Lo digo á V. en contestacion de su oficio relativo fecha 8 del pasado Octubre.

Libertad y Constitucion. La Paz, Noviembre 19, 1881.—J. M. RANGEL.
F. CORTES, Srio.

Al Sub Prefecto del Partido Norte. Real del Castillo.

SUB PREFECTURA POLITICA.

Un sello. Certifico: que no hay estampillas del presente año en este lugar.
Real del Castillo, Enero 2 de 1882.
—A Querejazu

Señor Subprefecto Político:

Rafael Serrano, C. mexicano y vecino de este Partido, ante vd. con el respeto debido expongo: que en virtud de las quejas que algunas personas han hecho ante esa Subprefectura de su digno cargo, es perjudicial al tránsito público el cambio del camino que he hecho en mi rancho dejando siempre transitable el antiguo camino, solamente con el pequeño inconveniente de dos puertas que se pueden abrir y cerrar con facilidad; pero como dichas puertas son la causa de la queja.

A V. suplico se sirva nombrar una comision para que inspeccione el camino nuevo y el inconveniente del viejo, á fin de que en su informe diga si el expresado camino nuevo está tan bueno ó mejor que el viejo y si las puertas del camino viejo perjudican el tránsito, y en vista del dicho informe se sirva disponer que queden tal como están las puertas, pues al quitarlas recibiria un grave perjuicio en mis intereses. Es gracia que solicito protestando lo no malicia.—Real del Castillo. Enero 2 de 1882.—R. SERRANO

Subjefatura Política del Partido Norte de la Baja California.—Núm. 1.—En contestacion á su ocurso de esta fecha digo á V. que puede cerrar el antiguo camino siempre que en el nuevo se hagan las reformas que crea necesarias, el perito I. Sanchez, nombrado por esa Subprefectura para el efecto, en la inteligencia de que V debe hacer todos los gastos que sean necesarios, tanto para satisfacer los honorarios del Sr. Sanchez como para cubrir los erogados en la compostura del camino nuevo.

Presentará V. esta comunicacion al Sr. Catarino para que quede sin efecto la orden que se le dió de quitar las puertas.

The January 14, 1882, edition of *El Fronterizo*. Courtesy of Antonio Padilla Corona, Instituto de Investigaciones Históricas, Universidad Autónoma de Baja California, Tijuana.

subprefecto residing in Real del Castillo, Zeferino Castañeda, to the minister of the interior in Mexico City. He had arrived about the same time as Ramírez but had still not received any part of his $800 annual salary:

> It has been three months since I undertook the office with which the supreme government has honored me, and during that time I have not received one cent of my salary. Instead, I have had to pay from my own pocket the expense of operating my government office, the rent, and wages of a person to clean and keep the office in order. In spite of having informed the jefe político of this situation, he has done nothing to remedy it and I find myself in the necessity of asking you to make the appropriate orders for payment.[29]

Castañeda had immediate personal needs, but it took months to receive a reply from Mexico City. An ocean voyage to La Paz, over 1,000 miles away, took three weeks. The fastest round-trip possible would require at least six weeks. A trip overland across the peninsula's brutal deserts would take even longer. Mexico City was nearly 500 miles more distant than La Paz. Officials in the remote Partido Norte had to patiently endure.

Unfortunately, Ramírez's work on *El Fronterizo* cannot be followed through every edition. Only eight issues still exist, separated by gaps in time. There are six editions from 1881 and two from 1882. Those in 1881 are dated August 20, October 29, November 5, November 12, December 24, and December 31. The last two issues were on January 14 and January 21, 1882.[30] Ramírez's first edition of *El Fronterizo*, dated August 20, 1881, was entirely filled with dreary edicts and government notices, reflecting its official character. The October 29 issue had only one local news item, an announcement of the marriage of Lorenzo Guarello, twenty-four years old, to Hilaria Acevedo, nineteen years old, both natives of the Partido Norte, before Judge Francisco Arenas in Real del Castillo. The wedding was necessarily of a civil nature since Real del Castillo had no church.

By and large, the content of *El Fronterizo* was dull. A major reason for this is found in the October 29, 1881, edition, where an item concerning a major storm in Mazatlan was preceded by Ramírez's acknowledgment of its source: "The subprefecto has received through the kindness of John Powers a copy of the *San Diego Union* newspaper, dated October 20, which contained a telegram about a storm in Mazatlan that we translate below." Having access to a San Diego newspaper was unusual. Publications from the outside world were seldom seen in Real del Castillo. This was a severe handicap facing Ramírez since an absolute necessity of the time for newspaper editors everywhere was to regularly receive copies of other periodicals from around the world. In this way the most interesting parts could be culled out and reprinted to inform and enliven the local press. Ramírez's isolation prevented regular receipt of newspapers and kept him ignorant of world affairs, something that would surely distress a man of his curiosity and intelligence.

The October 29, 1881, issue of *El Fronterizo* had quite a bit to do with Ramírez himself. He placed an advertisement for translations and legal services on two different pages in identical terms. Both were printed in English, no doubt with an eye toward the last of the Americans still engaged in mining:

FRANCISCO RAMIREZ

Translator and Interpreter of the English, French, and Spanish Languages. Attorney and Counselor at Law. Deeds, Mortgages, Powers of Attorney, Petitions for Mining Claims and Public Lands carefully drawn under the formalities of Mexican and American Laws.

Nothing came of Ramírez holding himself out as an interpreter and lawyer. There were simply not enough people in Real del Castillo to generate any business. His advertisement only appeared once. In another column an official petition for an abandoned gold mine called La Rosarita was made by "Francisco Ramirez and Mrs. Jesus Villa." The published petition was a copy of one submitted to the subprefecto. It bound the claimants to dig a shaft thirty feet deep and four and a half feet wide within sixty days or lose the claim. This venture must have failed since there was only one further mention of it.

The method of subsidizing Ramírez's newspaper was disclosed in an official account of the municipal treasury published by Ramírez on October 29, 1881. The expense was set forth as "ten pesos to F. P. Ramirez editor of El Fronterizo for 20 subscriptions." The municipality paid for varying numbers of subscriptions at fifty cents each from time to time, giving the newspapers to government officials, employees, and favored residents. Ramírez clearly needed the money since his October 29 edition contained no advertisements except his own.

A week later, on November 5, Ramírez was probably gratified to produce an edition with six new commercial advertisements. Each publicized a business in San Diego, practically the sole source of life's necessities in the

Partido Norte. In every issue Ramírez published the name of *El Fronterizo*'s agent in San Diego, G. Raffi, who owned a general store there. Raffi must have recruited advertisers for the newspaper in San Diego since Ramírez could not cross the border without the risk of arrest. Three general stores placed advertisements: the one owned by Raffi, a place called the Combination Store, and a store owned by a merchant named G. Caravia. Two hotels bought advertisements, each owned by Frenchmen. One was the Hotel and Restaurant of Paris, property of H. Aillaud, and the other was the Hotel France, owned by Joseph Jean. The largest advertisement was for a Mexican saddle maker in San Diego named R. Montijo.

Most of the edition of *El Fronterizo* on November 5, 1881, was taken up with several columns in which Ramírez printed a long 1862 statute describing a proposed judicial system for Baja California, signed by the former president, Benito Juárez, who had already been dead for ten years. Ramírez obviously did this because he had nothing else to print. The next edition, on November 12, was equally devoid of genuine news. It was not reasonable to ask fifty cents for a month's subscription to an official newspaper that contained little more than boring edicts and statutes, especially when that amount often represented a day's wages on the border and when the paper offered almost nothing about the world outside Real del Castillo.

Ramírez tried a different tactic in *El Fronterizo* on December 24, 1881, when he published a bilingual version of the paper. The entire front page was a reprint of an article in English dealing with mining in Baja California that had been taken from the *San Diego Sun*. Below the normal title and masthead in Spanish, a kind of subtitle appeared above the article in English: "Real del Castillo, Frontier Times." The third page was also in English, a copy of yet another article on mining in the region from the San Diego *News*. Little original writing was done by Ramírez except a column in Spanish about the virtues of Christianity, a recognition that the edition was appearing on Christmas Eve. The San Diego articles had little relevance to Real del Castillo. The best days of the gold strike had long been over.

A notable improvement in the December 24 issue was the use of foreign newspapers from San Diego, probably obtained by Ramírez's agent there, G. Raffi. A *New York Times* article on a trade agreement between Mexico and Germany was translated by Ramírez. There was also an item respecting a railroad line from Yuma to southern California, taken from *La Crónica* in Los Angeles. The same six advertisements for businesses in San Diego were published as before, with an accounting from the municipal treasury showing the purchase of another ten subscriptions to Ramírez's newspaper. For the first time Manuel Clemente Rojo was listed as the agent for *El Fronterizo* in Santo Tomás. After their acquaintance in Los Angeles more than thirty years before, it was probably gratifying for both of them to be associated in some way again.

The December 31, 1881, edition of *El Fronterizo* did not continue Ramírez's bilingual experiment of the week before. It was entirely in Spanish, with the largest item being an editorial by Ramírez commemorating New Year's Eve. He declared that the prospects for 1882 were favorable since the Partido Norte was controlled by excellent government officials. Each politician was mentioned by name with some laudatory comment. There were no negative statements concerning conditions in Baja California whatever. Ramírez's position as a recently arrived outsider was too precarious for him to engage in criticism.

The penultimate edition of *El Fronterizo* was dated January 14, 1882. The municipal treasury again paid Ramírez ten pesos for another twenty subscriptions. However, the content of the paper consisted purely of government edicts and announcements. It had no news of any kind, not even reprints from San Diego newspapers. The last edition appeared on January 24, 1882. Its main feature was a list of seventy-five men chosen to act as jurors during 1882. They were residents from all over the Partido Norte, including some Americans like John Powers and George Furlong who were so far integrated into local society that their probable lack of Mexican citizenship was ignored. Ramírez accompanied the juror list with a statement of the rights and duties of jurors in criminal cases under Mexican law, based on a fairly tedious review of the Code of Penal Procedure, which few people would have bothered to read. After this, Ramírez stopped publishing *El Fronterizo*.

Aside from its lack of news, the main reason for the suspension of *El Fronterizo* was that Real del Castillo's population was reduced to the point where it could no longer afford to subsidize a newspaper. Ramírez's efforts were supported by money from the municipal treasury without contributions from the Partido Norte. The subprefecto had no ability to share the expense of a newspaper. He had to rely on higher authorities in La Paz and Mexico City to cover the Partido's expenses, but he seldom received any payment, not even for his own salary or that of his subordinates. The cost of an official newspaper had become too great for Real del Castillo alone and had always been out of reach of the Partido Norte's subprefectura.

Almost simultaneously with the closure of *El Fronterizo*, the Ayuntamiento decided it had a better use for Ramírez than as editor of a newspaper. It hired him as the municipal schoolteacher at a salary of $40 per month.[31] He was given charge of a small adobe school with an enrollment of forty-three boys in different grades. Ramírez would act as *preceptor*—school master—for more than three years. Whether he was regularly paid for his services is doubtful. Schoolteachers seldom received their full salaries promptly, if at all. For example, María Lamadrid taught a class of girls in Real del Castillo for six months but was not paid as agreed. She sent a letter of complaint to the jefe político, which was lodged in the La Paz archives, but whether she received her money is unknown.[32] The continuous reduction of Real del Castillo's population and the consequent loss of income is shown by the number of children that Ramírez taught. His pupils declined from forty-three boys in 1882 to seventeen boys and two girls in 1883.[33]

Ramírez's employment as a schoolteacher began at a time when the subprefecto, Zeferino Castañeda, proposed changing the capital of the Partido Norte from Real del Castillo to Ensenada. In a letter of February 12, 1882, to the minister of the interior in Mexico City, Castañeda argued that Ensenada's harbor, now the site of a customhouse, offered better communication with the rest of Mexico than an inland capital. This idea, supported by José María Rangel, jefe político in La Paz, was favorably received in Mexico City. Not long after urging a change of capitals, Castañeda was granted a leave of absence to have a complicated fracture of his right leg looked after in Mexico City since there was no one in the Partido Norte with the medical knowledge necessary to treat him.[34]

After Castañeda departed on his painful trip, the president of the Ayuntamiento of Real del Castillo, Jorge Ryerson, was required by law to act as his temporary substitute. When Ryerson learned that Castañeda would not return, he attempted to prevent the appointment of another subprefecto to take his place. Ryerson circulated a petition throughout the Partido Norte asking the authorities in La Paz and Mexico City to name him as the permanent subprefecto. Despite an irregular salary and general disregard of the office by the central government, Ryerson made an intense campaign to become subprefecto.[35] Except for some time spent on adventures elsewhere in Mexico and the United States, Ryerson had lived in the Partido Norte for thirty years. He was a popular figure and had been elected president of the Ayuntamiento by a large majority. Ryerson had an intimate knowledge of the Partido Norte, as well as the respect of its people, advantages not enjoyed by subprefectos sent from the interior of Mexico. Practically every adult male resident of the Partido Norte signed his petition, including Francisco P. Ramírez.

Ryerson was disappointed when his petition was ignored and Antonio Jáuregui was sent from Mexico City as the new permanent subprefecto. Jáuregui arrived on July 15, 1882, with orders to transfer the capital to Ensenada. Ryerson resisted the move, sending another petition to Mexico City, this time requesting that the capital remain at Real del Castillo, perhaps fearing that he would be excluded from public office after a change of capitals. Ramírez also signed this second petition since he was indebted to Ryerson for helping him. As head of Real del Castillo's municipal government, Ryerson had necessarily been involved with setting up Ramírez as editor of *El Fronterizo* and giving him employment as a school teacher.

The new subprefecto, Antonio Jáuregui, aggressively set about making Ensenada the capital. Ryerson opposed him as much as possible, even going to San Diego to telegraph the minister of the interior in Mexico City, making supplications on behalf of Real del Castillo's Ayuntamiento not to move the capital. Ryerson's reluctance to make a change to Ensenada had unpleasant results. Jáuregui became fed up with Ryerson's resistance, especially after he ignored an order to take the Partido Norte's official archive to Ensenada. He had his aides arrest Ryerson on charges of sedition. After a few months of confinement, Ryerson was released by order of the minister of the interior in Mexico City, Carlos Diez Gutiérrez, a friend of Ryerson from the days when they fought against the French together in Tamaulipas. Not only was Ryerson vindicated, he was appointed as president of the newly established Ayuntamiento in Ensenada.[36] He would achieve his ambition of becoming subprefecto of the Partido Norte three years later, in 1885, when President Porfirio Díaz appointed him to the position.

While a transfer of the capital to Ensenada was under way, Ramírez remained in Real del Castillo, teaching school. Toward the end of 1882, he was elected as the *juez de paz*—justice of the peace—of the little settlement. As a lawyer, newspaper editor, and schoolteacher, he had gained considerable status among many local residents, most of whom were illiterate. They recognized that there were few people in the Partido Norte with Ramírez's knowledge and sophistication. His election as juez de paz was duly noted in the government archive in La Paz on January 28, 1883.[37]

Curiously, although Ramírez now occupied an official judicial position authorized by the Mexican constitution, no one thought to question his citizenship. Under Mexican law Ramírez was ineligible to be a juez de paz because he was an American citizen. This was overlooked by the authorities in La Paz, who, if they had inquired, would have found that Ramírez had taken an oath to support the constitution of the United States when admitted to practice law before the Los Angeles courts in 1869 and the California Supreme Court in 1879. By his conduct he had elected to be an American citizen under the terms of the Treaty of Guadalupe Hidalgo, which ended the war between the United States and Mexico in 1848. Still, Ramírez exercised his Mexican judicial office throughout 1883, choosing not to run for reelection after a one-year term. He was replaced in 1884 when Tomás Lamadrid was elected.

No records exist of cases handled by Ramírez while acting as a justice of the peace in Real del Castillo. It is doubtful that he had much judicial business because the population had greatly decreased. It was reported to the jefe político that only 163 people lived in Real del Castillo during 1883. The judicial hearings would have been conducted in a room in the government house or in a borrowed corner of a private adobe since Real del Castillo had no courthouse. In years to come, Ramírez would often be addressed by Americans as "Judge" because he was once a Mexican justice of the peace, a custom brought from the United States, where former judges of every sort retained their titles for life.

On December 14, 1882, the subprefecto Jáuregui requested 6,000 pesos from the minister of the interior in Mexico City to construct government offices in Ensenada. This money was denied, but forty-five soldiers and two officers from the Twenty-First Battalion of the federal army arrived in March 1883 to keep order in the Partido Norte. After this, the federal government lapsed into its old neglectful ways toward Baja California. Salaries of the twenty-six government employees in Ensenada were not paid. The soldiers likewise received no money or provisions, a situation that would lead to a mutiny of the troops on January 10, 1885. The only general store in Ensenada refused credit to government employees since they could seldom pay their debts, making it extremely difficult for them to obtain the necessities of life.[38]

The Gastélum family owned the land where Ensenada was slowly developing. Before the lack of federal support for the new capital was evident, they hired Salvador Z. Salorio to create a subdivision map so that they could sell lots to incoming residents. Salorio drew up a plan with eighteen urban blocks divided into lots for housing construction.[39] Most of those who purchased lots were merchants and government employees. During 1883 sales of lots in the nascent town were good, but they dropped off when government salaries and support began to evaporate. Deeds to lots sold by the Gastélum family were recorded in a newly formed government office called El Registro Público de la Propiedad de Ensenada—the Public Registry of Property in Ensenada.

A contract drawn up on April 30, 1882, made Francisco P. Ramírez one of the first purchasers of land in Ensenada. The seller was not the Gastélum family but a widow, Luz Reyna de López.[40] Her family had purchased two lots on Ensenada's principal street from the Gastélum family, where they constructed a large two-story wooden building that briefly operated as a hotel. The widow had earlier owned a kind of boardinghouse in Real del Castillo that was advertised in *El Fronterizo* on August 28, 1878. The hotel was the largest structure in Ensenada. The two lots that the building straddled contained 10,500 square feet, with the hotel covering nearly all of it. The building was so well constructed that after Ramírez's death it stood as a landmark in downtown Ensenada, until it was demolished in 1983 to make room for a restaurant and a nightclub.

The terms of the sale suggest that the widow was reluctant to sell it. The price was $300 in Mexican silver coin. However, she insisted that her contract with Ramírez contain a provision that she could return his money and cancel the transaction at any time for a period of six months after the sale on May 1, 1882. Ramírez was bound not to occupy or mortgage the property during the time the lady had to change her mind. However, she paid Ramírez the amount of $2.50 per month as rent while she lived in the building pondering whether to complete the sale. Although the price of $300 seems small, it was fair at the time, the second-largest sale to an individual in Ensenada during a period from 1882 to 1886, when seventy such transactions were recorded. The widow was advised by her son, a government official. He had to sign the contract for his mother since she was illiterate.

Six months after Ramírez's contract with the widow, she had not cancelled the sale. Although Ramírez was now the definite owner with a right to occupy the large structure, he remained in Real del Castillo as a schoolteacher. There was no point in moving to Ensenada yet. It was only partly built, a stagnant incomplete beginning of what was originally intended, because the federal government had withdrawn support for it. Ramírez would not move to his property for over a year. Meantime, his was one of the few buildings actually standing in Ensenada.

On January 31, 1884, Ramírez sent a report to the government in La Paz concerning the condition of the school in Real del Castillo. He was now teaching twenty-nine children, an increase of ten over the prior year. The usual subjects were imparted: reading, writing, arithmetic, Spanish grammar, geography, and English. Ramírez included a detailed inventory of the classroom accoutrements, such as a blackboard, chalk, desks, and children's textbooks. He indicated that there was not quite enough of everything to go around.[41]

At this time Ramírez was in close contact with Los Angeles. For example, he corresponded with his sister Isabel concerning a claim he had against her. Their dispute led to a lawsuit that Ramírez filed in Los Angeles on February 28, 1884.[42] He set up an elaborate legal proceeding against his sister, even though he was confined to Baja California.

According to the complaint in the lawsuit, Ramírez had borrowed $2,000 from Isabel on July 26, 1879, to repay a loan he had taken with the Savings and Loan Society of San Francisco. On that date Ramírez gave her a deed to a brick building and lot that he owned at the northeast corner of Alameda and Aliso streets, a gift from Jean Louis Vignes that he held separately from the rest of the family. Ramírez said that the deed he gave to his sister was merely to provide her with security for repayment of the loan. It was intended to be like a mortgage, not an absolute transfer. The value of the property was far greater than the amount of Isabel's loan. Ramírez asserted that he still owned the property, and by paying his sister, could sell it.

Ramírez's ability to keep in touch with Los Angeles was shown by his preparation of the lawsuit. To represent him, he hired Salisbury Haley, an attorney Ramírez had known when they both had offices in the Temple Block. This was done entirely by correspondence, Ramírez instructing Haley on the facts of the case and providing him with a fee. Another person in Los Angeles, Andronico Sepúlveda, the brother of Judge Ignacio Sepúlveda, accepted a power of attorney authorizing him to file the lawsuit on Ramírez's behalf. All this required a great deal of communication between Los Angeles and Real del Castillo, which Ramírez handled by having someone post his letters and pick up his mail in San Diego. Ramírez was close enough to Los Angeles to receive visits from friends and relatives. His older brother, Juan Bernardo, actually moved to Baja California to live with Ramírez. According to Ensenada judicial records, after the death of Juan Bernardo in 1906, Ramírez handled the probate of his brother's small estate there.

Ramírez's lawsuit against his sister Isabel finally went to trial without a jury on September 11, 1885. She was represented by the firm of Bicknell and White. The judge was Anson Brunson, an old acquaintance of Ramírez. Brunson and Ramírez had practiced law in Los Angeles at the same time and had been on friendly terms while both were leading members of the Republican Party. Brunson agreed with defense arguments that Ramírez needed to be personally present in court to testify about the transaction with his sister. Not being subject to cross-examination, written affidavits by Ramírez were inadmissible hearsay. The lack of personal testimony by Ramírez resulted in the dismissal of the case. This disposition of the matter was inevitable. Basic hearsay difficulties should have been anticipated by Ramírez and his lawyer. It is unclear why both men thought they could use the court system in Los Angeles from afar while Ramírez was absent as a fugitive from justice. The ill-advised lawsuit represented a substantial loss for Ramírez.

A sign that Ramírez had money while in Real del Castillo is shown by the fact that he lent $120 to an American named Dick C. Allen on July 31, 1884. The borrower was the managing director of the Continental Bullion Mine, which also promised repayment. After four years Ramírez had received nothing toward the principal or interest. A suit was filed in Ensenada, but Ramírez had to settle for less than was owed since the borrowers, like most miners, were nearly broke.[43] The significance of the transaction was that Ramírez was not in desperate financial straits, or he would not have let such a sum of money leave his hands to dubious borrowers on the prospect of receiving a little interest.

Ramírez could have immensely improved his life if he had left Baja California for Mexico City or some other large urban center in the interior. His tenacious residence amid the poverty in the Partido Norte stood in stark contrast to the experience of Ignacio Sepúlveda in Mexico. During 1884 Sepúlveda left Los Angeles to permanently live in Mexico City. Sepúlveda chose not to run for reelection to the Los Angeles Superior Court in 1883 because of a dramatic change in the electorate. The Southern Pacific Railroad established a second transcontinental connection to Los Angeles in December 1881, when its tracks drove eastward beyond Yuma, meeting the Texas Pacific Railroad at Sierra Blanca near El Paso, Texas. As a consequence Los Angeles was suddenly flooded with thousands of immigrants who brought violently racist attitudes with them. Their arrival increased the population of Los Angeles County from about 40,188 in 1881 to an estimated 60,609 in 1884. They became the new majority of voters, sweeping away the old aristocratic Southern Chivalry that had once supported a few elite Mexicans in public office. The newcomers were surprised to find men like Sepúlveda in responsible positions. They were convinced that Latins were a lesser breed who should never be allowed a place in public life. This was made clear to Sepúlveda when some of his old constituents proposed him at different times as a justice of the California Supreme Court and a United States senator. The Democrats, now mainly composed of new arrivals, rejected Sepúlveda's candidacy for such offices out of hand.[44]

Barred from further advancement, Sepúlveda believed that he faced the probable loss of his judgeship in the next election. He therefore resigned in 1883, to accept an offer from Wells Fargo to represent the company in Mexico City. Sepúlveda's assessment of the new American electorate was correct. Their prejudice was so great that after Sepúlveda left there was no Mexican judge on the Los Angeles Superior Court for the next seventy-four years, until Carlos Teran was appointed to the bench in 1957. After leaving

A group of train passengers arriving in Los Angeles during 1885. After the establishment of a second transcontinental rail link through Texas in 1882, vast numbers of settlers arrived, becoming a new majority of voters. Their prejudice against Mexicans was so great that they refused to support any for public office. Reprinted by permission of the University of Southern California Special Collections.

Los Angeles, Sepúlveda had a career in Mexico City completely dissimilar to Ramírez's residence in Baja California.

The rule of President Porfirio Díaz from roughly 1876 to 1911, called the *porfiriato*, emphasized foreign investment as a way to develop the country. Sepúlveda acted as a lawyer for many American investors, individual and corporate, to obtain concessions, privileges, monopolies, and licenses from Díaz's government. By sheer luck the military officer in charge of guarding the national palaces turned out to be General Agustín Pradillo, a former imperial army officer who had been confined with Sepúlveda in the Morelia Public Jail after Maximilian's execution. Like many other imperial army officers, Pradillo successfully made a transition to the military of President Díaz's regime. Pradillo introduced his old comrade to President Díaz, who saw Sepúlveda as a useful person in attracting American investment. Acting as interpreter, Sepúlveda frequently brought groups of investors from California to the national palace for an introduction to President Díaz. Such events were occasionally reported in the Los Angeles press.[45] Sepúlveda eventually became so close to Díaz that he could see the president anytime without an appointment. His clients usually obtained whatever favors they asked from the president.

Sepúlveda was appointed secretary of the United States legation in Mexico City in January 1896.[46] In this position he was in charge of all U.S. interests in Mexico. When diplomatic relations were upgraded by establishing an embassy during 1898, Sepúlveda was the chief advisor to the first ambassador, General Powell Clayton. In exchange, Ambassador Clayton referred all legal matters and investors seeking a lawyer in Mexico to Sepúlveda.[47] In 1898, Sepúlveda met Phoebe Hearst at the embassy—an encounter that led to a close friendship and the representation of the Hearst family's interests in Mexico, including the two-million-acre Rancho Babicora in Chihuahua. Phoebe's son, William Randolph Hearst, was presented to President Díaz more than once by Sepúlveda.[48] Eventually the relationship between Sepúlveda and the young Hearst developed to the point that on December 6, 1906, they left Mexico City together, with their respective families, in a private railcar for a trip to New York, where they stayed at the Hearst estate.[49]

American corporations brought railroads, a telephone system, electricity, banks, oil wells, and the manufacture of modern consumer goods to Mexico. Sepúlveda had important clients from nearly every sector of investment. He was the founder and first president of an organization called the Society of the American Colony, which drew its membership from the most affluent of the more than 10,000 Americans residing in Mexico City.[50] Sepúlveda also helped initiate the American Club, another prestigious expatriate group. President Díaz accepted honorary memberships in both of them. He was conspicuously escorted by Sepúlveda to uniquely American holiday celebrations like the Fourth of July and Thanksgiving.[51]

A daily English-language newspaper called the *Mexican Herald*, edited by Paul Hudson, was begun in 1895 to serve the American colony. It was a first-class newspaper in every sense, subsidized in part by the Mexican government to print propaganda to attract American investors. Sepúlveda's activities—at the very highest levels of Mexican society—were constantly reported in the newspaper. Together with his wife, Herlinda de la Guerra, a first cousin whom Sepúlveda had married just before leaving Los Angeles in 1883, he was a celebrity in Mexico City. As leaders in Mexican high society, the Sepúlvedas were often in the company of President Díaz at events such as diplomatic receptions, balls, banquets, state dinners, theatrical performances, and the opera.

All this would end with the Mexican revolution. President Porfirio Díaz was forced into exile in Paris during May 1911. His successor, Francisco Madero, was assassinated a little more than a year later on the orders of General Victoriano Huerta. Huertas's efforts to take over the presidency, called *la decena trágica*—the tragic ten days—brought about street fighting and artillery bombardments in downtown Mexico City, resulting in scores of deaths and massive property damage. Most of the American colony abandoned the city in the face of the danger and the impossibility of protecting their interests. Sepúlveda lost his home and money in the chaos. On December 3, 1913, he was forced to return to Los Angeles with his wife.[52] Their daughter had already been sent there ahead of them. Sepúlveda attempted to practice law again, but he was now seventy-one years of age and the Los Angeles he had known was gone. His daughter, later married to an Italian nobleman, was a longtime society columnist for the Hearst-owned *Los Angeles Examiner*, under the name of Princess Conchita Sepúlveda de Pignatelli. During a brief residence in Los Angeles that ended with his death on December 3, 1916, Sepúlveda and his wife were charitably supported by Phoebe Hearst, who sympathized with the misfortune of her old friends.

While Sepúlveda enjoyed a spectacular ascent in Mexico, becoming a confidante of the president, Ramírez endured the hardships of life in the Partido Norte. Other people he had known in Los Angeles were also involved in the prosperity and pleasures of the Mexican capital, far from the desolation of Baja California. One of them, Pastor de Celis, left his position as editor of Los Angeles's *La Crónica* to become an executive of the Mexican Central Railway. The *Mexican Herald* sometimes noted his presence at upper-class social functions in the capital.[53] Another was Lastania Abarta, the lady once engaged to Ramírez. She lived in a luxurious house on an elegant part of the Paseo de la Reforma, just a few blocks from Sepúlveda's residence on Calle Pane. The two could have easily met since Lastania's French husband inhabited the higher levels of Mexican society for many years.[54] A social encounter between Lastania and Sepúlveda would likely have been uncomfortable since he had presided over her trial for the murder of Chico Forster, in which she was acquitted on a theory of temporary insanity.

Sophisticated men like Sepúlveda, who were well grounded in the culture and language of both countries, were perfect intermediaries between American investors and the Mexican government. Splendid opportunities to make money awaited them in the graceful ambience of Mexico City, where they were needed to fully exploit the accommodating economic policies of President Porfirio Díaz. Ramírez was as qualified as Sepúlveda to undertake the representation of American investors in the capital. He could have contended for some of the prosperity and luxury that Sepúlveda enjoyed had he gone to Mexico City. Instead, he remained amid difficulties and privation in Baja California. He wanted to stay as close as possible to Los Angeles.

Judge Ignacio Sepúlveda in Los Angeles, about 1915. The massive influx of anti-Latin immigrants brought by the railroad forced him to resign his judgeship in 1883 and go to Mexico. After three decades as a confidante of President Porfirio Díaz, he returned home in 1913 to escape the Mexican Revolution. Reprinted by permission of the Los Angeles Public Library.

CHAPTER FOURTEEN
Exile in Ensenada

An opportunity for Ramírez to leave Real del Castillo came on April 25, 1885, when the secretary of public education in La Paz appointed him as the schoolmaster in Ensenada.[1] He moved to the new capital, where he could occupy the large two-story wooden building he had bought three years before. Ensenada was still sparsely populated, with little commercial activity, but an exciting new prospect of development was unfolding when Ramírez arrived. Everyone in the place was aware that the central government in Mexico City had made a concession of nearly the whole northern half of the peninsula to an American enterprise called the Compañía Internacional de Mexico—the International Company of Mexico—to develop and colonize the region. It was known that the headquarters of the American company would be in Ensenada and that the little harbor settlement was destined to be urbanized by laying out streets and erecting buildings. The person designated as the company's agent in Ensenada, Maximiliano Bernstein, arrived with his family in October 1885 to begin buying land for the construction of a new city. Ramírez realized that an influx of Americans in Baja California would require the services of local lawyers. He put a law office on the first floor of his building and furnished a residence above it. Now holding himself out as a lawyer, Ramírez resigned as Ensenada's schoolmaster, effective January 31, 1886.

The advent of the International Company of Mexico would radically change the Partido Norte.[2] It was born from the new *Ley de Colonización*—Law of Colonization—promulgated by the federal government in Mexico City on December 15, 1883. The law was intended to promote immigration to the vast, nearly unpopulated areas in the north and south of Mexico. Baja California was a particularly notable example of the kind of place where the law was intended to operate. The federal government offered to contract with individuals or corporations to grant them ownership of great expanses of land, subject to certain conditions. The grantee first had to survey the entire area in detail. When this was accomplished, one-third of the land was provisionally awarded. After that, the other two-thirds could be conditionally purchased at a special low price fixed in advance by the government. To obtain permanent title the grantee had to settle at least 100 families on parcels ranging from 37 to 247 acres within two years. Each family was to receive the necessary tools and agricultural equipment at the expense of the grantee. Within ten years, the grantee was obligated to settle 1,971 families on the land. Although the entry of foreign immigrants was encouraged, at least thirty percent of the families were required to be Mexican citizens. Preference was given to Mexicans living abroad who desired repatriation. If the grantee failed to settle the minimum number of families demanded by law within the established time limits, the contract and land grant were subject to cancellation. Compliance with the law regarding the settlement of families was imperative. Otherwise, the grantee could lose everything.[3]

The Mexican government's proposition was highly attractive. The size of the grants could be enormous. An individual or corporation with a contract for a grant could fully exploit the resources of a particular region without limitation. Luis Hüller, a naturalized Mexican citizen from Germany, obtained a grant of nearly the entire northern half of the Baja California peninsula from the twenty-ninth parallel in the south to the United States border in the north, a landmass consisting of 13,325,623 acres. Hüller was well connected in Mexico City. He was the owner of mining interests in Sonora, but he could not bear the expense of the required surveys and land purchases by himself. He therefore consulted with George Sisson, a wealthy American lawyer and financier who a few years earlier had met with Hüller in Sonora concerning Mexican investments. After initially forming a partnership to operate the grant, it became clear that they would need outside financial support. Both men were stretched too thin with other Mexican concessions and enterprises to afford the large output of cash needed for the northern Baja California enterprise.

Sisson and Hüller went to New York, where they aroused the enthusiasm of several major investors. A corporation called the International Company of Mexico (and usually referred to as the American company) was formed in Hartford, Connecticut, with its treasury in New York. Hüller assigned his grant to the new company, as well as two others he had acquired that had originally been given to Adolphe Bülle and Telésforo García. It was claimed that the total area transferred by Hüller to the company approached 18,000,000 acres. Branches of the company were set up in Hamburg, London, San Francisco, San Diego, and Mexico City. The initial capital of the enterprise was $1,000,000 but soon grew to $20,000,000. The first president of the corporation, Edgar T. Wells, a former secretary of the navy, was the president of several banks and a director on the boards of various large corporations of national importance.[4]

The company's resident agent, Maximilian Bernstein, began buying up land around Ensenada from private owners in 1885, as well as purchasing 8,676 acres from the Gastélum family in May 1886. This latter purchase included a portion around the Bay of Todos Santos, already surveyed into blocks and lots by the Gastélums, that became the heart of urban Ensenada. Streets were laid out in the midst of a rush of building construction. A wharf was extended into the Bay of Todos Santos to unload cargo and passengers. The company had at least three steamers regularly running between San Diego and Ensenada. To further improve communication with San Diego and points north, a telegraph line was run from Ensenada up to the border and beyond. Sisson invited an American, Charles Bennett, to open a sawmill in Ensenada to cut urgently needed lumber for the company's building program. Bennett was a great entrepreneur and innovator. He also supplied the locality with water from a large tank on an elevation above Ensenada fed by two wells. Residents were charged the same amount for water as those living in San Diego.

Encouraged by the company, a great many Americans came to Ensenada to start various kinds of businesses. Between 1885 and 1888 several manufactories owned by Americans and Mexicans were started up. They made fruit preserves, soap, candles, brooms, furniture, woolen goods, matches, and carbonated water. There also appeared a lumber yard, a winery and distillery, a wagon maker, a tannery, two metal-working shops, and two flour mills.[5] The supplies, food, and services once only available in San Diego could now be found in Ensenada. By 1887 there were three hotels—including the company's famous and luxurious Hotel Iturbide—five grocery stores, two Chinese laundries, a barber shop, several restaurants, two protestant churches, three printing shops, and enough saloons to satisfy the thirst of even a larger town.[6]

The intent of the Law of Colonization was to allow capitalists to control and exploit vast rural areas called *terrenos baldíos*—unclaimed empty lands—in exchange for settling a definite number of families on them within specified time limits. In the case of Baja California, the resources to be exploited included mining, fishing, and some limited agriculture. The contract with the International Company of Mexico for a grant of northern Baja California was predicated on the Mexican belief that the American company would proceed with rural development and the settlement of families to work the land. However, the actual course followed by the Americans was different. Their conduct soon alarmed conservative Mexican critics of the Law of Colonization.

Instead of perfecting its title to the virtual gift of nearly 18,000,000 acres by settling immigrant families on the land, the International Company of Mexico began selling as much of its enormous concession as possible. It mounted an intense publicity campaign announcing that all its land in Baja California was available for sale, even though it had not yet placed the required number of settlers on it. A bombardment of newspaper advertisements, pamphlets, and subsidized books published in English for American consumption contained exaggerated claims and occasional lies concerning the land's fertility, water supply, climate, and beauty. Publicists for the company held out the Partido Norte as a paradise on earth.[7] Representations were freely made to prospective American purchasers that the company could deliver perfect legal title to the land immediately. Such claims were false since the grant was conditioned on the contractual obligation to populate the region with settlers. The American company generally ignored its promises to the Mexican government in this regard, engaging in a frenzy of land sales even though the Mexican government retained the power to cancel its grant.

The behavior of the International Company of Mexico was the direct result of a land boom occurring at the time in southern California. The Santa Fe Railroad had broken the monopoly of the Southern Pacific Railroad on transcontinental railway travel by establishing its own link to southern California in 1885. The subsequent competition between the railroads drove the cost of tickets to such low levels that tens of thousands of immigrants could suddenly afford to move to southern California, most with an urgent need to locate a place to build a home. In response, through gaudy advertising and cleverly manipulated auctions real estate promoters offered to sell subdivisions of land divided into lots suitable for home building. Prospective buyers were given free lunches and transportation to see empty areas staked out as the future sites of cities, blocks, and lots. A fantastic rush of speculation by investors accompanied an enormous number of real estate purchases. The peak of the Los Angeles land boom during the three summer months of 1887 saw the unprecedented amount of $38,000,000 change hands through land transfers.⁸ In San Diego a similar phenomenon was taking place. In the final months of 1887, land sales there sometimes totaled more than $200,000 per day.⁹

The flamboyant efforts by the International Company of Mexico to sell land in Baja California represented an attempt to duplicate the boom north of the border. The company saw its concession in the Partido Norte as a natural extension of southern California, and it used the same kind of exaggerated publicity and sales methods that were successful in Los Angeles and San Diego. It hired Hanbury & Garvey, a San Diego real-estate firm, to sell off its properties, based on a commission arrangement. A large, three-story triangular office building made of brick was constructed as their headquarters. The impressive building gave American visitors a sense of permanence and security. It looked like a piece of San Diego set down in the center of Ensenada. This building, together with the surrounding wooden structures built in the American style, gave Ensenada the appearance of a place located somewhere north of the border.

The phenomenal rise of an American infrastructure in Ensenada greatly improved the quality of Ramírez's life. Within a short time he went from living in the rude adobe village of Real del Castillo to enjoying the amenities of an urban center much like a contemporary American town. Unlike his failed start in Real del Castillo, he was now able to conduct a law practice, owing to the presence of many more people. The majority of his clients were Americans or other foreigners. A small courthouse behind a building used as military headquarters for a company of Mexican troops was less than 100 yards southwest of Ramírez's home. The court, known as the Juzgado de Primera Instancia—Court of the First Instance—was roughly the equivalent of the Superior Court in California. The first appointed judge, Pedro Rendón, later became the principal attorney for the International Company of Mexico. The cases heard in the court were preserved in a judicial archive that still exists.¹⁰ Ramírez appeared in scores of cases, both as a lawyer and as an interpreter. The polyglot intermingling of Americans, Mexicans, Europeans, and Chinese in Ensenada often created a need for interpreters to help resolve disputes. The first record of an appearance by Ramírez as a lawyer in the Ensenada court is dated July 6, 1886; it was a case in which he filed a claim for attorney fees against the estate of a deceased client named Jacob B. Hanson.

At this time Ramírez was interested in increasing his personal wealth by acquiring real property.¹¹ Opportunities existed in Ensenada to purchase

A view of Ensenada toward the south, about 1887. The large building on the hill is the Hotel Iturbide. Beyond it lies the town built by the American company. Courtesy of Dr. Fernando Araujo, Ensenada.

Ensenada seen from a point near the Hotel Iturbide, looking southeast, about 1888. The three-story triangular brick building in the middle left is the property of Hanbury & Garvey, real-estate agents from San Diego. Just behind it to the left is Ramírez's two-story house. It was basically an American town, and English was the dominant language. Courtesy of Dr. Fernando Araujo, Ensenada.

Headquarters of the American company, circa 1886. It is now a museum. Courtesy of Dr. Fernando Araujo, Ensenada.

downtown urban lots described in the subdivision map prepared for the Gastélum family, the original owners of the land. Their subdivision map laid out the central area into twenty-eight city blocks, each containing lots of various sizes, a plan officially adopted by the Registry of Public Property in Ensenada and still used today. Ramírez bought his first parcel of property on April 3, 1883. It was lot C of block 14, purchased from Adolfo Bareño, the agent and son-in-law of the owner, Pedro Gastélum. The price is unknown; however, it later proved valuable since the courthouse and military headquarters were partly built on it. Ramírez next purchased two vacant lots in 1884, a large one from Félix Jordan for $177 on November 17 and a smaller one from Pedro Gastélum for $40 on December 31. During 1886 he acquired four lots from Adolfo Bareño on April 3 for a total price of $50 and a week later paid Bareño another $50 for four additional lots. He acquired his last lot on May 7, 1886, from Santos Cota for $150, a property next to the telegraph office installed by the International Company of Mexico. In all, Ramírez bought eleven vacant lots in the center of Ensenada from 1883 to 1886 by paying cash in the total amount of $467. During the following years he would make many real-estate transactions, including the purchase of rural properties, such as a ranch near Santo Tomás and another at Real del Castillo.

The International Company of Mexico subsidized two weekly newspapers in Ensenada during 1887. The first, called the *Lower Californian*, appeared on August 9, 1887, entirely in English. The editor was Francis R. Bennett, an experienced American newspaperman, assisted by two of his sons. The second was *La Voz de la Frontera de la Baja California*, roughly translated as *The Voice of the Border of Baja California*.[12] The newspaper was initially a four-page journal, half in Spanish and half in English. The first editor was Jesús María Cadena, who was at the same time the clerk of the Court of the First Instance. Originally, just the printing of *La Voz* was done by Ramírez. However, by the beginning of 1888, he had taken over as both editor and printer of the newspaper.

Now, seven years after leaving Los Angeles, Ramírez was editing his third newspaper in Mexico. He was not, however, in charge of an independent enterprise. The paper existed because of financial support from the International Company of Mexico. The front page stated, "Circulation: 3,000," but this was more than twice the number of Ensenada's residents. Half of the copies printed were sent to the United States as publicity for the company's land sales in Baja California. Ramírez was, in effect, an employee of the International Company of Mexico. A considerable part of his income at this time depended on not giving offense to the company. The newspaper always contained upbeat, optimistic reports about conditions in Ensenada. A large part of the paper was used to present advertisements with exaggerated claims about the fertility and beauty of Baja California land. The *Lower Californian* was like a twin to Ramírez's publication. Both were organs of propaganda for land sales, with no rivalry between them. Ramírez had surrendered his journalistic abilities to the company. The fiery youth who once wrote impassioned social criticism in the pages of *El Clamor Público* no longer existed.

At fifty-one years of age, Ramírez's turn as an editor for the company was not brilliant, but he produced a creditable newspaper with its resources. He had access to a wide selection of newspapers that he could use to provide his readers with genuine news, a luxury he did not have in Real del Castillo while editing *El Fronterizo*. The March 24, 1888, edition of *La Voz* cited reports from San Diego's *Sun*, Mexico City's *El Tiempo*, Tabasco's *El Independiente*, and Chicago's *Mail*. Ramírez was able to report the execution of the Indian rebel Cajeme in Sonora, the virtual reelection of President Porfirio Díaz, the death of Emperor Wilhelm I of Germany, and a failed treaty between Russia and the Vatican. Ramírez published items of local interest too, such as the dates that school would begin and a schedule of examinations for

The March 24, 1888, issue of *La Voz de la Frontera de la Baja California*, edited by Ramírez for the American company. Courtesy of the Sherman Library, Corona del Mar, California.

the pupils. A surprising number of Ensenada's businesses paid for advertising, as did the usual San Diego hotels and general stores.

A revealing instance of Ramírez's subservience to the company appeared in the March 21, 1888, edition of *La Voz*. Ramírez defended the International Company of Mexico from accusations that it willfully refused to pay Mexican customs for merchandise brought from San Diego. In response to a refusal by customs officials to allow the goods to leave their warehouse for lack of payment, Ramírez claimed that the shipment was destined for the use of settlers who were exempt from such charges. The contention was absurd, a makeshift argument raised by the company to conceal the fact that it did not have the $35,000 necessary to pay customs. This incident involving Ramírez as an apologist for the company was one of the first signs that it was in severe financial distress.

In response to charges of fraud and abuse by the International Company of Mexico, President Porfirio Díaz ordered administrative changes in northern Baja California to increase his authority over it. He abolished the Partido Norte as a political entity and removed it from the control of the jefe político in La Paz. Instead, the region from the twenty-eighth parallel to the United States border would be known as the Distrito Norte—Northern District—under a jefe político who would report directly to the president. General Luis E. Torres was appointed as the first jefe político of the new Northern District. He was a military and political figure of national importance, who enjoyed the utmost confidence of the president. When Torres was asked to take charge of the Northern District, he was the governor of Sonora, a position that placed him among the very highest officials in the country. His selection as jefe político in northern Baja California was a sign of the importance that President Díaz now placed on it.[13]

Torres arrived in Ensenada with a contingent of troops in January 1888. He was instructed to render monthly reports directly to President Díaz on the activities of the International Company of Mexico. Díaz relied on Torres to keep him informed and to formulate an official policy in dealing with the American presence in Baja California. Torres was met in Ensenada by Jorge Ryerson, the last subprefecto of the now defunct Partido Norte, who surrendered his authority to Torres. In one of his first letters to the president, Torres wrote that he had found the government of northern Baja California under the control of foreigners. Although he did not identify the foreigners involved, Ryerson was probably one of those he had in mind.

Ryerson deserves special mention because his career in Baja California was one of the most fantastic in all of Mexican history. He first appeared in Baja California when he was about twenty-three. Ryerson explained in fluent Spanish that, despite his name and Anglo appearance, he was a Mexican citizen, having been born in Texas during 1830, when it was still a province of Mexico. His parents might have been American, but his allegiance was to Mexico, his native country. He claimed his loyalty was such that he fought on the Mexican side as a teenage soldier during the war with the United States. Ryerson's story was made entirely credible during William Walker's 1853 invasion of Baja California. There was no one more zealous or exposed to greater danger in fighting the American filibusterers than Ryerson. He was one of the chief lieutenants of Antonio María Meléndrez, head of the Mexican armed resistance. Ryerson's leadership and bravery under fire in opposing the Americans endowed him with the reputation of a true Mexican patriot.[14]

In 1856 Ryerson married Guadalupe Serrano in Santo Tomás. He acquired the Rancho Vallecitos, about thirty miles south of Tecate, where he struggled to raise wheat and cattle. During the Civil War, without a word to anyone, he disappeared from Mexico to join the Confederate Army. Instead of returning to his wife when that war was over, he next served in the Mexican army in the war against the French, which ended in 1867. Ryerson was stationed in the region of Tamaulipas, where he was given the rank of major. It was believed in the Partido Norte that he had died during his long absence, since he had made no attempt to communicate with anyone. In the belief that she was a widow, his wife married an American, Francis Bragg, and had a daughter with him, named Victoria. Her marriage certificate with Bragg stated that she was "the widow of George Ryerson, who died in Tucson more than two years ago." There was great surprise and consternation, then, when word arrived that Ryerson, far from dead, was on his way to Baja California to reclaim his wife and home on the Rancho Vallecitos. Bragg abandoned his new wife and daughter to head for the border, not wishing to challenge a man with Ryerson's reputation for ferocity. Ryerson resumed his marriage as if nothing had happened, thereafter holding out Bragg's daughter as his niece. As has been seen, he subsequently became president of the Ayuntamiento of Real del Castillo, a position he held when Ramírez met him in 1881. After occupying the office twice temporarily, he became the legitimately appointed subprefecto of the Partido Norte in 1885.[15]

Ryerson's career as a Mexican politician began to unravel in 1887 because of a most improbable scenario. In that year an old impoverished prospector,

George Ryerson, living in Austin, Nevada, read that the wealthy philanthropist Martin Ryerson had died in Chicago. The prospector realized that the dead man was his brother. He had also been reading about another George Ryerson, a kind of governor of northern Baja California. The elder George Ryerson contacted his dead brother's son, Martin Ryerson, Jr., who made a trip west from Chicago, where the two men met. The elder Ryerson, more or less a derelict, was taken back to Chicago. The old man told his nephew that he had left his wife and two children, a son and a daughter, in Paterson, New Jersey, during 1834 and had never seen them again. A grand family reunion sponsored by Martin Ryerson, Jr., was held in Chicago during April 1888.[16] The old prospector's son, now known as Jorge Ryerson, accepted an invitation to the reunion, taking a train from San Diego to Chicago, probably in the expectation that he would receive some part of his uncle's enormous estate. He did not know that his participation in the family reunion would be widely publicized in the American and Mexican press.[17]

It became clear from reports in Chicago newspapers covering the family reunion that George Ryerson's story about being born in Texas when it was still Mexican territory was a lie. He had actually been born in Paterson, New Jersey, in 1830, with no Mexican connection whatever. He solemnly repeated the fictitious story of his birth in a narrative written for the historian Hubert Howe Bancroft in 1888, saying, "I was born in Texas when it belonged to Mexico, in the year 1830."[18] Ryerson had cultivated the myth of his Mexican origin so well that it was accepted as a matter of course. In an interview published in the *Los Angeles Times* on October 16, 1887, the reporter wrote, "Gov. Ryerson was born in Texas, of American and Mexican parentage, when Texas was yet a part of Mexico, and is therefore unqualifiedly a Mexican citizen."

Ryerson's claims were not always accepted. After Zeferino Castañeda withdrew as subprefecto in 1882, he was succeeded by Ryerson on an interim basis. A military officer in Real del Castillo, Lieutenant Carlos Rodriguez, wrote a letter to his superior on April 30, 1882, protesting Ryerson's taking the position of subprefecto because he was "a foreigner who knows nothing of our laws."[19] Lieutenant Rodriguez stated that he refused to obey a subprefecto who was not a genuine Mexican. The jefe político in La Paz, General José María Rangel, saw the letter and regarded the lieutenant's behavior as insubordination. He ordered the young officer confined to quarters for three days as punishment.[20]

After the revelation of Ryerson's true national origin, he held no further

George Ryerson and his wife, Guadalupe Serrano, date unknown. His neatly tailored clothing and placid demeanor belie a reputation for great physical strength and ferocity. Reprinted by permission of the San Diego Historical Society.

public offices in Baja California. He continued to live there but began spending more time in San Diego. His trips north involved much alcohol and poker playing. Ryerson's gambling debts cost him the Rancho Vallecitos, which he unsuccessfully tried to sell in 1895, before creditors could seize it. A heart attack took his life on January 23, 1896, while he was visiting San Diego. The *Los Angeles Times* published his obituary two days later, saying, "One of his weaknesses was an inordinate love for the game of poker, and although once possessed of large ranches and herds of stock, he dies without means of consequence." Ryerson was buried in San Diego's Mt. Hope Cemetery, in the Masonic section, with a tombstone written in Spanish. His deception did not diminish his standing as a notable figure in Baja California, however. One of Ensenada's principal downtown streets, Avenida Ryerson, is still named after him. Unhappily, Ryerson's death was not the only misfortune to befall his family. His wife, Guadalupe Serrano de Ryerson, was the subject of a criminal proceeding in Ensenada three years after her husband's death.[21] She was sentenced to jail during 1899 for the murder of a ten-year-old houseboy she employed. Even her daughter, Victoria, was not immune to the family's degradation. During 1895 she was arrested and served jail time in San Diego for assault with a deadly weapon.[22]

After succeeding Jorge Ryerson in 1888 as the Mexican official in charge of northern Baja California, Torres sent letters to President Díaz that were not favorable to the International Company of Mexico. His observations sharply conflicted with those of Teófilo Masac, a government agent who had been sent from Mexico City to inspect the progress of the American company a few months earlier. Masac's report of November 3, 1887, praised the Americans. He described the construction of magnificent buildings, broad avenues, parks, and monumental public works. Torres wrote to President Díaz that, after reading Masac's account and comparing it with what he saw himself, he did not know whether to laugh at its absurd exaggerations or feel indignation because of the lies presented for the government's reliance.[23] The truth of the matter, according to Torres, was that, besides the Hanbury & Garvey brick building and the Iturbide Hotel, only about a dozen decent wooden buildings had been put up by the Americans. Little of the splendor claimed by Masac actually existed. It was later shown that Masac had been bribed with gifts of land by the American company to present an unrealistic report.

The messages written by Torres to his old friend, the president of Mexico, frankly stated that Baja California was in danger of being overrun by Americans. Practically the only money in circulation came from the United States. English was the language most commonly spoken in Ensenada because the majority of the people living there were from across the border. The purchasers of land from the American company nearly always came from the United States since Mexican nationals could not afford the prices demanded. Torres said that the Americans in Ensenada were a "wealthy, industrious, hard-working and energetic" people, who regarded Baja California as an adjunct of their own country.[24] He pointed out the dangers arising from Baja California's being the only place on the border in close proximity to American urban centers like San Diego and Los Angeles. The rest of the dividing line confronted nothing but empty ranch lands in Arizona, New Mexico, and Texas.

A sophisticated man, Torres had an excellent command of English, which enabled him to better assess the American threat. He often visited San Diego, where he noted a pronounced sentiment in favor of annexing Baja California, something he duly reported to President Díaz. Torres believed that the American company was in clear violation of its obligations. He advised the president that the company had never seriously intended to introduce Mexican settlers into the territory as contemplated. It had done almost nothing in that regard, although bringing settlers to the region had been Mexico's basic motivation in making the contract in the first place. The company had ignored its promises of rural development in order to carry out sales of property in proposed urban areas, frankly imitating the land boom promoters across the border. Torres reminded the president that absolute legal title to the land depended on the company's attracting settlers in the agreed-upon numbers. Until the condition of bringing settlers had been met, the company could not deliver good title to land purchasers.

Torres thought that the American company should be reminded of its obligations with a threat to cancel its contract if there was a further lack of compliance. Another person sent to report on the American company, Manuel Sánchez Facio, arrived at about the same time as Torres. He was a severe critic of the Law of Colonization and a conservative member of a faction in the Mexican Congress opposed to President Díaz. His report to Mexico City on June 4, 1888, was not as restrained as that of Torres. Outraged over what he considered both a fraud on Mexico and the American land buyers who could not receive good title, he demanded an immediate rescission of the contract. When his recommendation was not accepted, he went to San Francisco, where in 1889 he published a book entitled *The Truth about Lower California*, with the provocative subtitle, *Frauds Committed by the International Company under the Protection and Sanction of the Present Administration of Mexico*. The embarrassed government in Mexico City secretly mounted a campaign to silence Sánchez Facio by having him jailed in San Francisco on false charges. Never mentally stable, he suffered a complete breakdown and was confined to an insane asylum on his return to Mexico City.[25]

Despite Torres's caution and Sánchez Facio's inflammatory accusations, the two agreed on several essential points. Both complained that the American company had not made efforts to attract settlers as promised. Another was that title to land sold by the company was tainted by fraud since it knowingly failed to comply with the conditions for perfecting its ownership. Finally, both men were adamantly against a proposal by the American company to build a railroad connection between Ensenada and San Diego. The former subprefecto, Jorge Ryerson, had enthusiastically endorsed such a project, but Torres and Sánchez Facio realized that this would mean the end of Mexican sovereignty over Baja California. A census ordered by Torres on his arrival in 1888 placed the population of Ensenada at only 1,280, mostly

Americans. Torres and Sánchez Facio warned that a railroad would bring thousands more, flooding the area with so many Americans that Mexico would end up ceding northern Baja California to the United States.[26]

Tensions between Mexico and the American company disappeared in 1889, the result of economic forces outside the control of either party. The boom in Southern California ended that year, causing a huge drop in land prices throughout the region, including in Baja California. The fortunes of the American company depended entirely on the boom occurring north of the border, of which it was an extension. When promoters saw land sales plummet in Southern California, the American company in Baja California experienced the same downturn.

Even before a general collapse of land sales, the American company's financial situation was precarious. We have already seen that Ramírez attempted to rationalize the inability of the American company to pay $35,000 in customs charges in the March 31, 1888, edition of *La Voz*. At about the same time Hanbury & Garvey, sales agents for the American company, filed suit against it for past-due commissions of over $500,000.[27] Disgruntled land purchasers who discovered that their titles were defective began to load up the courts in Ensenada and San Diego with lawsuits against the company. In view of an approaching financial failure, investors in the International Company of Mexico decided to cut their losses by a sale of the company's assets and a departure from Mexico.

The directors of the American company succeeded in convincing a group of British capitalists to purchase their concession in northern Baja California. This transfer required the consent of the Mexican government, which was obtained through a series of meetings with President Porfirio Díaz and other high officials in Mexico City. A new company formed in London on May 11, 1889, the Mexican Land and Colonization Company Limited, took an assignment of all the American company's interests in Baja California in exchange for assuming its debts. To manage its affairs the British company, known in Spanish as La Compañía Mexicana de Terrenos y Colonización, sent Major Buchanan Scott to establish his headquarters in Ensenada. Scott, a graduate of the Royal Military Academy, took a two-year leave of absence from the British army in India to administer the enterprise. He was an officer of engineers specializing in railroads and transportation, who was highly regarded in India, where he acted as a deputy consulting engineer for railways in 1887.[28] One of his first instincts was to build a railroad from Ensenada to

San Diego, a project opposed by General Luis E. Torres and Manual Sánchez Facio and which was eventually abandoned.

The chairman of the British company, Sir Edward Jenkinson, authorized payment of the debts left by the American company, as well as substantial improvements to Ensenada. Electric power and a telephone system were among the innovations eventually introduced by the British company. Major Buchanan Scott proved to be an excellent administrator, whose tenure took an upswing in early 1889, when a gold rush began to flower at a place called El Alamo, about fifty miles southeast of Ensenada.[29] Some 5,000 Americans went there, so many that businesses in San Diego complained that their employees had abandoned them. Ensenada's commercial houses briefly enjoyed an increase in business from the surging crowds of prospectors crossing the border. The international flavor of Ensenada was captured by a photograph of the period showing a Union Jack above the British company's headquarters, the American flag over a hotel, and the Mexican flag atop the customhouse, all within the distance of a single city block.

Judicial records for 1887 do not mention any appearances by Ramírez.

Ensenada in 1891, while under the control of the British company. In the left foreground the Union Jack flies over the British company's headquarters. The Mexican flag is high in the middle over the former Hanbury & Garvey building, now Ensenada's customhouse. Note Ramírez's house on the left behind it. To the middle right, the American flag is flying above the Hotel Pacheco owned by J. M. Martin. Courtesy of Dr. Fernando Araujo, Ensenada.

He was then actively engaged as editor of *La Voz de la Frontera de la Baja California* in the service of the American company. There was little time to aggressively pursue his law practice. The newspaper that Ramírez edited was suspended by the American company because of financial distress in early 1888. After the last edition appeared on March 31 of that year, Ramírez resumed his law practice. He was involved in four small cases representing American clients in collection matters and three in which he was a party himself. Ramírez separately sued Dick K. Allen and G. O. Hoffman for money he had lent them in different transactions, and he was a defendant in a lawsuit brought by Charles Bennett for $2,116.17. Ramírez owed Bennett for lumber he had contracted to buy for the construction of houses on some of his vacant lots. However, he could not pay for the building materials on time. The large debt owed to Charles Bennett was eventually discharged when Ramírez sold the improved properties.

The full extent of Ramírez's law practice cannot be measured by the number of times he appeared in court. A large part of his practice took place outside of it and involved the filing of mining claims for the approval of the jefe político, Luis E. Torres. Ramírez was necessarily well acquainted with Torres and his staff. Such filings were preceded by searches for conflicting claims and advice given to mining investors, mostly Americans. Ramírez was beginning to be recognized as a local authority on Mexican mining law. Another lucrative feature of his practice that did not involve court appearances was guiding Americans through the sometimes confusing Mexican documents and procedures required for business transactions. Ramírez could counsel Americans in their own language about what had to be done to achieve the desired legal results. He drafted Spanish and English contracts, deeds, mortgages, liens, receipts, wills, trusts, and other needed instruments. He was among the very few attorneys in Ensenada, if not the only one, capable of telling Americans precisely what they needed to know in perfect English. A fair amount of American money must have found its way to the office on the first floor of his building, which, with the advances in Ensenada's urbanization, was no longer standing alone in an empty space. It could now be found among other buildings on the recently laid-out northwest corner of First Street and Ruiz Avenue.

Although Ensenada was beginning to offer improved material circumstances in his exile, Ramírez did not abandon hope for a return home. This was shown by a rather long article in the *Los Angeles Tribune* of June 5, 1889, entitled "Ramirez Homesick—And He Wants Permission to Come to Los Angeles." The newspaper reported that Ramírez had hired two lawyers, C. C. Hamilton and O. W. Pendleton, to request a dismissal of the charges against him on the ground that there was insufficient evidence for a conviction. The *Tribune* stated that several attempts had been made before this one to have the charges dismissed, but "these efforts have proved futile for the reason that the man was not willing to come in and surrender himself—a necessary proceeding before any relief could be extended to him." In Ramírez's absence Judge J. W. McKinley summarily rejected the motion for dismissal on June 10, 1889. This proceeding and others like it were indicative of an important reason that Ramírez stayed in Baja California, regardless of its hardships. From northern Baja California he could better wage a battle for personal redemption in the courts of Los Angeles.

The building of Ensenada reached its peak by 1889. After that, the directors of the British company invested as little money as possible in Baja California. The collapse of the Baring Brothers Bank in London set off the Panic of 1890, which was followed by a profound depression. The British company's resultant shortage of money is shown by the report of its chairman, Sir Edward Jenkinson. Its expenditures in Baja California were reduced from £72,000 in 1889 to £25,000 in 1890, and then to only £8,600 in 1891.[30] The Mexican government observed that Ensenada was falling into decay under the British company. In early 1892 the British were ordered to repair the wharf in Ensenada's harbor because it had so deteriorated that ships were refusing to use it. The resident British executive director, Major Buchanan Scott, bitterly complained about the refusal of the company to provide funds for improvements. He departed on May 15, 1890, because the British Army refused to extend his leave of absence. Scott returned to India, where he had great success. He was awarded a knighthood before his death in England during 1937. After Sir Edward Jenkinson was denied money by the British company to build a railroad and a system of irrigation in Baja California, he protested by resigning his office in 1892. The March 4, 1919, *London Times* obituary for Sir Edward called his experience with Baja California "brief and burdensome."

The directors of the British company were not interested in putting more money into Mexico without an immediate large return. Successors to Major Buchanan Scott were sent to Ensenada, but the company's reticence to invest further amounts eventually killed the enterprise. By 1906 the British had mostly withdrawn from the Baja California peninsula. The Mexican government, delayed by an intervening revolution, finally declared its contract with the British company at an end in 1917.

Many Americans chose not to remain in Baja California during the last decade of the nineteenth century. Depressed economic conditions accompanied by a drought from 1892 to 1896 induced a movement back to the United States. The American departure accounts for a decline in Ensenada's population from 2,133 in 1896 to 1,726 in 1900.[31] With the gradual disappearance of the Americans, the little town became more Mexican during the 1890s. It was a decade when Ensenada was suffering from a depression, losing population, and was no longer the object of foreign investment. These factors tended to slow further growth, but the population stabilized, and the place tranquilly persisted as a small commercial center for the Northern District. General Luis E. Torres was no longer needed to monitor the American company or its more passive British successor. President Díaz sent Torres to Yucatan in early 1893 to deal with a crisis there. A year later he returned to Sonora, where he continued as governor until driven into exile by Mexican revolutionaries in 1911. Torres took refuge in Los Angeles, securing employment as an inspector for the Atchison, Topeka & Santa Fe Railroad. He died in Los Angeles in 1935 at the age of 91.[32]

Torres represented the best type of Mexican politician. Early in his tenure as jefe político in northern Baja California, he was aware of secret plots by American filibusterers to seize the Distrito Norte. Some were fantastic schemes dreamed up by Americans in San Diego without the means to carry them out. However, at least one serious proposal to take over northern Baja California was made by a powerful group consisting of British and American capitalists who wanted to buy it. Their representative, J. A. Drought, was the director of the Lower California Development Company, a subsidiary of the British company. Unfortunately for Drought, he suggested over dinner with Luis E. Torres at San Diego's Hotel Del Coronado that the region should be acquired by foreign interests and that any high Mexican official who helped promote a purchase of Baja California would be rewarded with a great fortune.[33]

This obvious attempt to enlist Torres in the purchase scheme resulted in Torres's sending a letter to President Díaz on December 16, 1891, describing the whole conversation. Díaz insisted that the British company discharge Drought, which was immediately done. Torres had proven himself absolutely incorruptible. Ironically, his sense of honor and loyalty to Mexico did not work in his favor once he was ejected from the country by revolutionaries. His later exile in Los Angeles might not have involved the burdensome employment with a railroad corporation that he was forced to take in his old age if he had cooperated with Drought.

Ramírez had a very limited law practice in Ensenada during the first half of the 1890s. Even assuming that he did a certain amount of office work outside of court, Ramírez was not overwhelmed by business. In 1890 he was in court twice as an interpreter, nothing more. During 1891 he visited the court only once. That single appearance was in connection with a probate case on April 4.[34] Ramírez's lack of clients may be attributed to Ensenada's small population and diminishing business activity. However, he was also engaged in another enterprise. The April 23, 1891, edition of the *Lower Californian*, which had survived the collapse of the American company, published this item:

> Messrs. Judge Ramirez and John C. Maupin have started up the brick-kiln east of town and expect to furnish all the bricks needed hereabouts. Mr. Maupin made the first bricks used in this part of the peninsula.

The title "judge" shown in the item was occasionally applied to Ramírez by Americans since he had once been a justice of the peace in Real del Castillo. The brick factory probably had little success since there was no further mention of it in the press.

The year 1892 was a little better for Ramírez, who had eight court appearances as a lawyer and two as an interpreter. He was in court on ten occasions in 1893, six times as a lawyer and four times as an interpreter. There were no new legal clients in 1894. Ramírez did nothing in court that year, except to act as an interpreter in three cases. Ramírez filed five new cases as a lawyer in 1895, with no activity as an interpreter.[35] During the whole period from 1890 to 1895, Ramírez made court appearances as a lawyer in only 23 cases and was an interpreter in eight more. Other attorneys, such as Pedro Rendón and Juan B. Uribe, had more clients. Nearly all the people represented by Ramírez were Americans. Out of the twenty-three cases he filed during the five-year period mentioned, only three were filed on behalf of Mexicans. Fourteen of his cases involved the collection of loans that Americans had made to one another. The other nine consisted of one divorce, one contract matter, two actions to recover horses, two evictions, and three probate matters. One of his most important clients was the Lower California Development Company, owned by the British Company. He filed three suits for this entity. He also twice represented Charles Bennett on collection matters. Bennett owned the local water company and three factories. Finally, Ramírez obtained a divorce for the naturalized Basque immigrant Francisco Andonaegui, one of the most prominent businessmen and politicians in Ensenada.

In the otherwise quiet year of 1894, Ramírez received some gratifying news. The secretary of state for Sonora, Ramon Corral, sent Ramírez a copy of an order dated August 3, 1894, directing the state treasurer of Sonora to pay him 2,871 pesos for salary owed during the time he was editor of Sonora's official newspaper, *La Estrella del Occidente*, from 1860 to 1862.[36] Incredibly, after more than thirty-two years of indebtedness to Ramírez for his salary, an order was finally issued to pay it. This could only have been the result of a dogged campaign by Ramírez to collect his back salary from recalcitrant state officials. It will be remembered that Ramírez had published complaints about not receiving his salary while editing the official newspaper in Sonora. This was one of the reasons for his return to Los Angeles. It is not known why Ramon Corral, who ten years later would be the vice president of Mexico, signed the order. Payment was no doubt brought about by Ramírez's efforts to collect it. Receipt of the money from Sonora was a tribute to his persistence.

Throughout his life Ramírez's relationship with women was obscure. Some romantic poetry published in *El Clamor Público* before he was twenty-three years old suggests that he suffered from the usual stirrings of passion common to young men. However, there is little evidence of a liaison with any particular young lady other than Lastania Abarta during his forties.

At a rather advanced age Ramírez was finally married. His bride was María Saint Raymond, a twenty-eight-year-old widow from San Antonio, a fishing and mining settlement on the central west coast of Baja California. She had two small children, Luis and Angela García, by her deceased husband.[37] The motives for Ramírez's marriage and the true feelings of both spouses toward one another are too murky to evaluate, but a few features of their union appear problematic. When they married in Ensenada on September 2, 1895, Ramírez was already fifty-eight, some three decades older than his wife.[38] A great difference in age between married couples was socially acceptable in that era, as long as the male was the older. From María Saint Raymond's point of view as a widow, social and economic factors would have urgently demanded remarriage, even if accompanied by major concessions regarding her partner. Both the American and Mexican social systems of the time were rigidly patriarchal. Women had almost no civil or political rights. They were expected to occupy a subordinate place in a household headed by a male. The survival of a widow and her children free of poverty and hardship often depended on finding an appropriate husband.

A further complication was that Ramírez may have married María Saint Raymond out of a sense of moral obligation. She was already pregnant when the ceremony took place. Their first child, Reginaldo Crisótomo, was born on February 7, 1896, about five months after they were married.[39] A tragic

María Saint Raymond about the time of her marriage to Ramírez in 1895. Courtesy of Victor Manuel Ramírez, Seattle.

event took the infant's life shortly afterward. Ramírez's maid negligently covered him with blankets in such a way that he suffocated in the cradle. After recovering from this horrible incident, and despite Ramírez's age, during the next twelve years María Saint Raymond gave birth to seven more children: Francisco, María Rosa, Ysidoro, Casimiro Pedro, Marcial Valentín, María Bibiana, and Lorenzo.[40]

By 1896 Ensenada had settled into a placid state under the rule of jefe políticos sent by Mexico City. The early excitement and expansion brought by the American and English companies had ended. There was little criminal or political violence to disturb the quiet community. A growing Mexican presence caused by an American withdrawal from Baja California was reflected in Ramírez's law practice. During the twelve years between 1896 and his death in 1908, Ramírez represented eighty-two clients in court as a lawyer. Of this number thirty-eight were Mexican.[41] This was a large increase over the previous five years, when only three of his clients were Mexicans compared to twenty-eight Americans.

The nature of Ramírez's law practice did not change dramatically from 1896 until his death. During that twelve-year period he handled thirty-six collection cases, eighteen probate matters, thirteen real-estate cases, eleven contract disputes, two lawsuits over mining claims, and one divorce.

A book published in 1899, subsidized by the Mexican government, presented Ramírez as he would have liked to see himself. Entitled *Baja California Illustrated*, the text appeared in both English and Spanish, with the obvious intention of attracting American investors and tourists. The author, John R. Southworth, wrote brief biographical sketches about people in Ensenada whom he thought Americans might find useful.[42] He included a flattering and somewhat exaggerated statement about Ramírez:

> One of the prominent attorneys of Lower California is Mr. F. P. Ramirez of Ensenada. Mr. Ramirez is qualified to attend to all legal matters in all the courts of the Mexican Republic, and his able handling of the many important cases that have come to him during his years of practice has won for him the highest esteem of his clients and the public in general. Mr. Ramirez makes a specialty of mining and commercial law, and is agent for the purchase and sale of lands and mining properties in the territory of Lower California. He is also an interpreter of the first order, and speaks English and French fluently. Mr. Ramirez is one of Ensenada's most esteemed and influential citizens.

This kind of publicity would please Ramírez's vanity and possibly help his

A 1901 photograph of Francisco P. Ramírez in Ensenada at the age of sixty-four. Courtesy of the Acervo Histórico Diplomatico, Secretaría de Relaciones Exteriores, Mexico, D.F.

practice in Ensenada. Southworth's book shows that the Mexican government still wanted Americans to invest in Baja California. It was willing to pay for propaganda presenting the region in the most favorable manner possible.

To improve his position as both a landowner in Ensenada and a practicing attorney, Ramírez formally applied for Mexican citizenship in 1901. An elaborate certificate of citizenship was prepared by the Secretaría de Relaciones Exteriores—the Ministry of Foreign Relations—and a copy was forwarded to Ramírez in Ensenada.[43] The original of the document still remains in the archives of that ministry in Mexico City. It was signed by President Porfirio Díaz, with a photograph of Ramírez attached, one of only two such images known to exist.

At this point Ramírez's life in Ensenada was fairly secluded. Proof of this is found in a newspaper, *El Progresista*, published between April 19, 1903, and June 26, 1904.[44] The paper was started by Carlos R. Ptacnik, a native of Chihuahua, when he was only twenty-three years old. Ptacnik's unusual last name arose from the fact that his father was a mining engineer from Munich, Germany, who had migrated to Mexico. Ptacnik's mother, María, was the daughter of Luis Terrazas, a fabulously wealthy landowner in Chihuahua, who had once been governor of the state. After studying to be an engineer in St. Louis, Missouri, Carlos Ptacnik arrived in Ensenada in 1901, a youth of independent means because of his connection with the Terrazas family. His newspaper, which lasted only some fourteen months, presented Ensenada as an almost idyllic community. No evidence of social or political discontent appeared in *El Progresista*. The newspaper exalted both President Porfirio Díaz and the new jefe político, Coronel Celso Vega, as leaders of an ideal society. With apparent satisfaction, it reported all Ensenada's social and public events in great detail.

If Ramírez was a prominent person, he would have been mentioned in the pages of *El Progresista*. However, his name never appears in a single issue except one published on June 5, 1904, which contained a list of annual municipal taxes paid by businesses and professions operating in Ensenada. It was a compilation of taxpayers' names and the amounts they were required to pay based on their estimated income. The English company paid $125 for running the largest general store in town. Most merchants paid less than twenty pesos. The cosmopolitan nature of Ensenada is revealed by the list. Out of seventy-five merchant taxpayers, twenty-three were American or European and eight were Chinese. There were six lawyers on the list, all of them Mexican. The attorney for the English company, Pedro Rendón, was the most prosperous, paying five pesos in taxes. He was followed by Roberto Otañez, who paid three pesos. Juan B. Uribe and A. Guerrero y Porrez were each charged two pesos. The last two lawyers on the list were deemed to have such modest practices that they only had to contribute one peso each. They were Francisco P. Ramírez and Luis G. Caballero. Lawyers paying the highest taxes consistently advertised in *El Progresista*, but not Ramírez. At this point he never advertised and was not regarded as prosperous.

Ramírez continued with his small number of law cases almost down to the time of his death. Some fragments of his last few cases still exist. One of them is a letter dated February 18, 1907, from W. B. White, manager of the Cox Investment Company's mining department in Philadelphia, inquiring about some documents that were probably mining claims. Another was a typewritten letter in English from Ramírez to M. H. Jolliff, an American in San Antonio, Baja California. Ramírez discussed some deeds in a land transaction and requested $40 from Jolliff. His letter mentioned a prior telephone conversation with Jolliff, a reference making it clear that near the end of his life Ramírez was no longer isolated in a primitive section of Mexico. His office now had electric lighting and telephone service.[45]

One of the last cases ever handled by Ramírez was an unsuccessful attempt to prevent the extradition from Ensenada of an accused American forger named William F. Walker. The *Reno Evening Gazette* of May 4, 1908, published an item stating that Walker had sought refuge in Ensenada after absconding with a large amount of money from a bank in New Britain, Connecticut, where he had been employed as a cashier. The newspaper identified Ramírez as Walker's attorney. Eventually, over Ramírez's objections, a Mexican judge in Ensenada gave custody of Walker to Connecticut authorities sent to retrieve him. Ramírez's representation of Walker was ironic since he was a fugitive himself. For some reason, the law enforcement officials in Los Angeles had little interest in extraditing Ramírez. He had no fear that this would happen as long as he remained below the border; consequently, he never made his presence in Baja California a secret.

Ramírez died in Ensenada on December 28, 1908. His death certificate stated that chronic bronchitis was the cause.[46] This diagnosis is suspect, however, since it was made by L. Y. Ketcham, not a medical doctor, but a druggist trained at the New York College of Pharmacy. He opened a drug store in Ensenada at first, then later held himself out as a physician and surgeon, although he had never attended medical school.[47] Most Ensenada residents avoided such quackery by going to San Diego for serious medical problems, but Ramírez was prevented from doing so because he risked arrest if he crossed the border.

An inventory filed in Ramírez's probate on January 30, 1909, shows that he left an estate worth $11,770, a fairly sizeable amount at the time. Included was $3,250 worth of personal property such as furniture, a library, and other belongings. His library alone was estimated as being worth $500 and amounted to one of the largest private book collections in Baja California. The value of his real property amounted to about $8,520. Besides his two-story house, he owned part or all of thirteen lots in the center of Ensenada, as well as a ranch in Santo Tomás and another in Real del Castillo.[48] Unfortunately, Ramírez left no will. This would cause his wife problems since it unnecessarily complicated his probate, which dragged on for years.

Ramírez's wife left Ensenada after his death, taking their children to Los Angeles. She periodically went to Ensenada to attend to the convoluted probate left by her husband. As adults, some of her children remained in the United States while others went to Tijuana, Ensenada, and other parts of

After Ramírez's death in 1908, his widow rented out the family homestead to various tenants. Among them was this Italian restaurant, well-known during the 1920s. Courtesy of Dr. Fernando Araujo, Ensenada.

Mexico. No one is certain about what became of them. The youngest child, Lorenzo, born just before his father's death, was one of those who returned to Ensenada. There he had two children rather late in life, who are still living: Jesús Lorenzo Ramírez of Ensenada and Victor Manuel Ramírez of Seattle, Washington. Lorenzo took possession of the family homestead to operate it as a hotel, its original purpose. Until the building was demolished in 1983, it stood as the Hotel Ramírez, a landmark in downtown Ensenada.

The widowhood of María Saint Raymond de Ramírez lasted thirty-seven years, until her death on November 22, 1945, in Tijuana at the age of eighty. She lived modestly on rents and the money left by her husband until it gradually dissipated over the years. Her body was taken to San Diego's old Calvary Cemetery.

Ramírez's death went unnoticed in Los Angeles. There was no mention of his passing in the press. His long connection with Los Angeles and his days as editor of *El Clamor Público* were forgotten. An article written in 1913 on the history of the Ramírez family by his niece, Petra Pelanconi, for the magazine *The Grizzly Bear*, made no reference to her uncle. Her omission of the best-known member of her family probably resulted from the disgrace of his having been a fugitive from justice. Ramírez's passage from the brilliant days of youth to the shadows of an old age in exile is a story of self-inflicted damage and the vagaries of the human condition. He lies buried somewhere in the Ensenada Municipal Cemetery in an unmarked grave.

Portrait of Lorenzo Ramírez, the youngest son of Francisco P. Ramírez and María Saint Raymond, date unknown. After his mother's death Lorenzo operated the family homestead for many years as the Hotel Ramírez. Courtesy of Victor Manuel Ramírez, Seattle.

The Hotel Ramírez shortly before its demolition in 1983. The building was a landmark in downtown Ensenada for a hundred years. Courtesy of Dr. Fernando Araujo, Ensenada.

CLAMOR PUBLICO

Periodico Independiente y Literario.

LOS ANGELES, CALIFORNIA, MARTES, JUNIO 19 DE 1855.

COMISION DE LOS ESTADOS UNIDOS

PARA LA APROBACION DE LOS TITULOS DE TERRENOS.

[*Sesion de 22 de mayo de* 1855.]

Opinion di Comisionado Farwell.

APROBADOS.

N.° 250.—El título del Sr. M G. Vallejo por 10 legus cuadradas y 5 mas en el condado de Petluma.

N.° 291.—Otro del mismo, por un terreno en el condado de Solano.

N.° 291.—El título de John Rose, seis leguas cuadadas en el condado de Yuba.

N.° 462.—El título de los herederos de Juan B. Alvrado, por el Rincon del Diablo en el condao de San Diego.

N.° 550.—El título de Jno P. Davison, cuatro legus cuadradas en Santa Paula y Santicoy, cudado de Sta. Barbara.

N.° 461.—El título de Juan Foster ocho leguas cuaradas en el valle de S. Felipe, condado deSan Diego.

N.° 664—El título de los herederos de David Littejohn, una legua cuadrada en Los Carneos, condado de Monterey.

N.° 509—El título de Samuel G. Reid, tres leguacuadradas en el rancho del Puerto, condado de San Joaquin.

N.° 248—El título de Chas Convilland, parte de 1 leguas concedidas primero a J. A. Sutter Concesion por recompensa y con condiciones en 1841. El terreno esta situado en Feather River.

DESAPROBADO.

N.° 688—El título de Temple y Alexander, por 100 varas cuadradas en el condado de Los Angeles. Concedidas provisionalmente en 1854.

Mexico.

El General Alvarez ha espedido el siguiente decreto para favorecer a las personas que deseen emigrar a Mexico para esplotar los ricos placeres de oro que se han descubierto en Ajutechlan, cerca de Acapulco:

El Capitan Juan Alvarez, General de Division de la República Mexicana y en Gefe del ejército restaurador de la Libertad—á los habitantes de la República, sabed:

Que usando de las amplias facultades que me concede el "Plan de Ayutla," para promover por cuantos medios me sean posibles la prosperidad y engrandecimiento de la nacion, he tenido a bien decretar:

ART. 1. El laboreo de los placeres de San Francisco del Oro, situados en el distrito deAjutichlan del departamento de Guerrero, se declara libre para mexicanos y extrajeros desde la publicacion de este decreto.

ART. 2. Todo individuo, ya sea nacional ó extranjero, que se dirija al distrito mencionado con objeto de trabajar los placeres, se presentará a las autoridades políticas para obtener de ellas "gratis," sus correspondientes resguardos.

ART. 3. Es libre de todo derecho la introducion que se haga por el puerto de Acapulco, de maquinaria, instrumentos y proviciones para el trabajo de las minas.

ART. 4. Los metales preciosos del distrito mineral, que se extraigan fuera de la república, solo pagarán al erario el 1 por 100, cayendo en pena de comiso los que contravengan a esta disposicion.

ART. 5. Todo trabajador de placeres referidos, ya sea nacional ó extranjero, que desee adquirir terrenos para fabricar ó dedicarse a la agricultura, ocurrirá a la autoridad política, que facilitará de los terrenos valdios el que se le pidiere, a precios convencionales o equitativos.

ART. 6. Las diferencias que ocurran entre los mineros, se resolverán por quien corresponda con sujecion a la ordenanza del ramo.

Por tanto, etc. Dado en en cuartel general del Ejército Restaurador en Texca, a 20 de Abril de 1855. JUAN ALVAREZ.

Sud America.

CHILE.—Segun las últimas noticias continúa su marcha pacífica y progresiva. Las elecciones para miembros del Congreso han pasado sin ocurrencia alguna notable. Entre los Senadores electos vemos con suma satisfaccion el nombre del ilustre colombiano D. Andrés Bello.

PERU.—El general Flores había llegado á Lima, y protestado contra el tratado que celebró Echenique con el gobierno del Ecuador, por el cual se le niega á aquel el asilo en el Perú. Parece que el gobierno provicional tiene por ominoso el tratado, y lo concidera humillante para el honor nacional. Pero el ministro del Ecuador protestó, y le han seguido losdemás Ministros de la América septentrional residentes en Lima. Piden que Flores salga del Perú inmediatamente. "Si Flores (dice un diario del Sur) ha sido siempre una amenaza para los Estados Colombianos, hoy es mayor esa amenaza, mediante la expedicion que se quedaba formando en los Estados Unidos por él, con el fin de tomar las islas de los Galápagos."

Es un hecho imposible que salga de aquí expedicion contra el Ecuador, por mas que hagan Flores y su edecan Clemens.

BOLIVIA,—No son menores las inquietudes en Bolivia con motivo del anunciado regreso del general Santa Cruz. El Presidente Belzu ha dictado un decreto, ordenando el secuestro de los bienes de todo el que tome parte en alguna sedicion, invacion etc. etc. Uno de los artículos de ese decreto manda conciderar sin efecto las transacciones que se hubieren celebrado sobre dichos bienes, desde seis meses antes de cometido el delito, en cuando fueren aquellos necesarios para indemnizar al Gobierno y a los particulares de los perjuicios causados por los perturbadores. Se ha dado a luz una carta que se dice dirijida por el general Santa Cruz al coronel Puch, fechada en Bruselas a 15 de nobiembre del año próximo pasado, y en la cual manifiesta el Protector su determinacion de "regresar á America á oponerse á la reeleccion en que está empeñado Belzu, adoptando al efecto el sistema de Rosas."

BRASIL Y PARAGUAY.—Por los extractos que ofrecen los diarios del Istmo de Panamá sabemos que la guerra del imperio del Brasil contra el Uruguay se está ya haciendo, y segun parece, sin una declaratoria que la precediera, "siendo lo mas extraño (dice el *Panameno*) ver que la marina de guerra de los Estados Unidos ayude a S. M. I; en su agrecion contra los paraguayos. Estos, empero, oponen fuerzas considerables á sus adversarios, y hasta ahora alcanzan el triunfo en los combates habidos."—He aquí lo que dice el *Constitucional* de Mendoza, en el asunto: "Se hacia serio nos informa uno de los pasajeros llegados en la mensajeria, el conflicto del Paraguay, atacado por una fuerte escuadra brasilera y un vapor norteamericano; dos potencias poderosas han llevado la guerra contra esta naciente y pequeña república; el Almirante del Paraguay, hijo del Presidente Lopez, de dos vapores que habian comprado en Europa, no habia conseguido introducir sino uno antes que la escuadra brasilera ocupase los rios. Habia tenido lugar un combate entre el vapor norteamericano que hemos mensionado y una bateria paraguaya, la que causó con sus fuegos algunas averías en el vapor matándole dos hombres ademas. Este desmontó algunas piezas de aquella. En la frontera con el Brasil, en las guardias ó fuertes se trataban encuentros parciales entre paraguayos y brasileros, en los que aquellos habian salido vencedores."

Los periódicos de Buenos Ayres dan la noticia de que una fuerza paraguaya de 8,000 hombres habia obtenido á inmediaciones de Villareal un triunfo sobre las fuerzas brasileras invasoras. Sobre el Paraná tenian los paraguayos 20,000 hombres estacionados, habian tapado dos de las tres bocas del rio Paraguay, echando á pique piraguas cargadas de piedras, y estando le-

FRANCIA.—Un decreto del Emperador aumenta al ejército en 90,000 hombres.—Cada regimiento de linea tendrá un refuerzo de 900.

Esperando la visita de la Reina Victoria á Paris, el Emperador ha mandado poner el Liceo Imperial en un pie de espléndida magnificencia.

Por decreto de 31 de marzo, Mr. de Thounevel Ministro Plenipotenciario de primera clase y director de los asuntos políticos, se encargará durante la aucencia del Ministro Secretario de Estado de Negocios Extranjeros, Mr. Drouyn de Lhuys, de la direccion de los trabajos de ese departamento y de la correspondencia diplomática.

El gobierno francés se ha quejado oficialmente al belga, á instancias del Príncipe Napoleon, por un opúsculo publicado contra el Emperador sobre la guerra y que se atribuyó al Príncipe.

EL PROXIMO CONGRESO,—Hasta hoy los miembros electos para el próximo Congreso son como sigue: Administracion 31; Oposicion 129. Todavía resta que elejir 37 miembros en los Estados donde las elecciones congrecionales aun no han tenido lugar.

INTERESANTE.—Un astrónomo Aleman dice que en veinte millones de años la tierra será destruida por una cometa!

LA MEDALLA RUSA.—En los cuerpos de algunos soldados rusos que cayéron en Eupatoria se encontró la medalla de plata de la decoracion de San Jorge. En un lado está grabada el águila rusa, con dos cabezas, teniendo en los pies el globo terrestre y el cetro del soberano; sobre el águila esta la corona imperial y una paloma iluminada. Sobre estas figuras tiene las siguientes palabras en lengua rusa:

"Arrodillense, idolatras, porque Dios es con nosotros."

En el otro lado tiene la siguiente divisa también en ruso:

"Para la sumision de Hungria y Transilvania.

☞ Dícese que casi todo el vino de la Moselle ha sido comprado por el gobierno Francés para mandarlo al ejercito de Crimea.

☞ La *Union* de Sacramento hablando del San Francisco *Chronicle* dice: "No se encuentra dentro de los límites de este Estado otro periódico mas cortéz, independiente y elegante."

☞ Los soldados heridos y enfermos que han muerto en Lìverpool, (Inglaterra) serán enterrados en un mismo lugar, sobre el cual se erijirá un monumento por suscricion pública.

PISCATORIO.—Mr. Joseph S. McIntyre, de la armada de los E. U. estacionada en Benicia, publica una carta en el *Herald* de San Francisco, anunciando que sacó un pescado y abriéndolo encontro un látigo de veinte pulgadas y media de largo y montado en plata. Se ha dudado mucho la veracidad de esta historieta.

POZO ARTESIANO.—Se ha cavado un nuevo pozo artesiano en San José, y segun el *Tribune* es una curiosidad.

CONVENCION DEMOCRATICA.—El dia 27 de Junio tendrá lugar una convencion democratica en Sacramento con el objeto de nombrar oficiales para la eleccion general en Setiembre próximo.

EL CENSO.—La Constitucion del Estado proviene que se tome el censo este año, pero como la legislatura no dispuso nada sobre esto, se tomara el año de 1860.

PELEGRINOS PARA PALESTINA.—Una caravana de pelegrinos se embarcó recientemente en Marsella para la Tierra Santa.—Antes de su salida fuéron invitados al palacio por el Obispo y cada uno recibió una crucesita de plata, con la fecha de su partida. Se esta organizando otra caravana

La ley del Dom

SECCION 1. Toda divers
bullicíosa será en lo sucesi
dias domingos.

SEC. 2. Todo individuo
ayudase á abrir en este di
miento público, tal como
juego, cuarto ó salon, juego
lugares propios para carre
combate de osos, de toros,
diversiones barbaras y b
prendido por un delito esp
ley, y despues de convicto,
á una multa cuyo minimu
cuenta pesos y el maximum
cuenta.

SEC. 3. Todo individuo
un billete de entrada á uno
de las diversiones enumer
gunda seccion de esta acta,
te castigado con una mult
al minimum, y de cincuent

SEC. 4. Los jueces de
en todos casos de infraccion
ciones de esta ley.

SEC. 5. Esta ley estará
desde Junio de 1855.

PAPEL DE TULE.—El Exm
BIGLER en su último mensa
los terrenos innundados y
presa como sigue:

"Y ya que estoy tocan
acaso no sea fuera de lugar
llegan á tener buen éxito lo
que ahora se están haciendo
del Atlántico, no tan solo s
sino que aumentará necesar
lor. Nadie ignora que un
los terrenos adquiridos po
virtud de la ley de Sept
está cubierta de lozano T
este suelo, y que por termi
toneladas por acre.

"Durante el último otoñ
sido cuidadosamente esan
bricantes esperimentados,
presado que, en su opinion,
con él un papel de calidad
perior.

"Puesto que el tallo de
está maduro y antes que s
la lluvia, es casi blanco, se
to del blanqueo seria com
pequeño. Estando cubierto
y compacta fibra, é interior
un tejido cecular con nume
fibras longitudinales, se
todas las cualidades requer

"Se han remitido vari
Tule á algunos fabricantes
Estados del Atlántico, con
hagan ensayos con él, y pr
el resultado de estos impo
mentos.

"A fin de poder apreciar
la importancia de este esper
que tenga feliz éxito, se ha
explicacion de algunos hec
rentes.

"El precio medio, en l
Atlántico, del material co
fabrica el papel es de uno
la libra. A dos centavos la
tercera parte del precio act
los trapos, cada acre produc
ochenta pesos ($80) ó sea
cientos pesos ($12,800) cada
acres, y esto, sin mas gast
se orijinen al tiempo de la
ño despues que haya comp
durado.

"Sin embargo, cualquier
sultado de los esperimentos
haciendo acerca de la prim
papel de cartas ó de impr
duda han los hombres ent
han ocupado de esta mater
el *Tule* se puede fabricar p
na calidad.

NOTES

Chapter One

1. Petra Pelanconi, Untitled article in the *Grizzly Bear* (1913), 1.
2. Leonce Jore, "Jean Louis Vignes of Bordeaux, Pioneer of California Viticulture," *Southern California Quarterly* 4, no. 4 (1963): 289–303.
3. Ibid., 298.
4. Los Angeles County Prefecture Records, vol. 1: 321.
5. Ibid., vol. A: 685.
6. Hubert Howe Bancroft, *History of California*, 7 vols., San Francisco: History Co., (1885–1888); reprint by Wallace Hebberd, Santa Barbara, CA (1966), 3: 636.
7. Deed dated November 17, 1855, Keller Collection.
8. Ibid. In the Mexican tradition both Juan and Petra Ramírez placed a little cross in the space for their signatures.
9. Jane Apostol, "Don Mateo Keller: His Vines and His Wines," *Southern California Quarterly* 84 (Summer 2002): 93–114.
10. Baptismal certificates, Archival Center, Archdiocese of Los Angeles.
11. Neal Harlow, *California Conquered: War and Peace on the Pacific, 1846–1850* (Berkeley: University of California Press, 1982), 217. W. W. Robinson, *Los Angeles from the Days of the Pueblo* (San Francisco: California Historical Society, 1981), 58.
12. Bancroft Library, dictation from Francisco P. Ramírez: ms. [circa 1888].
13. Leonard Pitt, *The Decline of the Californios, A Social History of the Spanish-Speaking Californians, 1846–1890* (Berkeley: University of California Press, 1966), 184. Douglas Monroy, *Thrown among Strangers: The Making of Mexican Culture in Frontier California* (Berkeley: University of California Press, 1990), 219.
14. Bancroft Library, dictation from Francisco P. Ramírez: ms. [circa 1888].
15. Manuel Clemente Rojo, *Apuntes Históricos de la Frontera de la Baja California* (Ensenada: Museo de Historia de Ensenada, 2000), 15–21.
16. Gerald McKevitt, *The University of Santa Clara: A History, 1851–1977* (Palo Alto, CA: Stanford University Press, 1979), 27.
17. Mary Dominica McNamee, *Light in the Valley, The Story of California's College of Notre Dame* (Berkeley, CA: Howell-North Books, 1967), 39–40.
18. McKevitt, *University of Santa Clara*, 325.

[348]   Notes

19. Ibid., 28.
20. William F. James and George M. McMurry, *History of San Jose, California* (San Jose, A. H. Cawston, 1933), 92–93.
21. Emerson Daggett, *History of Journalism in San Francisco* (San Francisco: Works Projects Administration, 1939–1941), 16.
22. Ibid., 14–15.
23. William B. Rice, *The Los Angeles Star, 1851–1864: The Beginnings of Journalism in Southern California* (Berkeley: University of California Press, 1947), 70–71.
24. Ibid., 70
25. Joseph Lancaster Brent, *The Lugo Case: A Personal Experience* (New Orleans, LA: Searcy and Pfaff, 1926), 5.
26. Pitt, *Decline of the Californios*, 184.
27. Monroy, *Thrown among Strangers*, 219.
28. Richard Griswold del Castillo, *The Los Angeles Barrio, 1850–1890: A Social History* (Berkeley: University of California Press, 1979), 31.
29. Paul Bryan Gray, *Forster vs. Pico: The Struggle for the Rancho Santa Margarita*, (Spokane, WA: Arthur H. Clark, 1998), 72–79.
30. H. D. Barrows, "J. Lancaster Brent," *Annual Publications of the Historical Society of Southern California* (1897): 238.
31. Gloria E. Miranda, "Racial and Cultural Dimensions of *Gente de Razón* Status in Spanish and Mexican California," *Southern California Quarterly* 70 (Fall 1988): 274.
32. Monroy, *Thrown among Strangers*, 138.
33. Griswold del Castillo, *Los Angeles Barrio*, 53.
34. Pitt, *Decline of the Californios*, 133.
35. Gray, *Forster vs. Pico*, 116.
36. Harris Newmark, *Sixty Years in Southern California*, 4th rev. ed. (Los Angeles: Zeitlin and Ver Brugge, 1970), 42.
37. Griswold del Castillo, *Los Angeles Barrio*, 91.
38. Ibid., 35–38.
39. Tomás Almaguer, *Racial Fault Lines: The Historical Origins of White Supremacy in California* (Berkeley: University of California Press, 1994), 36.
40. Pitt, *Decline of the Californios*, 85–89.
41. M. Colette Standart, "The Sonora Migration to California, 1848–1856: A Study in Prejudice," *Southern California Quarterly* 58 (Fall 1976): 348–50.
42. Informe de la visita oficial a la Municipalidad del Sáric in the Archivo del Gobierno del Estado de Sonora.

Chapter Two

1. "Beyond Commentary" in *El Clamor Público*; see Pitt, *Decline of the Californios*, 162–66, and Lawrence E. Guillow, "Pandemonium in the Plaza: The First Los Angeles Riot, July 22, 1856," *Southern California Quarterly* 77 (Fall 1995): 183–94.

2. Walter R. Bacon, "Fifty Years of California Politics," *Annual Publications of the Historical Society of Southern California* (1902): 35.
3. Bancroft, *History of California*, 5: 434.
4. Bayard Taylor, *El Dorado; or, Adventures in the path of Empire*. (New York: G. P. Putnam and Son, 1868), 53.
5. Andrew F. Rolle, *John Charles Frémont, Character as Destiny* (Norman: University of Oklahoma Press, 1991), 168.
6. Rice, *Los Angeles Star*, 121–22.
7. *Los Angeles Star*, August 23, 1856.
8. Newmark, *Sixty Years*, 207.
9. *El Clamor Público*, February 21, 1857.
10. *Los Angeles Star*, July 26, 1856.
11. Ibid., February 7, 1857.
12. Statutes of California (1851), Title 11, Ch. 1, Sec. 394.
13. Statutes of California (1855), Ch. 175, Secs. 1 and 2. This law was specifically directed against "persons commonly known as 'Greasers' or the issue of Spanish and Indian blood."

Chapter Three

1. Jean Louis Vignes was declared legally incompetent by Judge William G. Dryden on July 31, 1857. Manuel Requeña was appointed his guardian. *Guardianship of Jean Louis Vignes*, Los Angeles County Court, Case No. 201 (1857). Vignes died in 1862.
2. *El Clamor Público*, September 5, 1857.
3. Ibid., September 19, 1857.
4. *Los Angeles Star*, August 22, 1857.
5. *El Clamor Público*, September 19, 1857.
6. Bancroft, *History of California*, 5: 767.
7. *El Clamor Público*, March 27, 1858.
8. Gray, *Forster vs. Pico*, 88–89.
9. *Los Angeles Star*, September 4, 1858.
10. *El Clamor Público*, September 4, 1858.
11. David Lavender, *California, Land of New Beginnings* (New York: Harper and Row), 252.
12. *Los Angeles Star*, August 31, 1859.
13. *El Clamor Público*, September 10, 1859.

Chapter Four

1. Bancroft Library, dictation from Francisco P. Ramírez: ms. [circa 1888].
2. *La Estrella de Occidente*, May 4, 1860.
3. Francisco R. Almada, *Diccionario de Historia, Geografía y Biografía Sonorenses* (Hermosillo, Sonora: Instituto Sonorense de Cultura, 2009), 508.

[350] Notes

4. Rodolfo F. Acuña, *Sonoran Strongman: Ignacio Pesqueira and His Times* (Tucson: University of Arizona Press, 1974), 5–6.
5. José Francisco Velasco, *Noticias Estadísticas del Estado de Sonora* (Mexico, D.F.: Imprenta de I. Cumplido, 1850), 96.
6. Miguel Tinker Salas, *In the Shadow of the Eagles: Sonora and the Transformation of the Border during the Porfiriato* (Berkeley: University of California Press, 1997), 20.
7. Ibid., 21.
8. Ibid., 68.
9. *La Estrella de Occidente*, September 7, 1860.
10. Laureano Calvo Berber, *Nociones de Historia de Sonora* (Mexico, D.F.: Librería Porrúa, 1958), 216.
11. *La Estrella de Occidente*, January 4, 1861.
12. Eduardo W. Villa, *Historia del Estado de Sonora* (Hermosillo, México: Editorial Sonora, 1951), 277–78.
13. Ibid., 278.
14. Acuña, *Sonoran Strongman*, 73–74.
15. Ibid., 74.

Chapter Five

1. Griswold del Castillo, *Los Angeles Barrio*, 35.
2. Robert Glass Cleland, *The Cattle on a Thousand Hills* (San Marino, CA: Huntington Library, 1975), 102–16.
3. Ibid.,127–28.
4. Ibid., 313n40.
5. Gray, *Forster vs. Pico*, 99–100.
6. John W. Robinson, *Los Angeles in Civil War Days, 1860–1865* (Los Angeles: Dawson's Book Shop, 1977), 50–51.
7. Ibid., 59.
8. Ibid., 85.
9. Ibid., 75–77.
10. Judson A. Grenier and Robert C. Gillingham, *California Legacy* (Carson, CA: Watson Land Co.), 176–82.
11. *Los Angeles Star*, September 7, 1861.
12. *Los Angeles Semi-Weekly Southern News*, May 15, 1861.
13. Ibid., August 7, 1861.
14. Rice, *Los Angeles Star*, 233.
15. Statutes of California (1859) Ch. 65, Sec. 1.
16. Newmark, *Sixty Years*, 54.
17. *Los Angeles Star*, September 6, 1862.
18. Ibid., November 15, 1862.

19. David Hayes-Bautista, "Empowerment, Expansion, and Engagement: Las Juntas Patrióticas in California, 1848–1869," *California History* 85, no. 1 (2007): 8.
20. Several of Ramírez's speeches were published in their entirety by *La Voz de Méjico*. See the issues of June 6, 1863; September 15, 1863; October 1, 1864.
21. Records of the Bureau of Land Management, Records Group 49, Records of the Los Angeles Register, National Archives, Laguna Niguel, California.
22. George Cosgrave, *Early California Justice, The History of the United States District Court for the Southern District of California* (San Francisco: Grabhorn Press, 1948), 50.
23. Ibid., 49.
24. Ibid., 52.
25. *Los Angeles Semi-Weekly Southern News*, August 20, 1862.
26. See the letters written by Ramírez to his superior, J. M. Edmunds, in the National Archives, Laguna Niguel, California, cited in note 21 above.

Chapter Six

1. Letter from C. R. Johnson to Abel Stearns, February 6, 1863, Stearns Collection (Huntington Library).
2. Cleland, *Cattle*, 165–78.
3. *Los Angeles Star*, January 24, February 7 and 14, 1863; John Robinson, *Los Angeles*, 113–14.
4. *Los Angeles Semi-Weekly News*, September 25, 1863.
5. William B. Rice, "Paul R. Hunt—An Account of an Eccentric Angeleno." *Historical Society of Southern California Quarterly* 24 (1942): 63–65.
6. Report of the Senate Committee on Elections (1864).
7. Ibid.
8. Ibid.

Chapter Seven

1. Frank Soulé, *The Annals of San Francisco* (New York: D. Appleton, 1855), 471.
2. Bancroft, *History of California*, 6: 169.
3. Alessandro Baccari and Andrew M. Canepa, "The Italians of San Francisco in 1865: G. B. Cerruti's Report to the Ministry of Foreign Affairs," *California History* 60 (Winter 1981/82): 356–57.
4. Deanna Paoli Gumina, *The Italians of San Francisco, 1850–1930* (New York: Center for Migration Studies, 1978), 27.
5. Soulé, *Annals of San Francisco*, 472.
6. Baccari and Canepa, "Italians of San Francisco," 354–57.
7. K. Ángel María Garibay, *Diccionario Porrúa de Historia, Biografía y Geografía de México* (Mexico D. F.: Editorial Porrúa, 1964), 1178–79.
8. Robert Ryal Miller, "Plácido Vega: A Mexican Secret Agent in the United States, 1864–

1866," *Americas* 19 (October 1962): 137.
9. Antonio Nakayama, *Realidad y Mentira de Plácido Vega* (Culiacán Rosales, Sinaloa: Apoyos Educativos, 1993), 67–96.
10. Robert Miller, "Plácido Vega," 138–39.
11. Robert Ryal Miller, "Californians against the Emperor," California Historical Quarterly 37 (1958): 196–204.
12. Ibid., 194–95.
13. *El Tiempo Ilustrado*, "José María Vigil," January 1, 1906, 39. Garibay, *Diccionario Porrúa*, 1555–56.
14. Francisco P. Ramírez, *Ligeras Observaciones Sobre el Manifesto de la Junta Central Democrática del Estado a los Hispanos que Tienen Voz o Interés en California* (San Francisco: Tipografía de la Voz de Méjico, 1864), 1–8.
15. Gerardo López del Castillo, *Al Público*, Hoja Suelta (1863).
16. The most notable was a broadside by a half-Mexican member of San Francisco's Spanish-speaking community: Tomás M. Jewett, *Los Siete Pecados Capitales de Antonio Mancillas*, Hoja Suelta (1863).
17. David Hayes-Bautista, who has made a profound study of the juntas patrióticas, writes that they were sending about $1,000 to the Juárez government every two weeks or so. This amount would represent $35,000 in 2009 money based on the consumer price index. See Hayes-Bautista, "Empowerment," 10.
18. Robert Miller, "Plácido Vega," 144.
19. Roberto Hernández Cornejo, *Los Chilenos en San Francisco de California* (Valparaíso, Chile: Imprenta San Rafael, 1930), 1: 357–58.
20. Henry G. Langley, *San Francisco Directory for the Year Commencing September 1867* (San Francisco, 1870), 691.
21. Robert Miller, "Plácido Vega," 146.
22. This famous gunfight and its causes are described in detail by Esther Boulton Black in *Rancho Cucamonga and Doña Merced* (Redlands, CA: San Bernardino County Museum Association, 1975), 133–43.
23. Egon Caesar Corti, *Maximilian and Charlotte of Mexico* (New York: A. A. Knopf, 1928), 2: 580, 930–31.
24. Ibid., 2: 505–6, 590, 644.
25. Jack Autrey Dabbs, *The French Army in Mexico, 1861–1867; A Study in Military Government* (The Hague: Mouton, 1963), 69, 265–66.
26. Thomas R. Eldredge and Ramírez jointly translated such documents as the *Biannual Report of the State Controller Concerning the 17th and 18th Fiscal Years* (1867).
27. Hubert Howe Bancroft, *Literary Industries* (New York: Harper and Brothers, 1891), 356–57.

Chapter Eight

1. *Los Angeles News*, August 19, 1865.
2. James J. Ayers, *Gold and Sunshine, Reminiscences of Early California* (Boston: R. G. Badger, 1922), 228.
3. Ibid., 230–33.
4. Rice, *Los Angeles Star*, 259.
5. Cleland, *Cattle*, 227.
6. Ibid., 268–71.
7. *Los Angeles Weekly Republican*, August 1, 1868.
8. Bancroft, *Literary Industries*, 487.
9. Gray, *Forster v. Pico*, 102–3.
10. Newmark, *Sixty Years*, 99–100.
11. *Los Angeles Evening Express*, April 26, 1875. Undated notebook of Thomas Mott. Sepúlveda-Mott Collection (Seaver Center).
12. Jorge Ramírez López, "Tecate," in *Panorama Histórico de Baja California* (Tijuana, Baja California: Centro de Investigaciones Históricas, UNAM-UABC, 1983), 315–16.
13. Remi A. Nadeau, *City-Makers* (Los Angeles: Trans-Anglo Books, 1965), 36–37.
14. *Los Angeles Star*, March 28, 1868. John W. Robinson, *Southern California's First Railroad* (Los Angeles: Dawson's Book Shop, 1978), 26–32.
15. Nadeau, *City-Makers*, 34.
16. Ayers, *Gold and Sunshine*, 255–56.
17. Griswold del Castillo, *Los Angeles Barrio*, 35.
18. *El Nuevo Mundo*, March 27, 1865, and various subsequent editions.
19. Gordon Morris Bakken, *Practicing Law*, 18, 21–27.
20. *Los Angeles Weekly Republican*, February 8, 1868; October 17, 1868.
21. *Los Angeles Times* obituary of A. J. King, October 14, 1923.
22. Lyman Copeland Draper, *A Biographical Sketch of the Honorable Charles H. Larrabee* (Madison: Wisconsin State Historical Society, 1882), 1–25.
23. Pitt, *Decline of the Californios*, 234–39.
24. Sepúlveda's attendance at the Ellis School for Boys is confirmed by a letter he sent to his sisters on October 20, 1854, giving his return address as "in care of Wylie R. Ellis, Esq., Kingston, Massachusetts." Sepúlveda-Mott Collection Item number 768 (Seaver Center). The Kingston Public Library, 6 Green Street, Kingston, MA 02364, has numerous documents concerning the Ellis School.
25. Roll of Attorneys of the Los Angeles District Court, Courtney Collection, Box 4 (Huntington Library).
26. A compilation of imperial officers describes Sepúlveda as "a notable and magistrate." Leonardo Márquez, *Manifiestos (El Imperio y Los Imperiales)* (México, D. F.: F. Vásquez, 1904), 391. Another states that Sepúlveda was a major in the imperial army. Ignacio de la Peza and Agustín Pradillo, *Maximiliano y los Últimos Sucesos del Imperio en Querétaro y México* (México, D. F.: Imprenta de I. Cumplido, 1870), 105. He appears to have been a field grade officer and a magistrate of the imperial military courts.

27. Ernst Pitner, *Maximilian's Lieutenant: A Personal History of the Mexican Campaign, 1864-7* (Albuquerque: University of New Mexico Press, 1992), 182-83.
28. Márquez, *Manifiestos*, 425.
29. A telegram from Volney E. Howard and Phineas Banning to U.S. Senator Cornelius Cole on July 27, 1867, began efforts by the State Department to release Sepúlveda from Mexican custody. Official correspondence concerning the case is recorded in *Papers Relating to Foreign Affairs* (Department of State, 1868), 444, 454, and 466.
30. *Alta California*, August 1, 1868. *Los Angeles Star*, August 8, 1868.
31. United States census of 1860, Schedule 1, County of Sacramento, California, 608.
32. Her parents and their occupations are found in the United States census of 1840, Schedule 1, Worcester County, Maryland. It is interesting to note that their household included two "free colored persons."
33. Almaguer, *Racial Fault Lines*, 58.
34. *Nicolas Colima v. Custodio Ramirez*, Los Angeles District Court Case No. 1482 (1869), and *Jose D. Talamantes v. E. A. Preuss*, Los Angeles District Court Case No. 1553 (1869).
35. *Los Angeles Evening Express*, July 17, 1871; *Los Angeles Star*, July 29, 1871.
36. *Daily Alta California*, September 5, 1871.
37. *Los Angeles Star*, July 30, 1871.
38. *Los Angeles Evening Express*, August 8, 1871.
39. *Los Angeles Star*, September 13, 1871.
40. United States census of 1860 and 1870, County of Los Angeles, California.
41. The "unterrified" was a term applied to loyal Democrats.
42. Andrew F. Rolle, *California: A History* (Wheeling, IL: Harlan Davidson, 2003), 219-20.
43. William McCawley, *The First Angelinos: The Gabrielino Indians of Los Angeles* (Banning, CA: Malki Museum Press and Ballena Press, 1996), 9, 10, 42.
44. *Los Angeles Times*, February 10 and 12, 1921.
45. *Congressional Globe*, December 20, 1859, 173.
46. Los Angeles District Court Case Number 1797, filed April 8, 1871.
47. Los Angeles District Court Case Number 1907.

Chapter Nine

1. Bancroft, *History of California*, 6: 374-75n5.
2. Grenier and Gillingham, *California Legacy*, 38, 40-41, 45-46.
3. Samuel Lanner Kreider, "Volney Erskine Howard: California Pioneer," *Historical Society of Southern California Quarterly* 31 (March and June 1949): 124.
4. John W. Shore to Joseph Lancaster Brent, June 9, 1865, Brent Collection.
5. L. J. Rose, Jr., *L. J. Rose of Sunny Slope, 1827-1899* (San Marino, CA: Huntington Library, 1959), 46.
6. John W. Robinson, "Colonel Edward J. C. Kewen; Los Angeles' Fire-Eating Orator of the Civil War Era," *Southern California Quarterly* 61 (Summer 1979): 159-81.

7. William Wilcox Robinson, *Lawyers of Los Angeles* (Los Angeles: Los Angeles County Bar Association, 1959), 45–46. *Los Angeles Times* (Obituary), February 3, 1915.
8. Ibid., 46.
9. Ibid., 50.
10. John Steven McGroarty, *Los Angeles From the Mountains to the Sea* (Chicago: American Historical Society, 1921), 345, 348–49.
11. W. W. Robinson, *Lawyers*, 49–51. *Los Angeles Times* (Obituary), October 14, 1923.
12. The firm of Glassell, Chapman, and Smith is described in Gray, *Forster v. Pico*, 145–50.
13. Ibid., 140–45.
14. W. W. Robinson, *Lawyers*, 49, 50, 53.
15. *The Los Angeles Evening Express*, July 6, 1872. This paper published Sepúlveda's entire speech, "which was received with great applause. . . . [T]hree cheers were proposed and given with a will for Judge Sepúlveda."
16. Ayers, *Gold and Sunshine*, 243–44.
17. *Los Angeles Star*, January 9, 1872.
18. *R. M. Widney v. Fredric Foyal*, Los Angeles District Court Case No. 1949.
19. *Verdugo v. Urías*, Los Angeles District Court Case No. 1938, filed February 15, 1872.
20. *Mariano G. Santa Cruz v. Gertrudes Araiza*, Los Angeles District Court Case No. 1969, filed April 19, 1872.
21. *Teresa Lastra v. Carlos Ortega, et al.*, Los Angeles District Court Case No. 1974, filed April 25, 1872.
22. *Andrea Elizalole de Dávila, et al. v. Prudencio Yorba, et al.*, Los Angeles District Court Case No. 1978, filed April 29, 1872.
23. R. W. Hent, *Forms and Use of Blanks: Being over One Thousand Forms in Ordinary Legal and Business Transactions* (San Francisco: H. H. Bancroft, 1866).
24. The organization of the California courts described below is based on that mandated by the Statutes of California Passed at the Fourteenth Session of the Legislature (1863), Chapters 1, 2, 3, 4, 5, 6, 7, and 8. Each county had to conform to the statutory requirements. See also, Willoughby J. Rodman, *History of the Bench and Bar of Southern California* (Los Angeles: W. J. Porter, 1909), 36–38.
25. John J. Stanley, "Bearers of the Burden: Justices of the Peace, Their Courts and the Law, in Orange County, California, 1870–1907," *Western Legal History* 5 (Winter and Spring 1992): 47–48.
26. This example of different verdicts by juries in the justice court and county court involving the same case and factual situation is *Manuel Lopez v. A.F. Coronel*, Los Angeles County Court Case No. 768, appeal filed March 6, 1876.
27. Ibid.
28. *Thomas Alvitre v. M. F. Quinn*, Los Angeles County Court Case No. 770, filed May 18, 1876.
29. Kathleen L. Miller, "The Temple Block, A Core Sample of Los Angeles History," *Journal of the West* 33 (April 1994): 67.

[356] Notes

30. Granville Arthur Waldron, "Courthouses of Los Angeles County," *Historical Society of Southern California Quarterly* 41, no. 4 (1959): 362–65.
31. Ibid., 364.
32. Kathleen Miller, "Temple Block," 69–70.
33. Paul R. Spitzzeri, *The Workman and Temple Families of Southern California, 1830–1930* (Dallas, Seligson Publishing, 2008), 145–46.
34. *La Crónica*, April 2, 1873, and April 5, 1903.
35. *Los Angeles Times*, May 26, 1903.
36. Clifford H. Bissell, "The French Language Press in California," *California Historical Society Quarterly* 39, no. 1 (1960): 326–29.
37. *Los Angeles Star*, May 20, 1872.
38. John Walton Caughey, *California* (New York: Prentice-Hall, 1953), 433.
39. Ibid., 435.
40. William Francis Deverell, *Railroad Crossing: Californians and the Railroad, 1850–1910* (Berkeley: University of California Press, 1994), 29.
41. Caughey, *California*, 448–49.
42. *Los Angeles Evening Express*, July 10, 1872.
43. *Los Angeles Evening Express*, July 24, 1872.

Chapter Ten

1. Theodore Henry Hittell, *History of California*, 4 vols. (San Francisco, N. J. Stone, 1898), 4: 519.
2. *Los Angeles Star*, July 2, 1873.
3. *Los Angeles Star*, November 6, 1873.
4. *Alta California*, November 13, 1873.
5. Los Angeles District Court Case No. 2103.
6. *Los Angeles Times*, April 25, 1891.
7. *Los Angeles Star*, January 6 and January 22, 1873.
8. *Alta California*, August 26, 1873.
9. Winfield J. Davis, *History of Political Conventions in California: 1849–1892* (Sacramento: Publications of the California State Library, No. 1, 1893), 322.
10. *Los Angeles Evening Express*, July 22, 1873.
11. Newmark, *Sixty Years*, 446–47.
12. *New York Times*, July 30, 1916.
13. Reflecting on Greely's candidacy later, Howard called him a "bad egg" who was never a Democrat. *Los Angeles Herald*, August 18, 1875, and August 26, 1877.
14. *Los Angeles Evening Express*, September 1, 1873.
15. Spitzzeri, *Workman and Temple Families*, 76.
16. McGroarty, *Los Angeles*, 925.
17. *Guerrero v. Ballerino*, 48 Cal. 118 (1874).
18. *Breon v. Strelitz*, 48 Cal. 645 (1874).

Notes   [357]

19. *Keller v. Ruiz de Ocana*, 48 Cal. 638 (1874).
20. *Macy v. Davila*, 48 Cal. 646 (1874).

Chapter Eleven

1. Newmark, *Sixty Years*, 477.
2. *Los Angeles Star*, March 12, 1875.
3. Nadeau, *City-Makers*, 113–17.
4. *Los Angeles Star*, March 9, 1875.
5. Los Angeles District Court Case No. 2511, filed July 11, 1874.
6. *Baptiste Amestoy v. Francisca L. Amestoy*, Los Angeles District Court Case No. 2703, filed March 19, 1875.
7. *Bernard Dubordieu v. Gregorio Gonzalez*, Los Angeles District Court Case No. 2640. Newmark, *Sixty Years*, 332.
8. *Romain Grand v. Manuel Dominguez*, Los Angeles District Court Case No. 2669.
9. *Los Angeles Star*, July 14, 1875.
10. Bancroft, *History of California*, 4: 764.
11. *Los Angeles Star*, March 9, 1875.
12. *Los Angeles Star*, August 5, 1875.
13. *Los Angeles Star*, July 29, 1875.
14. *Los Angeles Star*, August 5, 1875.
15. *Los Angeles Star*, August 8, 1875.
16. *Los Angeles Herald*, August 15, 1875.
17. Bancroft, *History of California*, 7: 674–78.
18. The *Los Angeles Star* published lengthy articles on the collapse of the Bank of California, describing the catastrophe in great detail, on August 27 and 28, 1875.
19. *Los Angeles Star* and *Los Angeles Evening Express*, September 2, 1875.
20. Spitzzeri, *Workman and Temple Families*, 166–76. Robert Glass Cleland, *Isaias W. Hellman and the Farmers and Merchants Bank* (San Marino: CA: Huntington Library, 1965), 35–42. Nadeau, *City-Makers*, 133–39.
21. *Los Angeles Star*, September 3 and 8, 1875.
22. Newmark, *Sixty Years*, 474.
23. Spitzzeri, *Workman and Temple Families*, 172–74. Sandra Lee Snider, *Elias Jackson "Lucky" Baldwin, California Visionary* (Los Angeles: Stairwell Group, 1987), 8–10.
24. *F. P. F. Temple v. E. W. Squires*, Los Angeles District Court Case No. 2798, filed June 27, 1875.
25. Los Angeles District Court Case No. 2935, filed October 20, 1875.
26. Los Angeles District Court Case No. 3010, filed December 20, 1875.
27. Spitzzeri,*Workman and Temple Families*, 182–83.
28. Los Angeles District Court Case No. 3079, filed February 5, 1876.
29. Los Angeles District Court Case No. 2911, filed October 1, 1875.
30. *Walter J. Welch v. M. D. Hare*, Los Angeles District Court Case No. 3170, filed April

4, 1876.
31. This case is absent from court records but was given extensive coverage in the *Los Angeles Star* on May 16, 1876.
32. *Los Angeles Star*, May 18, 1876.
33. Nadeau, *City-Makers*, 139.
34. Ibid., 150.
35. *La Crónica*, June 14, 1876.
36. *Los Angeles Herald, Star,* and *Evening Express*, July 6, 1876.
37. *Los Angeles Star*, August 1, 1876.
38. *Los Angeles Star*, September 6, 1876.
39. Nadeau, *City-Makers*, 129.
40. *La Crónica*, September 20, 1876.
41. *John McFadden v. Wilson Beach*, Los Angeles District Court Case No. 3417, filed July 27, 1876.
42. *La Crónica*, June 24 and October 7, 1876.
43. *Los Angeles Star*, July 19, 1877.
44. *Los Angeles Star*, July 29, 1877.
45. Kevin Starr, *Endangered Dreams: The Great Depression in California* (New York: Oxford University Press, 1996), 6.
46. Ira B. Cross, *A History of the Labor Movement in California* (Berkeley: University of California Press, 1935), 88–90.
47. Starr, *Endangered Dreams*, 8.
48. Cross, *Labor Movement*, 92.
49. Los Angeles County Recorder's Office, Book 53, Page 384 (April 12, 1877).
50. Ibid., Book 55, Page 459 (August 1, 1877).
51. Ibid., Book 61, Page 397 (April 18, 1878).
52. The National Association of Hispanic Journalists inducted Ramírez into their Hall of Fame on July 25, 2008.

Chapter Twelve

1. *Ramon Ybarra v. Juan C. Lorenzana*, Los Angeles District Court Case No. 4083, filed September 11, 1877.
2. *A. B. Peltier v. J. P. Jordan*, Los Angeles District Court Case No. 4317, filed January 24, 1878.
3. Los Angeles District Court Case No. 4443, filed April 24, 1878.
4. Los Angeles District Court Case No. 4524, filed June 25, 1878.
5. Cross, *Labor Movement*, 95–96.
6. Ibid., 96.
7. Ibid., 100.
8. Ibid., 103–4.
9. Neil L. Shumsky, *The Evolution of Political Protest and the Workingmen's Party of Cali-*

fornia (Columbus: Ohio State University Press, 1991), 15–16.

10. Ibid., 152.
11. Ibid., 74–75.
12. Cross, *Labor Movement*, 96–97.
13. Shumsky, *Political Protest*, 194–96, 198.
14. *Los Angeles Star*, February 2, 1878.
15. *Los Angeles Star*, February 27, 1878.
16. Shumsky, *Political Protest*, 207–9.
17. Carl Brent Swisher, *Motivation and Political Technique in the California Constitutional Convention, 1878–79* (Claremont, CA: Pomona College, 1930), 24.
18. Ibid., 33–34.
19. David E. Hayes-Bautista, "Reginaldo Francisco del Valle, UCLA's Forgotten Forefather," *Southern California Quarterly* 88 (Spring 2006): 4–5.
20. *Los Angeles Herald*, September 17, 1878.
21. *Los Angeles Times*, April 9, 1911. Newmark, *Sixty Years*, 330, 372, 445.
22. *Los Angeles Herald*, November 17, 1878.
23. *Los Angeles Star*, December 3, 1878.
24. *Los Angeles Star*, December 4, 1878.
25. *Los Angeles Star*, March 19, 1879.
26. Cross, *Labor Movement*, 114–15.
27. *Los Angeles Herald*, March 22, 1879.
28. *Los Angeles Star*, March 23, 1879.
29. *Los Angeles Herald*, April 1, 1879.
30. *Los Angeles Herald*, September 7, 1879.
31. Ibid.
32. Shumsky, *Political Protest*, 105.
33. *Los Angeles Herald*, September 17, 1879.
34. 58 Cal. 11 (1881).
35. Los Angeles District Court Case No. 4899, filed January 20, 1879, and Los Angeles District Court Case No. 4936, filed February 12, 1879.
36. Los Angeles District Court Case No. 5088, filed May 19, 1879.
37. *Los Angeles Evening Express*, January 24, 1880.
38. Shumsky, *Political Protest*, 206–7.
39. The killing of Francisco "Chico" Forster caused a sensation in Los Angeles. The *Los Angeles Herald* of March 16, 1881, devoted a great deal of space to the incident.
40. *Evening Express*, April 30, 1881.
41. Testimony of Lastania Abarta as reported in the *Los Angeles Herald*, April 29, 1881.
42. The marriage of Lastania Abarta in Los Angeles took place on January 20, 1883. The story of how she was traced to Mexico City can be seen in Paul Bryan Gray, "Searching for Miss Abarta," *Branding Iron* (Summer 2000). This article is in the California index at the Los Angeles Public Library under the author's name.

43. *Los Angeles Herald*, December 2, 1880.
44. *People v. Ramirez*, Los Angeles Superior Court Case No. 648 (1881).
45. Ibid., testimony of Ramon Hidales.
46. Ibid., testimony of Adolfo Celis.
47. Ibid., testimony of William R. Rowland.
48. Ibid., testimony of Thomas H. Botello.
49. Los Angeles County Recorder's Office, Book 75, p. 196 (1881).
50. This comment was republished by the *Los Angeles Herald*, March 27, 1881.

Chapter Thirteen

1. Ramírez's opening of *El Ferrocarril* is only known from a statement he gave to Hubert Howe Bancroft's investigators in Ensenada. Bancroft Library, dictation from Francisco P. Ramírez: ms. [circa 1888].
2. The population of Real del Castillo was declining when Ramírez arrived. Two years later the official 1883 census showed only 163 inhabitants. Archivo Histórico "Pablo L. Martínez" de La Paz, Baja California Sur, Gobernación #43, Caja 179.
3. Antonio Padilla Corona, "Escenario Político en el Partido Norte." In *Baja California: Un Presente con Historia* (Mexicali, Baja California: Universidad Autónoma de Baja California, 2002), 1: 189.
4. Ibid., 192–98.
5. Ibid., 199–200.
6. Hilarie J. Heath, "Treinta Años de Minería en Baja California, 1870–1900," *Meyibó* 1 (1998), 32.
7. Padilla Corona, "Escenario Político," 1: 200.
8. *Alta California*, February 20, 1865.
9. Manuel Clemente Rojo, *Apuntes Históricos*, 36–37.
10. W. W. Robinson, *Lawyers*, 30, 38, 253.
11. Newmark, *Sixty Years*, 56.
12. Antonio Padilla Corona, "Real del Castillo: Subprefectura Política del Partido Norte de la Baja California, 1872–1882," in *Ensenada: Nuevas Aportaciones para su Historia*, (Mexicali, Baja California: Universidad Autónoma de Baja California, 1999), 118.
13. Ibid., 117–18.
14. Ibid., 118–20.
15. Ibid., 123–24.
16. Heath, "Treinta Años," 42.
17. *San Diego Union*, November 21, 1874.
18. Padilla Corona, "Escenario Político," 1: 207–8.
19. Víctor Manuel Lozano Montemayor, "Pedro Vadillo, El Pata de Oso," in *Ensenada: Nuevas Aportaciones para su Historia*, 125. The name of Six-Toed Pete could be spelled either Badillo or Vadillo.
20. The Indian uprising and Villagrana's reaction are described by Padilla Corona, "Real

del Castillo," 136-38.
21. Ibid., 138.
22. Ibid., 139-40.
23. Heath, "Treinta Años," 42.
24. Pablo L. Martínez, *Historia de Baja California* (Mexicali, Baja California: Universidad Autónoma de Baja California, 2003), 482-88.
25. Padilla Corona, "Real del Castillo," 151.
26. Ibid., 157-58.
27. Ibid., 158-59.
28. Heath, "Treinta Años," 42.
29. Padilla Corona, "Real del Castillo," 159.
30. These surviving issues are in the Archivo del Instituto de Investigaciones Históricas, Universidad Autónoma de Baja California, Tijuana.
31. Archivo Histórico "Pablo L. Martínez" de La Paz, Baja California Sur, Justicia #1, Caja 173, Escuelas 1882.
32. Ibid., Justicia #1, Caja 181, Escuelas 1884.
33. Ibid., Justicia #1, Caja 177, Escuelas 1883.
34. Padilla Corona, "Real del Castillo," 160-61.
35. Ibid., 160.
36. Hesíquio Treviño Calderón, *Historia y Personajes de Ensenada* (Ensenada, Baja California: Tipográfica Castañeda, 2003), 102.
37. Archivo Histórico "Pablo L. Martínez" de La Paz, Baja California Sur, Justicia #33, Caja 178, Escuelas 1883.
38. David Piñera Ramírez, "Las Compañías Colonizadores en Ensenada, 1886-1910," in *Ensenada: Nuevas Aportaciones para su Historia*, (Mexicali, Baja California: Universidad Autónoma de Baja California, 1999), 166-67.
39. Ibid., 166.
40. This sale and its circumstances are described in detail by Hesíquio Treviño Calderón. See "Fundadores de Ensenada, Lic. Francisco P. Ramírez," *Vivir en Ensenada* 2 (Julio 1992): 26-27.
41. Archivo Histórico "Pablo L. Martínez" de La Paz, Baja California Sur, Justicia #33, Caja 181, January 31, 1884.
42. *Andronico Sepúlveda v. Isabel Pelanconi de Tononi*, Los Angeles Superior Court Case No. 3011, filed February 28, 1884.
43. Archivo Judicial de Ensenada, Expediente 23.7, Instituto de Investigaciones Históricas, Universidad Autónoma de Baja California, Tijuana.
44. The *Los Angeles Times* of June 30, 1882, cited a Democratic refusal to nominate Sepúlveda for the California Supreme Court as a deliberate snub based on his ethnicity.
45. For example, see *Los Angeles Times*, September 7, 1888, and April 15, 1906.
46. *Los Angeles Times*, January 23, 1896.

[362] Notes

47. An Iowa newspaper, the Davenport *Republican* of November 25, 1900, had an advertisement for shares in a mahogany plantation with an explicit recommendation by the ambassador that investors consult Sepúlveda.
48. See, for example, *Mexican Herald*, December 2, 1906.
49. *Mexican Herald*, December 16, 1906.
50. William Schell, Jr., *Integral Outsiders: The American Colony of Mexico City, 1876–1911* (Wilmington, DE: Scholarly Resources, 2001), 12.
51. *Los Angeles Times*, November 22, 1903; *Mexican Herald*, December 1, 1905.
52. *Los Angeles Times*, February 14, 1914.
53. *Mexican Herald*, May 11, 1902.
54. Lastania's husband, Auguste Cazaux, was mentioned in the *Mexican Herald* of September 1, 1909, with reference to his wealth and his ownership of race horses.

Chapter Fourteen

1. Archivo Histórico "Pablo L. Martínez" de La Paz, Baja California Sur, Instrucción Pública #9, Caja 9, April 25, 1885.
2. A good description of the International Company and the emergence of Ensenada is Ángela Moyano Pahissa, *California y Sus Relaciones con Baja California* (México, D.F.: Fondo de Cultura Económica, 1983), 70–92.
3. David Piñera Ramírez, "Las Compañías Colonizadores," 167–69.
4. Ibid., 169–71.
5. Hilarie J. Heath, "La Época de las Grandes Concesiones," in *Baja California: Un Presente con Historia* (Mexicali, Baja California: Instituto de Investigaciones Históricas, Universidad Autónoma de Baja California), 1: 252.
6. Ibid.
7. Piñera Ramírez, "Las Compañías Colonizadores," 173–76.
8. Glenn S. Dumke, *The Boom of the Eighties in Southern California* (San Marino, CA: Huntington Library, 1944), 49.
9. Ibid., 139.
10. Archivo Judicial de Ensenada at the Instituto de Investigaciones Históricas, Universidad Autónoma de Baja California, Tijuana.
11. The list of Ramírez's land purchases in this paragraph is taken from Antonio Padilla Corona, *Inicios Urbanos del Norte de Baja California* (Mexicali, Baja California: Universidad Autónoma de Baja California, 1998), 200–211.
12. The only copies of these newspapers available to researchers in either Mexico or the United States are located at the Sherman Library and Gardens, Corona del Mar, CA.
13. Piñera Ramírez, "Las Compañías Colonizadores," 177–85.
14. Treviño Calderón, *Historia y Personajes*, 93–95.
15. Ibid., 97–103.
16. Donald Chaput, "Governor Jorge Ryerson," Baja California Symposium 28, June 17–18, 1989. Donald Chaput, William M. Mason, and David Zarate Loperena, *Modest*

Fortunes: Mining in Northern Baja California (Los Angeles: Natural History Museum of Los Angeles County, 1992), 40–44.

17. While Francisco P. Ramírez was editor of *La Voz de la Frontera de la Baja California*, the newspaper republished an article from the *Chicago Mail*, describing the Ryerson family reunion. The items appeared on March 24, 1888, with information that would lead to the conclusion that Ryerson was an American.

18. Dictation of Gov. Jorge Ryerson for the historical works of Hubert Howe Bancroft (1888).

19. Archivo Histórico "Pablo L. Martínez" de La Paz, Baja California Sur, Guerra #29, Caja 172, April 30, 1882.

20. Ibid.

21. *Los Angeles Times*, August 31, 1900.

22. *San Diego Union*, June 18, 1895.

23. Piñera Ramírez, "Las Compañías Colonizadores," 179.

24. Ibid., 182.

25. Ibid., 185–87.

26. Hilarie J. Heath, "El Ferrocarril Fantasma: Intrigas, Fraude y Crisis," Seminario de Historia de Baja California, *Memoria* (2000), 133.

27. Heath, "La Época," 269.

28. Donald Chaput, "The British Are Coming! Or, The Army of India and the Founding of Ensenada," *Journal of San Diego History* 33 (Fall 1987), 141–42.

29. Heath, "La Época," 277–79.

30. Ibid., 287.

31. Censo General de la República Mexicana, Verificado en 1900. Secretaría de Fomento, 1905.

32. The *Los Angeles Times* published several articles about General Luis E. Torres down to his death. See August 29, 1904, July 14, 1913, and September 10, 1935.

33. Piñera Ramírez, "Las Compañías Colonizadores," 210.

34. Archivo Judicial de Ensenada.

35. Ibid.

36. Jesús Lorenzo Ramírez Collection, Ensenada. These are papers kept by the grandson of Francisco P. Ramírez, who kindly gave copies to the author in 2004.

37. Treviño Calderón, "Fundadores de Ensenada," 26.

38. Pablo L. Martínez, *Guía Familiar de Baja California* (México, D.F.: Editorial Baja California, 1965), 770.

39. Ibid., 826.

40. Treviño Calderón, "Fundadores de Ensenada," 26.

41. Archivo Judicial de Ensenada.

42. John R. Southworth, *Baja California Illustrated* (La Paz: Gobierno del Estado de Baja California Sur, 1899), 28.

43. A copy of this document is in the Jesús Lorenzo Ramírez Collection, Ensenada. A

photograph of Ramírez is part of the certificate, but it is blurred beyond recognition. Fortunately, Ramírez's file survives in Mexico City in the Acervo Histórico de la Secretaría de Relaciones Exteriores. This ministry provided the author with a clear photo that appears in this book.

44. A book containing facsimiles of every edition of *El Progresista* was published jointly by the Universidad Nacional Autónoma de México and the Universidad Autónoma de Baja California in 1982. The biographical material relating to Carlos R. Ptacnik is taken from the book's introduction by David Piñera Ramírez.
45. These letters are in the Jesús Lorenzo Ramírez Collection, Ensenada.
46. This document is one of many originating in the Registro Civil de Ensenada but now transferred to the Archivo del Instituto de Investigaciones Históricas, Universidad Autónoma de Baja California, Tijuana.
47. Ketcham advertised himself as a druggist in *El Progresista*. After 1904 he claimed to be a physician and surgeon.
48. Ramírez's probate is in the Archivo Judicial de Ensenada at the Instituto de Investigaciones Históricas, Universidad Autónoma de Baja California, Tijuana. See Caja 98, Núm. 98.7, January 1, 1909.

BIBLIOGRAPHY

Manuscripts

Archival Center, Archdiocese of Los Angeles, Mission Hills, CA: Birth and baptismal records.
Archivo del Gobierno del Estado de Sonora, Hermosillo: Correspondencia de Jesús Islas. Reportes al prefecto del Distrito de Altar, 1883.
Archivo del Instituto de Investigaciones Históricas, Universidad Autónoma de Baja California, Tijuana: Archivo Judicial de Ensenada. Colección Donald Chaput.
Archivo Histórico "Pablo L. Martínez" de La Paz, Baja California Sur: Acervo del Jefe Político.
Bancroft Library, University of California, Berkeley, CA: Dictation from Francisco P. Ramírez: ms., circa 1888. Dictation of Gov. Jorge Ryerson, 1888. Hearst, Phoebe: Hearst Collection. Plácido Vega Papers. Mexican broadsides.
Huntington Library, San Marino, CA: Brent, Joseph Lancaster: Brent Collection. Courtney Collection. Keller, Matthew: Keller Collection. Los Angeles Area Court records. Los Angeles County prefecture records. Stearns, Abel: Stearns Collection.
Jesús Lorenzo Ramírez Private Collection, Ensenada, Baja California: Letters, receipts, citizenship certificate.
Los Angeles County Recorder's Office: Deeds and mortgages. Records of the San Francisco Savings and Loan Society.
Los Angeles Superior Court Archives: *People v. Ramirez*, Case No. 648.
Museum of Natural History (Seaver Center), Los Angeles, CA: Sepúlveda-Mott Collection. Sepúlveda family letters. Del Valle Collection.
National Archives, Laguna Niguel, CA: Francisco P. Ramírez letters. Bureau of Land Management records. Los Angeles Office, Records of the Register, 1862–1865.
Palacio Municipal, Sáric, Sonora: Papers and interviews.
Sherman Library, Corona del Mar, CA: Baja California newspapers.

Legal Cases

County, District, and Superior Court cases are in the Huntington Library's Los Angeles Area Court Records collection. California Supreme Court cases involving Ramírez are published in *California Reports* as follows:

Guerrero v. Ballerino, 48 Cal. 118.
Breon v. Strelitz, 48 Cal. 645.
Macy v. Davila, 48 Cal. 646.
Keller v. Ruiz de Ocana, 48 Cal. 638.
People v. Ardaga, 51 Cal. 371.
Kraemer v. Kraemer, 52 Cal. 302.

Newspapers

Daily Alta California (San Francisco), 1855–1881.
El Clamor Público (Los Angeles), 1855–1859.
El Fronterizo (Real del Castillo), 1881–1882.
El Fronterizo (Tucson), 1889.
El Nuevo Mundo (San Francisco), 1864–1868.
El Pájaro Verde (Mexico City), 1864–1867.
El Progresista (Ensenada), 1904.
La Crónica (Los Angeles), 1872–1881.
La Estrella de Occidente (Ures, Sonora), 1860–1862.
La Voz de la Frontera de la Baja California (Ensenada), 1887–1888.
La Voz de Méjico (San Francisco), 1862–1866.
Los Angeles Evening Express, 1875–1881.
Los Angeles Herald, 1874–1882.
Los Angeles Mirror, 1873–1880.
Los Angeles News, 1865–1868.
Los Angeles Semi-Weekly Southern News, 1860–1865.
Los Angeles Star, 1851–1879.
Los Angeles Times, 1882–1923.
Los Angeles Tribune, 1889.
Los Angeles Weekly Republican, 1867–1870.
Lower Californian (Ensenada), 1888–1891.
Mexican Herald (Mexico City), 1895–1913.
New York Times, 1856–1916.
Reno Evening Gazette, 1908.
San Diego Union, 1882–1900.

Books and Articles

Acuña, Rodolfo F. *Sonoran Strongman: Ignacio Pesqueira and His Times.* Tucson: University of Arizona Press, 1974.
Almada, Francisco R. *Diccionario de Historia, Geografía, y Biografía Sonorenses.* Hermosillo, Sonora: Instituto Sonorense de Cultura, 2009; reprinted from 1962.

Almaguer, Tomás. *Racial Fault Lines: The Historical Origins of White Supremacy in California*. Berkeley: University of California Press, 1994.

Apostol, Jane. "Don Mateo Keller: His Vines and His Wines." *Southern California Quarterly* 84 (Summer 2002): 93–114.

Ayers, James J. *Gold and Sunshine, Reminiscences of Early California*. Boston: R. G. Badger, 1922.

Baccari, Alessandro, and Andrew M. Canepa. "The Italians of San Francisco in 1865: G. B. Cerruti's Report to the Ministry of Foreign Affairs." *California History* 60 (Winter 1981/82): 351–69.

Bacon, Walter R. "Fifty Years of California Politics." *Annual Publications of the Historical Society of Southern California* (1902): 31–42.

Bakken, Gordon Morris. *Practicing Law in Frontier California*. Lincoln: University of Nebraska Press, 1991.

Bancroft, Hubert Howe. *History of California*. 7 vols. San Francisco: History Co., 1885–1888; reprint by Wallace Hebberd, Santa Barbara, CA: 1966.

———. *Literary Industries*. New York: Harper and Brothers, 1891.

Barrows, H. D. "J. Lancaster Brent." *Annual Publications of the Historical Society of Southern California* (1897): 238–41.

Bissell, Clifford H. "The French Language Press in California." *California Historical Society Quarterly* 39, no. 1 (1960): 311–53.

Black, Esther Boulton. *Rancho Cucamonga and Doña Merced*. Redlands, CA: San Bernardino County Museum Association, 1975.

Brent, Joseph Lancaster. *The Lugo Case, A Personal Experience*. New Orleans, LA: Searcy and Pfaff, 1926.

Calvo Berber, Laureano. *Nociones de Historia de Sonora*. México, D. F.: Librería Porrúa, 1958.

Caughey, John Walton. *California*. New York: Prentice-Hall, 1953.

Chaput, Donald. "The British Are Coming! Or, The Army of India and the Founding of Ensenada." *Journal of San Diego History* 33 (Fall 1987): 151–64.

———. "Governor Jorge Ryerson." Baja California Symposium 28–June 17 and 18, 1989.

Chaput, Donald, William M. Mason, and David Zarate Loperena. *Modest Fortunes: Mining in Northern Baja California*. Los Angeles: Natural History Museum of Los Angeles County, 1992.

Cleland, Robert Glass. *The Cattle on a Thousand Hills*. San Marino, CA: Huntington Library, 1975; reprint of 1951 edition.

———. *Isaias W. Hellman and the Farmers and Merchants Bank*. San Marino, CA: Huntington Library, 1965.

Corti, Egon Caesar. *Maximilian and Charlotte of Mexico*. 2 vols. New York: A. A. Knopf, 1928.

Cosgrave, George. *Early California Justice, The History of the United States District Court for the Southern District of California*. San Francisco: Grabhorn Press, 1948.

Cross, Ira B. *A History of the Labor Movement in California*. Berkeley: University of California Press, 1935.

Dabbs, Jack Autrey. *The French Army in Mexico, 1861–1867; A Study in Military Government*. The Hague: Mouton, 1963.

Daggett, Emerson. *Frontier Journalism in San Francisco*. San Francisco: Works Project Administration, Project 10008, 1939.

———. *History of Journalism in San Francisco*. San Francisco: Works Projects Administration, 1939.

Davis, Winfield J. *History of Political Conventions in California: 1849–1892*. Sacramento: Publications of the California State Library, No. 1, 1893.

Deverell, William Francis. *Railroad Crossing: Californians and the Railroad, 1850–1910*. Berkeley: University of California Press, 1994.

Draper, Lyman Copeland. *A Biographical Sketch of the Honorable Charles H. Larrabee*. Madison: Wisconsin State Historical Society, 1882.

Dumke, Glenn S. *The Boom of the Eighties in Southern California*. San Marino, CA: Huntington Library, 1944.

Eldredge, Thomas R., and Francisco P. Ramírez. *Informe Bienal del Controlador del Estado*. Sacramento: Charles T. Botts, State Printer, 1866.

El Tiempo Ilustrado, "José María Vigil." (January 1, 1906): 39.

Garibay, K. Ángel María. *Diccionario Porrúa de Historia, Biografía y Geografía de México*. México D. F.: Editorial Porrúa, 1964.

Gray, Paul Bryan. *Forster vs. Pico: The Struggle for the Rancho Santa Margarita*. Spokane, WA: Arthur H. Clark, 1998.

———. "Francisco P. Ramirez, a Short Biography." *California History* 84, no. 2 (2006–2007): 20–39.

———. "Francisco P. Ramírez: Un Desterrado en Ensenada." In *Baja California: Un Presente con Historia*, vol. 1. Mexicali, Baja California: Instituto de Investigaciones Históricas, Universidad Autónoma de Baja California, 2002.

———. "Searching for Miss Abarta." *Branding Iron* (Summer 2000): 11–14.

Grenier, Judson A., and Robert C. Gillingham. *California Legacy*. Carson, CA: Watson Land Co., 1987.

Griswold del Castillo, Richard. *The Los Angeles Barrio, 1850–1890: A Social History*. Berkeley: University of California Press, 1979.

Guillow, Lawrence E. "Pandemonium in the Plaza: The First Los Angeles Riot, July 22, 1856." *Southern California Quarterly* 77 (Fall 1995): 183–97.

Gumina, Deanna Paoli. *The Italians of San Francisco, 1850–1930*. New York: Center for Migration Studies, 1978.

Harlow, Neal. *California Conquered: War and Peace on the Pacific, 1846–1850*. Berkeley: University of California Press, 1982.

Hayes-Bautista, David E. "Empowerment, Expansion, and Engagement: Las Juntas Patrióticas in California, 1848–1869." *California History* 85, no. 1 (2007): 4–23.

———. "Reginaldo Francisco del Valle, UCLA's Forgotten Forefather." *Southern California Quarterly* 88 (Spring 2006): 1–35.

Heath, Hilarie J. "El Ferrocarril Fantasma: Intrigas, Fraude y Crisis." Seminario de Historia de Baja California, *Memoria* (2000): 131–43.

———. "La Época de las Grandes Concesiones." In *Baja California: Un Presente con Historia*, vol. 1. Mexicali, Baja California: Instituto de Investigaciones Históricas, Universidad Autónoma de Baja California, 2002.

———. "Treinta Años de Minería en Baja California, 1870–1900." *Meyibó* 1 (1998): 25–64.

Hent, R. W. *Forms and Use of Blanks: Being over One Thousand Forms in Ordinary Legal and Business Transactions.* San Francisco: H. H. Bancroft, 1866.

Hernández Cornejo, Roberto. *Los Chilenos en San Francisco de California.* 2 vols. Valparaíso, Chile: Imprenta San Rafael, 1930.

Hittell, Theodore Henry. *History of California.* 4 vols. San Francisco: N. J. Stone, 1898.

James, William F., and George H. McMurry. *History of San Jose, California.* San Jose: A. H. Cawston, 1933.

Jewett, Tomás M. *Los Siete Pecados Capitales de Antonio Mancillas.* Hoja Suelta, 1863.

Jore, Léonce. "Jean Louis Vignes of Bordeaux, Pioneer of California Viticulture." *Southern California Quarterly* 4, no. 4 (1963): 289–303.

Kreider, Samuel Lanner. "Volney Erskine Howard: California Pioneer." *Historical Society of Southern California Quarterly* 31 (March and June 1949): 119–34.

Langley, Henry G. *San Francisco Directory for the Year Commencing September 1867.* San Francisco, 1870.

Lavender, David. *California: Land of New Beginnings.* New York: Harper and Row, 1972.

López del Castillo, Gerardo. *Al Público.* Hoja Suelta, 1863.

Lozano Montemayor, Víctor Manuel. "Pedro Vadillo, El Pata de Oso." In *Ensenada: Nuevas Aportaciones para su Historia.* Mexicali, Baja California: Universidad Autónoma de Baja California, 1999.

Márquez, Leonardo. *Manifiestos (El Imperio y Los Imperiales).* México, D. F.: F. Vásquez, 1904.

Martínez, Pablo L. *Guía Familiar de Baja California.* México, D. F.: Editorial Baja California, 1965.

———. *Historia de Baja California.* Mexicali, Baja California: Universidad Autónoma de Baja California, 2003.

McCawley, William. *The First Angelinos: The Gabrielino Indians of Los Angeles.* Banning, CA: Malki Museum Press and Ballena Press, 1996.

McGroarty, John Steven. *Los Angeles from the Mountains to the Sea.* Chicago: American Historical Society, 1921.

McKevitt, Gerald. *The University of Santa Clara: A History, 1851–1977.* Palo Alto, CA: Stanford University Press, 1979.

McNamee, Mary Dominica. *Light in the Valley, The Story of California's College of Notre*

Dame. Berkeley, CA: Howell-North Books, 1967.

Miller, Kathleen L. "The Temple Block, A Core Sample of Los Angeles History." *Journal of the West* 33 (April 1994): 62–74.

Miller, Robert Ryal. "Californians against the Emperor." *California Historical Quarterly* 37 (1958): 193–214.

———. "Plácido Vega: A Mexican Secret Agent in the United States, 1864–1866." *Americas* 19 (October 1962): 137–48.

Miranda, Gloria E. "Racial and Cultural Dimensions of *Gente de Razón* Status in Spanish and Mexican California." *Southern California Quarterly* 70 (Fall 1988): 265–78.

Monroy, Douglas. *Thrown among Strangers: The Making of Mexican Culture in Frontier California*. Berkeley: University of California Press, 1990.

Nadeau, Remi A. *City-Makers*. Los Angeles: Trans-Anglo Books, 1965.

Nakayama, Antonio. *Realidad y Mentira de Plácido Vega*. Culiacán Rosales, Sinaloa: Apoyos Educativos, 1993.

Newmark, Harris. *Sixty Years in Southern California*. 4th rev. ed. Los Angeles: Zeitlin and Ver Brugge, 1970; originally published in 1916.

Padilla Corona, Antonio. "Escenario Político en el Partido Norte." In *Baja California: Un Presente con Historia*. Mexicali, Baja California: Universidad Autónoma de Baja California, 2002.

———. *Inicios Urbanos del Norte de Baja California*. Mexicali, Baja California: Universidad Autónoma de Baja California, 1998.

———. "Real del Castillo: Subprefectura Política del Partido Norte de la Baja California, 1872–1882." In *Ensenada: Nuevas Aportaciones para su Historia*. Mexicali, Baja California: Universidad Autónoma de Baja California, 1999.

Pahissa, Ángela Moyano. *California y Sus Relaciones con Baja California*. México, D.F.: Fondo de Cultura Económica, 1983.

Papers Relating to Foreign Affairs. Washington, D.C.: Department of State, 1870.

Pelanconi, Petra. "The Ramirez Family." *Grizzly Bear* (1913), 1.

Peza, Ignacio de la, and Agustín Pradillo. *Maximiliano y los Últimos Sucesos del Imperio en Querétaro y México*. México, D.F.: Imprenta de I. Cumplido, 1870.

Piñera Ramírez, David. "Las Compañías Colonizadoras en Ensenada, 1886–1910." In *Ensenada: Nuevas Aportaciones para su Historia*. Mexicali, Baja California: Universidad Autónoma de Baja California, 1999.

Pitner, Ernst. *Maximilian's Lieutenant: A Personal History of the Mexican Campaign, 1864–7*. Albuquerque: University of New Mexico Press, 1993.

Pitt, Leonard. *The Decline of the Californios, A Social History of the Spanish-Speaking Californians, 1846–1890*. Berkeley: University of California Press, 1966.

Ramírez, Francisco P. *Ligeras Observaciones Sobre el Manifiesto de la Junta Central Democrática del Estado a los Hispanos que Tienen Voz o Interés en California*. San Francisco: Tipografía de la Voz de Méjico, 1864.

Ramírez López, Jorge. "Tecate." In *Panorama Histórico de Baja California*, edited by

David Piñera Ramírez, 315–21. Tijuana, Baja California: Centro de Investigaciones Históricas, UNAM-UABC, 1983.

Rice, William B. *The Los Angeles Star, 1851–1864: The Beginnings of Journalism in Southern California.* Berkeley: University of California Press, 1947.

———. "Paul R. Hunt—An Account of an Eccentric Angeleno." *Historical Society of Southern California Quarterly* 24 (1942): 63–65.

Robinson, John W. "Colonel Edward J. C. Kewen: Los Angeles' Fire-Eating Orator of the Civil War Era." *Southern California Quarterly* 61 (Summer 1979): 159–81.

———. *Los Angeles in Civil War Days, 1860–1865.* Los Angeles: Dawson's Book Shop, 1977.

———. *Southern California's First Railroad.* Los Angeles: Dawson's Book Shop, 1978.

Robinson, William Wilcox. *Lawyers of Los Angeles.* Los Angeles: Los Angeles County Bar Association, 1959.

———. *Los Angeles from the Days of the Pueblo.* San Francisco: California Historical Society, 1981.

Rodman, Willoughby J. *History of the Bench and Bar of Southern California.* Los Angeles: W. J. Porter, 1909.

Rojo, Manuel Clemente. *Apuntes Históricos de la Frontera de la Baja California.* Ensenada: Museo de Historia de Ensenada, 2000.

Rolle, Andrew F. *California: A History.* Wheeling, IL: Harlan Davidson, 2003.

———. *John Charles Frémont, Character as Destiny.* Norman: University of Oklahoma Press, 1991.

Rose, L. J., Jr. *L. J. Rose of Sunny Slope, 1827–1899.* San Marino, CA: Huntington Library, 1959.

Schell, William, Jr. *Integral Outsiders: The American Colony of Mexico City, 1876–1911.* Wilmington, DE: Scholarly Resources, 2001.

Shumsky, Neil L. *The Evolution of Political Protest and the Workingmen's Party of California.* Columbus: Ohio State University Press, 1991.

Snider, Sandra Lee. *Elias Jackson "Lucky" Baldwin: California Visionary.* Los Angeles: Stairwell Group, 1987.

Soulé, Frank. *The Annals of San Francisco.* New York: D. Appleton, 1855.

Southworth, John R. *Baja California Illustrated.* La Paz: Gobierno del Estado de Baja California Sur, 1899.

Spitzzeri, Paul R. *The Workman and Temple Families of Southern California, 1830–1930.* Dallas: Seligson Publishing, 2008.

Standart, M. Colette. "The Sonora Migration to California, 1848–1856: A Study in Prejudice." *Southern California Quarterly* 58 (Fall 1976): 333–57.

Stanley, John J. "Bearers of the Burden: Justices of the Peace, Their Courts and the Law in Orange County, California, 1870–1907." *Western Legal History* 5 (Winter and Spring 1992): 37–67.

Starr, Kevin. *Endangered Dreams: The Great Depression in California.* New York: Oxford

University Press, 1996.

Swisher, Carl Brent. *Motivation and Political Technique in the California Constitutional Convention, 1878–79.* Claremont, CA: Pomona College, 1930.

Taylor, Bayard. *Eldorado; or, Adventures in the path of Empire.* New York: G. P. Putnam and Son, 1868.

Tellez Duarte, Miguel Agustín. "Francisco P. Ramírez: Un Pionero en Ensenada." Seminario de Historia de Baja California, *Memoria* (2002): 199–228.

Tinker Salas, Miguel. *In the Shadow of the Eagles: Sonora and the Transformation of the Border during the Porfiriato.* Berkeley: University of California Press, 1997.

Treviño Calderón, Hesíquio. "Fundadores de Ensenada, Lic. Francisco P. Ramírez." *Vivir en Ensenada* 2 (Julio 1992): 26–29.

———. *Historia y Personajes de Ensenada.* Ensenada, Baja California: Tipográfica Castañeda, 2003.

Velasco, José Francisco. *Noticias Estadísticas del Estado de Sonora.* Mexico, D.F.: Imprenta de I. Cumplido, 1850.

Villa, Eduardo W. *Historia del Estado de Sonora.* Hermosillo, México: Editorial Sonora, 1951.

Waldron, Granville Arthur. "Courthouses of Los Angeles County." *Historical Society of Southern California Quarterly* 41, no. 4 (1959): 345–68.

INDEX

Abarta, Lastania, 272–74, 316, 338
Adams, John Quincy, 26
admission to California Bar, 149–50
agriculture, 145–47, 149
Ailland, H., 305
Alamos, Sonora, Mexico, 71, 76, 78–79, 81
Alas, Ignacio, 297–99, 301
Alexander, David W., 229
Allen, Dick C., 312
Almada, Toribio, 81
Alta California, Daily (San Francisco)
    on Booth, Newton, bolting Republican Party, 210
    Brother Jonathan (steamer), passenger list, 104
    El Clamor Público, praise for, 15
    "Dolly Varden Gathering", 211
    on election fraud in Los Angeles, 165
    on Frémont, John Charles, favorable senate votes by native Californians, 37
    on notary fees, 88
    on peoples' and tax-payers elections, 160
    Ramírez, praise for, 124–25
    Senate Elections Committee, contest for seat, 104, 106
    Sepúlveda, Ignacio, wedding of, 155–56
Altar, Sonora, Mexico, 69–70
Anaheim, California
    Anaheim Gazette newspaper, 281
    Evey, Edward, candidate from, 162
    farmers, objecting to Los Angeles' domination of, 160–61

    Howard, Volney E., railroad money raised in, 223
    Mendelson, Louis, departure from, 291
    People's Ticket, site of convention for, 160
    Ramírez, Francisco P., Republican speaker at, 249
    Santa Ana River, drains flow from, 144
    Southern Californian, newspaper, 192
    Strobel, Max, ex-mayor organizes People's Ticket in, 160
Anderson, Elizabeth, 155
Anderson, Ora, 155, 158
antislavery positions, 28, 39, 43, 48, 79, 182
Apaches, 30, 69–70, 72
Arévalo, Manuel, 226
Arguello, Santiago, 6
Atíl, Sonora, Mexico, 70
Austin, Henry C., 214
Ávila, Cornelio, 3
Ávila, Francisco, 3, 9
Ávila, Juan, 75
Ávila, Petra, 3, 7, 234
Ayers, James J.
    California Constitutional Convention of 1878–79, delegate to, 259
    Daily Hawaiian Herald, co-editor of, 141–42
    Evening Express, editor of, 259
    Los Angeles Star, editor of, 208
    Sonoratown, description by, 148

Badillo, Pedro "Six-Toed Pete," 292, 294–96

Index

Baily, Alexander, 228
Baja California
   crime, 286–87, 291–92
   Ensenada, capital of Partido Norte, 308–10. *See also* Ensenada
   gold, 290–91, 333
   jefe políticos, 284
   La Paz, capital of Partido Sur, 284
   International Company of Mexico (American), 318–32
   Law of Colonization of 1883, 317–18
   Márquez León, Manuel, revolt in, 296–97
   Mexican Land and Colonization Company (British), 332–33
   political organization of, 284
   Real del Castillo, capital of Partido Norte, 290
   subjefes, 284
   Walker, William, invasion of, 284–85
Baldwin, Elias J. "Lucky Baldwin," 232, 234–36
Bank of California (San Francisco), 230–31
Banning, Phineas, 116, 146–47, 155, 195
Bareño, Adolfo, 323
Barrows, Henry D., 86
Barter, George Washington, 201, 207–8
Barton, James R., 44–48
Bazaine, Marshal François Achille, 134–35
Beach, Wilson, 243
Bell, Alexander, 39
Bell, Horace, 253
Benavides, Loreto, 219
Bennett, Charles, 319
Bennett, Francis R., 324
Bernstein, Maximilian, 319
Bidwell, John, 210, 226–27
black Republicans, 39, 42
blacks
   Buchanan, James, on similarity with Mexicans, 43
   as colonists in Los Angeles, 193
   exclusion of, in Los Angeles, 239
   Frémont, John Charles, association with, 38
   Hamilton, Henry, racism toward, 39, 176
   Larrabee, Charles Hathaway, rejection of equality for, 176
   in Los Angeles County, number of, 171
   and Ramírez, Francisco P., 26, 175
   San Francisco Herald, on, 68
   voting rights of, 139, 149, 151
Booth, Newton
   anti-railroad campaign, 198, 210
   as Dolly Varden candidate, 210–11
   corruption of governorship, 198
   Independent Party, platform adoption, 210–11, 227
   as Republican governor, 165
   and U.S. Senate, 227
   Widney, Robert M., appointment by, 184
Botello, Thomas H., 278–79
brandy, 6, 145
Brent, Joseph Lancaster
   Chivalry Democrats, leader of, 18, 260
   and Confederate Army, 180
   Domínguez, Manuel, defends as witness, 48
   and excluding free blacks, 49
   Ramírez, Francisco P., accusations against, 48
   and ranchero elite, 29
   and Sepúlveda, Ignacio, 154, 155, 183
Broderick, David C., 16, 28
Brown, George W., 262–63
Brunson, Anson, 162, 182, 184, 249, 312
Bülle, Adolfo, 318
Burrill, George Thompson, 288
Bush, Charles W., 213
Butler, Jesse H., 257, 263

Caballero, Luis G., 342
Caborca, Sonora, Mexico, 49, 70, 144
Cadena, Jesús María, 324
California Constitutional Convention of 1878–79, 258–59, 264, 266
Camarena, Jesús, 122, 124

Index

Caravia, G., 305
Carlisle, Robert, 132
Carlton, Capt. James Henry, 85
Carriega, Ferdinand, 34
Carrillo, José Antonio, 75
Carrillo, Ramon, 65, 75
Castañeda, Zeferino, 299, 303, 307, 328
Castrejón, Brigido, 295–97
Castro, José María, 286
Catholic Standard, 13, 14, 25, 109
Caystile, Thomas, 208
Celis, Adolfo, 277
Central Pacific Railroad Company
  Big Four, 196
  Booth, Newton, campaigns against, 210
  Charles Crocker Company swindles shareholders of, 197
  and corruption of government officials, 198–99
  Dolly Varden Party, organized against, 204–5
  Houghton, Samuel O., backed by, 229
  immigrants, passengers on, 247
  Independents, succumb to, 221
  Judah, Theodore H., first envisioned railroad, 196
  Kearney, Denis, incites violence against, 255
  Los Angeles, contracts with, 199–201
  monopoly, greatest in state, 256
  public resentment toward, 198
  Ramírez, Francisco P., leader of Independent opposition to, 204–5, 215–16
  resistance to, 198–99, 202–5, 210–11, 214
  Sierra Nevada, route through, 146
  Southern Pacific Railroad, owned by, 196
  transcontinental railroad, completed by, 195
  subsidies to, 196–97
  workingmen protest against, 255–57
Cerro Gordo silver mines, 146–47, 222

Chaffin, Carl, xvi
Chapman, Alfred Beck, 181
Chaput, Don, xv
Cheesman, David W., 52
Chileans
  Fierro, Felipe, assistant at *El Nuevo Mundo*, 121, 140
  Mancillas, Antonio, accuses Fierro of not being Chilean, 130
  North Beach community of, 109, 121
  Splivato, Augusto D., Chilean politician in San Francisco, 135, 164
  as subscribers to *El Nuevo Mundo*, 122, 134, 139
children of Francisco P. Ramírez, 339–40
Chinese (in California)
  blacks, compared to, 109
  Crocker, Charles, recruiting of, 198
  exclusion of, demands for, 254, 261
  Larrabee, Charles Hathaway, denounces, 176
  and wages, 27
  workingmen's organizations, threats and violence against, 247, 254–55
Chinese (in Ensenada), 319, 321, 342
Chinese (in Los Angeles)
  Los Angeles Star, unusually fair article on, 259
  "Negro Alley", presence in, 166, 223
  prejudice against, 245–46, 260, 262, 266
  press, ridicule of, 166–67
  prostitution, accusations of, 223
  San Fernando Tunnel, built by, 239
  workingmen's clubs, protests against, 257
Chinese massacre in Los Angeles, 166, 168–69, 188
Chivalry Democrats
  and Brent, Joseph Lancaster, recruits ranchero elite to, 18, 29
  and Civil War Los Angeles as bastion of Confederacy during, 84–85, 99, 179

[376] Index

Deep South, origination in, 18
elections, defeats all opponents, 43, 66, 87, 90–91, 99, 102
Gwin, Sen. William M., state leader of, 28
legislature, majority in, 37
Los Angeles, citizens' support of, 17, 57, 86, 151
Mexican voters, controlled by, 41, 57, 91
racism of, 18, 68
and ranchero elite, early adherents with aristocratic pretensions, 18, 41
Rosewater, leadership of, 53–54
slavery, supported with fanatical enthusiasm, 28, 60, 68
Clay, Henry, 26
Clayton, Gen. Powell, 314
Club Patriótico Mexicano de San Francisco, 110, 127–28, 136, 137
Cohn, Bernard, 263
Committee of One Hundred (Los Angeles), 247–48
Compromise of 1850, 26
Confederate support in Los Angeles, 84–86, 142–43, 151, 179
Comonfort, Ignacio, 288
Conway, Charles R., 67, 69, 70, 76, 87, 90–91
Corral, Ramon, 338
Cota, Santos, 323
county court, 187–88
Couts, Cave, 287
Covillaud, Charles, 14
Cox Investment Company, 342
Crabb, Henry, 49, 70
Crank, James F., 269, 271
Crocker, Charles, 196–97, 239, 255
Cucapás, 285
Cueva Pelayo, Jesús, xvi

Daily Express (Los Angeles), 218
Daniel, Pancho, 45, 54, 55, 59

Dávalos, Bibiano, 287–88
Day, John G., 256
de Aguilar, José, 78
de Cazotte, Charles, 131
de Celis, Eulogio
   Cinco de Mayo, remarks on magic of night, 209
   education, 193–94
   La Crónica, as new editor of, 193
   Mexican Benevolent Society, as founder of, 237–38
   People's Reform Ticket, rejected by, 215
   Ramírez, Francisco P., friendship with, 193
   report of funeral (*Los Angeles Times*), 262
   as Republican Party delegate, 226
   as Union Club member, 226
de Celis, Pastor, 194, 244, 316
de la Guerra, Pablo, 153
del Valle, Ignacio, 84, 260
del Valle, Reginaldo, 260–61, 267, 270–71
Demke, Siegfried, xvi
Derbec, Etienne, 121
Desmond's Store, 202
Diez Gutiérrez, Carlos, 308
Dimmick, Kimball H., 86
district court, 188
Dolly Varden Party, 204–5, 211
Domínguez, Manuel, 42, 48
Domínguez, Ramon, 206
Downey, John G.
   Farmers and Merchants Bank, president of, 230–31
   as governor, former, 143
   Los Angeles and San Pedro Railroad Company, president of, 146
   opens first bank in Los Angeles, 148
   and railroads, promotes line to Los Angeles, 195, 199
   and ranch land, subdivides, 143, 186
   wife of, 171
Dred Scott case, 49, 52

Drum Barracks (U.S. Army post), 85, 91
Dryden, William G., 95, 157

Eastman, James G., 182, 248
Eaton, Benjamin S., 103
El Clamor Público (Los Angeles)
   American press, arose from example of, 16
   ethnic press, influenced by, 16
   financial collapse of, 62–67
   and foreigners, French and American, 22
   format, 22–23
   last edition of, 68
   Mexican liberalism, 17
   name, origin of, 15
   sale of printing press and equipment, 67
   subscriptions, Mexican resistance to, 17
Eldredge, Thomas R., 136
El Eco del Pacífico (San Francisco), 28, 121
El Ferrocarril, (Mazatlan), 283
El Fronterizo, (Real del Castillo), 31, 300–307, 324
Elliot, John M., 277
El Nuevo Mundo (San Francisco)
   conflict and affray with Gen. Plácido Vega in, 124–28
   Fierro, Felipe, buys newspaper, 140
   French withdrawal from Mexico, collapse of juntas and newspaper, 134–35, 139
   juntas patrióticas, recognize editor Ramírez as de facto treasurer, 134–35
   Mancillas, Antonio, refuses to support editor Ramírez, 121–22, 126
   promotion of Ramírez's aspirations in, 119–21
   Ramírez, Francisco P., takes ownership by assuming debts, 119
   rivalry with *La Voz de Méjico*, 122, 126
   Vigil, José María, begins but cannot continue newspaper, 114–15, 118

El Pájaro Verde (Mexico City), 126
El Progresista (Ensenada), 341
English, William, 155
Ensenada, Baja California
   American appearance of, 321
   ayuntamiento, 308
   building construction, 319
   business development, 319–20
   capital, changed to, 307–8
   census (1888), 331–32; (1900), 336
   English, predominant language of, 330
   filibusterers at, 285
   fraud, by International Company of Mexico (American company), 320, 326, 329–32
   Gastelum family, original owners of land, 310
   Hanbury and Garvey, real estate agents, 321
   International Company of Mexico (American), beginnings in, 317
   judicial records of, 312
   land sales in, by International Company of Mexico (American), 320–21
   La Voz de la Frontera de la Baja California (newspaper, edited by Ramírez, 324
   Lower California (newspaper, edited by Francis R. Bennett, 324
   Mexican Land and Colonization Company Limited (British), 332–33
   El Progresista (newspaper, edited by Carlos Ptacnik, 341–42
   Public Registry of Property in Ensenada, 310
   railroad to San Diego, denied, 331
   Rancho de Ensenada de Todos Santos, 283, 285
   Ryerson, George (Jorge), subprefecto, 327
   Sánchez Facio, Manuel, criticizes American company, 331
   steamships, between Ensenada and San Diego, 319

[378]　Index

streets laid out by International Company of Mexico (American), 319
Tapia, Lt. Col. Andrés, arrival of, 295
Torres, Gen. Luis E., as jefe político, agent of President Porfirio Díaz, 326, 330
Espinosa, José Jesús, 45
Esteves, Antonio, 80, 114
Evey, Edward, 162
Evening Express, 159, 162, 214

Farmers and Merchants Bank (Los Angeles), 230–31
farming, 144–46, 161, 222
Fierro, Felipe, 121, 126, 130, 139
filibusterers, 38–39, 49, 180, 284–46
Fisher, James A., 275–76, 279
Flores, Juan, 44–46
forgery, 274–75
Forster, Francisco "Chico," 272–73, 316
Forster, John, 44, 181, 272
free Black anti-immigration law, 49
Freeman, Daniel, 234
Frémont, John Charles, 36–41, 43, 51–52, 54, 63
French in Los Angeles, 6, 44, 51, 56–57, 251
Friedlander, Isaac, 256
Furlong, George, 290

Gabrielinos, 171, 173–75
Gage, Henry T., 276, 278
Ganahl, Frank, 156, 158–59, 181, 226
Gándara, Manuel, 76
Garabalini, Mateo, 233
García, Angela, 338
García, Luis, 338
García Morales, Gen. Jesús, 76, 114
García, Telesforo, 318
Garfias, Manuel, 101
Garibaldi, Lorenzo, 245
Garvey, Richard, 236
Gastelum, family, 309
Gastelum, Pedro, 323
Getman, William C., 34
Gibbs, George C., 206

Gitchell, Joseph R., 89–90, 102
Glassell, Andrew, 128, 157, 181, 218
Glenn, Hugh, 256
Godfrey, John F., 262–63
Godoy, José A., 127, 133, 137
González, Gen. Jesús, 100
González, José Elías, 28
Grange, 210
Granger, Lewis, 39
Grant, Ulysses, 129, 150, 201–2, 204
"Greaser Law," 49
"greasers," 18, 44, 165–66
Greely, Horace, 201–2, 206
Green, P.M., 267
Guaymas, Sonora, Mexico, 69, 71, 73 82, 113
Guerrero y Porrez, A., 342
Guinn, James Miller, 213
Gwin, William M., 28, 29, 60

Haight, Fletcher M., 94, 95
Haight, Henry H., 139, 165
Haley, Salisbury, 311
Hamilton, Henry
　Arizona, removes to, 116
　arrest for supporting Confederacy, 92
　Ayers, James J., partnership with, 141
　blacks, virulent hatred of, 39
　Chivalry, outspoken advocate of, 39
　Los Angeles Star, promotes Confederacy in, 87
　Ramírez, Francisco P., rivalry with, 39, 58, 60
　railroad, envisions expansion of, 146
　state senate, defeats Ramírez in election for, 102
Hanbury & Garvey, 321, 330 332
Hancock, Henry, 56, 58
Hancock, Capt. Winfield Scott, 85, 152
Hare, M.D., 235
Hartman, Isaac, 7
Hawaii, 6, 141, 208
Hayes, Benjamin I., 54, 151, 153 171
Hazard, Henry T., 176, 182, 226, 228, 233 241, 249

Hearst, Phoebe, 314–15
Hearst, William Randolph, 314
Heath, Hilarie, xvi
Heathman, William F., 270
Hellman, Isaias, W., 148, 230–31
Hermosillo, Sonora, Mexico, 71, 77–78, 80–81, 129
Herrera, José María, 132
Hewitt, Joshua, 235
Hidales, Ramon, 274–79
Higbie, A., 213
Hill, Ramon J., 117
Hoffman, Abraham, xvi, xviii
Hopkins, Mark, 196, 198, 255
Hotel del Coronado (San Diego), 336,
Hotel Montgomery, 56
Houghton, Samuel O., 228–29
Howard, Volney E.
   antebellum values of, "Southernized" in youth, 179
   attorney, successful law practice of, 223
   California Constitutional Convention (1878–1879), leading delegate to, 259, 264–65
   Chivalry, leader of, 154
   district attorney, elected as, 216
   Independent Party, joins to combat railroad, 213–14, 229
   Los Angeles Superior Court, elected as judge, 267
   major general, state militia, 179
   and Ramírez, Francisco P. (sets bail), 279
   and Sepúlveda, Ignacio (obtains release from Mexican prison,), 155
   Southern Pacific Railroad, antagonist of, 223, 240
   Stanford and Ramírez, involvement in lawsuits with, 187, 218–19, 224, 234–35, 268
Hudson, Paul, 315
Hudson, Rodney J., 229
Hüller, Luis, 318
Hunt, Paul R., 103, 105

Huntington, Collis, 196, 198, 199–200
Hutton, Aurelius W., 180–81

illiteracy, 21
Indians (in California)
   appearance of, as similar to Mexicans, 48, 169
   extinction of, 171, 173–74, 175
   lack of immunity to disease of, 98
   poverty of, 268–69
   Ramírez, Francisco P., sympathy for, 174
   Santos Juncos, José de los, 174
Indian tribes. *See individual entries.*
inferior municipal courts, 186–87
International Company of Mexico (American), 318–24, 326–32
irrigation, 144–46
Irwin, Gov. William, 228–29
Islas, Jesús, 29–31, 70

Jáuregui, Antonio, 308
Jean, Joseph, 305
Jenkins, William W., 33–36
Jenkinson, Sir Edward, 333, 335
Jofre, Javier, 25
Johnson, J. Neely, 28, 57, 179
Jolliff, M.H., 342
Jones, Sen. John T., 222
Jordan, Félix, 323
Juárez, Benito
   California Mexicans, earns support of, 116, 118, 137
   French, resistance to, 137
   juntas patrióticas, organized to aid financially, 119
   and Lincoln, Abraham, common struggle with, 116
   and Maximilian, defeat and execution of, 138–39, 287
   Puebla, defense of, 92
   Ramírez, Francisco P., influence upon, 17, 130, 154, 217
   and Ramírez, Ignacio (El Nigromante), appointment of, 112

sends military to Baja California, 286
and Vega, Plácido, sent to San Francisco by, 114; turns against, 138
Judah, Theodore H., 196–97
judge of the plains, 7
Junta Central Directiva (San Francisco), 93, 117
Junta for the Promotion of Hispano-American Migration to Sonora, 56
Junta Patriótica de Los Angeles
   Cinco de Mayo celebrations, 99, 115–16, 209
   Fourth of July, participation in, 238
   Godoy, José A., invites nomination for treasurer from, 133
   La Voz de Méjico, announces formation of, 194
   Mancillas, Antonio, demands he publish proceedings of, 122
   Mexican Independence Day observed by, 102, 166, 216, 232–33
   Mexican ex-prisoners feted by, 133
   Ramírez, Francisco P., as leader and spokesman for, 94
   Sepúlveda, Ignacio, ironic celebration of election as judge, 218
   Treasurer, Junta Central, proposes Ramírez for, 128, 237
   Vega, Plácido, criticizes for assault on Ramírez, 129
Junta Patriótica de Marysville, 135
Junta Patriótica de Sacramento, 134
Junta Patriótica de San Andrés, 135
Junta Patriótica de Wilmington, 126, 133
justice courts, 185–86

Kay, James, 238, 278
Kearney, Denis, 254–57, 263–65, 269, 271,
Kearny, Gen. Stephen Watts, 37
Keller, Matthew, 7, 9
Ketcham, L.Y., 343
Kewen, Edward John Cage
   arrest, 91–92, 181
   as assemblyman, 91,101
   as attorney, 182, 184, 243
   birth of (Columbus, Mississippi), 180
   as California attorney general, 180
   as candidate for Congress, 266
   and Chivalry, partisanship of, 66, 180–81, 195, 227
   and Warner, J.J. (insults for antislavery views), 66
   and Walker, William (filibusterer with in Nicaragua), 180
King, Andrew J., 66, 149, 151, 156–57, 181
King, Frank, 132
King, Houston, 132
King, Thomas, 54
Kino, Eusebio, 30, 70
Knight, H.L., 256
Knights of the Columbian Star, 86
Knights of the Golden Circle, 86

labor violence, 246–48
La Crónica (Los Angeles)
   Cinco de Mayo, description in, 209
   La Compañía Publicista, ownership of, 244
   Coronel, Antonio, newspaper company president, 244
   de Celis, Eulogio, editor of, 193
   de Celis, Pastor, saves from bankruptcy, 244–45
   latin unity, promoted by, 194, 238–39
   People's Reform Ticket, rejected by, 194, 238–39
   Ramírez, Francisco P., interim editor of, 192
   Teodoli, Eduardo F., establishment of, 191–92
La Estrella de Los Angeles, 11, 14, 15
La Estrella de Occidente
   circulation, 72
   on Hermosillo (assault), 81
   on Indian attacks, reported weekly, 73
   official newspaper, format of, 72–73
   politics of, fictitious election campaign by, 79
   Pesquiera, Ignacio, editorials exalting, 80

Ramírez, Francisco P., as editor, 73–76, 82
   on Ures, rebel attack, 70–71
   Urrea, Miguel, insults Ramírez as editor, 78
   on Yaquis, warfare with, 76, 79
La Junta Patriótica de Juárez, 216, 218, 226, 232–33
Lamadrid, María, 307
Lanbourn, Fred, 228–29
Land Act of 1851, 28–29, 37, 52
land boom, 320–21, 331
Larrabee, Charles Hathaway, 151–53, 156–59, 175–76
Lastra, Teresa, 185
Latin Quarter (San Francisco), 110–13
law
   admission to the California Bar, 149–50
   fence law, 161
   forgery, 274–75
   free blacks, anti-immigration law, 49
   "Greaser Law," 49
   judge of the plains, 7
   Land Act of 1851, 28–29, 37, 52
   libel, 130, 224, 243
   lynching, 35–38, 44–45, 47
   notary public, 88–89
   squatters, 52–53
   vagrancy law, 48–49
Law of Colonization (Mexican), 317, 319–20, 331
Ledyard, Henry S., 231
Lewis, David, 101
Little Mexico (San Francisco), 110
López, Andrea, 233
López, Luz Reyna de, 310
Los Angeles and Independence Railroad, 222–23
Los Angeles and San Pedro Railroad Company, 146, 199–201
Los Angeles Evening Express, 160, 163–64, 183, 209, 292
Los Angeles Herald, 231, 263, 265
Los Angeles News, 149, 159

Los Angeles Republican
   acknowledgment of voting power of Southern majority, 150–51
   on building mania in Los Angeles, 147
   on Chinese, ridicule of, 166–67
   on Indians, probable extinction of, 173
   Larrabee, Charles Hathaway, pro-Union views of, 152–53
   on rail transportation, laments lack of, 145
Los Angeles Star
   Barter, George Washington, abandons newspaper, 207–8
   Chivalry Democrats, promotes and defends, 39, 42–42, 66
   Confederacy, advocated without restraint, 87
   El Clamor Público, rivalry with, 58
   emancipation of slaves, outraged reaction to, 97
   financial problems, 250
   first edition, 10
   Hamilton, Henry, sells to Benjamin C. Truman, 212
   Lincoln, Abraham, criticism of, 87
   Rojo, Manuel Clemente, editor of Spanish page, 9
   Semi-Weekly Southern News, competition with, 87
   U.S. mail, exclusion from for treasonous articles, 88
   Truman, Benjamin C., sells newspaper, 249–50
   Workingmen's Party, becomes an organ of, 262–63
Los Angeles Times, 159, 209 262, 328–29
Low, Gov. Frederick F., 102, 114
Lower California Development Company, 337
Lugo, Vicente, 42, 84
Lux, Charles, 256
lynching, 35, 45–48, 55, 59

Macy, Obed, 39
Macy, Oscar, 163

Madero, Francisco, 315
Mancillas, Antonio
    Fierro, Felipe, accuses of American citizenship, 130
    Juárez, Benito, 137–38
    Junta Patriótica de San Franciso, secretary of, 117–18
    La Voz de Méjico, editor of, 93
    Ramírez, Francisco P., first meeting, 110; offers editorship, 112
    Ramírez, Ignacio (El Nigromante), publishes letters of, 112–13
    rivalry with Ramírez, 126, 128; hatred for, 117
    Rodríguez, Manuel E., loses libel lawsuit to, 130
    treasurer of Junta Central, helps defeat Ramírez, 126
    Union Party, pays for political tract, 117
    Vega, Plácido, subsidizes as editor, 125
Márquez de León, Gen. Manuel, 296–97
Masac, Teófilo, 330
Mason, Biddy, 171
Maupin, John C., 337
Maximilian, Archduke Ferdinand
    Baja California, resistance to, 135–36
    El Nuevo Mundo, denounces, 154
    French, support for, 115; withdrawal, 135
    Imperial Army, desertion of, 135
    juntas patrióticas, opposition to spurs growth of, 118
    L'Echo du Pacifique (San Francisco), endorses empire, 122
    Mexican ultraconservatives, persuade to accept throne, 115
    Queretaro, Mexico, capture and execution in, 138–39, 155, 287
    Ramírez, Francisco P., as enemy of, 126; opposes execution of, 139
    San Francisco Spanish-language press, opposition to, 118
    Sepúlveda, Ignacio, offers services to, 154–55

Vega, Plácido, on mission against in San Francisco, 113
Mazatlan, Sinaloa, Mexico, 29, 113, 283, 296, 303
McClellan, Gen. George B., 117
McConnell, John R., 228
McDaniel, E. H., 156, 157–58, 159
McFatridge, J.W., 279
McKinley, Isaac, 263
McPherson, William, 151
Medina, Modesto, 132
Meléndrez, Antonio María, 327
Mendelson, Louis, 291, 294
Mendoza, Juan, 286–87
Mejía, Gen. Tomás, 138
Mexican Land and Colonization Company Limited (British), 332
Mexican political apathy, 20, 25, 91, 148–49
Miller, Henry, 256
Miramón, Gen. Miguel, 38
Mondran, F.V.C. de, 194
Montijo, R., 305
Moore, Alfred, 248
Mora, José María Luis, 17
Moreno, José, 294
Moreno, José Matías, 286
Morrison, Murray, 66, 151, 157–58, 177, 184
Mott, Thomas D., 103

Nadeau, Remi, 147
Napoleon III, 134
Negro Alley, 166, 169
Newmark, Harris, 144, 199, 221, 288
newspapers
    Alta California, Daily (San Francisco). See entry.
    Catholic Standard (San Francisco), 13, 109
    Daily Express (Los Angeles), 218
    El Clamor Público (Los Angeles). See entry.
    El Eco del Pacífico (San Francisco), 28, 121

El Ferrocarril (Mazatlan, Sinaloa, Mexico), 283
El Fronterizo (Real del Castillo, Baja California, Mexico), 31, 300–307, 324
El Nuevo Mundo (San Francisco). *See entry.*
El Pájaro Verde (Mexico City), 126
Evening Express (Los Angeles), 159, 162, 214
Herald (San Francisco), 42
La Crónica (Los Angeles). *See entry.*
La Estrella de Los Angeles, 11, 14, 15
La Estrella de Occidente (Ures, Sonora, Mexico). *See entry.*
La Voz de la Frontera de la Baja California (Ensenada), 324–26, 334
Los Angeles Evening Express, 160, 163–64, 183, 209, 292
Los Angeles Herald, 231, 263, 265
Los Angeles News, 149, 159
Los Angeles Republican. See entry.
Los Angeles Star. See entry.
Los Angeles Times, 209
San Francisco Daily Morning Call, 105, 139–40
San Francisco Examiner, 110
San Francisco Herald, 33–34, 55
Semi-Weekly News (Los Angeles). *See entry.*
Southern Vineyard (Los Angeles), 55, 57, 59
Tri-Weekly News (Los Angeles), 117, 131
Weekly California Express (Marysville), 14
Weekly Mirror (Los Angeles), 208–9
Newton, Frank Q., xvi
Nigger Alley, 166, 169
no-fence law, 161
Nobili, Giovanni, 13
Norton, Myron, 56
notary public, 88–90, 100, 102, 149
Nunis, Jr., Doyce B., xv

Ocaranza, Jesús, 301
Ogier, Isaac Stockton Keith, 94, 288
Olvera, Agustín, 153
O'Melveny, Harvey K. S., 188, 195, 236
Ópatas, 71
Oquitoa, Sonora, Mexico, 70
Ord, Edward O. C., 4, 5
Osa, David de la, 206
Osborne, W.M., 213
Otis, Harrison Gray, 209
Owens, Robert, 171
Owens, Winney, 171

Pacheco, Romualdo, 114, 163–64, 227, 229, 241, 260
Padilla, Antonio, xvi
Palmer, A.D., 96
Panic of 1875, 230, 236, 243, 250
Patton, Gen. George S. Jr., 181
Peel, Bryant Lorenzo, 186–87, 258
Pelanconi, Antonio, 275
Pelanconi, Petra, 344
People's Ticket
    Anaheim, as site of first convention for, 160
    elections, disappears prior to, 164
    non-partisan nature of, 161
    opposition to by Los Angeles press, 162–63
    People's Independent Party, influenced by, 204
    railroad, rejects subsidies to, 161
    Ramírez, Francisco P., candidate for assembly on, 161; withdraws, 164
    taxes, demands reductions of, 161
Pérez García, Antonio, 110
Pérez, Guillen, Eulalia, 235
Perkins, George C., 267
Pesqueira, Gov. Ignacio, 67, 73–76, 79–81, 113–14
Pflugardt, George, 44
Phelps, Timothy G., 228
Pico, Andrés
    candidate for assembly, 56–57

[384]   Index

Chivalry Democrats, early ranchero elite member, 56–57
elections, chooses not to run for assembly again, 64
financial difficulties of, 84
hangs outlaws near San Juan Capistrano, 45
Mexican lancers, commands company of, 44, 46
Territory of Colorado, proposes southern California be converted to, 60
witness, Ramírez's election contest, 103–4
Pico, Antonio María, 86
Pico, Pío
board of supervisors, nominated for, 42
Castro, José María, former rival of, 286
financial problems, helps his brother avoid, 84
Frémont, John Charles, endorses for president, 41
Glassell, Andrew, law client of, 181
Pico, Andrés, brother of Pío Pico, 56
Ramírez, Francisco P., greets Pío Pico and others from Sonora, 75
Pignatelli, Conchita Sepúlveda de, 315
Piñera, David, xvi
Pitt, Leonard, xvii
political parties and factions
Chivalry Democrats. *See entry*.
Dolly Varden Party, 204–5, 210–11
Free Soil Democrats, 16, 55
Greenback-Labor Party (Los Angeles), 271
Know-Nothing (American Party), 23, 25, 28
New Constitution Party, 266, 271
People's Reform Party (Los Angeles), 212–16
People's Ticket (Los Angeles). *See entry*.
Republican Party. *See entry*.
Rosewater Chivalry, 53, 54, 61–62
Union Party. *See entry*.
Workingmen's Party of California, 247, 249, 253–59, 264–66, 269–70, 271
Pollorena, María Candelaria, 33
postmaster in Los Angeles, 124
Powers, John, 290
Pradillo, Gen. Agustín, 314
Prieto, Guillermo (Fidel), 112
Ptacnik, Carlos R., 341–42
Puebla, Battle of (Mexico), 92–93, 100
Puebla, Second Battle of (Mexico), 99, 132

Raffi, G., 305
railroad plans, 195–96
Ralston, William C., 230
Ramírez, Casimiro Pedro (son), 340
Ramírez, Cirilo, 73
Ramírez, Francisco (grandfather), 3
Ramírez, Francisco (son), 340
Ramírez, Francisco P.
autodidactic education, 10
bank fraud, arrest for, 275
becomes a lawyer, 151–52
birth, 10
Catholic Standard (San Francisco), employee of, 13–14
Chinese immigration, in favor of, 26–27
Chivalry Democrats, rejection of, 29
Cinco de Mayo, orator at first celebration, 99
death, 343
economic depression affects law partnership, 237, 243, 250
education, views on, 60–61
El Clamor Público
begins, 15–18
sells assets of, 67
El Fronterizo (Real del Castillo, Baja California), editor of, 300–306
El Nuevo Mundo
editor of, 118–19
sale of, 139–40
engagement to Lastania Abarta, 272

Ensenada, Baja California
  acquires real estate in, 310, 321–23
  editor of *La Voz de la Frontera de la Baja California,* 324–26, 334
  opens law practice in, 317
family, 1–6, 9
financial distress of, 62–64
flees to Mexico, 279, 281
Frémont, John Charles, campaigns for, 38–43
"Greaser laws," attacks, 48–49
Hamilton, Henry, rivalry with, 39
Indians, protests mistreatment of, 166, 174–75
juntas patrióticas
  attempts to lead state-wide, 119–22
  collapse of, 134–35
La Estrella de Los Angeles
  compositor for, 10–11
  editor of, 14–16
La Estrella de Occidente (Ures, Sonora), editor of, 72–75
La Junta Patriótica de Los Angeles, spokesman for, 94
La Voz de la Frontera de la Baja California, editor of, 324–26, 334
Land Act of 1851, criticism of, 28–29
law partnership dissolves, 250–51
leads anti-railroad Independent political movement, 215–16
learns French language, 10
lynching of Mexicans by Americans, condemnation of, 47
marriage to María Saint Raymond, 338–40
as Mexican liberal, 17
moves to San Francisco, 116
moves to Sonora, Mexico, 69–71
notable trials (with Stanford), 184–85, 223–24, 224–25, 234
Real del Castillo, Baja California
  editor of *El Fronterizo,* 300–306
  elected justice of the peace in, 308
  school teacher in, 307–8
Republican Party, joins, 36, 42
returns to Los Angeles, 83–85, 141–42
schools attended in San Jose, 12–13
slavery, opposition to, 25–26, 36, 49, 60
Stanford, Frederick A., forms law partnership with, 171
state assembly candidate in 1858, 56–58
state assembly candidate in 1859, 64–67
state assembly candidate in 1880, 269–70
state senate candidate in 1864, 100–102
urges withdrawl of Mexican Americans to Sáric, Sonora, Mexico, 30
Vega, General Plácido, rivalry and fight with, 124–29
Vignes, Jean Louis, godson of, 6
Weekly California Express (Marysville), employee of, 14
Ramírez, Ignacio (El Nigromante), 112–13
Ramírez, Isabel (sister), 12–13
Ramírez, Jesús Lorenzo (grandson), 344
Ramírez, Juan (father), 3
Ramírez, Juan Bernardo (brother), 206
Ramírez, Juan de la Resurrección, (brother) 69
Ramírez, Lorenzo (son), 344
Ramírez, Marcial Valentín (son), 340
Ramírez, María Bibiana (daughter) 340
Ramírez, María Rosa (daughter), 340
Ramírez, Petra Ávila de (mother), 234
Ramírez, Petra (daughter of Juan Bernardo), 206
Ramírez, Rosa Quijada de (grandmother), 3
Ramírez, Víctor Manuel (grandson), 344
Ramírez, Ysidoro (son), 340
Ramonet, Francisco G., 134
Rancho Babicora, Chihuahua, Mexico, 314
Rancho Camulos, 84
Rancho Las Mariposas, 37

Rancho San Rafael, 281
Rancho Santa Margarita, 84
Rancho Vallecitos, Baja California, Mexico, 329
Rangel, José María, 296–99, 307
Real del Castillo, Baja California, Mexico, 290
Reed, John, 54
Registry of Public Property in Ensenada, 323
Rendón, Pedro, 337
Republican Party
   antislavery principles of, 36
   assembly, Ramírez as Republican candidate for, 270–71
   County Central Committee, Ramírez appointed to, 159–60
   county conventiom, 160
   Independent movement, subordinates to, 210–12, 226
   Los Angeles, support for, 39–41
   People's Ticket, seen as rival, 162
   Ramírez, Francisco P., joins party in support of Frémont, 36–43
   Stanford, Leland, wins governorship for, 66
   Union Party, formed by, 87
Rentería, José, 110
Requeña, Manuel, 42
Retes, Manuel, 58, 67
Richardson, N.P., 213
Ridge, Martin, xvi
Rivera, Francisco, 132
Robinson, Alfred, 143
Rodríguez, Lt. Carlos, 328
Rodríguez, Manuel E., 121, 130
Rojo, Manuel Clemente, 11, 20, 287–90, 291
Ronstadt, Col. Federico A., 77
Ross, Erskine M., 180
Rowland, William R., 214, 267, 274–75, 277–78
Rubio, José, 32, 41
Ruiz, Antonio, 33–36
Ruiz de Esparza, Feliciano, 286

Ryerson, George (father), 327–28
Ryerson, George (Jorge}, 299, 307–8, 326–29
Ryerson, Martin, 328
Ryerson, Martin, Jr., 328

Sainsevain, Pierre, 12
Saint Raymond, María, 338
Sánchez Facio, Manuel, 331,
Sánchez, Juan Matías, 232
Sánchez, Tomás, 42, 103
San Bernardino Guardian, 142
San Francisco Daily Morning Call, 139–40
San Francisco Examiner, 110
San Francisco Herald, 33–34, 55
San Jose, California, 9
San Juan Capistrano, 44
San Luis Obispo, 55
San Vicente, Baja California, Mexico, 284
Santa Anna, Antonio López de, 288
Santa Clara College, 12–13
Santacruz, Mariano, 185
Santa Fe Railroad, 320
Santo Tomás, Baja California, Mexico, 288–89
Sargent, Aaron, 196
Sargent, William, 291
Sáric, Sonora, Mexico, 30–31, 58, 67, 70
Scott, Buchanan, 332
Scott, Thomas A., 200
Seebold, Lathar, 213
Semi-Weekly News
   begins with press sold by Ramírez to Conway and Waite, 67
   Chivalry Democrats, in fervent opposition to, 87, 90–91, 98, 101–2
   Hamilton, Henry, approves of rival's incarceration, 91–92
   Ramírez, Francisco P., favorable mention of, 94–95, 102
   state senate, supports election of Ramírez to, 104, 106
   Union Party, adheres to, 87
Sepúlveda, Ignacio
   Americans, accepted by, 183–84, 218, 225

Index   [387]

American Club, Mexico City, founded by, 315
American investors, represents in Mexico, 314
Anderson, Ora, marries, 155
assemblyman, elected as, 100
attorney, 100, 105, 157
Brent, Joseph Lancaster, law apprentice of, 154
Chinese massacre, calls for grand jury inquiry, 168
County Court, election as judge, 158
death of first wife, Ora Anderson, 158–59
de la Guerra, Herlinda, marries, 315
death of Sepúlveda, 315
Díaz, President Porfirio, friend and confidante of, 314
District Court, elected as judge, 218
elections, selling of votes, investigates with grand jury, 166
Hearst family, friend of, 315
Howard, Volney E., helps get release from Mexican prison, 155
Howard and Sepúlveda, law partnership, 156
Massachusetts, boarding school, 154
Maximilian, Emperor of Mexico, offers services to, 155
Mexican Imperial Army, holds rank of major, 155
Mexican revolution forces return to Los Angeles, 315
Ramírez, Francisco P., contrast with, 153–54
U.S. Legation, secretary of, 314
Sepúlveda, José Andrés, 144
Sepúlveda, Juan María, 75
Seri, 71
Serrano, Guadalupe, 327
Shore, John W., 54
Signoret, Felix, 244
Silva, Jesús, 129
Sisson, George, 318–19
Slauson, Jonathan S., 278

slavery
California Constitution prohibits, 179
Chivalry Democrats, zealously support, 18, 28, 97
Emancipation Proclamation, Los Angeles protest against, 97
Free Soil Democrats, oppose, 28
Frémont, John Charles, antislavery views, 37–38
Los Angeles, majority of residents in favor of, 17, 26, 149, 152, 179
Mexican liberalism, rejects, 26
Ramírez, Francisco P., opposition to, 17, 25–26, 36, 182
Republican Party, arose in protest to, 36, 38, 41, 51
Territory of Colorado, would allow slavery in southern California, 60
Smallpox epidemic, 98
Smith, George H., 181, 249
Sociedad Hispano-de Beneficencia Mutua, 237–38
Society for the Promotion of Emigration of Native Californians to Sonora, 30–31, 47
Sonoita, Sonora, Mexico, 70
Sonoratown
Ayers, James J., description of, 148
elections in, 164–65
fiestas in, 166, 209, 216–17, 249
Junta Patriótica de Los Angeles, center of, 226
Mexicans move to, 83
neglect of, 244
Ramírez, Francisco P., relation to, 154, 163, 183–84, 216, 219, 221, 233
smallpox in, 98
Soto, Miguel, 46
Southern Pacific Railroad Company
Central Pacific Railroad, owned by, 196
Howard, Volney E., dedicated opponent of, 214, 223
Los Angeles, contract with, 199–200, 205

Ramírez, Francisco P., opposes subsidies to, 200
resistance to, 200, 227, 245
San Francisco–Los Angeles connection by, 239–40
Texas Pacific Railroad, competitor, 200
Yuma, line to "by way of Los Angeles," 200
Southern Vineyard, 55, 57, 59
Southworth, John R., 340
Spanish-American Republican Club, 150, 164–65
Spence, Edward F., 234
Splivato, Augusto D., 133, 164
Squatters, 52–53
Stanford, Cornelia, 177
Stanford, Frederick A.
  Arizona, removes to, 250
  arrives from Texas, member of Houston bar, 177
  born in New York, 177
  death of wife in Los Angeles, 241
  dissolution of partnership, 250–51
  educated Ramírez on conducting trials, 184–85
  financial difficulties of partnership, 243–44
  Mexican Independence Day, speaker at, 216, 233
  military rank of colonel, source unknown, 177–78
  Ramírez, Francisco P., forms law partnership with, 177
  Spanish language, forced to learn, 207
  Widney, Judge Robert M., friendship with, 184
Stanford, Frederick, Jr., 177
Stanford, Mary Elizabeth, 177
Stanford, Leland, 66, 86, 89, 196, 199, 255, 267
Stanly, Edward, 52
Stearns, Abel, 116, 143
Stearns, Arcadia Bandini de, 143
Still, William G., 89, 90
Strobel, Max, 160–61

Taggart, Charles P., 204
Tánori, Refugio, 76
Tapia, Andrés L., 295–96
Tapia, Luciano, 54
Temple, Antonia Margarita, 189
Temple Block (Los Angeles), 189–91, 214, 253, 257, 280
Temple, John, 189
Temple, Francis Pliny Fisk
  arrival in Los Angeles, 189
  Baldwin, Elias J. ("Lucky Baldwin"), makes loan to, 232
  county treasurer, candidate for, 214; elected as, 229
  foreclosure, loses all property to Lucky Baldwin, 234–36
  Temple Block, constructs in 1871, 189–91
  Temple, John, brother of, inherits property from, 189–91
  Temple-Workman Bank, formed in 1871, 191; panic and failure, 230–32, 234
  Workman, Antonia Margarita, married to, 189
  Workman, William, bank failure causes suicide of, 236
Tena, Francisco D., 73
Teodoli, Eduardo F., 191–92, 226, 238, 244
Terrazas, Gov. Luis, 342
Terrazas, María, 342
Territory of Colorado, 60
Texas Pacific Railroad, 200–201, 205
Thom, Cameron E., 157–58, 161, 180, 229, 249
Tiffany, George A., 159
Toberman, James R., 262–63
Tohono O'odham (formerly Papagos), 71
Tomlinson, John J., 147
Tononi, Giacomo, 275
Torres, Gen. Luis E., 326–36
translator, official California, 136
Tri-Weekly News (Los Angeles), 117, 131
Truman, Benjamin C., 212, 215, 221, 232, 249–50

Tubutama, Sonora, Mexico, 70
Tucson, Arizona, 71

Union Club of Los Angeles, 71
Union Party
   dissolution of, 139
   legislature, majority of members, 106–7
   Low, Frederick F., elected as governor by, 102
   juntas patrióticas, support Union Party, 119–20, 131
   Mancillas, Antonio, has Ramírez write political tract for, 117
   Maximilian refuses to recognize as emperor, 127
   official state Spanish translator, appoints Ramírez as, 136
   Ramírez, Francisco P., Union Party candidate for state senator, 100–101
   Republican Central Committee, changes name to Union Party, 87
   Semi-Weekly News, embraces Union Party, 87
United States Commissioner, 77–78
United States Land Office Receiver, 78, 80
Ures, Sonora, Mexico, 71
Uribe, Juan B., 337
Urrea, Miguel, 78

vagrancy law, 48–49
Valade, Julio, 124–25, 127, 129
Valdez, José, 294
Vallejo, Mariano, 114
Vega, Plácido
   assault on Ramírez, 127–30
   arrival in San Francisco, 113
   Bancroft, Hubert Howe, documents entrusted to, 138
   commission to raise arms, money and volunteers, 113
   death of, 138
   Juárez, Benito, joins movement against, 138
   juntas patrióticas, attempts to control, 114
   Pacheco, Romualdo, introduces to high state officials, 114
   prohibition of arms exportation, frustrates, 114, 131
   Ramírez, Francisco P., contests leadership of juntas, 124
   San Francisco Union Club, becomes vice-president of, 120
   Sinaloa, Mexico, governor of, 113–14
   subsidizes *La Voz de Méjico*, 114
Vigil, José María, 114–15, 118
Vignes, Jean Louis, 5–6, 51, 62, 250, 311
Villagrana, José María, 291–95
Vineyard, James R., 86

Wagner, Jacob, 290
Waite, Alonzo, 67, 69, 87, 90
Waite, James S., 14, 69
Walker, William (filibusterer), 284–85
Walker, William E. (embezzler), 343
Warner, Andrés, 238
Warner, Juan José (Jonathan Trumbull), 55, 59, 66, 102, 178
Watson, Jack, 86
Weekly California Express, 14
Weekly Mirror (Los Angeles), 208–9
Wells, Edgar T., 319
Wheeler, John O.
   appoints Ramírez as U.S. commissioner and deputy federal clerk, 94
   county clerk, Republican candidate for, 65
   El Clamor Público, contributes English articles to,
   federal court, clerk of, 94
   Frémont, John Charles, campaigns for with Ramírez, 40
   Ramírez, Francisco P., associate of, 57
   Union Club, member of, 226
White, Stephen M., 228, 236
White, W.B., 342
Widney, Robert M., 143, 182, 184, 217

Wigginton, Peter D., 228–29
Wilson, Benjamin Davis, 156, 195, 200
Wilson, John, 235
wine, 6, 9, 11
Woodworth, John D., 103
Workingmen's Club, No. 1 of Los Angeles, 257–58
Workingmen's Party of California, 256–59
Workingmen's riots (San Francisco), 247
Workman, William, 236–37
Worth, John H., 148–49

Yaquis, 69, 71, 76–77, 78, 79
Yarnell, Jesse, 208
Yorba, Bernardo, 185
Yuma, 70, 133, 199–200, 305, 312